Pages listed are first occurrences.

Topography of a Bird

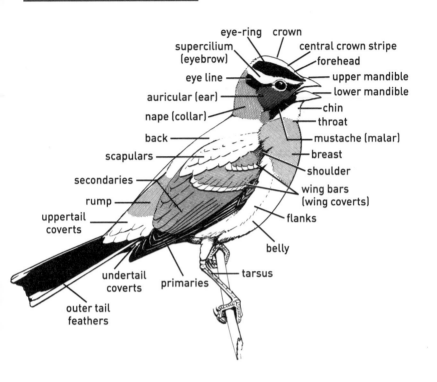

eye-ring   crown
supercilium (eyebrow)   central crown stripe
eye line   forehead
auricular (ear)   upper mandible
nape (collar)   lower mandible
back   chin
scapulars   throat
secondaries   mustache (malar)
rump   breast
uppertail coverts   shoulder
undertail coverts   wing bars (wing coverts)
outer tail feathers   flanks
primaries   belly
tarsus

Undersurface of Wing

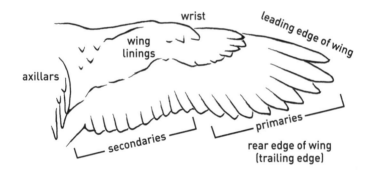

wrist
leading edge of wing
wing linings
axillars
secondaries
primaries
rear edge of wing (trailing edge)

On the upper surface of the secondaries, some waterfowl have a bright-colored patch, called a *speculum*.

BIRDS OF WESTERN NORTH AMERICA

PETERSON FIELD GUIDE TO

BIRDS OF WESTERN NORTH AMERICA

FIFTH EDITION

Roger Tory Peterson

WITH CONTRIBUTIONS FROM
Michael DiGiorgio
Paul Lehman
Peter Pyle
Larry Rosche

Mariner Books
An Imprint of HarperCollins*Publishers*
BOSTON   NEW YORK

Library of Congress Cataloging-in-Publication Data

Names: Peterson, Roger Tory, 1908–1996, author. | DiGiorgio, Michael, editor.
Title: Peterson field guide to birds of western North America / Roger Tory Peterson ;
with contributions from Michael DiGiorgio, Paul Lehman, Peter
 Pyle, Larry Rosche.
Description: Fifth edition. | Boston : HarperCollins Publishers, 2020. |
 Series: Peterson field guides | Includes bibliographical references and index.
Identifiers: LCCN 2020009023 (print) | LCCN 2020009024 (ebook) | ISBN
 9781328762221 | ISBN 9780358346258 (ebook)
Subjects: LCSH: Birds—West (U.S.)—Identification. | Birds—Canada,
 Western—Identification.
Classification: LCC QL683.W4 P4 2020 (print) | LCC QL683.W4 (ebook) | DDC
 598.0978—dc23
LC record available at https://lccn.loc.gov/2020009023
LC ebook record available at https://lccn.loc.gov/2020009024

Book design by Eugenie S. Delaney

Printed in Vietnam

23 SCP 10 9 8 7 6 5 4

ROGER TORY PETERSON INSTITUTE
OF NATURAL HISTORY

Continuing the work of Roger Tory Peterson
through Art, Education, and Conservation

In 1984, the Roger Tory Peterson Institute of Natural History (RTPI) was founded in Peterson's hometown of Jamestown, New York, as an educational institution charged by Peterson with preserving his lifetime body of work and making it available to the world for educational purposes.

RTPI is the only official institutional steward of Roger Tory Peterson's body of work and his enduring legacy. It is our mission to foster understanding, appreciation, and protection of the natural world. By providing people with opportunities to engage in nature-focused art, education, and conservation projects, we promote the study of natural history and its connections to human health and economic prosperity.

Art—Using Art to Inspire Appreciation of Nature
The RTPI Archives contain the largest collection of Peterson's art in the world— iconic images that continue to inspire an awareness of and appreciation for nature.

Education—Explaining the Importance of Studying Natural History
We need to study, firsthand, the workings of the natural world and its importance to human life. Local surroundings can provide an engaging context for the study of natural history and its relationship to other disciplines such as math, science, and language. Environmental literacy is everybody's responsibility—not just experts and special interests.

Conservation—Sustaining and Restoring the Natural World
RTPI works to inspire people to choose action over inaction, and engages in meaningful conservation research and actions that transcend political and other boundaries. Our goal is to increase awareness and understanding of the natural connections between species, habitats, and people—connections that are critical to effective conservation.

For more information, and to support RTPI, please visit rtpi.org.

CONTENTS

PETERSON FIELD GUIDE TO

BIRDS OF
WESTERN
NORTH AMERICA

INTRODUCTION

How to Identify Birds

Veteran birders will know how to use this book. Beginners, however, should spend some time becoming familiar in a general way with the illustrations. The plates, for the most part, have been grouped into taxonomic families. However, in cases where there is a great similarity of shape and action, similar-appearing families have been grouped outside their current taxonomic order, to aid in field identification.

Birds that could be confused are grouped together when possible and are arranged in identical profile for direct comparison. The arrows point to outstanding field marks, which are explained opposite. The text also gives aids such as voice, actions, and habitat, not visually portrayable, and under a separate heading discusses species that might be confused. The general range is not described for most species in the text. The annotated three-color range maps next to the species accounts provide range information.

In addition to the plates of birds normally found in western North America north of Mexico, and on the Hawaiian Islands, there are also some plates depicting accidental vagrant species from Eurasia, offshore pelagic areas, and the Tropics, as well as some plates of the exotic escapees that are sometimes seen.

What Is the Bird's Size?

Acquire the habit of comparing a new bird with some familiar "yardstick" — a House Sparrow, robin, pigeon, etc. — so that you can say to yourself, for example, "Smaller than a robin, a little larger than a House Sparrow." The measurements in this book represent lengths in inches (with centimeters in parentheses) from bill tip to tail tip of specimens on their backs as in museum trays. For species that show considerable size variation, a range of measurements is given. For less variable species, only one measurement is given.

What Is Its Shape?

Is it plump like a starling (left) or slender like a cuckoo (right)?

What Shape Are Its Wings?

Are they rounded like a bobwhite's (left) or sharply pointed like a Barn Swallow's (right)?

What Shape Is Its Bill?

Is it small and fine like a warbler's (1), stout and short like a seed-cracking sparrow's (2), dagger-shaped like a tern's (3), or hook-tipped like a bird of prey's (4)?

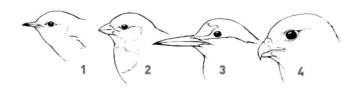

What Shape Is Its Tail?

Is it deeply forked like a Barn Swallow's (1), square-tipped like a Cliff Swallow's (2), notched like a Tree Swallow's (3), rounded like a jay's (4), or pointed like a Mourning Dove's (5)?

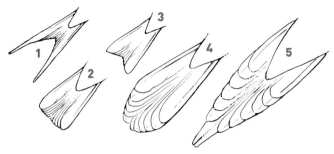

How Does It Behave?

Does it cock its tail like a wren or hold it down like a flycatcher? Does it wag its tail? Does it sit erect on an open perch, dart after an insect, and return as a flycatcher does?

Does It Climb Trees?

If so, does it climb upward in spirals like a creeper (left), in jerks and using its tail as a brace like a woodpecker (center), or go down headfirst like a nuthatch (right)?

How Does It Fly?

Does it undulate (dip up and down) like a flicker (1)? Does it fly straight and fast like a dove (2)? Does it hover like a kingfisher (3)? Does it glide or soar?

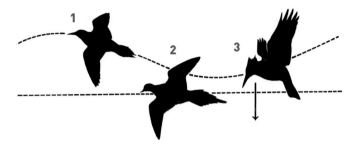

Does It Swim?

Does it sit low in the water like a loon (1) or high like a gallinule (2)? If a duck, does it dive like a scaup or a scoter (3) or dabble and upend like a Mallard (4)?

Does It Wade?

Is it large and long-legged like a heron or small like a sandpiper? If one of the latter, does it probe the mud or pick at things? Does it teeter or bob?

What Are Its Field Marks?

Some birds can be identified by color alone, but most birds are not that easy. The most important aids are what we call field marks, which are, in effect, the "trademarks of nature." Note whether the breast is spotted as in a thrush (1), streaked as in a thrasher (2), or plain as in a cuckoo (3).

Tail Pattern

Does the tail have a "flash pattern" — a white tip as in the Eastern Kingbird (1), white patches in the outer corners as in the Eastern and Spotted Towhees (2), or white sides as in the juncos (3)?

Rump Patch

Does it have a light rump like a Cliff Swallow (1) or flicker (2)? Northern Harrier, Yellow-rumped Warbler, and several shorebirds also have distinctive rump patches.

Eye Stripes and Eye-ring

Does the bird have a stripe above, through, or below the eye, or a combination of these stripes? Does it have a striped crown? A ring around the eye, or "spectacles"? A "mustache" stripe? These details are important in many small songbirds.

Wing Bars

Do the wings have light wing bars or not? Their presence or absence is important in recognizing many warblers, vireos, and flycatchers. Wing bars may be single or double, bold or obscure.

Wing Pattern

The basic wing pattern of ducks (shown below), shorebirds, and other water birds is very important. Notice whether the wings have patches (1) or stripes (2), are solidly colored (3), or have contrasting black tips.

Bird Songs and Calls

Using sounds to identify birds can be just as useful as using visual clues. In fact, in many situations, birds are much more readily identified by sound than by sight. The species accounts here include a brief entry on voice, with interpretations of these songs and calls, in an attempt to give birders some handle on the vocalizations they hear. Authors of bird books have attempted, with varying success, to fit songs and calls into syllables, words, and phrases. Musical notations, comparative descriptions, and even ingenious systems of symbols have also been employed. To supplement this verbal interpretation, there are recording collections available for nearly every region of the world and for individual groups of birds. The Peterson *Birding by Ear* CDs provide a step-by-step method for learning how to develop your listening and identification skills. Preparation in advance for particular species or groups greatly enhances your ability to identify them. Some birders do a majority of their birding by ear, and there is no substitute for actual sounds — for getting out into the field, tracking down the songster, and committing the song to memory. However, an audio library is a wonderful resource to return home to when attempting to identify a bird heard in the field. Many such collections can now be taken into the field on mobile devices. *Caution:* When using recordings to attract hard-to-see species, limit the number of playbacks, and do not use them on threatened species or in heavily birded areas.

Bird Nests

The more time you spend in the field becoming familiar with bird behavior, the more skilled you'll become at finding bird nests. It is as exciting to keep a bird nest list as it is to keep a life list. Remember, if you happen to find a nest during the breeding season, leave the site as undisturbed as possible. Back away, and do not touch the nest, eggs, or young birds. Often squirrels, raccoons, several other mammals, crows, jays, grackles, and cowbirds are more than happy to have you "point out" a nest and will raid it if you disrupt the site or call attention to it. Many people find juvenile birds that have just left the nest and may appear to be alone. Usually they are not lost but are under the watchful eye of a parent bird and are best left in place rather than scooped up and taken to a foreign environment. In the winter, nest hunting can be great fun and has little impact, as most nests will never be used again. They are easy to see once the foliage is gone, and it can be a challenge to attempt to identify the maker.

The Maps and Ranges of Birds

The ranges of many species have changed markedly over the past 50 or more years. Some species are expanding because of protection given them, changing habitats, bird feeding, or other factors. Other avian species have diminished alarmingly and may have been extirpated from major parts of their range. The primary culprit here has been habitat loss, although other factors, such as increased competition and predation from other species, may sometimes be involved. Many bird species will face challenges from impending changes in our climate. Species that are in serious decline in North America run the gamut, from Ivory Gull to Lesser Prairie-Chicken and Loggerhead Shrike to Bewick's Wren, Rusty Blackbird, and Red Knot.

Successful introductions of some species, such as Trumpeter Swan and Eurasian Collared-Dove, have resulted in self-sustaining, growing populations (the latter was either introduced to the Bahamas or flew over from Africa, then dispersed throughout the U.S. and Canada on its own). And a good number of additional vagrant species — out-of-range visitors from faraway lands — continue to be found (such as a Red-footed Falcon in Massachusetts, Rufous-necked Wood-Rail in New Mexico, and Chatham Albatross in California). Some species that were formerly thought to occur only exceptionally have, over the past several decades, become much more regular or widespread visitors (such as Cave Swallow and Lesser Black-backed Gull) and sometimes even become local breeders (such as Clay-colored Thrush). Such changes in status can be the result of actual population increases or may also reflect better observer coverage and advances in field identification skills.

The maps in this book are approximate, giving the general outlines of the range of each species. Within these broad outlines may be many gaps — areas ecologically unsuitable for the species. A Marsh Wren must have a marsh, a Ruffed Grouse a woodland or a forest. Certain species may be extremely local or sporadic for reasons that may or may not be clear. As noted previously, some birds are extending their ranges — a few explosively — while others are declining or even disappearing from large areas where they were formerly found. Winter ranges are often not as well-defined as breeding ranges. A species may exist at a very low density near the northern limits of its winter range, surviving through December in mild seasons but often succumbing to or moving south to avoid the bitter conditions of January and February. Varying weather conditions and food supplies from year to year may result in substantial variations in winter bird populations.

The maps are specific only for the area covered by this field guide.

The Mallard, for example, is found over a large part of the globe. The map shows only its range in western North America and, where appropriate, Hawaii. Species found regularly in both western North America and Hawaii may have range maps for each area.

The maps are based on data culled from many publications (particularly from monographs detailing the status and distribution of a state or province's avifauna, as well as from breeding bird atlases), from such journals as *North American Birds*, and from communication with many state and provincial experts throughout western North America and Hawaii.

Range maps don't depict how abundant a particular species is within its range. The following list defines terms of abundance used throughout the book. The definitions presume you're in the habitat and season in which a species would occur, but note that this in itself can vary throughout the continent.

COMMON: Always or almost always encountered daily, usually in moderate to large numbers.

FAIRLY COMMON: Usually encountered daily, generally not in large numbers.

UNCOMMON: Occurs in small numbers and may be missed on a substantial number of days.

SCARCE: Present only in small numbers or difficult to find within its normal range.

RARE OR VERY RARE: Annual or probably annual in small numbers but still largely within its normal range.

CASUAL: Beyond its normal range; occurs at somewhat regular intervals but usually less frequently than annually.

ACCIDENTAL VAGRANT: Beyond its normal range; one record or a very few records.

LOCAL: Limited geographic range within the U.S. and Canada.

ENDEMIC: Found only in the described region; here most often used for Hawaiian species.

INTRODUCED OR EXOTIC: Not native; population derived from deliberately released or escaped **individuals.** These terms can be used for species that are present in limited numbers and may or may not be breeding, or for well-established species such as House Sparrow and European Starling.

UNESTABLISHED EXOTIC: Nonnative releasee or escapee that does not have a naturalized breeding population, though some may be breeding in very localized areas.

Habitats

Gaining a familiarity with a wide range of habitats will greatly enhance your overall knowledge of the birds in a specific region, increase your skills, and add to your enjoyment of birding. It is unlikely you will ever see a meadowlark in an oak woodland or a Wood Thrush in a meadow. Birders know this, and if they want to go out to run up a large day list, they do not remain in one habitat but shift from site to site based on time and species diversity for a given type of habitat.

A few birds do invade habitats other than their own at times, especially on migration. A warbler that spends the summer in the boreal forests of Canada might be seen, on its journey through the southern U.S., in a palm, or in coastal scrub. In cities, migrating birds often have to make the best of it, like the American Woodcock found one morning on the window ledge of a New York City office. Strong weather patterns can also alter where a bird happens to appear. Hurricanes, for example, can be a disaster for many species. As these violent storms sweep over the ocean, the eye can often "vacuum" up oceanic species that seek shelter in its calmness. Upon reaching land, these normally offshore species are faced with an entirely strange habitat and account for sightings such as a Yellow-nosed Albatross heading up the Hudson River, a White-tailed Tropicbird in downtown Boston, and numbers of storm-petrels on inland reservoirs in the desert Southwest.

Most species, however, are quite predictable for the major portion of their lives, and for the birder who has learned where to look, the rewards are great.

To start, familiarize yourself with individual habitat types. Become familiar with the dominant plant types that are indicators — for example, oak-beech woods, cactus desert, grass-shrub meadows, native Hawaiian cloud forest, salt- or freshwater wetlands — and keep accurate records of what species you find in each. In a short time you will have a working knowledge of the predominant species in each habitat, and this will help you with identification by allowing you to anticipate what might be found there.

The seasonal movements of birds at your sites will provide an overview of migrant species that come through at a given time and will be a reference point for future visits during these migration periods. A forest dotted with migrant warblers in spring may revert to relative quiet accented by the repetitive calls of a Red-eyed Vireo or the drawn-out call of a Western Wood-Pewee in midsummer.

Be sure not to overlook cities and towns, where well-adapted species can be found. Peregrine Falcons have shown remarkable adaptability, nesting on strategic ledges in the "walled canyons" of many cities. The fertile grounds for hunting Rock Pigeons and European Starlings seem to suit this raptor quite well.

Ecotones are edges where two habitat types interface — a forest and a shrub meadow, for example. As this is not a gradual change, ecotones offer habitat for species from both of the adjoining areas and are therefore rich in bird life.

The changes in habitat over the years will also affect your favorite birding areas. Fields turn to shrubby lots and then woodlands. Bobwhite, Savannah Sparrows, and meadowlarks may move on, but Indigo or Lazuli Buntings and Field or Lincoln's Sparrows establish themselves. This dynamic is normal in the natural world. However, humankind's alterations to this process have had a great impact. Forest fragmentation is an example. Land development has affected numerous species. Sudden disruptions have a more drastic effect than slow changes, which allow for adaptation. As we have divided up habitat with roadways, range lands, and agricultural fields, we have created a greater edge effect, and this has allowed Brown-headed Cowbirds to penetrate into forest areas where they would not have ventured in the past. They now parasitize many more species than before, and such parasitization has led to marked declines in total numbers of many species. Forest fragmentation has also affected the success rate of nestling fledging by increasing the access of some predators and by altering prime habitat requirements for obtaining food to raise young.

Some species are obligates to a specific habitat type, and searching these areas greatly improves your chances of finding such birds. These include Golden-crowned Kinglet nesting in coniferous woodlands and Kirtland's Warbler in Michigan, which breeds only in jack pine woodlands of a specific height. Even in migration, many species remain faithful to selected habitats, such as waterthrushes along watercourses. Running or dripping water has proven to be an important attractant for migrating land birds, and in areas where fresh water is scarce, a water drip can be a gold mine for migrant warblers and other passerines.

Subspecies and Geographic Variation

Many species of birds inhabit wide geographic areas. The Song Sparrow (*Melospiza melodia*), for example, breeds throughout North America, from Mexico north into Alaska and from California to Newfoundland. In such a wide-ranging species, there are geographic subsets within the population that show distinct plumage patterns and/or song variants. When these reach a point when individuals are recognizably different from nearby populations, they may formally be designated as subspecies by attaching a third, subspecific name to the scientific name of the species. Thus, the pale Song Sparrow of the southwestern deserts of North America is called *Melospiza melodia fallax,* to distinguish that form from up to 25 other subspecies found throughout North America. The Song Sparrow ranks among the most geographically variable of North American birds.

Often subspecific groups are so distinct that they can be easily recognized in the field by bird watchers. Good examples of this are subspecies within Dark-eyed Junco (*Junco hyemalis*). With 12 subspecies, at least five subspecies groups are easily discerned: the "Oregon," "Pink-sided," "White-winged," "Slate-colored," and "Gray-headed" Juncos (p. 340). For the birder, identification of subspecies can add greater challenges to birding and, when documented, valuable information, especially when subspecies are reclassified to full species status. Such has been the case, for example, with the splitting of Solitary Vireo (*Vireo solitarius*) into Blue-headed (retaining *V. solitarius*), Cassin's (*V. cassinii*), and Plumbeous (*V. plumbeus*) Vireos (p. 294). Field studies of Sage Grouse (*Centrocercus urophasianus*) leading to the separation of Greater Sage-Grouse (*C. urophasianus*) and the rare and threatened Gunnison Sage-Grouse (*C. minimus*) prove how valuable these studies of subspecific populations can be. The differences between Bicknell's Thrush (*Catharus bicknelli*) and Gray-cheeked Thrush (*C. minimus*) illustrate how subtle field marks can be between species and why they had once been considered subspecies. The shifting of this line between subspecies and species is ongoing. Recording data on location and numbers can prove helpful in completing a picture of a species' and subspecies' distribution.

In this edition, distinct subspecies that are easily recognized, such as those of Yellow-rumped Warbler (*Setophaga coronata*) and Dark-eyed Junco (*J. hyemalis*), are represented. When in the field, challenge yourself to discern the subspecies. It will increase your visual and listening skills and add a new level of understanding and enjoyment of birds.

Identifying the Age and Sex of Birds

In many species, the ages and sexes of birds can be identified to various degrees, and being able to accurately determine age/sex groups can add fulfillment to your birding experience. It can also be important in assessing the degree to which less common species are reproducing. In this new edition, we have made an effort to point out every identifiable age/sex classification of each species, illustrating many of them. We have also refined and standardized our terminology, replacing such imprecise terms as "immature" with specific age groupings (such as juvenile, adult, first-year, second-winter, etc.) and, for plumages, we have replaced the labels "breeding" and "nonbreeding" with "spring/summer" and "fall/winter," respectively, to better align with age classifications and because plumage state does not directly equate to breeding state.

Conservation

Birds undeniably contribute to our pleasure and quality of life. But they also are sensitive indicators of the environment, a sort of "ecological litmus paper," and hence more meaningful than just chickadees and cardinals that brighten the suburban garden, grouse and ducks that fill the sportsman's bag, or rare warblers and shorebirds that excite the field birder. The observation and recording of bird populations over time lead inevitably to environmental awareness and can signal impending changes. In this edition we have indicated the status of species or populations as threatened or endangered according to the curent U.S. Endangered Species List.

Please help the cause of wildlife conservation and education by contributing to or taking part in the work of the following organizations: American Bird Conservancy (abcbirds.org), American Birding Association (www.aba.org), BirdLife International (www.birdlife.org), Cornell Laboratory of Ornithology (www.birds.cornell.edu), Defenders of Wildlife (www.defenders.org), Ducks Unlimited (www.ducks.org), National Audubon Society (www.audubon.org), National Wildlife Federation (www.nwf.org), The Nature Conservancy (www.nature.org), Partners in Flight (www.partnersinflight.org), Roger Tory Peterson Institute of Natural History (www.rtpi.org), and World Wildlife Fund (www.wwf.org), as well as your local land trust and natural heritage program and your local Audubon and ornithological societies and bird clubs. These and so many other groups are on the forefront of bird conservation and merit your support.

PLATES

GEESE, SWANS, and DUCKS Family Anatidae

Web-footed waterfowl. **RANGE:** Worldwide.

GEESE

Large, gregarious waterfowl; heavier bodied, longer necked than ducks; bills thick at base. Noisy in flight; some fly in lines or V formations. Sexes similar. Geese are more terrestrial than ducks, often grazing. **FOOD:** Grasses, seeds, waste grain, aquatic plants; eelgrass (Brant); shellfish (Emperor Goose).

GREATER WHITE-FRONTED GOOSE   Fairly common
Anser albifrons (see also p. 22)

28 in. (71 cm). Gray-brown with *pink* bill. *Adult:* Has *white patch on front of face* and sparse to heavy *black bars* on belly. The only other N. American goose with yellow or orange feet is Emperor Goose. *First-year:* Dusky with dull pinkish bill; gradually acquires white at bill base and black on belly. May be confused with some domestic Graylag Geese. **VOICE:** High-pitched tootling, *kah-lah-a-luk,* in chorus. **HABITAT:** Marshes, prairies, agricultural fields, lakes, bays; in summer, tundra.

EMPEROR GOOSE *Anser canagicus* (see also p. 22)   Scarce, local

26 in. (66 cm). Alaskan. *Adult:* A small blue-gray goose, *scaled* with black and white; identified by its *white head and hindneck.* Throat *black* (not white as in dark-morph Snow and Ross's Geese). Golden or *orange legs. Juvenile:* Has dark head and bill; quickly becomes white in first fall. **HABITAT:** In summer, tundra; in winter, rocky shores, mudflats, seaweed.

SNOW GOOSE   Locally very common
Anser caerulescens (see also p. 22)

White morph: 25–33 in. (64–84 cm). *White* with *black primaries.* Head sometimes rust-stained from feeding in muddy or iron-rich waters. Bill pink with black "lips." Feet pink. Base of bill curves back slightly toward eye. *Juvenile and first-winter:* Pale gray; dark bill and legs. Dark morph ("Blue Goose"), 25–30 in. (64–76 cm), uncommon in West. Suggests Emperor Goose, but has *white throat, dark "lips,"* and lacks scaly pattern. *Juvenile and first-winter:* Similar to young Greater White-fronted Goose but blacker, feet and bill *dark.* **VOICE:** Loud, nasal, double-noted *houck-houck,* in chorus. **SIMILAR SPECIES:** Ross's Goose. **HABITAT:** Marshes, grain fields, ponds, bays; in summer, tundra.

ROSS'S GOOSE *Anser rossii* (see also p. 22)   Locally fairly common

23 in. (58 cm). Like a small Snow Goose, but neck shorter, head rounder (steeper forehead). Bill has *gray-blue or purple-blue base,* stubbier (with *vertical border* between base and facial feathering), *lacking distinctive "grinning black lips"* and with warts at bill base (can be difficult to see). *Juvenile and first-winter:* Whiter than young Snow Goose. *Rare dark morph* has more extensively dark neck, whiter wing patches and abdomen than "Blue" Snow Goose; hybrids with Snow Goose occur. **VOICE:** Higher than Snow's, suggesting Cackling Goose. **SIMILAR SPECIES:** Snow Goose. **HABITAT:** Same as Snow Goose; often together.

GEESE

juvenile/
first-winter

GREATER
WHITE-FRONTED
GOOSE

adult

adult

juvenile

EMPEROR
GOOSE

adult

adult

adult

juvenile/
first-fall

adults

SNOW GOOSE

dark morph
("Blue" Goose)

dark morph
(rare)

adults

ROSS'S
GOOSE

juvenile/
first-winter

adult

Snow

SNOW
GOOSE

white
morph

Ross's

adults

Snow

BRANT *Branta bernicla* (see also p. 22) Locally common

24–26 in. (59–66 cm). A small black-necked goose. Has white vent and undertail, conspicuous when it upends, whitish flanks, and band of white on neck. *First-year:* Shows smaller neck patch than adult and thin white wing bars. Travels in large irregular flocks. Western subspecies, "Black" Brant (*B. b. nigricans*), has *dark belly* and more complete white band across foreneck. Eastern subspecies, "Pale-bellied" Brant (*B. b. hrota*), a casual vagrant to West, has *lighter belly, less contrasty flanks,* and usually two separated neck patches; caution that worn Black Brants in spring and summer can be confused with pale-bellied subspecies. **VOICE:** Throaty *cr-r-r-ruk* or *krr-onk, krrr-onk.* **SIMILAR SPECIES:** Foreparts of Canada and Cackling Geese not black to waterline, and those species have large white face patch. Brant is more strictly coastal. **HABITAT:** Salt bays, estuaries; in summer, tundra. Rare migrant or vagrant inland.

CACKLING GOOSE *Branta hutchinsii* Fairly common

23–32 in. (58–81 cm). Recently elevated to full-species rank separate from larger Canada Goose, in the West, this species includes the variably sized smaller subspecies *taverneri* ("Taverner's"), *minima* ("Ridgway's"), and *leucopareia* ("Aleutian"). Like Canada Goose, shows variable breast color and neck collar. Ages similar. **VOICE:** High, cackling *yel-lik.* **SIMILAR SPECIES:** Told from Canada by smaller size; shorter neck; smaller, rounder head; stubbier bill; and higher-pitched voice. Distinctions between larger Cacklings (such as Taverner's) and smaller Canadas (such as Lesser) can be subtle. **HABITAT:** Lakes, marshes, fields; in summer, tundra. Individuals will sometimes occur with larger Canadas and are usually noticeably smaller and shorter necked. Aleutian subspecies increasing and now occurs in large flocks breeding in the Aleutian Is. and migrating and wintering along the Oregon and California coasts.

CANADA GOOSE *Branta canadensis* (see also p. 22) Common

30–43 in. (76–109 cm). The most widespread goose in N. America. Note black head and neck, or "stocking," that contrasts with pale breast and *white chin strap.* Ages similar. Flocks travel in strings or in Vs, "honking" loudly. Substantial variation in size and neck length exists among populations: in West, subspecies *moffitti* ("Greater"), *occidentalis* ("Dusky"), and *parvipes* ("Lesser") split from smaller Cackling Goose. **VOICE:** Deep, musical honking or barking, *ka-ronk* or *ka-lunk.* Lesser Canada Geese have higher-pitched calls but not as high as Cackling's. **SIMILAR SPECIES:** Cackling Goose. **HABITAT:** Lakes, ponds, bays, marshes, fields. Resident in many areas, frequenting parks, lawns, golf courses.

"Pale-bellied" (Atlantic)

adults

BRANT

"Black" (Pacific)

Pacific juvenile/ first-winter

Pacific adult

CACKLING GOOSE

"Aleutian"

"Taverner's"

"Dusky"

"Lesser"

CANADA GOOSE

"Greater"

SWANS

Huge, white, larger and longer necked than geese. First-year birds are pale gray-brown. Sexes alike. Feeds by immersing head and neck or by "tipping up." **FOOD:** Aquatic plants, seeds.

TUNDRA SWAN　　　　　　　　　　　Uncommon to locally common
Cygnus columbianus (see also p. 22)
52–53 in. (132–135 cm); wingspan 6–7 ft. (183–213 cm). More widespread in West than Trumpeter Swan. Bill *black,* usually with *small yellow basal spot.* Eurasian subspecies *bewickii* ("Bewick's" Swan), casual from AK to CA, has *much more yellow on bill* above nostrils. *Juvenile:* Dingy, with pinkish bill variably dark at base and tip; quickly becomes whiter during first year. **VOICE:** Mellow, high-pitched cooing: *woo-ho, woo-woo, woo-ho.* **SIMILAR SPECIES:** Trumpeter and Mute Swans. **HABITAT:** Lakes, marshes, bays, estuaries, grain fields; in summer, tundra.

TRUMPETER SWAN *Cygnus buccinators*　　　Locally uncommon
58–60 in. (147–152 cm). Larger than Tundra Swan, with longer, heavier, *all-black bill,* which has *straight ridge* recalling Canvasback. Black on lores wider, *embracing eyes* and lacking yellow spot (some Tundras also lack this spot). Bill base forms *V shape* (rather than U shape) on forehead. *Juvenile and first-year:* Keeps dusky body color later into first year than does Tundra. **VOICE:** *Deeper, more nasal calls* than Tundra Swan, often described as bugle-like. **HABITAT:** Lakes; in winter, also grain fields. Scarce vagrant south of range, though beware escapees.

MUTE SWAN *Cygnus olor*　　　　　　Very local, introduced
60 in. (152 cm). Introduced from Europe. Swims with an S curve in neck; wings arched over back. *Black-knobbed orange bill tilts downward. Juvenile and first-winter:* Dingy with dull pinkish bill, lacking knob. **VOICE:** Hissing and wheezing sounds. **RANGE:** Small local populations around Victoria, BC, and in northern California; exotic escapees rarely observed elsewhere. **HABITAT:** Ponds, marshes.

WHISTLING-DUCKS

These ducks have long necks and legs. Ages and sexes similar. Named for their high-pitched calls. Gregarious. **FOOD:** Seeds of aquatic plants.

FULVOUS WHISTLING-DUCK　　　　　　　　Very rare
Dendrocygna bicolor (see also p. 44)
20 in. (51 cm). Note *tawny body, dark back, pale side stripes, black underwings, white band* on rump. **VOICE:** Squealing slurred whistle, *ka-whee-oo.* **SIMILAR SPECIES:** Black-bellied Whistling-Duck, female Northern Pintail. **HABITAT:** Freshwater marshes, irrigated land, rice fields. Active at dusk and night. Seldom perches in trees. Casual vagrant well north of breeding range.

BLACK-BELLIED WHISTLING-DUCK　　Locally rare to uncommon
Dendrocygna autumnalis
21 in. (53 cm). Rusty with *black belly,* gray face, bright *coral red* bill. Broad *white patch* along forewing, visible in flight. Frequently perches in trees. **VOICE:** Four- or five-part high-pitched squealing whistle. **HABITAT:** Ponds, freshwater marshes. Casual vagrant well north of breeding range.

SWANS AND WHISTLING-DUCKS

juvenile

TRUMPETER SWAN

juvenile/ first-winter

adult

TUNDRA SWAN

adult

MUTE SWAN

adult

adult

juvenile

TUNDRA SWAN

TRUMPETER SWAN

adult

FULVOUS WHISTLING-DUCK

Black-Bellied Whistling-Duck

Fulvous Whistling-Duck

BLACK-BELLIED WHISTLING-DUCK

GEESE and SWANS in FLIGHT

CANADA GOOSE *Branta canadensis* p. 18

Large, slow wingbeats. Cackling Goose (p. 18) smaller, more Brantlike, faster wingbeats.

BRANT *Branta bernicla* p. 18

Small; black head and neck, black belly, white stern. "Black Brant" the regular species along Pacific North American Coast. "Pale-bellied Brant" a rare vagrant in West.

GREATER WHITE-FRONTED GOOSE *Anser albifrons* p. 16

Adult: Gray-brown neck, black bars or splotches on belly.
Juvenile and first-winter: Dusky, with light bill and feet.

EMPEROR GOOSE *Anser canagicus* p. 16

Gray with white head, black throat, white tail.

TUNDRA SWAN *Cygnus columbianus* p. 20

Very long neck. *Adult:* Plumage entirely white. Trumpeter Swan (p. 20) similar, larger.

SNOW GOOSE (WHITE MORPH) *Anser caerulescens* p. 16

Adult: White with black primaries. Juvenile and first-winter grayer.

SNOW GOOSE (DARK MORPH, "BLUE" GOOSE) p. 16
Anser caerulescens

Adult: Dark body, white head.
Juvenile and first-winter: Dusky, with dark bill and feet.

ROSS'S GOOSE *Anser rossii* p. 16

Smaller, slightly shorter necked and shorter billed than Snow Goose. Juvenile and first-winter grayer. Rare dark morph blacker than larger "Blue" Goose.

Many geese and swans fly in line or V formation.

GEESE AND SWANS

CANADA GOOSE

BRANT

"Pale-bellied"

adults

"Black"

juvenile/first-winter

EMPEROR GOOSE

adult

GREATER WHITE-FRONTED GOOSE

adult

juvenile/first-winter

adult

adult

TUNDRA SWAN

adult

adult

SNOW GOOSE dark morph ("Blue" Goose)

SNOW GOOSE white morph

adult

ROSS'S GOOSE

adult

DABBLING DUCKS

Feed by dabbling and upending; often feed on land. Take flight directly into air. Most species have an iridescent "speculum" on secondaries from above. Adult males brighter than females; in midsummer, males molt into drab "eclipse" (alternate) plumage, usually resembling females. Juvenile males also female-like but gain colorful plumage in first fall. **FOOD:** Aquatic plants, seeds, grass, waste grain, small aquatic life, insects.

NORTHERN PINTAIL *Anas acuta* (see also p. 42)   Fairly common

Male 25–26 in. (63–66 cm); female 20–21 in. (51–54 cm). Speculum brownish with pale tips. *Male:* Slender, slim-necked, white-breasted, with long, *needle-pointed tail* and *white point* on side of dark head. *Female:* Variably mottled grayish brown to cinnamon brown; note rather pointed tail, slender neck, *gray bill.* In flight both sexes have a *single light border* on rear edge of speculum. **VOICE:** Male, a double-toned whistle: *prrip, prrip;* wheezy notes. Female, a low *quack.* **SIMILAR SPECIES:** Female thinner- and longer-necked than other dabbling ducks. **HABITAT:** Marshes, prairies, ponds, lakes, salt bays.

AMERICAN WIGEON   Fairly common
Mareca americana (see also p. 42)

19–20 in. (48–51 cm). Speculum green. In flight, recognized by *large white patch on forewing.* Often grazes on land. *Male:* Warm brownish; head pale gray with green eye patch. Note *white crown* (nicknamed "Baldpate"). *Female:* Brown; gray head and neck; whitish belly and forewing. **VOICE:** Male, a two-part whistled *whee whew.* Female, *qua-ack.* **SIMILAR SPECIES:** See Eurasian Wigeon. Squarish head, small bluish bill, and whitish patch on forewing seperate wigeon from similar ducks. **HABITAT:** Marshes, lakes, bays, fields, grass.

EURASIAN WIGEON *Mareca penelope*   Rare

19–20 in. (48–51 cm). *Male:* Note *red-brown* head, *buff* crown. A *gray-sided* wigeon with rufous-pinkish breast. *Female:* Similar to female American Wigeon but head is less grayish, *brown or reddish brown.* In flight, shows grayish (not white) axillars, or wingpits. **VOICE:** Male, a long whistle, *wheeee-oo.* Female, a purr or quack. **HABITAT:** Same as American Wigeon, with which it is usually found. Rare winterer on coast; casual vagrant inland.

WOOD DUCK *Aix sponsa* (see also p. 42)   Fairly common

18–19 in. (45–49 cm). Highly colored; often perches in trees. Speculum steely blue and purple. In flight, white belly contrasts with dark breast and wings; note long dark tail, short neck, and squat, large-headed look. *Male:* Striking face pattern, sweptback crest, red coloration to bill, and rainbow iridescence unique. Juvenile and eclipse male like female but have reddish bill and muted head pattern. *Female:* Dull gray with dark crested head, gray bill, and *white eye patch;* see similar female Mandarin Duck (p. 50). **VOICE:** Male, hissing *jeeeeeeb,* with rising inflection. Female, a loud, rising squeal, *oo-eek,* and sharp *crrek, crrek.* **HABITAT:** Wooded swamps, rivers, ponds, marshes.

DABBLING DUCKS

NORTHERN PINTAIL

female

male

AMERICAN WIGEON

male

female

EURASIAN WIGEON

female

male

female

WOOD DUCK

male in eclipse (summer)

male

SILHOUETTES OF DUCKS ON LAND

dabbling ducks (dabblers)

sea and bay ducks (divers)

mergansers (divers)

Ruddy Duck (diver)

whistling-ducks (dabblers)

GADWALL
Fairly common to common

Mareca strepera (see also p. 42)

19–20 in. (48–51 cm). In flight, upperwing dark, speculum black and white. *Male: Gray* body with brown head and *black rump, white inner speculum* on rear edge of wing, and dark ruddy patch on forewing (may be difficult to see). When swimming, inner speculum may be concealed but often shows as a white square patch midwing. Belly white, feet yellow, bill dark. *Female:* Brown, mottled, with *white inner speculum,* yellow feet, orange sides on gray bill. **VOICE:** Male, a low, reedy *bek;* a whistling call. Female, a nasal quack. **SIMILAR SPECIES:** Female told from female Mallard by steeper forehead, wing pattern, more nasal call. A blockier duck than female Northern Pintail, without long neck or tail. White patch on flanks diagnostic but not always visible. **HABITAT:** Lakes, ponds, marshes.

MALLARD *Anas platyrhynchos* (see also p. 44)
Common

22–23 in. (55–59 cm). Speculum greenish blue to blue with broad white tips. *Male:* Note uncrested *glossy green head* and *white neck ring,* grayish body, chestnut chest, white tail, yellowish bill, orange feet. *Female:* Mottled brown with *whitish tail.* Dark bill patched with orange, feet orange. In flight, shows white bar *on both sides* of blue speculum. **VOICE:** Male, *yeeb;* a low *kwek.* Female, boisterous quacking. **SIMILAR SPECIES:** Female Gadwall, American Black Duck. **HABITAT:** Marshes, wooded swamps, grain fields, ponds, rivers, lakes, bays, city parks.

"MEXICAN" MALLARD *Anas platyrhynchos diazi* Uncommon, local

10–21 in. (51-54 cm). This subspecies of Mallard is often regarded as a distinct species called Mexican Duck. Intergrades with Mallard are frequent. Both sexes very similar to female Mallard but with *grayish brown* instead of whitish tail. Bill of male like bill of male Mallard (unmarked yellowish green). Yellow-orange bill of female has a dark ridge. Has white border *on both sides* of wing patch, thinner than in female Mallard. **VOICE:** Same as Mallard's. **SIMILAR SPECIES:** Mallard. **RANGE:** Resident in nw. Mexico and from se. AZ to sw. TX. **HABITAT:** Ponds.

DABBLING DUCKS

dabbling ducks
spring directly
from the water

dabbling ducks
tip up

female

male

GADWALL

female

male

MALLARD

(female similar
except for bill
orange, mottled
dusky)

male

"MEXICAN" MALLARD

BLUE-WINGED TEAL

Uncommon to fairly common

Spatula discors (see also p. 42)

15–16 in. (38–41 cm). A medium-small dabbling duck; speculum green. *Male:* Note *white facial crescent* and large *chalky blue* patch on *forewing.* Molting males hold eclipse plumage later in year than other dabbling ducks and resemble females. *Female, juvenile, and first-winter male:* Brown, mottled; dark eye line; partial eye-ring; pale loral spot; blue on forewing duller. **VOICE:** Male, quiet whistled peeping notes. Female, a high quack. **SIMILAR SPECIES:** Cinnamon and Green-winged Teal. **HABITAT:** Ponds, marshes, mudflats, flooded fields.

CINNAMON TEAL   *Spatula cyanoptera*

Fairly common

16–17 in. (41–43 cm). *Male:* A small, *dark chestnut* duck with large chalky blue patch on forewing. Adult has *red eye,* which it retains in eclipse plumage. *Female, juvenile, and first-winter male:* Very similar to female Blue-winged but tawnier; bill slightly larger (more shoveler-like), face pattern duller. In flight suggests Blue-winged Teal. Beware: juvenile Cinnamon can be more similar to female Blue-winged, with slightly smaller bill, sometimes somewhat bolder face pattern than adult female Cinnamon. **VOICE:** Like Blue-winged. **HABITAT:** Marshes, freshwater ponds, flooded fields.

NORTHERN SHOVELER

Fairly common

Spatula clypeata (see also p. 42)

18–19 in. (46–49 cm). The long *spoon-shaped bill* gives this duck a front-heavy look distinctive among puddle ducks. When swimming, it sits low, with bill angled toward or in water; often strains water. Speculum green. *Male: Rufous* belly and sides; *white breast;* pale blue patch on forewing; orange feet; dark bill. *Juvenile and female:* Brown. Note large spatulate bill, blue-gray forewing patch, white tail, orange feet; dusky orange bill. *First-winter male:* Variable between female and male; can have dark head with white crescent in front of bill. **VOICE:** Male, a soft *thup-thup.* Female, short quacks. **SIMILAR SPECIES:** Cinnamon Teal. **HABITAT:** Marshes, ponds, sloughs; in winter, also salt bays.

GREEN-WINGED TEAL   *Anas crecca* (see also p. 42)

Common

14–15 in. (36–39 cm). Our smallest puddle duck; flies in tight flocks. Green-wingeds lack light wing patches (speculum *deep green*). *Male:* Small, compact, gray with brown head (a green head patch shows in sunlight). On swimming birds note butter-colored streak near tail and, on common N. American subspecies (*carolinensis*), *vertical white mark* near shoulder. Uncommon (w. AK) to rare Eurasian subspecies, also known as "Common Teal" (subspecies *crecca*), considered separate species by some; shows *longitudinal* (not vertical) white stripe above wing, bolder buffy borders to eye patch. Integrades are encountered. *Female:* A nondescript, small speckled duck with *green* speculum, pale undertail coverts; subspecies not distinguishable. **VOICE:** Male, a high, froglike *dreep.* Female, a sharp *quack.* **SIMILAR SPECIES:** Female Blue-winged and Cinnamon Teal slightly larger and larger-billed, have light blue wing patches; in flight, males have dark belly. Green-winged has white belly, broader dark border to underwing. **HABITAT:** Marshes, rivers, bays, mudflats, flooded fields.

BLUE-WINGED TEAL

male

female

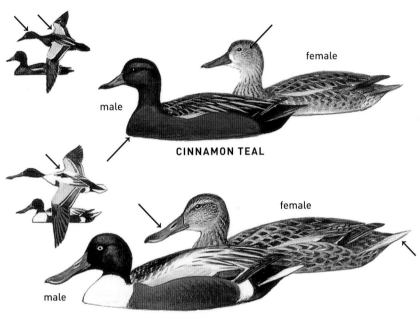

male

female

CINNAMON TEAL

male

female

NORTHERN SHOVELER

GREEN-WINGED TEAL

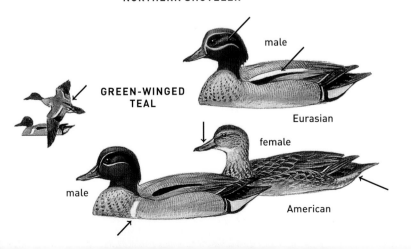

male

Eurasian

female

male

American

CANVASBACK *Aythya valisineria* (see also p. 46)   **Uncommon**

21–22 in. (53–56 cm). A large duck with *long, sloping head profile. Adult male:* White with *chestnut red* head sloping into *long blackish* bill. Red eye, black chest. *Female, juvenile, and first-year male:* Pale grayish brown with rust head and neck. **VOICE:** Cooing notes, a raspy *krrrr*, etc. **SIMILAR SPECIES:** Redhead grayer on body, lacks sloping forehead and bill. **HABITAT:** Lakes, salt bays, estuaries; in summer, freshwater marshes and lakes.

REDHEAD *Aythya americana* (see also p. 46)   **Uncommon**

19–20 in. (48–51 cm). *Adult male:* Gray; black chest and *round rufous head;* bill bluish with black tip. *Female, juvenile, and first-year male:* Brown overall; *diffuse light patch* near bill. Both sexes have indistinct *gray* wing stripe. **VOICE:** Harsh catlike *meow*, soft *krrr* notes. **SIMILAR SPECIES:** Male Canvasback. See female Ring-necked Duck, scaup. **HABITAT:** Lakes, salt bays, estuaries; in summer, freshwater marshes and ponds.

RING-NECKED DUCK *Aythya collaris* (see also p. 46)   **Fairly common**

17–17½ in. (43–46 cm). *Adult male:* Like a scaup but with *black back* and less distinct *gray* wing stripe in flight. *Vertical white mark* before wing; bill with white ring. *Female, juvenile, and first-year male:* Similar to female Lesser Scaup but with *indistinct* light face patch, darker eye, *white eye-ring, grayer* wing stripe, and *pale ring on bill.* **VOICE:** Low-pitched whistle, quacking growl. **SIMILAR SPECIES:** Redhead has rounder head, paler crown, browner (less gray) face. **HABITAT:** Wooded lakes, ponds; in winter, also rivers, bays.

LESSER SCAUP *Aythya affinis* (see also p. 46)   **Fairly common**

16½–17 in. (42–44 cm). Scaup have broad white stripes in wings, shorter (more confined to secondaries) in Lesser. *Adult male:* On water, black at both ends, whitish or pale gray in middle. Bill *blue;* head has "peaked" shape, often glossed dull purple. *Female, juvenile, and first-year male:* Dark brown, usually with white patch near bill. **VOICE:** A soft whistle; a loud *scaup;* also purring notes. **SIMILAR SPECIES:** Greater Scaup, Ring-necked Duck, Redhead; see Tufted Duck (p. 50). **HABITAT:** Lakes, bays, reservoirs; in summer, marsh and taiga ponds. Tends to inhabit fresher-water less-marine habitats than Greater Scaup.

GREATER SCAUP *Aythya marila* (see also p. 46)   **Common**

18–18½ in. (46–48 cm). Very similar to Lesser Scaup, but slightly larger, head more gently rounded, bill slightly wider with *larger black tip* (nail), *white wing stripe longer,* extending onto primaries. *Adult male:* Head often glossed dull green rather than dull purple, but use this with caution. *Female, juvenile, and first-year male* (not shown): White facial patch often larger; sometimes shows pale ear crescent. **VOICE:** Wheezy whistles, a raspy *scaup-scaup.* **SIMILAR SPECIES:** Lesser Scaup, Ring-necked Duck, Redhead, Tufted Duck (p. 50). **HABITAT:** Lakes, bays, estuaries, near-shore ocean waters; in summer, tundra and taiga ponds. Scarce migrant or vagrant in interior West.

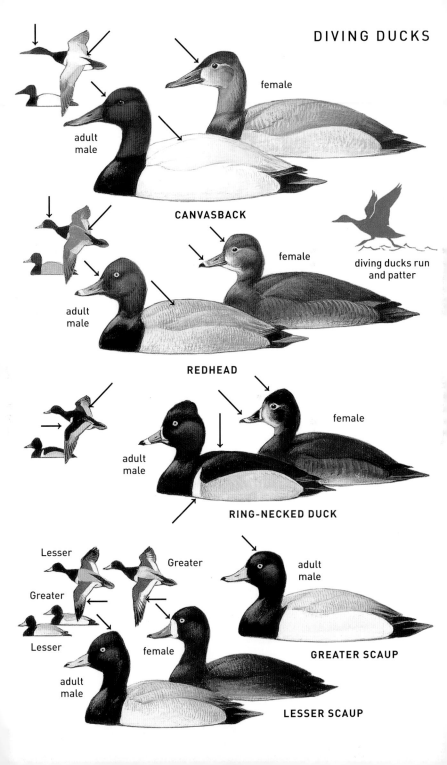

DIVING DUCKS

female

adult male

CANVASBACK

diving ducks run and patter

adult male

female

REDHEAD

adult male

female

RING-NECKED DUCK

Lesser

Greater

adult male

Greater

Lesser

female

GREATER SCAUP

adult male

LESSER SCAUP

DIVING DUCKS

Also called "sea ducks" or "bay ducks," but many are found on lakes and rivers and breed in marshes. All dive. Adult sexes differ but juvenile and first-winter males are female-like. **FOOD:** Small aquatic animals and plants. Seagoing species eat mollusks and crustaceans.

EIDERS

Eiders are found at sea and often mass in flocks off shoals and rocky coasts. Adult males are colorful and show white wing patches in flight; females are brown; adult males become brown ("eclipse" plumage), like females, during molt in late summer and early fall. **FOOD:** Mostly mollusks, crustaceans.

SPECTACLED EIDER *Somateria fischeri*   Rare, local, threatened

21–22 in. (53–56 cm). *Adult male:* Suggests male Common Eider, but head largely pale green, with large *white "goggles"* narrowly trimmed with black. *Female, juvenile, and fall/eclipse male:* Note pale *ghost image of goggles.* Feathering at base of bill extends far down upper mandible. **VOICE:** Mostly silent. Both sexes give calls similar to Common Eider's, but softer. **SIMILAR SPECIES:** Female Common and King Eiders lack goggles. **HABITAT:** In summer, Arctic coasts, tundra ponds; in winter, breaks in pack ice.

KING EIDER *Somateria spectabilis* (see also p. 48)   Rare to uncommon

22 in. (56 cm). *Adult male:* A stocky sea duck; foreparts appear white, rear parts black; crown and nape powder blue; protruding *orange bill-shield. Female, juvenile, and first-winter male:* Warm brown, weak pale eye-ring and thin stripe curving behind and down from eye, flanks barred with crescent-shaped marks. Note facial profile. *First-spring male:* Dusky brown with light breast; bill becomes orange; second-year male intermediate in plumage and bill characteristics. **VOICE:** Courting male, a low crooning phrase. Female, grunting croaks. **SIMILAR SPECIES:** Common Eider larger, with flatter head profile, longer bill-lobe before eye; adult male has *white back*, female evenly barred flanks. In flight, note position of white wing patches in male. **HABITAT:** Rocky coasts, ocean. Nests on tundra. Casual vagrant well south of winter range; accidental inland.

COMMON EIDER *Somateria mollissima* (see also p. 48)   Fairly common

24–25 in. (61–64 cm). A bulky, thick-necked, oceanic duck, often found in flocks near shoals. Flight sluggish and low; flocks usually in a line. *Adult male: Black belly and white back.* Forewing and back white; head white with black crown, greenish nape. *Female, juvenile, and fall/eclipse male:* Large, brown, *closely barred, with pale eyebrow;* long, flat profile. *First-spring male:* Dusky or chocolate with white breast and collar; white areas come in irregularly through second year; bill slowly becomes brighter yellow. **VOICE:** Male, a moaning *ow-ooo-urr.* Female, a grating *kor-r-r.* **SIMILAR SPECIES:** See King Eider. Female scoters smaller, lack heavy dark barring of female eiders. **HABITAT:** Rocky coasts, shoals; in summer, also islands, tundra. Accidental vagrant inland and south to n. CA.

EIDERS

summer/fall male (eclipse)

female

head of female Spectacled

adult male

SPECTACLED EIDER

first-spring male

female

head of female King

adult male

KING EIDER

first-spring male

female

adult male

head of female Common

COMMON EIDER

Common

King

Spectacled

STELLER'S EIDER *Polysticta stelleri*   Scarce, local

17 in. (43 cm). Unlike other eiders in shape, bill. *Adult male:* Black and white, with *yellow-buff underparts, white head,* black throat, and green bump on back of head. Note *round black spot* on side of breast. As in other eiders, white forewing is conspicuous in flight. *Female, juvenile, and fall/eclipse male:* Dark brown, mottled, with pale eye-ring; distinguished from other eiders by much smaller size and *shape of its small head and blue-gray bill.* Purple speculum bordered in white, visible at short range, suggests a female Mallard. First-spring and second-year male increasingly develops adult malelike plumage. **VOICE:** Usually silent. Male's crooning note resembles Common Eider's but is quieter. Female has a low growl. **SIMILAR SPECIES:** Other eiders, Long-tailed Duck. **HABITAT:** Coasts, ocean. Vagrant south to n. CA.

HARLEQUIN DUCK   Uncommon
Histrionicus histrionicus (see also p. 48)

16–17 in. (41–44 cm). A smallish dark duck. *Adult male:* Spectacularly patterned, slaty with chestnut sides and elaborate white patches and spots. In flight, has stubby shape of a goldeneye but appears uniformly dark. *Female:* A small dusky duck with three round white spots on each side of head; no wing patch. *First-year male:* Intermediate between male and female; eclipse male also female-like but can be tinged bluish and shows white in wing coverts and tertials. **VOICE:** Usually silent. Male, a squeak; also *gwa gwa gwa.* Female, *ek-ek-ek-ek.* **SIMILAR SPECIES:** Female Bufflehead has white wing patch and only one white facial patch. Female scoters larger, with larger bills. **HABITAT:** Turbulent mountain streams in summer; rocky coastal waters in winter. Casual to accidental vagrant inland and well to south of range.

LONG-TAILED DUCK   Uncommon to rare
Clangula hyemalis (see also p. 48)

Male 21–22 in. (53–56 cm); female 16 in. (41 cm). A small duck except for long tail in adult male. The only sea duck combining much *white on body and unpatterned dark wings.* It flies in bunched, irregular flocks, rocking side to side as it flies. *Fall/winter male:* Note needlelike tail, pied pattern, dark cheek. *Spring/summer male:* Dark with white flanks and belly. Note white eye patch, pink on bill. *Fall/winter female:* Dark unpatterned wings, white face with dark cheek spot, lacks long tail feathers. *Spring/summer female:* Similar but darker. Lacks pink on bill. *Juveniles and first-winter males:* Female-like but duller. Much individual variation in plumages. **VOICE:** Talkative; a musical *ow-owdle-ow* or *owl-omelet.* **SIMILAR SPECIES:** Bufflehead. In flight, sometimes confused with alcids because of dark underwings and rapid wingbeats. **HABITAT:** Ocean, harbors, large lakes; in summer, tundra pools and lakes. Widespread but rare winter visitor or vagrant inland across West.

DIVING DUCKS

summer/fall male (eclipse)

female

adult
male

STELLER'S EIDER

female

adult
male

HARLEQUIN DUCK

fall/winter
female

spring/summer
female

fall/winter
male

LONG-TAILED DUCK

spring/summer
male

SCOTERS

Scoters are heavy, blackish ducks seen in large flocks along ocean coasts. They often fly in thin line formation. Scoters are usually silent but during courtship and mating may utter low whistles, croaks, or grunting noises; wings whistle in flight. **FOOD:** Mainly mollusks, crustaceans.

WHITE-WINGED SCOTER *Melanitta fusca* (see also p. 48) Uncommon

21 in. (53 cm). Largest of the three scoters; bill is feathered to nostril. On water, white wing patch is often barely visible or fully concealed (wait for bird to flap or fly). *Adult male:* Black, with a "teardrop" of white near eye; bill orange with black basal knob. *Female and juvenile male:* Sooty brown, with white wing patch and two light oval patches on face. First-year male gradually becomes blackish; bill becomes orange; underparts bleached white on first-year birds of all three scoters. Asian subspecies *stejnegeri,* very rare in w. AK, has hornlike knob at base of bill. **SIMILAR SPECIES:** Other scoters. **HABITAT:** Salt bays, ocean; in summer, lakes. Rare winter visitor or vagrant to interior states.

SURF SCOTER *Melanitta perspicillata* (see also p. 48) Common

19–20 in. (48–51 cm). Medium-sized, the most common scoter by far along the Pacific Coast. *Adult male:* Black, with bold *white patches* on crown and nape. Sloping bill patterned with orange, black, and white. *Female and juvenile male:* Dusky brown; dark crown; two light spots on each side of head (sometimes obscure). First-year male gradually becomes blackish; bill becomes orange, swollen. **SIMILAR SPECIES:** Female White-winged Scoter slightly larger overall, has more extensive feathering on bill, more horizontal, oval face patches, and white wing patch (may not show until bird flaps). Black Scoter has rounder head profile (more like Redhead), lacks feathering on bill, and has silvery underside to flight feathers; female has pale cheeks. **HABITAT:** Ocean, salt bays; in summer, lakes. Rare winter visitor or vagrant to interior states.

BLACK SCOTER Rare to uncommon
Melanitta americana (see also p. 48)

18½–19 in. (47–48 cm). The smallest scoter. Bill upturned and not as bulbous as in other scoters. *Adult male:* Entirely black; bright *orange-yellow knob* on bill is diagnostic. In flight, silvery gray underwing more pronounced than in other scoters. *Female and juvenile male:* Sooty; *entirely light cheeks* contrast with dark cap. First-year male gradually becomes blackish, especially in head; bill becomes yellow, swollen. **SIMILAR SPECIES:** First-spring male Surf Scoter may lack white head patch and have messy orange coloration to mandible, but note higher-sloping bill. Female and juvenile scoters of other two species have smaller light spots on side of head, not entirely pale cheeks. **HABITAT:** Seacoasts, bays; in summer, tundra and taiga ponds. Very rare winter visitor or vagrant to interior states.

scoters can fly in V formation or in loose clumps

SCOTERS

Surf

Black

White-winged

adult male

female

first-winter/spring male

WHITE-WINGED SCOTER

adult male

female

first-winter/spring male

SURF SCOTER

first-winter/spring male

adult male

female

BLACK SCOTER

diving ducks (sea ducks and bay ducks) raft on water, skitter when taking wing

COMMON GOLDENEYE
Fairly common

Bucephala clangula (see also p. 46)

18½–19 in. (47–49 cm). *Adult male:* Note large, *round white spot* before eye. White with black back and blocky, green-glossed head. In flight, short-necked; wings whistle or "sing," show large white patches. *Female, juvenile, and first-year male:* Gray, with white collar and dark brown head; large square white patches that may show on closed wing. Bill black in males, with some yellow in winter/spring females. **VOICE:** Courting male has harsh nasal double note. Female, a harsh *gaak*. **SIMILAR SPECIES:** Barrow's Goldeneye. **HABITAT:** Forested lakes, rivers; in winter, also open lakes, salt bays, seacoasts.

BARROW'S GOLDENEYE *Bucephala islandica*
Uncommon

18 in. (46 cm). Similar to Common Goldeneye, but bill *shorter and "cuter."* *Adult male:* Note *white facial crescent.* Blacker above; head often glossed with *purple* (not green); nape blockier; shows *dark "spur"* on shoulder toward waterline, less white in back and wings. *Female and first-year male:* Similar to female Common but head slightly darker, with steeper forehead and blockier nape, less white in wing. Besides being smaller, bill can become entirely *yellow,* subject to seasonal change. Female Common Goldeneye's bill rarely all yellow. **VOICE:** Usually silent. Courting male, a grunting *kuk, kuk.* Female near nest, a soft *coo-coo-coo.* Wings of both species whistle in flight. **SIMILAR SPECIES:** Common Goldeneye, Bufflehead. **HABITAT:** Wooded lakes, ponds; in winter, lakes and rivers, protected coastal waters. Rare winter visitor or vagrant to most interior West areas; accidental to TX.

BUFFLEHEAD *Bucephala albeola* (see also p. 46)
Common

13½–14 in. (34–36 cm). Small. *Adult male:* Mostly white with black back; blocky head with *large, bonnetlike white patch.* In flight, shows large white wing patches. *Female and first-year male:* Dark and compact, with *white cheek spot,* small bill, smaller wing patch. **VOICE:** Male, in display, a hoarse rolling note. Female, a harsh *ec-ec-ec.* **SIMILAR SPECIES:** Male Hooded Merganser has spikelike bill, brown sides. **HABITAT:** Lakes, ponds, rivers; in winter, also salt bays.

STIFF-TAILED DUCKS

Small, chunky divers, nearly helpless on land. Spiky tail. Adult sexes not alike. **FOOD:** Aquatic life, insects, water plants.

RUDDY DUCK *Oxyura jamaicensis* (see also p. 46)
Fairly common

15 in. (38 cm). Small, chubby; note *white cheek* and dark cap. Often cocks tail upward. Flight "buzzy." *Spring/summer male:* Vivid rusty red with white cheek, black cap, large and strikingly *blue* bill. *Fall/winter male:* Gray with *white cheek,* dull blue or gray bill. *Female and juvenile male:* Similar to fall/winter male, but duskier cheek crossed by dark line. **VOICE:** Courting male, a sputtering *chick-ik-ik-ik-k-k-k-kurrrr,* accompanied by head bobbing. **SIMILAR SPECIES:** Female Bufflehead, Black Scoter. **HABITAT:** Freshwater marshes, ponds, lakes; in winter, also salt bays, harbors.

DIVING DUCKS

COMMON GOLDENEYE

female

adult
male

BARROW'S GOLDENEYE

winter/spring
female

adult
male

summer/fall
female

BUFFLEHEAD

female

adult
male

RUDDY DUCK

female

spring/
summer
male

fall/winter male

MERGANSERS

Long, slender-bodied, crested diving ducks with spikelike bill, saw-edged mandibles. In flight, bill, head, outstretched neck, and body are on a horizontal axis. Adult sexes not alike; first-year and eclipse males resemble female. **FOOD:** Chiefly fish.

COMMON MERGANSER
Fairly common

Mergus merganser (see also p. 44)

24–25 in. (62–64 cm). Whiteness of adult male and merganser shape (bill, outstretched neck, head, and body held horizontally) identify this species. *Adult male:* Note long whitish body, black back, green-black head; primarily white upperwing. Bill and feet red; breast can be tinged rosy peach. *Female and first-year male:* Gray with rufous head contrasting with white chin and clean white chest; wing patch on trailing edge. First-spring males can show dark green in face. **VOICE:** Male, in display, low staccato croaks. Female, a guttural *karrr.* **SIMILAR SPECIES:** Female Red-breasted Merganser very similar to female Common. Note distinct cut-off of rusty head and neck from breast in Common; this is diffuse in Red-breasted. **HABITAT:** Wooded lakes, ponds, rivers; in winter, open lakes, rivers, rarely coastal bays.

RED-BREASTED MERGANSER
Common

Mergus serrator (see also p. 44)

22½–23 in. (56–58 cm). *Adult male:* Rakish; black head glossed with green and *crested;* breast at waterline dark rusty; *wide white collar* between head and breast; bill and feet red. *Female and first-year male:* Gray, with crested, dull rusty head that *blends* into color of neck; red bill and feet. First-spring male can molt in dark green feathers in face and black feathers in back. **VOICE:** Usually silent. Male, a hoarse croak. Female, *karrr.* **SIMILAR SPECIES:** Male Common Merganser whiter, without collar and breast-band effect; lacks shaggy crest. See Common Merganser for female. Common's bill slightly thicker at base. **HABITAT:** Woodland and coastal lakes, open water; in winter, also bays, tidal channels, nearshore ocean waters.

HOODED MERGANSER
Uncommon to fairly common

Lophodytes cucullatus (see also p. 44)

17–18 in. (43–46 cm). *Male:* Note vertical *fan-shaped white crest,* which may be raised or lowered. Breast white, with two black bars on each side. Upperwing has white patch; *flanks rusty brown. Female and first-winter male:* Merganser-like silhouette and spikelike bill; small size, dusky look, and *dark head, bill, and chest.* Note loose *tawny crest.* First-spring male can molt in black and white feathers in head and breast. **VOICE:** In display, low grunting or croaking notes. **SIMILAR SPECIES:** Male Bufflehead smaller and chubbier, with *white* sides. Other female mergansers larger and *grayer,* with rufous head, reddish bill. In flight, wing patch and silhouette separate female Hooded Merganser from female Wood Duck. **HABITAT:** Wooded lakes, ponds, rivers; in winter, also tidal channels, protected bays. Rare in Southwest.

MERGANSERS

mergansers fly with bill, head, body, and tail on the same horizontal axis

saw-edged mandibles of merganser

female

adult male

COMMON MERGANSER

female

adult male

RED-BREASTED MERGANSER

crest down

adult males

first-winter male

crest up

female

HOODED MERGANSER

Common   Red-breasted   Hooded

FLIGHT PATTERNS of DABBLING DUCKS

Note: Only males are described below. Although females are unlike the males in body plumage, their wing patterns are quite similar. The names in parentheses are common nicknames used by hunters.

NORTHERN PINTAIL ("SPRIG") *Anas acuta*   p. 24
From below: Needle tail, white breast, thin neck.
Above: Needle tail, neck stripe, single thin white border on speculum.

WOOD DUCK ("WOODY") *Aix sponsa*   p. 24
From below: White belly, dusky wings, long square tail.
Above: Stocky; long dark tail, white border on dark wing.

AMERICAN WIGEON ("BALDPATE") *Mareca americana*   p. 24
From below: White belly, pointed dark tail.
Above: Large white shoulder patch.

NORTHERN SHOVELER ("SPOONBILL") *Mareca clypeata*   p. 28
From below: Dark belly, white breast, white tail, spoon bill.
Above: Large pale bluish shoulder patch, spoon bill.

GADWALL ("GRAYDUCK") *Mareca strepera*   p. 26
From below: White belly, white underwing, square white patch on rear edge of wing.
Above: White patch on rear edge of wing.

GREEN-WINGED TEAL ("ROCKET") *Anas crecca*   p. 28
From below: Small; light belly, dark head, broad dark borders to underwing.
Above: Small, dark-winged; green speculum.

BLUE-WINGED TEAL ("WHITEFACE") *Spatula discors*   p. 28
From below: Small; dark belly, narrow dark borders to underwing.
Above: Small; large chalky blue shoulder patch.
Note: Cinnamon Teal (*S. cyanoptera*) shows similar wing pattern to Blue-winged Teal.

upper wing of a dabbling duck showing the iridescent
speculum (secondaries)

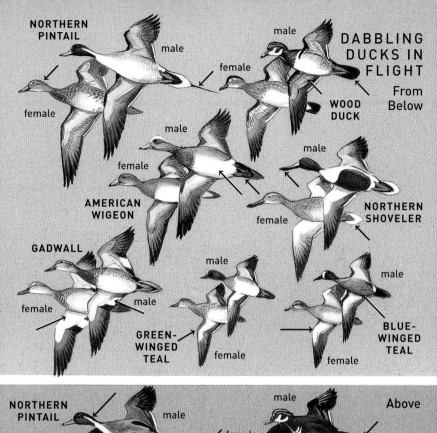

DABBLING DUCKS IN FLIGHT

From Below

NORTHERN PINTAIL — male, female
WOOD DUCK — male, female
AMERICAN WIGEON — male, female
NORTHERN SHOVELER — male, female
GADWALL — female, male
GREEN-WINGED TEAL — male, female
BLUE-WINGED TEAL — male, female

Above

NORTHERN PINTAIL — male, female
WOOD DUCK — male, female
AMERICAN WIGEON — male, female
NORTHERN SHOVELER — male, female
GADWALL — male, female
GREEN-WINGED TEAL — male, female
BLUE-WINGED TEAL — male, female

FLIGHT PATTERNS of
DABBLING DUCKS and MERGANSERS

Note: Only males are described below. Although most females are unlike the males, their wing patterns are quite similar. Mergansers have a distinctive flight silhouette. The names in parentheses are common nicknames used by hunters.

MALLARD ("GREENHEAD") *Anas platyrhynchos*   p. 26
From below: Dark chest, light belly, white neck ring, white tail.
Above: Dark head, neck ring, two white borders on bluish speculum.

FULVOUS WHISTLING-DUCK *Dendrocygna bicolor*   p. 20
From below: Tawny, with blackish underwing linings.
Above: Dark, unpatterned wings; white band on rump.

COMMON MERGANSER ("SAWBILL") *Mergus merganser*   p. 40
From below: Merganser shape; oustretched neck, dark head, white body, white underwing linings.
Above: Merganser shape; white chest, large white wing patches.

RED-BREASTED MERGANSER ("SHELDRAKE") *Mergus serrator*   p. 40
From below: Merganser shape; oustretched neck; dark chest band, white collar.
Above: Merganser shape; dark chest, large white wing patches.

HOODED MERGANSER ("HOODIE") *Lophodytes cucullatus*   p. 40
From below: Merganser shape; dusky underwing linings.
Above: Merganser shape; small white wing patches.

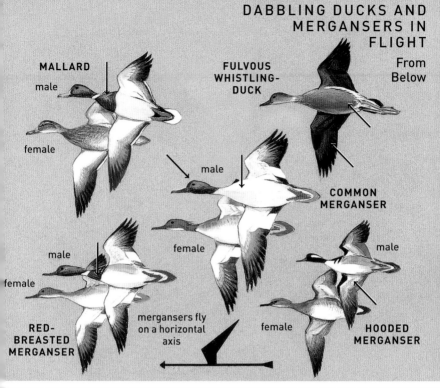

DABBLING DUCKS AND MERGANSERS IN FLIGHT

From Below

MALLARD
male
female

FULVOUS WHISTLING-DUCK

COMMON MERGANSER
male
female

RED-BREASTED MERGANSER
male
female

mergansers fly on a horizontal axis

HOODED MERGANSER
male
female

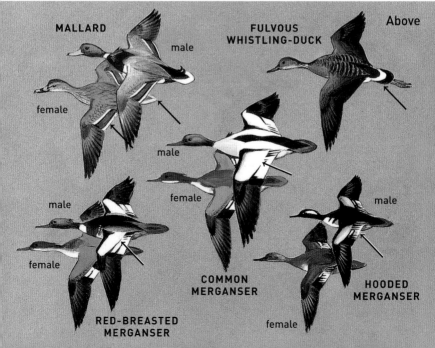

Above

MALLARD
male
female

FULVOUS WHISTLING-DUCK

COMMON MERGANSER
male
female

RED-BREASTED MERGANSER
male
female

HOODED MERGANSER
male
female

FLIGHT PATTERNS of DIVING DUCKS, etc.

Note: Only adult males are described below. The first five all have a black chest. The names in parentheses are common nicknames used by hunters.

CANVASBACK ("CANNIE") *Aythya valisineria* p. 30
From below: Black chest, long profile.
Above: White back, long profile. Lacks contrasty wing stripe of next four species.

REDHEAD ("POCHARD") *Aythya americana* p. 30
From below: Black chest, roundish rufous head.
Above: Gray back, broad gray wing stripe.

RING-NECKED DUCK ("BLACKJACK") *Aythya collaris* p. 30
From below: Not safe to tell from scaup from below; gray wing stripe sometimes evident.
Above: Black back, broad gray wing stripe.

GREATER SCAUP ("BROADBILL") *Aythya marila* p. 30
From below: Black chest, white stripe showing through wing.
Above: Broad white wing stripe (extending onto primaries).

LESSER SCAUP ("BLUEBILL") *Aythya affinis* p. 30
Above: Wing stripe shorter than in Greater Scaup.

COMMON GOLDENEYE ("WHISTLER") *Bucephala clangula* p. 38
From below: Dark underwing linings, white wing patches, rounded dark head.
Above: Large white square wing patch, short neck, dark head.

RUDDY DUCK ("STIFFTAIL") *Oxyura jamaicensis* p. 38
From below: Stubby; white face, dark chest, long tail.
Above: Small; dark with white cheeks, long tail.

BUFFLEHEAD ("BUTTERBALL") *Bucephala albeola* p. 38
From below: Like a small goldeneye; note head patch.
Above: Small; large wing patches, white head patch.

Silhouettes of Ducks on Land

| dabbling ducks (dabblers) | sea and bay ducks (divers) | mergansers (divers) | Ruddy Duck (diver) | whistling-ducks (dabblers) |

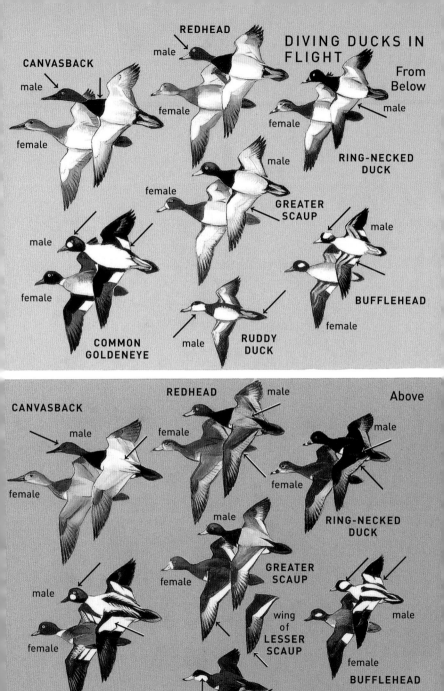

DIVING DUCKS IN FLIGHT

From Below

CANVASBACK — male, female

REDHEAD — male, female

RING-NECKED DUCK — male, female

GREATER SCAUP — male, female

BUFFLEHEAD — male, female

COMMON GOLDENEYE — male, female

RUDDY DUCK — male

Above

CANVASBACK — male, female

REDHEAD — male, female

RING-NECKED DUCK — male, female

GREATER SCAUP — female, male

wing of LESSER SCAUP

BUFFLEHEAD — male, female

COMMON GOLDENEYE — male, female

RUDDY DUCK — male

FLIGHT PATTERNS of DIVING DUCKS

Note: Only adult males are described below. The names in parentheses are common nicknames used by hunters.

LONG-TAILED DUCK ("KAKAWI") *Clangula hyemalis*   p. 34
From below: Dark unpatterned wings, white belly.
Above: Dark unpatterned wings, much white on body.

HARLEQUIN DUCK ("BLUEDUCK") *Histrionicus histrionicus*   p. 34
From below: Solid dark below, white head spots, small bill.
Above: Dark with white marks, small bill, long tail.

SURF SCOTER ("SKUNKHEAD") *Melanitta perspicillata*   p. 36
From below: Black body, white head patches (not readily visible from below), sloping forehead.
Above: Black body, white head patches, sloping forehead.

BLACK SCOTER ("BUTTERBILL") *Melanitta americana*   p. 36
From below: Black plumage, paler flight feathers, rounded forehead.
Above: All-dark plumage. Body slightly smaller and pudgier than Surf Scoter's, rounded forehead.

WHITE-WINGED SCOTER ("WHITEWING") *Melanitta fusca*   p. 36
From below: Black body, white wing patches.
Above: Black body, white wing patches.

COMMON EIDER ("IDAH") *Somateria mollissima*   p. 32
Above: White back, white forewing, black belly.

KING EIDER ("KING") *Somateria spectabilis*   p. 32
Above: Whitish foreparts, black rear parts.

DIVING
DUCKS
IN
FLIGHT
From Below

LONG-TAILED DUCK
male
female

HARLEQUIN DUCK
male
female

SURF SCOTER
male
female

BLACK SCOTER
male
female

WHITE-WINGED SCOTER
male
female

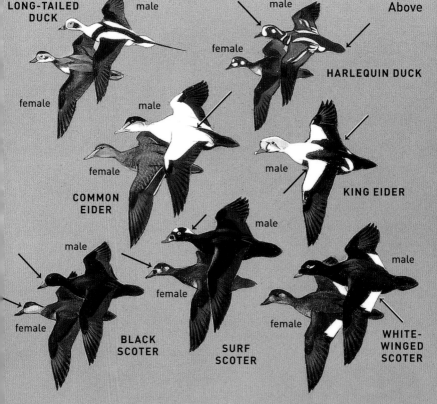

Above

LONG-TAILED DUCK
male
female

HARLEQUIN DUCK
male
female

COMMON EIDER
male
female

KING EIDER
male

BLACK SCOTER
male
female

SURF SCOTER
male
female

WHITE-WINGED SCOTER
male
female

VAGRANT WATERFOWL

GARGANEY *Spatula querquedula*   Casual vagrant

15–16 in. (38–41 cm). *Male:* Broad white eyebrow stripe, silvery shoulder patch (in flight). *Female:* Told from Blue-winged and Cinnamon Teal by bolder face pattern, grayer (less blue) upperwing patch, dark legs, and white borders on speculum. **RANGE:** Rare visitor from Asia to w. AK; casual elsewhere in West, primarily along coast.

TUFTED DUCK *Aythya fuligula*   Vary rare vagrant

16½–17 in. (41–43 cm). *Adult male:* Differs from male scaup and Ring-necked Duck by conspicuous wispy crest; note also black back, white sides, white wing stripe. *Female, juvenile, and first-year male:* Resembles female scaup but develops small tuft, broad band at bill tip, and lacks eye-ring and ring on bill of Ring-necked. May or may not have white at base of bill. **VOICE:** Similar to Ring-necked Duck. **RANGE:** Regular visitor from Eurasia to w. AK; very rare along Pacific Coast; casual elsewhere inland. **HABITAT:** Sheltered ponds, bays, reservoirs. Usually with scaup.

SMEW *Mergellus albellus*   Accidental vagrant

16 in. (41 cm). Smaller and shorter-billed than other mergansers. *Adult male:* Very white, with *black eye patch* and slight drooping black-and-white crest behind eye; conspicuous black-and-white wings. *Female, juvenile, and first-year male:* Small and gray, with *white cheeks, chestnut cap.* **RANGE:** Rare but regular spring visitor from Asia to w. AK; accidental elsewhere. Some birds might be escapees.

UNESTABLISHED EXOTIC WATERFOWL

BARNACLE GOOSE *Branta leucopsis*   Exotic

26–27 in. (66–69 cm). Accidental vagrant in East; occasional escapes observed in West.

PINK-FOOTED GOOSE *Anser brachyrhynchus*   Exotic or vagrant

25–30 in. (65–75 cm). Similar to Greater White-fronted Goose but head entirely brown, bill mostly dark, tail whiter. Accidental but increasing in e. North America; recent records in West (e.g., CO) may be vagrants.

EGYPTIAN GOOSE *Alopochen aegyptiacus*   Exotic

25–29 in. (63–73 cm). Has become established in FL and e. TX but still an exotic in West, where small numbers of escapees are found in CA.

MANDARIN DUCK *Aix galericulata*   Exotic

16–19 in (41–49 cm). Often found in parks. Female similar to female Wood Duck but bill smaller, often reddish; sides with more white markings; speculum with little or no blue.

COMMON SHELDUCK *Tadorna tadorna*   Exotic

23–26 in. (58–67 cm). A vagrant in East but birds in West are exotics.

RUDDY SHELDUCK *Tadorna ferruginea*   Exotic

24–26 in. (61–67 cm). Possible vagrant in East but records in West are escapes.

VAGRANT
WATERFOWL

GARGANEY

female

male

TUFTED
DUCK

female

adult
male

adult
male

female

SMEW

PINK-FOOTED
GOOSE

EGYPTIAN
GOOSE

BARNACLE
GOOSE

adult
male

COMMON
SHELDUCK

RUDDY
SHELDUCK

MANDARIN DUCK

adult male

CORMORANTS Family Phalacrocoracidae

Large blackish waterbirds that often stand erect on rocks, posts, or dead limbs. Breeding adults may have colorful facial skin, throat pouch, and eyes. Bill slender, hook-tipped. Sexes alike. Cormorants swim low and with bill tilted up at an angle. Silent except for occasional low grunts at nesting colonies. **FOOD:** Fish, crustaceans. **RANGE:** Nearly worldwide.

DOUBLE-CRESTED CORMORANT *Phalacrocorax auritus* Common

32–33 in. (81–84 cm). Cormorants found inland or on fresh water are largely this species except where range overlaps Neotropic Cormorant. Told from other Pacific cormorants by its *orangey to yellowish lower mandible, throat pouch, and bare face* including loral region. In flight, shows *kink* in neck. *Adult:* Glossy black, perches and flies with neck in an S. *First-year:* Brownish belly, pale throat and chest can become white by spring. **SIMILAR SPECIES:** Other cormorants, loons. **HABITAT:** Coasts, estuaries, lakes, rivers; nests colonially on islands, structures or trees near water (often with herons).

NEOTROPIC CORMORANT *Phalacrocorax brasilianus* Uncommon

25–26 in. (64–66 cm). *Adult and first-year:* Similar to Double-crested Cormorant, but smaller, slimmer, and with proportionally *much longer tail.* Note smaller throat pouch, in adult with *narrow white border,* forming a point at rear; bare orangey face does not extend to loral area; underparts of first-year not quite as pale. **SIMILAR SPECIES:** Other cormorants. **HABITAT:** Freshwater wetlands, reservoirs, ponds, lakes. Casual vagrant well north and west of range.

BRANDT'S CORMORANT *Phalacrocorax penicillatus* Common

34 in. (86–89 cm). *Adult:* Almost same size as Double-crested Cormorant but has dark chin (*blue* when breeding), shorter tail, longer bill, and flies without marked kink in neck. *Buff throat patch* behind pouch. *First-year:* Underparts extensively brown, becoming bleached by spring; *buff throat.* **SIMILAR SPECIES:** First-year Double-crested has yellow in bill, face, and throat pouch, paler breast; Pelagic and Red-faced show darker brown limited to breast. **HABITAT:** Ocean, coasts, rocky islets; nests colonially on flats of offshore islets.

PELAGIC CORMORANT *Phalacrocorax pelagicus* Fairly common

26–29 in. (66–73 cm). *Adult:* Noticeably smaller and more iridescent greenish or purplish than other cormorants, with more *slender neck* (no kinks in flight), longish tail, small head, and smaller, *thinner bill.* In late winter through midsummer shows *white patch* on flanks. Dull red throat pouch obvious only at close range. *First-year:* Deep brown on chest, brownish black elsewhere. **SIMILAR SPECIES:** Other cormorants, loons. **HABITAT:** Ocean, coasts, rocky islets, sounds. Breeds on cliff faces.

RED-FACED CORMORANT *Phalacrocorax urile* Uncommon, local

30–31 in. (76–79 cm). *Adult:* Note *bright red* face (extending to forehead and behind eye). Throat pouch *bluish; bill mostly pale.* Has white flank patches in spring/summer. *First-year:* Bill mostly pale; facial skin pinkish. **SIMILAR SPECIES:** Other cormorants, loons. Pelagic Cormorant is slightly smaller, has duller red pouch and face and thinner, all-dark bill. **HABITAT:** Ocean, coasts; nests on sea cliffs.

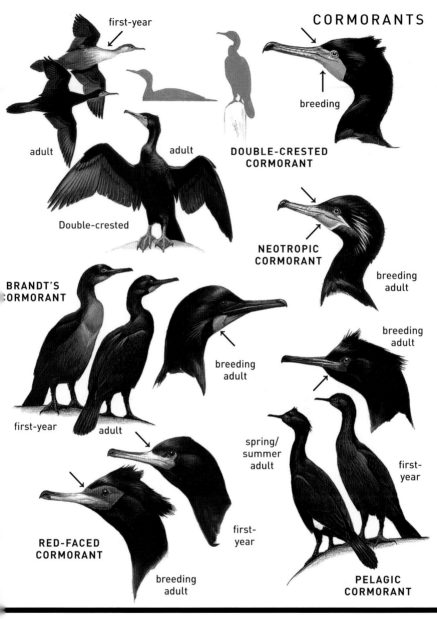

CORMORANTS

first-year

breeding

DOUBLE-CRESTED CORMORANT

adult

adult

Double-crested

NEOTROPIC CORMORANT

breeding adult

BRANDT'S CORMORANT

breeding adult

breeding adult

first-year

adult

breeding adult

spring/ summer adult

first-year

RED-FACED CORMORANT

first-year

breeding adult

PELAGIC CORMORANT

FIRST-YEAR CORMORANTS IN FLIGHT

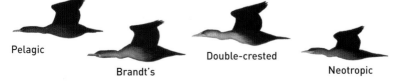

Pelagic

Brandt's

Double-crested

Neotropic

LOONS Family Gaviidae

Large, long-bodied, with daggerlike bills. Airborne, loons are slower and more hunchbacked than most ducks. Sexes alike. Juvenile and first-winter loons are more scaly above than winter adults. **FOOD:** Small fish, crustaceans, other aquatic life. **RANGE:** Northern parts of N. Hemisphere.

RED-THROATED LOON *Gavia stellata* Fairly common

25 in. (64 cm). Slimmer head and neck than other loons and note thin, slightly *upturned bill, often uptilted head.* Flies with neck drooped. *Spring/summer adult:* Plain brown back, gray head, *rufous throat patch. Fall/winter adult and second-year:* Back paler, *spotted white;* extensive white on neck and face includes eye. *Juvenile and first-year:* Face and neck smudgier. **VOICE:** When flying, a repeated *kwuk.* Guttural ptarmigan-like calls and wails on breeding grounds. **SIMILAR SPECIES:** Other loons, Western and Clark's Grebes. **HABITAT:** Nearshore ocean, bays, estuaries; in summer, tundra lakes. Rare inland.

PACIFIC LOON *Gavia pacifica* Common

25–26 in. (64–66 cm). Smaller than Common Loon, with slightly thinner straight bill. *Spring/summer adult: Pale gray nape;* black throat and fore-neck. Back divided into four checkered patches. *Fall/winter adult and second-year:* Note sharp, straight separation of dark and white on neck. Dark feathering around eye. **VOICE:** On breeding grounds, deep, barking *kwow;* falsetto wails; otherwise silent. **SIMILAR SPECIES:** Winter Red-throated Loon shows more white in face. Face of Common Loon smudgier. **HABITAT:** Ocean, large coastal bays; in summer, tundra lakes and sloughs. Very rare inland.

ARCTIC LOON *Gavia arctica* Rare, local

27–28 in. (69–73 cm). A bit larger than Pacific Loon, with more angular head, larger bill, and whiter sides and rear-flank patches. Spring/summer adult has bolder black-and-white streaking on neck. Juvenile and fall/winter adult have white flanks. Scarce vagrant along Pacific Coast in winter. **SIMILAR SPECIES:** Red-throated Loon also may have white flanks. **HABITAT:** Same as Pacific Loon.

COMMON LOON *Gavia immer* Fairly common

31–32 in. (78–81 cm). Large, long-bodied, low-swimming; bill *stout,* dag-gerlike. In flight shows large, trailing feet. *Spring/summer adult:* Blackish head and bill. Uniformly *checkered back,* broken white necklace. *Fall/winter adult and second-year:* Note *irregular or broken (half-collared) neck pattern. Pale partial eye-ring.* **VOICE:** In breeding locations, falsetto wails, weird yodeling, maniacal quavering laughter; at night, a tremulous *ha-oo-oo.* In flight, a barking *kwuk.* Usually silent in fall/winter season. **SIMILAR SPECIES:** Other loons and first-year cormorants. **HABITAT:** In summer, lakes, tundra ponds; in winter, larger lakes, bays, ocean.

YELLOW-BILLED LOON *Gavia adamsii* Rare

34–35 in. (86–89 cm). Similar to Common Loon but bill *pale ivory* (some-times with darker base), appears *yellowish* in summer, and slightly uptilted: straight above, angled below. In fall/winter, *paler* and with browner head and neck than Common, usually with small *dark ear patch.* **SIMILAR SPECIES:** Bill of fall/winter Common Loon can be pale, but cul-men (upper ridge) is *dark to tip* versus pale in Yellow-billed. **HABITAT:** Same as Common Loon. Casual winter vagrant inland.

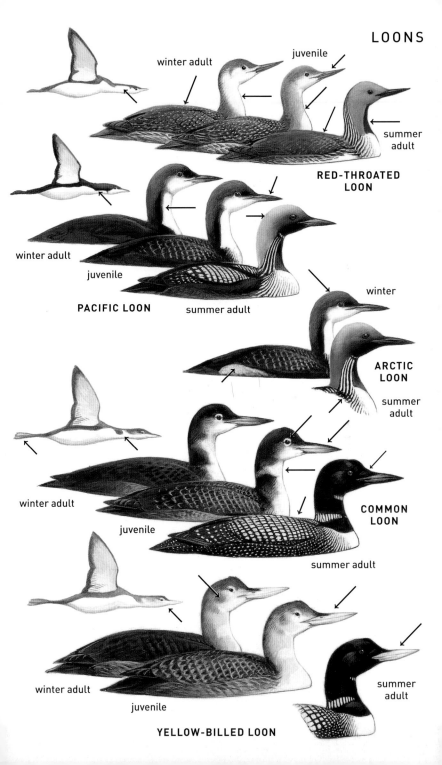

LOONS

winter adult

juvenile

summer adult

RED-THROATED LOON

winter adult

juvenile

summer adult

PACIFIC LOON

winter

ARCTIC LOON

summer adult

winter adult

juvenile

summer adult

COMMON LOON

winter adult

juvenile

summer adult

YELLOW-BILLED LOON

GREBES Family Podicipedidae

Somewhat ducklike divers with lobed toes, thin necks and bills; tailless. Sexes alike. Juvenile has striped head; thereafter ages largely alike. Flight labored. **FOOD:** Small fish, other aquatic life. **RANGE:** Worldwide.

PIED-BILLED GREBE *Podilymbus podiceps*　　　Fairly common
13–13½ in. (33–34 cm). Note "chickenlike" bill, puffy white undertail. *Spring/summer: Black throat patch* and *ring* around pale bill. *Fall/winter:* Lacks black bill markings. **VOICE:** Song *kuk-kuk-cow-cow-cow-cowp-cowp-cowp;* also a whinny and sharp *kwah.* **HABITAT:** Ponds, lakes, marshes; in winter, also salt bays and estuaries.

HORNED GREBE *Podiceps auritus*　　　Fairly common
13½–14 in. (34–36 cm). *Spring/summer: Golden ear patch* and *chestnut neck. Fall/winter:* Black cap *clean-cut to eye level;* white foreneck, thin straight bill. **VOICE:** Loud *gamp,* trills on breeding grounds; silent otherwise. **SIMILAR SPECIES:** Eared Grebe has longer neck, smudgy face; also note flatter crown, pale lores, straighter, pale-tipped bill. Red-necked Grebe larger, bill with yellow. **HABITAT:** Lakes, ponds, coastal waters. Rare migrant or winter visitor to Southwest.

EARED GREBE *Podiceps nigricollis*　　　Common
12½–13 in. (32–33 cm). Note peaked crown, skinny neck, slightly upturned all-dark bill. Floats high in water. Gregarious. *Spring/summer: Wispy golden ear tufts, black neck. Fall/winter:* Lower face and neck often dusky. **SIMILAR SPECIES:** Horned Grebe. **VOICE:** Musical *poo-ee-chk;* froglike *poo-eep* or *krreep.* **HABITAT:** Prairie lakes, ponds; in winter, open lakes, coastal estuaries; in fall congregates at salt lakes.

RED-NECKED GREBE *Podiceps grisegena*　　　Uncommon
18–19 in. (46–49 cm). A largish grebe. *Spring/summer:* Long *rufous neck, white cheek,* black cap. *Fall/winter:* Grayish brown (including neck); white crescent on face; variable dull *yellowish* base of bill. **VOICE:** Loud braying on breeding grounds. **SIMILAR SPECIES:** Loons, Red-breasted Merganser. **HABITAT:** Lakes, ponds; in winter, prefers salt water. Rare inland.

LEAST GREBE *Tachybaptus dominicus*　　　Casual
9½ in. (24 cm). Smaller, darker than Pied-billed Grebe, puffy undertail coverts, slender *black bill, golden eyes.* **VOICE:** A chattering whinny. **HABITAT:** Ponds, marshes, and lake edges. Accidental vagrant to CA.

WESTERN GREBE *Aechmophorus occidentalis*　　　Common
25 in. (64 cm). A large grebe with long neck. Bill long, greenish yellow with dark ridge (male's larger than female's). Black cap extends *below eye.* **VOICE:** Loud, reedy *crik-crick.* **SIMILAR SPECIES:** Clark's Grebe, Red-throated Loon. **HABITAT:** Rushy lakes, sloughs; in winter, large lakes, bays, coasts. Rare vagrant to Plains states.

CLARK'S GREBE *Aechmophorus clarkii*　　　Fairly common
25 in. (64 cm). Formerly regarded as a pale morph of Western Grebe. Bill *orange-yellow.* Dark eye *surrounded by white* (may be pale gray in first-year and winter plumages). Slightly paler than Western with narrower stripe on back of neck. Downy young are white, not gray. **VOICE:** Single-noted *creet* or *criik.* **HABITAT:** Similar to Western, but scarcer in ocean waters during winter. Very rare vagrant to Plains states.

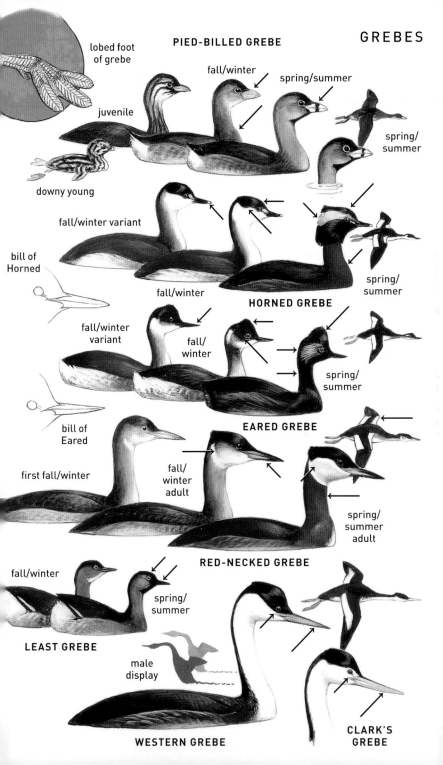

GREBES

lobed foot of grebe

PIED-BILLED GREBE

juvenile

fall/winter

spring/summer

spring/summer

downy young

bill of Horned

fall/winter variant

fall/winter

HORNED GREBE

spring/summer

fall/winter variant

fall/winter

spring/summer

bill of Eared

EARED GREBE

first fall/winter

fall/winter adult

spring/summer adult

RED-NECKED GREBE

fall/winter

spring/summer

LEAST GREBE

male display

WESTERN GREBE

CLARK'S GREBE

AUKS, MURRES, and PUFFINS Family Alcidae

The northern counterparts of penguins, but alcids are smaller and can fly, beating their small narrow wings in a whir, often veering. Most species nest on sea cliffs or in burrows, often in crowded colonies, and all winter on open ocean. Sexes alike. **FOOD:** Fish, squid, krill, zooplankton. **RANGE:** N. Atlantic, N. Pacific, and Arctic Oceans.

THICK-BILLED MURRE *Uria lomvia* Uncommon, local

18 in. (46 cm). Similar to Common Murre, but *blacker above.* Bill shorter, thicker, with *whitish line along gape. Spring/summer adult:* Head and face black, white of foreneck forms inverted V. *Fall/winter adult and first-year:* Face whitish with dark on head extending *well below eye;* no dark line through white ear coverts. White bill mark often less evident. Bill also much smaller, shorter, during first year. **VOICE:** Guttural "murre" calls. Juvenile gives loud whistles. **SIMILAR SPECIES:** Common Murre. **HABITAT:** Nests on coastal cliff ledges; in winter, offshore ocean waters.

COMMON MURRE *Uria aalge* Common

17–17½ in. (43–45 cm). Note slender, pointed bill. *Spring/summer adult:* Head, neck, back, and wings dark, *tinged brownish;* underparts, underwing linings, and line on rear edge of wing white. *Fall/winter adult and first-year:* Similar, but throat and cheeks white. *Black mark extends from eye to cheek* in most birds although some birds off CA retain mostly dark heads in winter. Bridled morph regular in Atlantic but rarely observed in Pacific. Murres often raft on water, fly in lines, stand erect on sea cliffs. Chicks may be mistaken for murrelets but accompany adults (fathers) until mostly grown. **VOICE:** Similar to Thick-billed Murre's. **SIMILAR SPECIES:** Thick-billed Murre. **HABITAT:** Same as Thick-billed Murre, but regularly seen from shore throughout year along Pacific Coast.

PIGEON GUILLEMOT *Cepphus columba* Fairly common

13½ in. (34 cm). *Spring/summer adult:* A medium-sized, black, pigeonlike waterbird, with large *white wing patches* (subdivided by variable black bar or wedge), *red feet,* pointed black bill, orange-red mouth lining, and mostly dark or dirty underwing. *Fall/winter adult, juvenile, and first-year:* Pale gray and white to whitish with dusky eye patch and back; wings with large white patches as in summer, mottled in first-year. **VOICE:** Wheezy or hissing whistle, *peeeeee.* **SIMILAR SPECIES:** Young juveniles can be confused with Marbled and other murrelets but have longer neck, rounder head, and dark reddish mouth lining and feet. See Black Guillemot. **HABITAT:** Inshore ocean waters; less pelagic than most other alcids.

BLACK GUILLEMOT *Cepphus grylle* Scarce, local

12½–13½ in. (32–24 cm). Very similar to Pigeon Guillemot but white wing patch lacks dark bar; underwing linings *white* with thin dark border (at least half dusky in Pigeon). Fall/winter and juvenile Black Guillemots average whiter than similar-plumaged Pigeon Guillemots, have slightly shorter bill. **VOICE:** As in Pigeon Guillemot. **SIMILAR SPECIES:** Pigeon Gullemot. **HABITAT:** Inshore Arctic Ocean waters; breeds on rocky shores, islands. Accidental vagrant inland.

ALCIDS (AUKS)

spring/summer adult

fall/winter

THICK-BILLED MURRE

spring/summer adults

bridled morph

COMMON MURRE

chick

fall/winter

juvenile

PIGEON GUILLEMOT

fall/winter adult

spring/summer adult

spring/summer adults

fall/winter

spring/summer adult

spring/summer adults

BLACK GUILLEMOT

TUFTED PUFFIN *Fratercula cirrhata*   **Uncommon**

15–16 in. (38–40 cm). A stocky, black seabird with large head and bill. *Spring/summer adult:* Blackish, with *massive, triangular, orange-red* bill; white face; and *long, curved, ivory yellow ear tufts.* Feet orange. *Fall/winter adult:* White face and ear tufts much reduced (a trace of dull buffy-yellowish); duller orange-red bill, smaller and not as triangular as in summer because of shedding of outer bill plate. *First-year:* Body brownish black with *broad brown swath behind eye,* belly pale grayish; bill smaller, with little or no red; lacks white face and head plumes during first summer. Three years generally required to reach full adult appearance. **VOICE:** Throaty growling in nesting colony; silent at sea. **SIMILAR SPECIES:** First-year Rhinoceros Auklet. First-year Horned Puffin has gray face, contrasting distinctly with black neck and throat (contrast is lower on breast and less distinct in Tufted Puffin). **HABITAT:** Same as Horned Puffin.

HORNED PUFFIN *Fratercula corniculata*   **Fairly common, local**

15 in. (38 cm). A puffin with *clear white underparts* and broad black collar. Feet bright orange. *Spring/summer adult:* Cheeks *white,* with small, dark erectile horn above each eye. Bill massive, *triangular,* laterally flat; *yellow with red tip. Fall/winter adult:* Cheeks dusky; bill duller, blackish with orange tip. *First-year:* Resembles fall/winter adult with dusky cheeks, but bill smaller and darker; keeps dusky cheeks through first summer. **VOICE:** Low, growling *arr.* **SIMILAR SPECIES:** Atlantic Puffin (not shown) very similar in winter but bill shape differs; malar area, throat, and neck have broader black band; vagrants to opposite coasts might be expected with melting polar cap. **HABITAT:** Nests on rocky ocean cliffs. Forages in offshore waters.

RHINOCEROS AUKLET *Cerorhinca monocerata*   **Fairly common**

15 in. (38 cm). A dark stubby seabird with a blocky wedge-shaped head. *Spring/summer adult* (plumage acquired in late winter): *White mustache* and narrow *white plume* a*bove and behind eye, short erect horn* at base of yellowish bill. *Fall/winter adult:* Note size and *uniform dark color with paler lower vent.* White plumes shorter, horn absent. *First-year:* Similar to fall/winter adult, with smaller, darker bill. **VOICE:** Wide array of barks, growls, groans. **SIMILAR SPECIES:** First-year Tufted Puffin. Cassin's Auklet smaller, rounder headed. Parakeet Auklet has longer eye stripe *originating at rear of eye,* red bill, whiter below. **HABITAT:** Nests colonially in burrows on islands. Found in both nearshore and offshore ocean waters.

CASSIN'S AUKLET *Ptychoramphus aleuticus*   **Fairly common**

9 in. (23 cm). A small stubby seabird; entirely dark gray except for white crescent above eye, white iris (darker in juvenile and first-year), and white belly; note pale spot at base of lower mandible. **VOICE:** In nesting colony, a series of ringing wheezy *kueek-kueek* notes; silent at sea. **SIMILAR SPECIES:** In winter, all other small alcids in its range have much more white. See Rhinoceros and Parakeet Auklets. **HABITAT:** Nests in island burrows and crevices. Forages for krill in open ocean.

ALCIDS

juvenile

fall/winter
adult

spring/
summer
adults

TUFTED
PUFFIN

juvenile

fall/winter adult

spring/summer adults

HORNED
PUFFIN

juvenile

fall/winter

spring/summer
adult

RHINOCEROS
AUKLET

adults

CASSIN'S
AUKLET

LONG-BILLED MURRELET *Brachyramphus perdix*   Casual vagrant

10–11 in. (25–28 cm). Similar to Marbled Murrelet but *lacks white collar* and shows two small pale *oval patches* on nape. Dark crown contrasts with white face in straighter line than in Marbled Murrelet, bill longer, head more wedge-shaped. **RANGE AND HABITAT:** Casual visitor from Asia; rarely at lakes, reservoirs, and rivers far inland. Declining.

MARBLED MURRELET   Uncommon, endangered
Brachyramphus marmoratus

9¾–10 in. (24–25 cm). *Spring/summer adult: Dark brown; heavily mottled* on underparts. *Fall/winter and first-year:* Dark above and white below, with *strip of white on scapulars,* white collar. **VOICE:** Sharp *keer, keer* or lower *kee.* **SIMILAR SPECIES:** Fall/winter Pigeon Guillemot slightly larger, with white patch on wing, not scapulars. See Long-billed Murrelet. **HABITAT:** Coastal ocean waters, bays. Breeds inland, mainly high on limbs of mossy old-growth conifers. Endangered.

KITTLITZ'S MURRELET   Scarce, local, endangered
Brachyramphus brevirostris

9¼–9½ in. (23–24 cm). *Spring/summer adult:* Buffy or tan overall, *mottled and freckled with white* above, giving a pale look. *Fall/winter and first-year:* Similar to Marbled Murrelet, but *white on face surrounds eyes.* White outer tail feathers in all plumages. **SIMILAR SPECIES:** Marbled Murrelet. **HABITAT:** Glacial waters; nests on slopes above timberline.

SCRIPPS'S MURRELET *Synthliboramphus scrippsi*   Uncommon, local

9½–9¾ in. (24–25 cm). Formerly lumped with Guadalupe Murrelet as "Xantus's Murrelet." A small alcid, contrastingly sooty black above, white below. Ages and sexes similar. **VOICE:** High-pitched twittering at colonies; occasionally at sea. **SIMILAR SPECIES:** Pure white underwings distinguish Scripps's and Guadalupe Murrelets from Craveri's Murrelet. Guadalupe Murrelet has white above eye in all plumages. **HABITAT:** Breeds in rocky island crevices; disperses to offshore waters.

GUADALUPE MURRELET   Scarce, local, threatened
Synthliboramphus hypoleucus

9½–9¾ in. (24–25 cm). Very similar to Scripps's Murrelet, but with distinctive white arc above eye. **RANGE AND HABITAT:** Breeds on islands off Baja CA, a rare late-summer and fall visitor north to BC, often farther offshore (in warmer water) than Scripps's Murrelet.

CRAVERI'S MURRELET   Rare, local, threatened
Synthliboramphus craveri

9¼–9½ in. (23–24 cm). Very similar to Scripps's Murrelet, but slightly browner, with *dark partial collar* extending down sides of breast, and *dusky* (not white) underwing linings. Bill very slightly longer and head shape slightly more rounded. Disperses irregularly north in summer and fall, often during warmer-ocean years.

ANCIENT MURRELET *Synthliboramphus antiquus*   Scarce

10 in. (25 cm). In all plumages, *gray back contrasts with black cap. Spring/ summer adult:* Sharply cut *black throat patch* and *white stripe over eye.* Bill yellow. *Fall/winter and first-year:* Throat whitish or mottled dusky; weaker head stripe. **VOICE:** Whistled trills. **SIMILAR SPECIES:** Other Pacific alcids lack back/crown contrast. **HABITAT:** Breeds on rocky and debris-strewn slopes. Accidental vagrant inland.

MURRELETS

LONG-BILLED MURRELET

fall/winter

MARBLED MURRELET

fall/winter

fall/winter

spring/summer adult

spring/summer

KITTLITZ'S MURRELET

spring/summer

fall/winter

spring/summer adult

fall/winter

GAUDALUPE MURRELET

SCRIPPS'S MURRELET

CRAVERI'S MURRELET

fall/winter

spring/summer

spring/summer adult

ANCIENT MURRELET

CRESTED AUKLET   *Aethia cristatella*   Fairly common, local

9½–10½ in. (24–27 cm). A droll auklet of the Bering Sea. *Spring/summer adult:* Slate gray; thin white plume behind eye. Stubby bill is *bright orange* and a curious crest *curls forward* over bill. Orange gape on bill lost and crest shorter in winter. *First-year:* Paler gray overall, with dark bill; juvenile lacks head stripe and plume. **VOICE:** Doglike bark in nesting colony. **SIMILAR SPECIES:** Whiskered and Cassin's Auklets. **HABITAT:** Nests on remote islands and coastal areas. Forages in open ocean.

WHISKERED AUKLET   *Aethia pygmaea*   Scarce, local

7¾–8 in. (20 cm). Similar to slightly larger Crested Auklet, but spring/summer adult has *three additional thin white plumes* (whiskers) on each side of face. In fall/winter and first-year plumages, plumes are shorter. Juvenile can lack head plumes. At all times flying birds show *paler lower belly and undertail coverts* (can be inconspicuous on sitting birds). **HABITAT:** Tidal rips, rocky coasts.

PARAKEET AUKLET   *Aethia psittacula*   Uncommon, local

10 in. (25 cm). A medium-sized alcid with *stubby, red bill* and whitish underparts. *Spring/summer adult:* Entire head black, with thin white plume behind eye. *Fall/winter and first-year:* Mostly whitish underneath; bill duskier, less red. Juvenile can lack white head stripe. **VOICE:** At nesting colony, a high whinny. **SIMILAR SPECIES:** Crested Auklet entirely dark. Least Auklet much smaller. Rhinoceros Auklet in winter larger, bill longer and not reddish, less white below. At sea, can look similar to smaller Cassin's Auklet but head plume is usually present, whiter underneath, including undertail coverts. **HABITAT:** Offshore occurs singly or in small loose groups (not in flocks like other small alcids); nests in scattered pairs or in colonies on sea cliffs and rubble slopes.

LEAST AUKLET   *Aethia pusilla*   Fairly common, local

6–6¼ in. (15–16 cm). The tiniest alcid; chubby, neckless. Black above, white below. In flight, a whirring ping-pong ball. *Spring/summer adult:* Has dark band across upper breast. *Fall/winter and first-year: White below, lacks plumes.* **VOICE:** High-pitched chattering in colony. **SIMILAR SPECIES:** Dovekie is much larger. **HABITAT:** Nests on remote rocky islands in colonies with other auklets. Forages in open ocean.

DOVEKIE   *Alle alle*   Scarce and very local

8–8¼ in. (20–21 cm). About the size of European Starling. Chubby and seemingly neckless, with very stubby bill. In flight, flocks bunch tightly. *Spring/summer adult:* Black above, white below; black hood. *Fall/winter and first-year:* White-chested. **VOICE:** Shrill chatter. Noisy on nesting grounds. **SIMILAR SPECIES:** Fall/winter Marbled Murrelet similar but more slender, bill thinner, white stripes on sides of back more distinct. Parakeet Auklet larger with larger reddish bill, lacks white in back. Fall/winter Least Auklet much smaller. **HABITAT:** Nests in high Arctic on coastal cliffs. Winters at sea.

CRESTED
AUKLET

juvenile

fall/
winter

spring/
summer
adult

spring/
summer

spring/
summer
adult

juvenile

fall/
winter

spring/
summer

WHISKERED AUKLET

fall/winter

spring/
summer

spring/summer adult

PARAKEET AUKLET

fall/winter

spring/
summer

LEAST
AUKLET

fall/winter

spring/summer

DOVEKIE

fall/winter

spring/
summer

fall/winter

spring/summer

SHEARWATERS and PETRELS Family Procellariidae

Somewhat gull-like birds of open sea. During windy conditions they bank, or arc, up and down like a roller coaster on stiffly held wings; in calm weather they sit on water or fly with several flaps and then a glide. Called "tubenoses" due to tubelike external nostrils present on bill. Ages and sexes similar. Largely silent at sea; but noisy at breeding colonies. **FOOD:** Fish, squid, crustaceans, ship refuse. **RANGE:** Oceans of world. Most species not seen from mainland shores.

NORTHERN FULMAR *Fulmarus glacialis* Uncommon to common

18½–19 in. (47–49 cm). Stockier than a shearwater, with larger head and shorter, rounder wings; flies like shearwater but aspect more horizontal, less gliding. Note rounded forehead; *stubby, yellowish/pinkish, tubenose bill with variable dark band.* Primaries show a *pale flash or patch.* Leg color pinkish to bluish. Polymorphic, with some intermediates. *Light morph:* Gull-like in plumage; white wing patches distinct. *Dark morph* (more common in Pacific): Uniformly smoky gray, wing patches reduced. First-spring birds worn and disheveled. **VOICE:** Hoarse, grunting *ag-ag-ag-arrr* or *ek-ek-ek-ek-ek.* **SIMILAR SPECIES:** Gulls fly differently and have longer bills; dark shearwaters browner (less gray), stiffer and more banking in flight. **HABITAT:** Open ocean; breeds colonially on sea cliffs.

MURPHY'S PETREL *Pterodroma ultima* Rare

15½–16 in. (40–41 cm). A dark brownish petrel, with bluish sheen when fresh; *underwing primaries pale with dark crescent,* faint dark M across back and wings, and *pale throat, extending around bill.* Flight in windy conditions quick and darting. Rare but regular offshore visitor, mostly in spring. **SIMILAR SPECIES:** Sooty Shearwater, dark-morph Northern Fulmar. Accidental Great-winged Petrel (*Pterodroma macroptera;* not illustrated) larger and stockier, bill stouter, more white on face.

COOK'S PETREL *Pterodroma cookii* Rare, threatened

10½–11 in. (27–28 cm). *Dark M* across gray back and upperwing and *gleaming white* underwings suggest much larger Buller's Shearwater, but note Cook's paler head with black ear patch and light sides of tail. Flight in windy conditions quick and darting. Occurs rarely and irregularly off W. Coast, primarily in summer and fall. **SIMILAR SPECIES:** Accidental Stejneger's Petrel (*Pterodroma longirostris;* not illustrated) similar but bill slightly smaller, *crown dark gray to black.*

MOTTLED PETREL *Pterodroma inexpectata* Rare

14 in. (36 cm). *Dark M* across back and upperwing and contrasting *dark belly* and *heavy diagonal black bar* across underwing. **RANGE:** Regular summer visitor to deep offshore AK waters; very rare though probably somewhat regular south to well off CA, mostly in late fall and winter.

HAWAIIAN PETREL *Pterodroma sandwichensis* Rare, endangered

17–18 in. (43–46 cm). Larger and longer-winged than other petrels off W. Coast; blackish to brownish upperparts with slightly darker M; *black hoodlike cap* with broad *white patch around bill*; broad dark diagonal *underwing carpal bars.* **RANGE:** Breeds in HI (see p. 374), rare but increasingly observed well off CA and OR, primarily in summer and early fall.

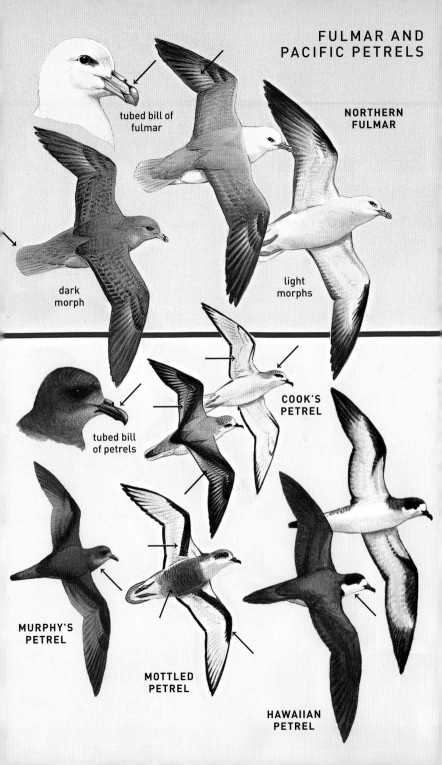

tubed bill of fulmar

NORTHERN FULMAR

dark morph

light morphs

tubed bill of petrels

COOK'S PETREL

MURPHY'S PETREL

MOTTLED PETREL

HAWAIIAN PETREL

SHORT-TAILED SHEARWATER · *Ardenna tenuirostris* · Uncommon

16–17 in. (40–43 cm). Very similar to Sooty Shearwater; best distinguished by *shorter bill, steeper forehead,* and *variably smoky gray* underwing linings, slightly smaller size and narrower wings, more rapid wingbeats. May have contrasty pale throat. **RANGE:** Common in Alaskan waters in summer; found only in small numbers in late fall and winter to south.

SOOTY SHEARWATER · *Ardenna grisea* · Common

17–18 in. (43–46 cm). Often seen in massive flocks in summer, regularly close to shore. Rises over and arcs above waves on narrow, rigid wings. Note *whitish linings* on underwings. Flight rapid and directed, often following each other during migration. **SIMILAR SPECIES:** Short-tailed and Flesh-footed Shearwaters, dark-morph Northern Fulmar. **RANGE:** Breeds in S. Hemisphere, long-distance migrant to our area, where it molts.

FLESH-FOOTED SHEARWATER · *Ardenna carneipes* · Rare

17–17½ in. (43–45 cm). Rare but regular visitor, mostly in fall. *Larger* than Sooty Shearwater; flight more sluggish. Distinguished by *pale pink bill* (with dark tip), *pinkish feet,* dark underwing linings. **SIMILAR SPECIES:** Dark-morph Northern Fulmar, Sooty Shearwater. Rare darker Pink-footed Shearwaters similar in size, shape, and bill, but plumage grayer (less brown), underparts and underwing usually whitish.

PINK-FOOTED SHEARWATER · Fairly common, threatened
Ardenna creatopus

19½ in. (50 cm). Larger than Sooty Shearwater, has dark-tipped pinkish bill and slower wingbeats. Underparts and underwing variably dusky, in darkest cases approaching all-gray (considered "dark-morph" by some). **SIMILAR SPECIES:** Buller's Shearwater; see Flesh-footed Shearwater. Black-vented Shearwater is *smaller,* bill dark, flight faster.

BULLER'S SHEARWATER · Uncommon, irregular, threatened
Ardenna bulleri

16 in. (41 cm). A *very white-bellied* shearwater, separated by distinct *dark M pattern* on back and wings; more buoyant flight. Cap dark. Occurs in fall (primarily late July through Oct.) in variable numbers interannually. **SIMILAR SPECIES:** Pink-footed Shearwater is larger with *dingier* underwings, more *uniform* upperparts, more *blended* face pattern.

BLACK-VENTED SHEARWATER · Fairly common, local
Puffinus opisthomelas

13½–14 in. (34–36 cm). A small shearwater, dark brown above and whitish below with dusky breast sides, dark undertail coverts, dark cap extending below eye. Small size, contrasting *dark-and-white* pattern, and rapid wingbeats with short glides are distinctive among regular Pacific Coast shearwaters. Less contrasting than Manx Shearwater, and rarely shows white patches on sides of rump. Often seen in flocks from shore, mostly in fall and winter. **SIMILAR SPECIES:** Manx and Pink-footed Shearwaters.

MANX SHEARWATER · *Puffinus puffinus* · Rare

13½ in. (34 cm). Similar to Black-vented Shearwater but shows *complete white undertail coverts* and can have white patches on rump; *white extends upwards from neck behind ear coverts.* Rare off Pacific Coast since 1994, when numbers apparently invaded Pacific from Atlantic. Probably breeds in our area, perhaps on islands of AK and BC. Often seen with Sooty and Pink-footed rather than Black-vented Shearwaters.

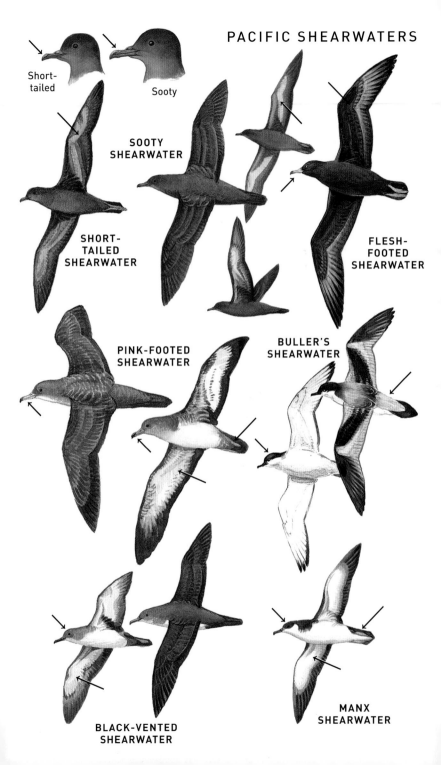

PACIFIC SHEARWATERS

Short-tailed

Sooty

SOOTY SHEARWATER

SHORT-TAILED SHEARWATER

FLESH-FOOTED SHEARWATER

PINK-FOOTED SHEARWATER

BULLER'S SHEARWATER

BLACK-VENTED SHEARWATER

MANX SHEARWATER

ALBATROSSES Family Diomedeidae

Majestic birds of open ocean, with rigid gliding and banking flight. Much larger than gulls; wings proportionately longer. "Tubenosed" (nostrils in two tubes); bill large, hooked, covered with horny plates. Sexes generally alike. Largely silent at sea. **FOOD:** Cuttlefish, fish, squid, other small marine life; some feeding at night. **RANGE:** Mainly cold oceans of S. Hemisphere; three species nest north of equator in Pacific.

LAYSAN ALBATROSS *Phoebastria immutabilis*   Scarce

32 in. (81 cm); wingspan 6½ ft. (198 cm). White body with *dark back and wings,* suggesting a huge, dark-backed gull with extra-long wings. Whitish underwing has variable *dark smudges.* Bill and feet pinkish gray. Ages similar. Found farther offshore than Black-footed Albatross. Hybrids with Black-footed Albatross observed occasionally in large breeding colonies but rarely at sea. **SIMILAR SPECIES:** Several southern albatross species formerly of the "Shy Albatross" group, including White-capped Albatross (*Thalassarche cauta*; not illustrated), casual off the Pacific Coast. Larger than Laysan, *bill variably dusky greenish to yellow; underwing white;* head variably white or washed dusky. **RANGE:** Breeds in HI (p. 378) and off nw. Mex. Casual vagrant up coastal rivers.

BLACK-FOOTED ALBATROSS *Phoebastria nigripes*   Uncommon

32–33 in. (81–84 cm); wingspan 7 ft. (213 cm). Bulky, *sooty color,* tremendously long saberlike wings, and rigid shearwater-like gliding identify this species, the albatross found most regularly off our Pacific Coast. Occasionally seen from shore; e.g., in Monterey Bay, CA. Breeds in HI (p. 378). At close range shows whitish face and pale areas toward wingtips. Bill and feet *dark.* Older adults and males develop more white on uppertail and undertail coverts; extensively white in males over 15 years old. Worn adults in summer can acquire bleached heads and whitish underparts, recalling other species or rare hybrids with Laysan Albatross. **SIMILAR SPECIES:** Juvenile and second-year Short-tailed Albatross slightly larger, has much larger, *pinkish bill and feet.*

SHORT-TAILED ALBATROSS *Phoebastria albatrus*   Rare, endangered

36–37 in. (91–94 cm); wingspan 7½ ft. (229 cm). *Adult: White back through uppertail coverts, pink bill,* yellowish nape. Upperwing dark with white patches proximally; underwing white with dark edge. *Juvenile through second-year:* Dark brown; bill and feet *pinkish.* Up to 15 years needed to acquire adult plumage; brown replaced by white, first in face and breast, then back, last on crown and nape. **SIMILAR SPECIES:** Black-footed and Laysan Albatrosses. **RANGE:** Breeds on islands off Japan and recently on Midway Atoll, nw. Hawaiian Is. (p. 378). *Formerly near extinction, slowly recovering.* **RANGE:** From Bering Sea to CA; most commonly found here in late fall and winter.

ALBATROSSES

LAYSAN ALBATROSS

worn summer adult

BLACK-FOOTED ALBATROSS

older birds with white tail coverts

second-year

SHORT-TAILED ALBATROSS

adults

fourth-year

STORM-PETRELS
Families Oceanitidae and Hydrobatidae

Small birds found over open ocean; nest on islands. **FOOD:** Plankton, small fish. **RANGE:** All oceans. Family Oceanitidae (Wilson's Storm-Petrel here), recently split from Hydrobatidae, have longer legs used to patter upon water.

WILSON'S STORM-PETREL *Oceanites oceanicus* Casual

7¼–7½ in. (18–19 cm). Found primarily off cen. CA in late summer through fall. From other Pacific storm-petrels by *white uppertail-covert (often called "rump") patch that wraps around sides;* tail rounded or square-cut, *not forked.* Feet yellow-webbed, show *beyond tail* in flight.

FORK-TAILED STORM-PETREL *Oceanodroma furcata* Uncommon

8½ in. (22 cm). *Pale gray* overall, with contrasting *slaty underwing linings;* all other Pacific storm-petrels are blackish overall. Dark eye patch; faint dark bar across upperwing; forked tail.

LEACH'S STORM-PETREL *Oceanodroma leucorhoa* Uncommon

8 in. (20 cm). Note obscurely divided (double-oval) *white uppertail-covert patch* and forked tail. In flight, bounds about erratically on angled wings, suggesting a nighthawk. "Dark-rumped" birds off s. CA can lack or have reduced white in uppertail coverts. **VOICE:** On breeding grounds, nasal chattering notes and trills. **SIMILAR SPECIES:** Wilson's, Black, and Ashy Storm-Petrels. See Townsend's Storm-Petrel. Wedge-rumped Storm-petrel (*O. tethys*), an accidental vagrant to CA and AZ, smaller; white uppertail coverts extend to tail or nearly so.

TOWNSEND'S STORM-PETREL *Oceanodroma socorroensis* Scarce

7 in. (17–18 cm). Recently split from Leach's Storm-Petrel and very similar. Slightly smaller, darker, with shorter and less-forked tail. Uppertail-covert patch often less divided but also beware individuals with darker uppertail coverts. **SIMILAR SPECIES:** Leach's Storm-Petrel. **RANGE:** Breeds off Mex.; uncommon visitor off s. CA in late summer.

ASHY STORM-PETREL Uncommon, endangered
Oceanodroma homochroa

8 in. (20 cm). From Black and "dark-rumped" Leach's Storm-Petrels by slightly smaller size, more direct flight (shallower wingbeats, lower to water). Plumage ashy colored; underwings and rump have *pale cast.* Feeds far offshore but aggregates into large molting flocks in Aug.–Sept.

BLACK STORM-PETREL *Oceanodroma melania* Fairly common

9 in. (23 cm). The largest all-black storm-petrel found off CA, primarily in fall. Forked tail. Larger than Ashy and "dark-rumped" Leach's Storm-petrels; flight languid, with slower wingbeats and more direct flight; Leach's tends to be farther offshore than Black. Irregular; numbers tend to be higher and occurrence more northerly during warm-ocean events.

LEAST STORM-PETREL Rare to scarce, local
Oceanodroma microsoma

5¾ in. (15 cm). A late-summer and fall visitor in variable numbers. Small. Our only storm-petrel with *very short rounded or wedge-shaped* tail. Flight similar to Leach's. **SIMILAR SPECIES:** Ashy Storm-Petrel is larger and grayer with notched tail, paler underwing, and quicker wingbeats; beware molting Ashies can resemble Least in tail shape and flight style.

STORM-PETRELS

WILSON'S STORM-PETREL

FORK-TAILED STORM-PETREL

LEACH'S STORM-PETREL

"dark-rumped"

"white-rumped"

TOWNSEND'S STORM-PETREL

ASHY STORM-PETREL

BLACK STORM-PETREL

LEAST STORM-PETREL

TROPICBIRDS Family Phaethontidae

Resemble large terns but with two greatly elongated central tail feathers (adults) and stouter, slightly decurved bills. Tropicbirds fly with shallow wing-beats, rarely glide, and swim with tail held clear of water. Sexes alike. **FOOD:** Squid, fish, crustaceans. **RANGE:** Tropical oceans.

RED-BILLED TROPICBIRD *Phaethon aethereus*   Rare

18 in. (45 cm), adults to 37 in. (94 cm) with tail-streamers. *Adult:* Mostly white with *two extremely long white central tail feathers, heavy red bill,* extensive black in primaries, and *finely barred back.* Juvenile lacks long tail. **SIMILAR SPECIES:** Juvenile Red-tailed Tropicbird has finer back markings, dark bill.

RED-TAILED TROPICBIRD *Phaethon rubricauda*   Casual

18 in. (46 cm), adults to 37 in. (94 cm) with tail-streamers. *Adult:* Whiter above than other tropicbirds; tail-streamers *red. Juvenile:* Lacks tail-streamers, thinly barred on back, bill dusky. **RANGE:** Nests in tropical Pacific, including HI (p. 384). Casual far off CA coast. Rare to uncommon regular visitor.

PELICANS Family Pelecanidae

Huge waterbirds with long flat bills and throat pouches. Neck long, body robust. Sexes alike. **FOOD:** Mainly fish, crustaceans. **RANGE:** N. and S. America, Africa, s. Eurasia, E. Indies, Australia.

AMERICAN WHITE PELICAN *Pelecanus erythrorhynchos*   Common

62 in. (157 cm). Huge; wingspan 8–9½ ft. (244–290 cm). White, with black primaries and a great orange-yellow bill and throat pouch. Breeding adult has keratinous appendage on ridge of bill in spring, drops off in fall. *First-year:* Dusky wash on head, neck; dark mottling to upperwing coverts; second-year birds intermediate. This pelican does not plunge from air but scoops up fish while swimming, often working in groups. Flocks circle high in air on thermals. **VOICE:** In colony, a low groan. Young utter whining grunts. **SIMILAR SPECIES:** Wood Stork flies with neck and long legs extended; Snow Goose much smaller, noisy. **HABITAT:** Lakes, marshes, estuaries.

BROWN PELICAN *Pelecanus occidentalis*   Common

48–50 in. (122–127 cm); wingspan 6½ ft. (198 cm). An unmistakable, ponderous dark waterbird. *Adult:* Much white and buff on head and front of neck. Dark chestnut brown on back of neck and reddish throat when breeding. *First-year:* Duskier brown overall, with dark head, paler underparts; second-year intermediate. Large size, head and bill shape, and powerful slow flight (a few flaps and a glide) indicate pelican; dark color and habit of *plunging bill-first* distinctive to this species. Lines or broken Vs of pelicans glide low over water, wingtips almost touching. **VOICE:** Adults silent (rarely a low croak). Nestlings squeal. **HABITAT:** Salt bays, beaches, ocean; more rarely inland lakes. Perches on rocks, buoys, jetties, beaches. Casual to accidental vagrant inland.

TROPICBIRDS AND PELICANS

RED-BILLED TROPICBIRD

RED-TAILED TROPICBIRD

AMERICAN WHITE PELICAN

spring/summer adult

first-year

adults

spring/summer adults

first-year

fall/winter adult

BROWN PELICAN

BOOBIES Family Sulidae

Larger and longer necked than most gulls, tapered at all four ends. Sexes largely alike. Boobies sit on buoys, rocks; fish by plunging from air. **FOOD:** Fish, squid. **RANGE:** Tropical seas. Nest colonially on islands.

BLUE-FOOTED BOOBY *Sula nebouxii*   Casual

32–33 in. (81–83 cm). *Adult:* White body; whitish head; *light patches on upper back and rump*; dark-mottled back and wings, underwing mostly dark; *blue feet*. *Juvenile:* Head and neck darker. **SIMILAR SPECIES:** First-year Masked and Brown Boobies. Adult male Brown Booby in w. Mex. also has pale head, grayish bill, but back entirely dark. Rare to casual vagrant inland, especially Salton Sea.

BROWN BOOBY *Sula leucogaster*   Rare to uncommon

29–30 in. (74–76 cm). *Adult:* Chocolate brown with *white belly in clean-cut contrast* to dark breast. White underwing linings contrast with dark flight feathers. *Feet yellowish*. Male of w. Mex. subspecies *brewsteri* ("Brewster's Booby") white around head (varies to largely white headed) and has paler breast and grayer bill (vs. yellower in other subspecies). *Juvenile:* Underparts mostly dark, with little or no contrast between breast and belly; bill grayish. Fairly common breeder in HI (p. 384). **SIMILAR SPECIES:** First-year Red-footed Booby (which has dark tail) more buffy overall with dark underwing; has blackish or pinkish-based bill; feet pinkish to pale reddish. First-year Masked Booby resembles adult Brown Booby, but brown of head not sharply demarcated from paler underparts and has white nape collar. Blue-footed Booby has weaker contrast below, shows whitish patches on upper back and rump. **RANGE:** Increasing off CA. Rare to casual vagrant inland, especially Salton Sea.

RED-FOOTED BOOBY *Sula sula*   Casual

27–28 in. (69–71 cm). The smallest booby. *Adult:* Feet *bright red,* tail *white.* Two color morphs. *White morph:* White with black tip and trailing edge of wing (except tertials), tail white. *Dark morph:* Brown back and wings, paler head; white tail and belly; in flight, *underwing dark,* thin dark trailing edge on upperwing. *Juvenile:* Brownish overall with *dark underwing,* blackish bill that becomes pink with dark tip by second year, *pink feet* that quickly become red. **SIMILAR SPECIES:** Juvenile Brown Booby is darker overall, has a more conical and paler grayish bill, yellowish feet. **RANGE:** Nests in Tropics, including commonly in HI (p. 384). Very rare off CA, accidental to AK.

MASKED BOOBY *Sula dactylatra*   Casual

31–32 in. (79–81 cm). *Adult:* White with *black tail,* black along *entire rear edge* of wing, and black in *face.* Yellowish bill; dark bluish facial skin; *feet dark olive to slate.* Mostly white underwing. *Juvenile:* Variably mottled with dark on upperwing and head, *white hind collar.* Uncommon breeder in HI (p. 384). **SIMILAR SPECIES:** Other boobies. Nazca Booby (*S. granti*), casual but increasing vagrant off CA and HI from Mex., similar but bill orangish in adult, becomes horn colored or tinged orange at base with deep yellow tip during first year. Also one Northern Gannet (*Morus brassanus*; not shown) has reached CA.

BLUE-FOOTED BOOBY

adult

adult

juvenile

adult

"Brewster's" adult male

female

adults

adult female

juvenile

BROWN BOOBY

first-year

MASKED BOOBY

adults

NAZCA BOOBY

adult

first-year

dark morph

white-tailed dark morph

juvenile

white morph

RED-FOOTED BOOBY

FRIGATEBIRDS Family Fregatidae

Primarily black tropical seabirds with extremely long wings. Bill long, hooked; tail deeply forked. **FOOD:** Fish, jellyfish, squid, other seabird chicks; scavenges and pirates from other seabirds. **RANGE:** Pantropical oceans.

MAGNIFICENT FRIGATEBIRD *Fregata magnificens*　　Scarce, local

36–46 in. (91–117 cm); wingspan 7–8 ft. (215–245 cm). A large black seabird with extremely long angled wings and *scissorlike* tail (often folded in a *point*). *Male:* All black with *red throat pouch* (inflated like a balloon in display). *Female:* White breast, dark head. *Juvenile:* Head and breast white. **SIMILAR SPECIES:** Great Frigatebird of w. Mex and HI (see p. 384) is accidental off CA and elsewhere. Lesser Frigatebird (*F. ariel*), accidental across N. America, is smaller, has white spur on axillars. **HABITAT:** Tropical oceans; declining off CA. Accidental to scarce vagrant away from coast.

SKUAS and JAEGERS Family Stercorariidae

Falconlike seabirds that harass gulls, terns, and shearwaters, forcing them to disgorge or drop their food. Light, intermediate, and dark morphs exist in at least two species; all have flash of white in primaries. Adult jaegers have two projecting central tail feathers, which differ in shape and length among the species and ages. In juveniles and molting birds these feathers can be shorter or lacking, or sometimes blunter-tipped than in adults. Separating jaegers in most plumages can be very difficult. Skuas are larger, powerful birds that lack elongated tail feathers and are broader winged. Sexes alike. **FOOD:** In Arctic, lemmings, eggs, young birds. At sea, food taken from other birds or from water. **RANGE:** Seas worldwide, breeding in subpolar regions. In w. N. America, all three jaegers occur as rare to accidental vagrants inland.

SOUTH POLAR SKUA *Stercorarius maccormicki*　　Uncommon

21 in. (53 cm). Skuas are near the size of a large gull, but stockier, with deep-chested, hunchbacked look. Dark, with short, slightly wedge-shaped tail and *conspicuous white wing patch at base of primaries visible on both upperwing and underwing. Adult:* Has *pale head and underparts* contrasting with darker wings; older adults can be much paler than shown. *Juvenile and first-year:* Darker and more uniform, with *paler nape* developing during first and second years. **SIMILAR SPECIES:** Dark jaegers, especially Pomarines, may lack elongated tail feathers, but South Polar Skuas are larger, their wings wider, with more striking white wing patches. **HABITAT:** In our area, open ocean; rarely seen from or close to shore.

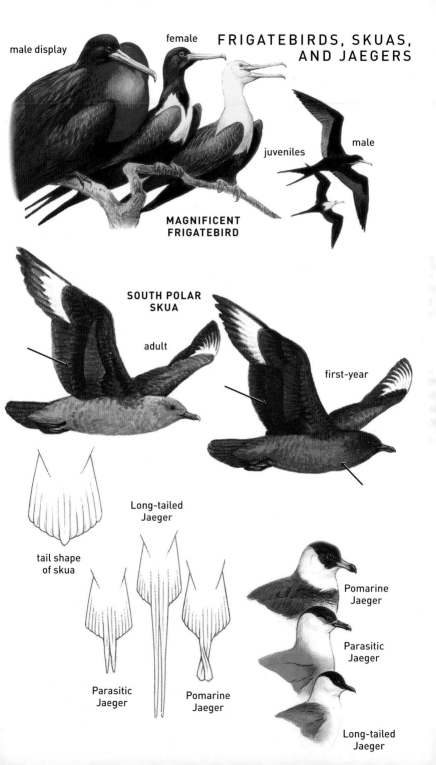

FRIGATEBIRDS, SKUAS, AND JAEGERS

male display

female

juveniles

male

MAGNIFICENT FRIGATEBIRD

SOUTH POLAR SKUA

adult

first-year

tail shape of skua

Long-tailed Jaeger

Parasitic Jaeger

Pomarine Jaeger

Pomarine Jaeger

Parasitic Jaeger

Long-tailed Jaeger

PARASITIC JAEGER *Stercorarius parasiticus* **Fairly common**

17–19 in. (44–49 cm). This is the jaeger most frequently seen from shore. Flies with strong, falconlike wing strokes. Smaller and less chesty than Pomarine Jaeger; larger and with a longer bill than Long-tailed Jaeger. Typically chases larger terns and medium-sized gulls. Like other jaegers, it shows variable white wing-flash. *Spring/summer adult:* Dark crown and pale underparts (light morph) to completely dark brown (dark morph). *Sharp central tail feathers* project up to 3½ in. (9 cm). Shows small *pale spot* above base of bill. *Juvenile and first-year:* Juvenile jaegers are highly variable in body plumage and have heavy barring, especially on underwing. Juvenile Parasitic often with *more distinct white patch on upperwing*; dark-morph is usually *warmer brown* than other juvenile jaegers. Up close, look for *streaked head* and *pale-edged primary tips*, along with size and structural differences. Second-years of all three jaeger species retain partial barring on underwing and elsewhere. Winter adult (not seen in our area) can lack dark crown and has barring on back and flanks. **SIMILAR SPECIES:** Pomarine and Long-tailed Jaegers; along coast, Heermann's Gull, which can occasionally show white wing patches and also sometimes harasses terns, small gulls. **HABITAT:** Primarily ocean, regularly seen from shore; in summer, tundra.

POMARINE JAEGER *Stercorarius pomarinus* **Fairly common**

19–21 in. (48–53 cm). Like Parasitic Jaeger, but slightly heavier with more gull-like flight style. Typically chases larger gulls, shearwaters. *Adult:* *Broad and twisted* central tail feathers are blunt-tipped and project 2–7 in. (5–18 cm); bill heavy and *pink-based*. In light morph, dark cap extends *farther down* sides of head and near bill base; breast-band *darker* and more barred than in Parasitic. Dark-morph averages sootier than dark-morph Parasitic. *Juvenile:* Plumage variable, but compared with juvenile Parasitic it lacks warm tones, and very short central tail feathers are blunt-tipped. Look for white-based primary coverts creating *double white flash* on underwing. Second-year and adult-winter plumages as described under Parasitic Jaeger. **SIMILAR SPECIES:** Plumages of Pomarine and Parasitic Jaegers are so variable that they are often best distinguished by structural features and behvaior. Large molting Pomarine Jaegers can resemble South Polar Skua but bills are more slender, white wing flashes not as extensive, especially from above. **HABITAT:** Open ocean, seen from shore in small numbers; in summer, tundra.

LONG-TAILED JAEGER *Stercorarius longicaudus* **Fairly common**

17–22 in. (44–56 cm). The smallest, slimmest jaeger with buoyant, tern-like flight style, and small short bill. Typically chases smaller terns and gulls. *Adult:* Plumage less variable than that of other jaegers, virtually all being light morph. Paler and grayer above, with distinctly *two-toned upperwing* in flight; *long attenuated tail streamers* project 8–15 in. (20–38 cm); black cap neat and *sharply defined; no breast-band; almost no white in wings. Juvenile:* Varies from light to dark morph. All have very *limited white on upperwing* (two or three primary shafts), *stubby bill,* and longer, blunter-tipped central tail feathers than Parasitic Jaeger. White patch on underwing variable but often smaller than in juvenile Parasitic Jaeger. Light morph juvenile has distinctively *pale grayish head and breast* and extensively *white belly.* Dark morph cold gray-brown and often with pale nape and *pale lower breast patch.* **HABITAT:** Open ocean; tundra in summer. Most pelagic of the jaegers; seldom if ever seen from shore.

JAEGERS

light morph

adults

Parasitic

Pomarine

Long-tailed

PARASITIC
JAEGER

dark morph

intermediate
morph

dark-
morph
juvenile
Parasitic

dark morph

adults

first-year

POMARINE
JAEGER

Pomarine

adult

light
morph

LONG-TAILED
JAEGER

light-morph
juvenile
Long-tailed

dark-morph
juvenile
Long-tailed

GULLS Family Laridae

Most gulls are more robust, wider winged, and longer legged than terns, and most have larger and slightly hooked bills. Tails square or rounded rather than forked. Gulls seldom dive. **FOOD:** Omnivorous; marine life, plant and animal food, refuse, carrion. **RANGE:** Nearly worldwide.

AGING GULLS

It is often important to determine the age of a gull before identifying it. Knowing what both adult and first-year plumages look like is helpful in placing gulls to species in intermediate, second- and third-year, stages. Plumage sequences in gulls can be divided into three groups based on age at which "adult" plumage is reached, generally equating to size but variable in all species, with some individuals reaching adult plumage a year before or after that described below. Most (but not all) gulls also have differing plumages in fall/winter and spring/summer, which become more distinct in each successive age class. It is helpful to first focus on the size and structure of easier-to-identify adults, then consider size and structure of younger birds.

SEQUENCE OF PLUMAGES IN SMALL GULLS

In the top panel of the opposite page, the Bonaparte's Gull illustrates the transition of plumages directly from first-year to adult, usually without a distinctive second-year plumage. Species in this category include Bonaparte's, Black-headed, Little, Ross's, Sabine's, and Ivory Gulls, and Red-legged Kittiwake. Adult Bonaparte's is also an example of a gull that has a distinctive spring/summer plumage for breeding.

SEQUENCE OF PLUMAGES IN MEDIUM-SIZED GULLS

In the middle panel of the opposite page, the Ring-billed Gull illustrates this transition with an additional, distinctive second-year plumage. Species in this category are mostly medium-sized gulls, including Ring-billed, Laughing, Franklin's, and Mew Gulls, and Black-legged Kittiwake. Of these, Laughing and Franklin's Gulls have distinctive spring/summer plumages in their second year and as adults, whereas in the others, winter plumages have slight dusky streaks to the head, lost for breeding.

SEQUENCE OF PLUMAGES IN LARGE GULLS

In the bottom panel of the opposite page, the Herring Gull illustrates the transition of plumages from first-year to adult, including distinctive second- and third-year plumages. Species in this category are mostly large gulls, including California, Herring, Lesser Black-backed, Great Black-backed, Slaty-backed, Western, Yellow-footed, Glaucous-winged, Glaucous, and Iceland Gulls. Plumages tend to be more similar between winter and summer, some showing head streaking in winter; the Yellow-footed Gull has a more-advanced second-summer plumage than other large gull species. The medium-sized Heermann's Gull is also a four-year species, the only one of these with distinct fall/winter and spring/summer plumages as adults.

Caution: There is extensive variation in plumage within species (particularly the second- and third-year plumages), resulting from variation in molt extents and timing, and plumage wear and bleaching. In addition, hybridization is a regular phenomenon among most large species, especially along the Pacific Coast (commonly between Glaucous-winged and Western, Herring, and Glaucous Gulls, and between Glaucous and Herring Gulls). Even expert birders leave some gulls unidentified.

BONAPARTE'S GULL

Plumages of Small Gulls

first-year

fall/winter adult

spring/ summer adult

RING-BILLED GULL

first-year

second-year

spring/ summer adult

Plumages of Medium-Sized Gulls

Plumages of Large Gulls

HERRING GULL

first-year

second-year

third-year

fall/winter adult

LAUGHING GULL *Leucophaeus atricilla*   Uncommon, very local

16–16½ in. (41–42 cm). *Adult: Dark mantle blends into black wingtips.* Head *black* in spring/summer plumage; pale in fall/winter plumage with dark gray smudge on head. Bill longish, often with slight droop to tip; reddish when breeding, mostly dark in winter. *Juvenile and first-winter:* See p. 92. **VOICE:** Nasal laughing *ha-a* and strident *ha-ha-ha-ha-ha-haah-haah-haah*, etc. **SIMILAR SPECIES:** Franklin's Gull is slightly smaller, shorter billed, rounder headed, has broader white eye-arcs, and *different wingtip pattern.* **HABITAT:** Salt marshes, coastlines, parks, farm fields. Regular at Salton Sea; rare vagrant north along Pacific Coast; accidental inland in West.

FRANKLIN'S GULL *Leucophaeus pipixcan*   Fairly common

14½–15 in. (37–38 cm). *Adult:* Note *white band* near wingtip, separating black from gray. In spring/summer, head black; breast often has rosy bloom; bill red. In fall/winter, head paler, dark cheeks and nape form partial hood; bill mostly dark. *First-year:* See p. 92. **VOICE:** Shrill *kuk-kuk-kuk;* also mewing, laughing cries. **SIMILAR SPECIES:** Laughing Gull. **HABITAT:** Prairies, inland marshes, lakes; in winter, coasts, ocean, primarily in S. America. Scarce migrant along Pacific Coast.

SABINE'S GULL *Xema sabini*   Fairly common

13½–14 in. (34–36 cm). A small, *ternlike* gull with slightly *forked tail. Adult:* Note *bold upperwing pattern* of black outer primaries and *triangular white wing patch.* Bill black with *yellow tip;* legs dark. *Juvenile:* See p. 92. **VOICE:** Various grating or buzzy ternlike calls, given mostly on breeding grounds. **SIMILAR SPECIES:** Bonaparte's Gull; Black-legged Kittiwake. **HABITAT:** Ocean; nests on tundra pools. Rare to casual vagrant inland.

BLACK-HEADED GULL *Chroicocephalus ridibundus* Accidental vagrant

15¾–16 in. (40–41 cm). *Adult:* Similar to Bonaparte's Gull, but slightly larger; mantle slightly paler; shows much *blackish gray on underside of primaries;* bill *dark red,* not black. *First-year:* See p. 92. **VOICE:** Harsh *kerrr.* **HABITAT:** Often with Bonaparte's Gulls; also beaches, lawns.

BONAPARTE'S GULL   Uncommon to fairly common
Chroicocephalus philadelphia

13–13½ in. (33–34 cm). A petite, almost ternlike gull. *Adult:* Note *wedge of white* on *fore edge* of wing. Legs red to pinkish; bill small, black. Head blackish in spring/summer, whitish with *black ear spot* in fall/winter. *First-year:* See p. 92; also Sequence of Plumages in Small Gulls, p. 82. **VOICE:** Nasal, grating *cheeer* or *cherr.* Some calls ternlike. **SIMILAR SPECIES:** Black-headed and Little Gulls. **HABITAT:** Ocean, bays, lakes, sewage-treatment ponds; in summer, muskeg.

LITTLE GULL *Hydrocoloeus minutus*   Accidental vagrant

11 in. (28 cm). This rare visitor is the smallest gull; usually associates with Bonaparte's Gull. *Adult:* Note *blackish undersurface* of *rather rounded wing* and absence of black above. Legs red. In fall/winter, head *dark-capped, black ear spot,* bill black. *First-year:* See p. 92. **VOICE:** Series of one- or two-syllable *key* notes. **SIMILAR SPECIES:** Bonaparte's Gull. **HABITAT:** Lakes, rivers, bays, sewage-treatment ponds; often with Bonaparte's Gulls.

SMALL HOODED GULLS
Adults

fall/winter

LAUGHING GULL

breeding adults flying

spring/summer

FRANKLIN'S GULL

fall/winter

spring/summer

SABINE'S GULL

fall/winter

spring/summer

BLACK-HEADED GULL

fall/winter

BONAPARTE'S GULL

fall/winter

spring/summer

spring/summer

LITTLE GULL

fall/winter

spring/summer

HEERMANN'S GULL *Larus heermanni* Common

19 in. (48 cm). A distinctive gull. *In all plumages, has black legs and feet. Adult: Dark gray body, black tail* with white tip, *red bill with black tip.* White head in winter/spring becomes gray in summer/fall. Occasionally shows white patches on upperwing. *First- and second-years:* See p. 92. **VOICE:** Whining *whee-ee,* repeated *cow-auk.* **SIMILAR SPECIES:** Can behave like jaegers, chasing other birds for food, but more buoyant gull-like flight eventually betrays Heermann's. **HABITAT:** Ocean and immediate coastlines. Accidental vagrant inland.

CALIFORNIA GULL *Larus californicus* Common

21–21½ in. (53–55 cm). *Adult:* Note *greenish to yellow legs,* medium-dark mantle, *darker eye,* bill with *both red and black spots.* Wings proportionally long, with more white in tips than Ring-billed Gull. In fall/winter, head streaked, bill and legs slightly duller, the latter often *grayish green. First- and second-years:* See p. 94. **VOICE:** Hoarser than Herring Gull's; also a high-pitched *keeer* in flight. **HABITAT:** Ocean and coasts, lakes, farms, dumps, urban centers.

RING-BILLED GULL *Larus delawarensis* Common

17–17½ in. (43–45 cm). Similar to Herring and California Gulls, but smaller, more buoyant and delicate. *Adult:* Shows *pale eye* and *light gray mantle* (paler than California and Mew); *legs yellow or greenish yellow.* Note *complete black ring* encircling bill. In fall/winter, shows fine dark streaking on head; bill and legs become duller. *First-year:* See p. 92. Also see Sequence of Plumages in Medium-sized Gulls, p. 82. **VOICE:** Higher pitched than Herring Gull's. **SIMILAR SPECIES:** Mew Gull has smaller unmarked bill, darker mantle, dark eye, and more extensive dark mottling on head in fall/winter. **HABITAT:** Lakes, bays, coasts, dumps, plowed fields, shopping malls; rarer on open ocean than other gulls.

MEW GULL *Larus canus* Common

16–17 in. (41–44 cm). *Adult:* Smaller than Ring-billed Gull, with more greenish legs in winter and *dainty, short, unmarked greenish-yellow bill.* Darkish eye. Mantle *medium gray,* noticeably darker than Ring-billed's. Shows larger white "mirrors" in its black wingtips than either California or Ring-billed Gull. In fall/winter head is streaked and bill is duller. *First-year:* See p. 92. **VOICE:** Low, mewing *queeu* or *meeu.* Also *hiyah-hiyah-hiyah,* etc., higher-pitched than in other gulls. **SIMILAR SPECIES:** Ring-billed Gull, Black-legged Kittiwake. **HABITAT:** In winter, ocean, coastlines, wet fields, tidal rivers; in summer, lakes, taiga, tundra. Casual vagrant well inland.

BLACK-LEGGED KITTIWAKE *Rissa tridactyla* Uncommon

16–17 in. (41–43 cm). A small, buoyant oceanic gull. *Adult:* Wingtips lack white spots, *solid black,* almost *straight across,* as if dipped in ink. Bill slightly curved, without angle to lower mandible of other gulls; pale yellow, unmarked. Legs and feet *black.* Eyes dark. Nape has dusky band in fall/winter. *First-year:* See p. 92. **VOICE:** At nesting colony, a raucous *kaka-week* or *kitti-waak.* **SIMILAR SPECIES:** Mew, Ring-billed, and Sabine's Gulls; in w. AK, Red-legged Kittiwake (p. 98). **HABITAT:** Chiefly oceanic; rarely on beaches, casual inland. Nests on sea cliffs. Rare to casual vagrant inland.

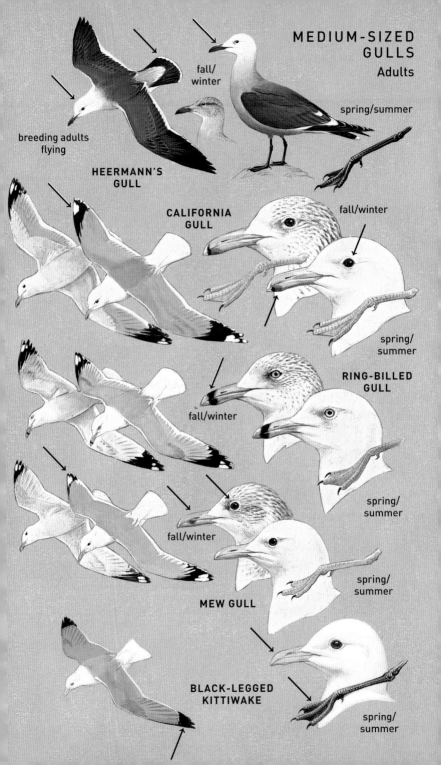

MEDIUM-SIZED GULLS
Adults

fall/winter

spring/summer

breeding adults flying

HEERMANN'S GULL

CALIFORNIA GULL

fall/winter

spring/summer

RING-BILLED GULL

fall/winter

spring/summer

fall/winter

spring/summer

MEW GULL

BLACK-LEGGED KITTIWAKE

spring/summer

HERRING GULL *Larus argentatus* **Fairly common**

24–25 in. (61–64 cm). A fairly large gull. *Adult: Pale gray* mantle, *pinkish* legs, *pale eye.* Outer primaries contastingly *black* with moderately extensive white spots or "mirrors." Bill somewhat thin, yellow, with red spot on lower mandible. In fall/winter, head and neck streaked brownish; bill and legs duller. *First- and second-years:* See p. 94 and also Sequence of Plumages in Large Gulls, p. 82. **VOICE:** A loud *hiyak . . . hiyak . . . hyiah-hyak* or *yuk-yuk-yuk-yuk-yuckle-yuckle.* Mewing squeals. Anxiety call of this and other gulls, *gah-gah-gah.* **SIMILAR SPECIES:** "Thayer's" (Iceland) and California Gulls. Adult of latter darker mantled, has dark eye, greenish yellow legs; first-years can be similar (see p. 86). **HABITAT:** Ocean, coasts, bays, beaches, lakes, dams, piers, farmland, dumps. Regularly hybridizes with Glaucous-winged Gull in AK.

GLAUCOUS-WINGED GULL *Larus glaucescens* **Common**

25–26 in. (63–66 cm). *Adult:* A *very large pinkish-legged* gull, with large bill, pale gray mantle, and *medium gray* primaries. Head streaked grayish and bill duller in fall/winter. *First- and second-years:* See p. 96. Hybridizes extensively with Western Gull in Pacific Northwest (see p. 96), and with Herring and Glaucous Gulls in AK. **VOICE:** Low *kak-kak-kak;* a low *wow;* a high *keer, keer.* **SIMILAR SPECIES:** Adult Glaucous Gull has whitish primaries, thinner bill, paler eye. See also Western, "Thayer's" (Iceland), and Herring Gulls. **HABITAT:** Ocean, coastlines, parks, dumps, lakeshores. Rare vagrant in the interior West (hybrids with Herring Gull?).

GLAUCOUS GULL *Larus hyperboreus* **Uncommon**

27–28 in. (68–72 cm). A large, chalky white gull with pinkish legs. *Adult:* Has pale gray mantle and *unmarked white outer primaries. Light eye.* Head slightly streaked and bill duller in fall/winter. *First- and second-years:* See p. 96. **VOICE:** Much like Herring Gull's. **SIMILAR SPECIES:** Iceland ("Kumlien's") Gull is smaller; head rounder, wings proportionately longer (extending well beyond tail when sitting). See also Glaucous-winged Gull. **HABITAT:** Mainly coastal; a few inland at large lakes and dumps. Rare inland and causal vagrant well south of normal winter range.

ICELAND GULL *Larus glaucoides* **Uncommon**

22–24 in. (56–61 cm). Western "Thayer's" Gull (subspecies *thayeri*), formerly a separate species, has blacker primary tips like Herring Gull but with *darker eye*, smaller bill (often tinged greenish in winter), and *more-extensive white mirrors* than other adult W. Coast gulls. Eastern N. American "Kumlien's" Gull (*kumlieni*), a scarce vagrant to West, resembles a small Glaucous Gull (which see). Variation in wingtip pattern between Kumlien's and Thayer's breeding in the high Arctic nearly continuous; thus often paler than Herring Gull's wingtip. *First- and second-years:* See p. 96. **VOICE:** Similar to Herring Gull but higher pitched; rarely heard away from breeding grounds. **SIMILAR SPECIES:** Herring Gull larger and has paler back and eye than Thayer's, wingtip jet black. First-year Glaucous-winged Gull can be very similar to first-year Thayer's (see p. 96). **HABITAT:** Ocean, coastlines, freshwater outflows, dumps. Rare to casual well inland.

breeding adults flying

fall/winter

LARGE PALE GULLS
Adults

HERRING GULL

spring/summer

GLAUCOUS-WINGED GULL

spring/summer

fall/winter

GLAUCOUS GULL

spring/summer

fall/winter

"Thayer's" Gull

fall/winter

spring/summer

pale

"Kumlien's" Gull

ICELAND GULL

typical

WESTERN GULL *Larus occidentalis* Locally common

25–26 in. (64–66 cm). A large, large-billed gull. *Adult:* Note *very dark mantle*, contrasting with snowy underparts. Legs and feet dull pinkish. Northern subspecies has paler mantle, but still noticeably darker than that of California Gull. Southern subspecies (*wymani*) blacker backed. From below, dark primaries and secondaries contrast with white wing lining more than in other gulls. *First- and second-years:* See p. 94. Hybridizes near-continuously with Glaucous-winged Gull (notably in the Olympic Pennisula, WA, south to CA and sometimes inland in winter). Hybrids have intermediate mantle and wingtip coloration (see p. 88). **VOICE:** Guttural *kuk kuk kuk;* also *whee whee whee* and *ki-aa.* **SIMILAR SPECIES:** Glaucous-winged, Herring, and California Gulls. Back and wingtips of hybrid Western × Glaucous-winged Gulls not as contrasting and note also the much larger and stouter bills. **HABITAT:** Offshore and coastal waters, beaches, piers, city waterfronts, parks, lower reaches of tidal rivers. Casual to accidental vagrant well inland.

SLATY-BACKED GULL *Larus schistisagus* Scarce, local

25–26 in. (64–67 cm). A dark-backed Asian gull. *Adult:* Similar to Western Gull, but with *paler "staring" eye*, deeper pinkish feet, more *extensive head markings in fall/winter plumage.* White subterminal tongues form *thin white bar* crossing dark outer primaries. *First-year:* Similar to Herring Gull but dumpier, legs darker purplish, bill stout and black, inner primaries not as pale. *Second- and third-years:* Follow plumage and bill color changes of Kelp Gull as shown on p. 98 but legs dark pink; eye paler than in similar-aged Western Gull. **SIMILAR SPECIES:** Siberian subspecies of Herring Gull (*vegae*), also found in w. AK, is darker mantled than N. American subspecies. **RANGE:** Regular visitor to w. AK, rare vagrant to CA, casual vagrant inland. **HABITAT:** Seacoasts, beaches, dumps.

YELLOW-FOOTED GULL *Larus livens* Fairly common, local

27 in. (69 cm). In the U.S., found regularly only at Salton Sea, CA. *Adult:* Closely resembles Western Gull, but adult has *yellow* (not pinkish) legs and feet and slightly thicker bill. *First-, second-, and third-years:* Similar to equivalent plumages in Western Gull (p. 94) but second-summer plumage more adultlike. Attain yellow legs and feet by second winter. **VOICE:** Deeper than Western's. **HABITAT:** Same as Western Gull. Accidental along CA coast.

GREAT BLACK-BACKED GULL *Larus marinus* Very rare vagrant

29–30 in. (73–76 cm). Much larger than Pacific Gulls with broad wings and heavy body and bill. *Adult:* Blacker backed than Western Gull. *First- and second-years:* See p. 94. **SIMILAR SPECIES:** See Lesser Black-backed and Slaty-backed Gulls. Accidental vagrant to W. Coast.

LESSER BLACK-BACKED GULL *Larus fuscus* Scarce vagrant

21–22½ in. (53–57 cm). Similar in size and shape to California Gull, with long wings, but mantle slate gray. *First- and second-years:* See p. 94. **VOICE:** Harsh *kyah.* **SIMILAR SPECIES:** Slaty-backed Gull. **HABITAT:** Same as other gulls; favors fresh water over marine habitats in CA.

LARGE DARK GULLS
Dark-backed Adults

breeding adults flying

WESTERN GULL

Southern

Northern

SLATY-BACKED GULL

YELLOW-FOOTED GULL

Great Black-backed Gull

LESSER BLACK-BACKED GULL

among the gulls on this plate, only Slaty-backed and Lesser Black-backed show heavy head streaking in fall/winter

GREAT BLACK-BACKED GULL

FIRST-YEAR and SECOND-YEAR GULLS

Younger gulls are generally more difficult to identify than adults. They are usually darkest the first year and become lighter and more adultlike during the second and third years, depending on when they reach adult plumage (see p. 82). Body and bill size and structure are useful for identification.

LAUGHING GULL *Leucophaeus atricilla* Adult, p. 84

Most reach adult plumage by third year. *Juvenile:* Dark brown with black tail, white rump, and *broad white* trailing edge of wing. *First-year:* Neck and back become smudged with gray. *Second-year:* Darker upperwing tips than fall/winter adult, and with traces of black in tail.

FRANKLIN'S GULL *Leucophaeus pipixcan* Adult, p. 84

Most reach adult plumage by third year. *First-year:* Similar to first-year Laughing Gull, but more petite with *smaller and straighter bill, blackish extensive half-hood,* outermost tail feather *white. Second-year:* Like second-year Laughing but with blackish half-hood, paler underwing.

BLACK-HEADED GULL *Chroicocephalus ridibundus* Adult, p. 84

Most reach adult plumage by second year. *First-year:* Similar to Bonaparte's but larger; bill longer, orange with dark tip; *sooty underwing.*

BONAPARTE'S GULL *Chroicocephalus philadelphia* Adult, p. 84

Most reach adult plumage by second year. *First-year:* Note dark ear spot, narrow black tail band, dark trailing edge to wings, and white in outer primaries. Pale underwing. See also p. 82.

LITTLE GULL *Hydrocoloeus minutus* Adult, p. 84

Most reach adult plumage by second year. *First-year:* Very small with bold *black and white M pattern* across back and wings, *dusky cap.*

SABINE'S GULL *Xema sabini* Adult, p. 84

Most reach adult plumage by second year. *Juvenile:* Dark grayish brown and white-scaled back, but with adult's bold *triangular wing pattern.* Note also *forked* tail. *First-spring:* Black hood partial.

HEERMANN'S GULL *Larus heermanni* Adult, p. 86

Most reach adult plumage by fourth year. *Juvenile:* Dark chocolate with pale-fringed feathers. Becomes grayer with broader white trailing wing edges and and broader white tail tip through third year. *Black legs and feet*, salmon to *reddish bill, tipped black.*

BLACK-LEGGED KITTIWAKE *Rissa tridactyla* Adult, p. 86

Reaches adult plumage by third year. *First-year:* Dark bar on nape, black M across back and wings. *Second-year:* Some dark markings to upperwing.

MEW GULL *Larus canus* Adult, p. 86

Most reach adult plumage by third year. *First-year:* Smaller than Ring-billed and darker overall, with smaller bill, rounder head, darker tail and uppertail coverts. *Second-year:* See second-year Ring-billed Gull.

RING-BILLED GULL *Larus delawarensis* Adult, p. 86

Most reach adult plumage by third year. *First-year:* Bicolored (pinkish-based) bill, mostly whitish underneath and on rump and upper tail, *pale gray back.* Well-defined subterminal tail band. *Second-year:* Like adult but upperwing with brown and black, tail with black. See also p. 82.

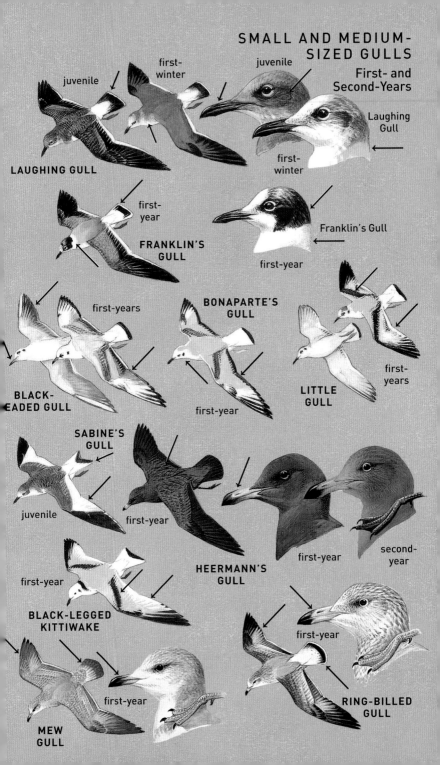

SMALL AND MEDIUM-SIZED GULLS

First- and Second-Years

juvenile

first-winter

juvenile

Laughing Gull

first-winter

LAUGHING GULL

first-year

FRANKLIN'S GULL

Franklin's Gull

first-year

first-years

BONAPARTE'S GULL

BLACK-HEADED GULL

first-year

LITTLE GULL

first-years

SABINE'S GULL

juvenile

first-year

first-year

second-year

HEERMANN'S GULL

first-year

BLACK-LEGGED KITTIWAKE

first-year

RING-BILLED GULL

first-year

first-year

MEW GULL

FIRST-YEAR and
SECOND-YEAR LARGE DARK GULLS

WESTERN GULL *Larus occidentalis* Adult, p. 90

Most reach adult plumage by fourth year. First-year is very dark; larger, larger-billed, and sootier brown than most California and Herring Gulls. Back and wing-covert fringing not as patterned as in first-year California Gull, and bill entirely black. *Second-year:* Similar to first-year but not as patterned; gains some gray upperpart feathers by spring; bill black with dull and messy pinkish base. *Third-year:* Resembles adult but upperwing washed brown and has more blackish to tip; bill has dusky ring or smudge; tail has some black. Hybridizes extensively with Glaucous-winged Gull; first-year hybrid shown.

CALIFORNIA GULL *Larus californicus* Adult, p. 86

Most reach adult plumage by fourth year. *First-year:* Like Herring Gull, but slimmer and bill longer and always distinctly bicolored. Wing lacks pale area on inner primaries. *Second-year:* Legs often dull gray-green. Somewhat similar to first-winter Ring-billed Gull, but larger, darker, retains dark eye, and tail mostly dark rather than with only a dark subterminal band. *Third-year:* Like adult but more black in wingtips, some black usually in tail, black of bill more extensive, sometimes forming ring (but red spot also present). In larger gulls, females have smaller bills and rounder heads than males, as shown here.

LESSER BLACK-BACKED GULL *Larus fuscus* Adult, p. 90

Most reach adult plumage by fourth year. *First-year:* Dark back and proportionally long wings; broad tail band; heavily streaked breast. White tail base, paler head and underparts, black bill. *Second- and third-years:* Follow plumages and bill colors of other large gulls; some are more adult-like in second spring/summer.

HERRING GULL *Larus argentatus* Adult, p. 88

Most reach adult plumage by fourth year. *First-year:* Variable; combine body and bill structure with plumage to identify. Brownish overall, with brownish-black wingtips and dark brown tail. Often shows much mottling or checkering on upperwing coverts and rump. *Pale area on inner primaries visible in flight.* Bill all dark in juvenile, becoming paler at base during first or second year (variable). *Second- and third-years:* Head and underparts variably become whiter; eye paler; back pale gray; bill pink, then yellow, dark-tipped. See Sequence of Plumages in Large Gulls, p. 82.

GREAT BLACK-BACKED GULL *Larus marinus* Adult, p. 90

Most reach adult plumage by fourth or fifth year. Large size and bill. *First-year:* Salt-and-pepper patterned, becoming whiter on head, rump, and underparts. Bill entirely black. *Second-year:* Similar to first-year but mantle becomes blacker during winter; bill becomes paler at base and often tipped yellow. *Third-year and some fourth-years:* Adultlike but secondaries and wing coverts washed brown; wingtips darker, with smaller white mirrors; tail with black; bill variably black and yellowish.

LARGE DARK GULLS
First-Years and Second-Years

second-year

first-year

juvenile

first-year
Glaucous-winged
x Western Gull

**WESTERN
GULL**

second-year

California
Gull

second-
year

first-
year

**CALIFORNIA
GULL**

second-year

variation in
first-years

male

**LESSER
BLACK-BACKED
GULL**

first-year

first-year

female

**HERRING
GULL**

first-
year

**GREAT
BLACK-BACKED
GULL**

second-year

FIRST-YEAR, SECOND-YEAR, and THIRD-YEAR LARGE PALE GULLS

ICELAND GULL *Larus glaucoides*   Adult, p. 88

Most reach adult plumage by fourth year. For Thayer's subspecies, first-year is tan-brown and checkered; similar to juvenile Herring Gull but lighter; primaries paler, usually *light tan-brown* (not brownish black) *with pale edges to tips; bill entirely or almost entirely blackish, more petite; underside of primaries pale.* Often has dark smudge through eye. Usually smaller and darker-winged than first-year female Glaucous-winged but can be rather similar. *Second-year:* Paler and grayer; primaries gray-brown with darker outer webs. Plumages of Kumlien's subspecies similar to Glaucous Gull's, but size and structure differ as in adults (p. 88); bill of most first-year Iceland Gulls mostly dark, only very rarely as sharply demarcated as in Glaucous. Most birds have at least a hint of a tail band as well as some dark in outer primaries, both lacking in Glaucous. *Third-year:* In both subspecies, similar to adults but tail and bill usually have some dusky; white mirrors to outer primaries smaller.

GLAUCOUS GULL *Larus hyperboreus*   Adult, p. 88

Most reach adult plumage by fourth year. *First-year:* Recognized by its large size, pale tan when fresh, becoming white by late winter; primaries white with small black marks when fresh. Brownish barring on undertail coverts and mottling in wing coverts and tail. Bill *pale pinkish* with *sharply demarcated* dark tip. *Second-year:* Pale gray back and pale eye acquired; first- and second-year plumages often become nearly pure white through bleaching by spring. *Third-year:* Like adult but bill usually retains a dark tip or smudge.

GLAUCOUS-WINGED GULL *Larus glaucescens*   Adult, p. 88

Most reach adult plumage by fourth year. Variable. Primaries are close to same tone as rest of wing, not markedly darker as in Western and Herring Gulls, or paler or translucent as in Glaucous Gull. Hybrids with Western or Herring Gulls have intermediate-colored primaries. *First-year:* Can vary from checkered to muddy olive-gray in plumage. Smaller first-year females can be difficult to separate from first-year Thayer's but bill is usually larger. Worn first- and second-year Glacous-wingeds in spring and summer may appear very white, but lack clean-cut two-toned bill of similar-aged Glaucous Gulls. Hybridizes extensively with Western Gull; see p. 90.

LARGE PALE GULLS
First-Years, Second-Years,
Third-Years

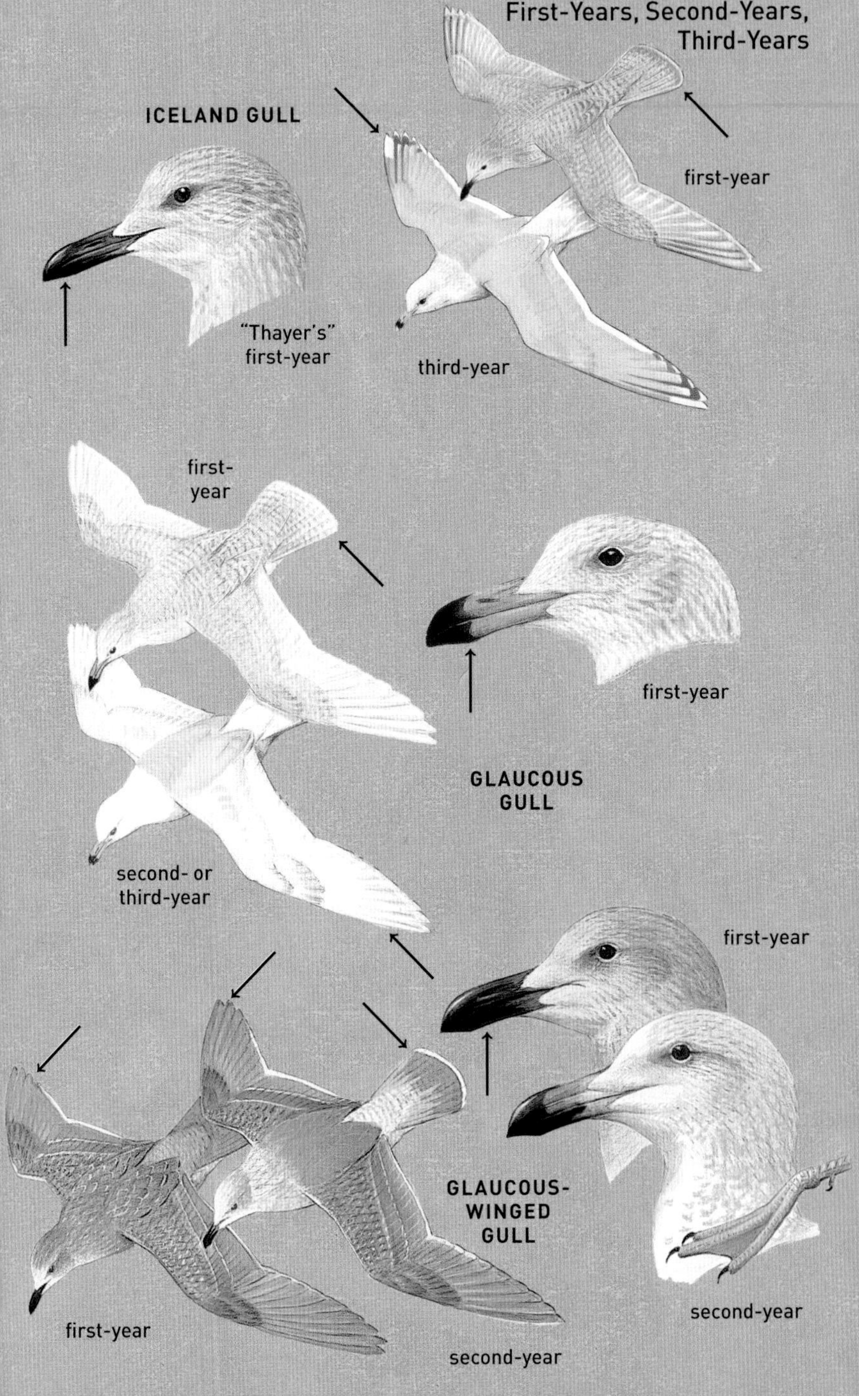

ICELAND GULL

"Thayer's"
first-year

first-year

third-year

first-year

GLAUCOUS
GULL

first-year

second- or
third-year

first-year

first-year

GLAUCOUS-
WINGED
GULL

second-year

first-year

second-year

RARE GULLS

BLACK-TAILED GULL *Larus crassirostris* Accidental vagrant

18–18½ in. (46–47 cm). Size and shape of California Gull, with slightly longer bill. Adult has red tip to black-banded bill, slate gray mantle, and wide black subterminal band on tail. First-year very dark with bright pink-based bill. **RANGE:** Casual visitor from e. Asia, with widely scattered records across w. N. America.

KELP GULL *Larus dominicanus* Accidental vagrant

22–25 in. (56–64 cm). A black-backed, stocky gull of S. America that has reached as far as CA as a vagrant. *Adult:* Black back, reduced mirrors to primaries (typically a *square patch on outermost primary* only), *bill very stout, legs bright greenish yellow.* Younger plumages and bill colors parallel those of other large dark-backed gulls. **SIMILAR SPECIES:** Lesser Black-backed Gull has similar plumages but is usually smaller, more slender, and has slimmer bill; juvenile and first-year Kelp Gulls have darker legs, blacker base to tail in flight.

RED-LEGGED KITTIWAKE Uncommon, very local, threatened
Rissa brevirostris

15 in. (38 cm). *Adult:* Similar to Black-legged Kittiwake but smaller, with *darker gray mantle* (noticeable when both species together); *shorter bill and rounder head* give it a more dovelike look; legs *bright red.* Wing pattern similar, although white trailing edge broader; *darkish gray underwing.* First-year (not shown) has wing and tail pattern similar to Sabine's Gull but back paler gray. Legs dull red. **VOICE:** High-pitched *tuu-WEE* near nesting colony. **HABITAT:** Open ocean, where it often forages at night. Nests in colonies on steep, rocky ocean cliffs. Accidental winter vagrant to WA and CA.

ROSS'S GULL *Rhodostethia rosea* Very rare

13–13½ in. (33–35 cm). A rare Arctic gull of drift ice. Note *wedge-shaped tail, medium gray underwing linings,* and *small black bill. Spring/summer: Rosy* blush on underparts, *fine black collar. Fall/winter:* Less rosy, lacks black collar. *First-year:* Similar in pattern to first-year Black-legged Kittiwake or Little Gull, but intermediate in size and note *longer wedge-shaped tail* with black tip and *gray* linings of underwing; lacks dark nape of young kittiwake. **HABITAT:** Arctic waters, tundra in summer. Vagrant well south of normal winter range.

IVORY GULL *Pagophila eburnea* Very rare

17 in. (43 cm). A declining species of Arctic pack ice; those that wander south of normal range are usually first-years. Bill dark greenish *with yellow tip. Adult:* Small, all-white gull with *black legs.* Pigeonlike in size and head shape; wings long, flight ternlike. *First-year:* White, with dark *smudge on face, black spots* above, wing and tail feathers tipped black. **HABITAT:** Open Arctic waters near pack ice; vagrants well south of winter range found on coasts, lakes.

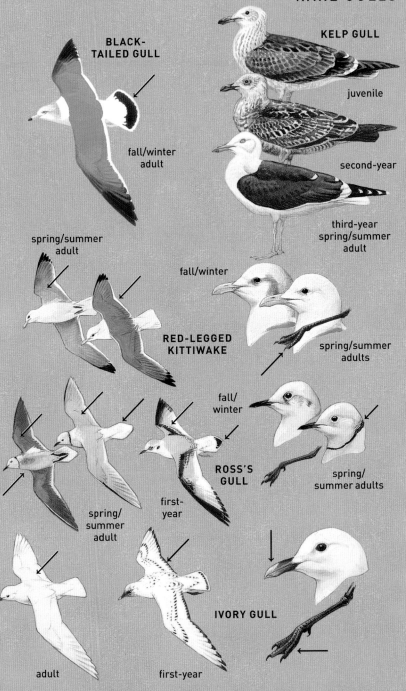

RARE GULLS

KELP GULL

juvenile

second-year

third-year
spring/summer
adult

BLACK-
TAILED GULL

fall/winter
adult

spring/summer
adult

fall/winter

RED-LEGGED
KITTIWAKE

spring/summer
adults

fall/
winter

ROSS'S
GULL

spring/
summer
adult

first-
year

spring/
summer adults

adult

first-year

IVORY GULL

TERNS Subfamily Sterninae

Wings more pointed than gulls, tail usually forked. Bill pointed, often tilted toward water when flying. Most terns are whitish with black cap in summer, the black crown replaced by white forehead in fall/winter. Sexes alike. Terns hover and plunge headfirst for fish; normally do not swim. **FOOD:** Small fish, marine life, large insects. **RANGE:** Almost worldwide.

FORSTER'S TERN *Sterna forsteri* Fairly common

14½ in. (37 cm). Similar to Common Tern, but paler; adults have *paler wingtips than rest of wing*, with more orange tone to thicker bill. Whitish below, lacking gray wash of spring/summer Common. Tail grayer. Fall/winter adult and first-year have isolated *black mask, usually not connecting around nape*; first-year Common has slightly darker gray carpal (shoulder) bar. Juvenile has upperpart fringing washed cinnamon and marked dark; tail short, forked. **VOICE:** Harsh, nasal *za-a-ap* and nasal *kyarr.* **HABITAT:** Fresh and salt marshes, lakes, bays, beaches, nests in marshes.

COMMON TERN *Sterna hirundo* Uncommon

14 in. (36 cm). A graceful, black-capped, slim bird with deeply forked tail. *Spring/summer adult:* Pearl gray mantle and black cap; bill red with black tip; feet orange-red. Similar to Forster's and Arctic Terns, but *dark wedge on upperwing primaries. Grayer below* than Forster's, bill and legs smaller than in Forster's, *larger than in Arctic. Fall/winter adult and first-year:* Cap, nape, and bill blackish. *Dark shoulder bar.* Juvenile: Upperparts washed brownish and marked dark. Asian subspecies (*longipennis*), a very rare visitor in w. AK, darker, with *black bill* in spring/summer and *blackish legs and feet.* **VOICE:** Drawling *kee-arr* (downward inflection); also *kik-kik-kik;* a quick *kirri-kirri.* **HABITAT:** Ocean, bays, marshes, beaches; nests colonially on small islands. Rare well inland.

ARCTIC TERN *Sterna paradisaea* Uncommon

15 in. (38 cm). A pelagic tern when away from nesting grounds. Similar to Common Tern, but bill smaller, neck shorter, head rounder. *Legs shorter.* From below, note translucent effect of primaries and *narrow black trailing edge. Spring/summer adult:* Bill usually *blood red* to tip, extensive wash of *gray below,* setting off white cheeks. *Fall/winter and juvenile:* Like Common, but black on head more extensive, shoulder bar *weaker, secondaries whitish,* and structural differences noted above. **VOICE:** *Kee-yak,* less slurred, higher than Common's. A high *keer-keer* is characteristic. **HABITAT:** Open ocean; in summer, taiga lakes, tundra; rare vagrant on coasts and casual inland.

ALEUTIAN TERN *Onychoprion aleuticus* Scarce, local

13½–14 in. (34–36 cm). A gray-backed tern of Alaskan coastal waters. *Blackish bill and legs, clean-cut white forehead, dark bar along underside of secondaries. Spring/summer adult:* Pale-to-medium gray plumage contrasts with white tail. *Fall/winter adult and first-year:* Not seen in our area; underparts and cap whitish. *Juvenile:* Upperpart feathers and wing coverts largely rusty brown; legs orange. **VOICE:** Three-syllable whistle, suggesting a shorebird. **HABITAT:** Summers/nests along AK coast on islands, sandbars.

SMALLER TERNS

first-year

fall/
winter

**FORSTER'S
TERN**

adult

spring/
summer
adult

adult

adult

fall/winter

first-year

COMMON TERN

spring/summer
adult

adults

**ARCTIC
TERN**

fall/
winter

first-
year

spring/
summer adult

**ALEUTIAN
TERN**

adults

spring/
summer adult

GULL-BILLED TERN *Gelochelidon nilotica* Uncommon, very local

14 in. (36 cm). Note *stout black* bill. Stockier and paler than Common Tern; tail much less forked; feet *black*. In fall/winter, head white with dark ear patch, nape pale. *First-year:* Similar to fall/winter adult; carpal (shoulder) bar dusky; crown mostly pale in spring/summer. *Juvenile:* Crown and upperparts washed pale brown; wing coverts grayish. Plucks food from water's surface and hawks for insects over marshes and fields. **VOICE:** *Kay-weck, kay-weck;* also a throaty, rasping *za-za-za*. **SIMILAR SPECIES:** Forster's Tern in winter, small gulls. **HABITAT:** Marshes, fields, coastal bays. Accidental vagrant inland.

ELEGANT TERN *Thalasseus elegans* Locally common

17 in. (43 cm). Smaller and slimmer than Royal Tern. Bill orange or orange-yellow, proportionately *longer, more slender,* and slightly droopier than deeper orange bill of Royal. Elegant's black crown extends farther down nape. In fall/winter and first-year plumages, dark of head *includes eye*. *Juvenile and first-year:* Like winter adult, tertials with dark centers, cap mostly white; upperpart feathers fringed dusky when fresh; bill yellower. Note head pattern of juvenile can be similar to Royal Tern. Following breeding, juveniles follow adults north along W. Coast. **VOICE:** Nasal *karrik* or *kerr-rik*. **SIMILAR SPECIES:** Royal and Caspian Terns. **HABITAT:** Ocean, coasts, beaches, salt bays. Accidental vagrant inland.

ROYAL TERN *Thalasseus maximus* Fairly common, local

20 in. (51 cm). A large tern, slimmer than Caspian, with medium-large *orange* bill. Tail forked. Keeps solid black crown for short time in spring; for most of year, *much white on forehead,* black crown feathers forming a crest. In fall/winter, black feathers behind eye usually *do not encompass eye* as in Elegant Tern. Dusky upperside and *pale underside to primaries,* opposite of Caspian. *First-year:* Like winter adult, tertials with dark centers, cap mostly white. *Juvenile:* Upperpart feathers and upperwing coverts with neat black crescents. **VOICE:** Sonorous *karr-rik,* mellower (slower and lower-pitched) than Elegant; also *kaak* or *kak*. **SIMILAR SPECIES:** Caspian Tern (a more-common inland species) has bill heavier, redder, tipped dark; Elegant's bill thinner, proportionally longer, paler orange or yellow-orange. **HABITAT:** Ocean, coasts, beaches, salt bays (accidental vagrant inland).

CASPIAN TERN *Hydroprogne caspia* Fairly common

21 in. (53 cm). Large size and *stout reddish bill with small dark mark near tip* set Caspian apart from all other terns. Royal's forehead is *clear white* in adult fall/winter plumage, whereas Caspian has *gray-streaked* forehead. Caspian shows obvious *grayish black on undersurface of primaries, but pale upper surface. First-year:* Rare in our area but cap like winter adult's. *Juvenile:* Upperpart feathers boldly marked gray and black; wing coverts have dusky markings. **VOICE:** Raspy, low *kraa-uh* or *karr,* also repeated *kak;* juvenile gives whistled *wheee-oo*. **SIMILAR SPECIES:** Royal and Elegant Terns. Caspian ranges inland, Royal usually does not. **HABITAT:** Large lakes, rivers, coastal waters, beaches, bays.

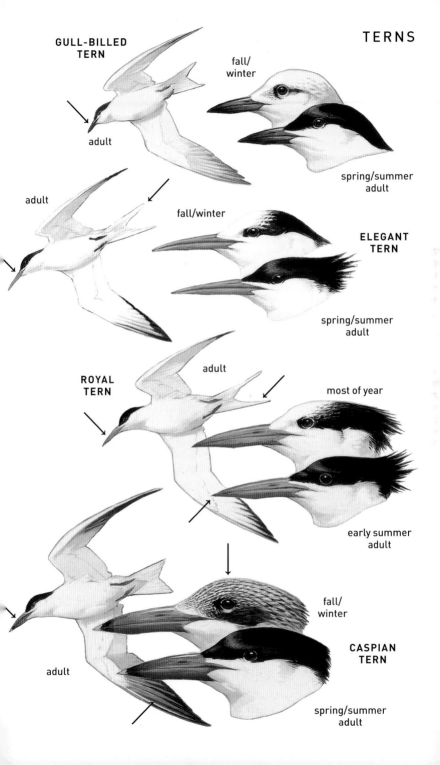

TERNS

GULL-BILLED TERN

adult

fall/winter

spring/summer adult

adult

fall/winter

ELEGANT TERN

spring/summer adult

ROYAL TERN

adult

most of year

early summer adult

fall/winter

CASPIAN TERN

adult

spring/summer adult

LEAST TERN *Sternula antillarum* Locally uncommon

9 in. (23 cm). A *very small* tern, with quicker wingbeats than other terns. *Spring/summer adult:* Dark-tipped *yellow bill, yellow legs and feet*, and *white forehead. Long black wedge on outer wing. First-year:* Dark bill, dark cheek and nape, dusky crown, dark carpal (shoulder) bar, duller legs. *Juvenile:* Upperpart feathers and wing coverts streaked dusky and fringed brownish cinnamon. **VOICE:** Sharp, repeated *ka-dec;* a harsh, squealing *zree-eek* or *k-zeek;* also a rapid *kitti-kitti-kitti.* **SIMILAR SPECIES:** Forster's Tern is much bigger. **HABITAT:** Beaches, bays, rooftops, abandoned runways. CA populations (subspecies *browni*) endangered. Casual vagrant inland.

BLACK TERN *Chlidonias niger* Uncommon

9½–9¾ in. (24–25 cm). A black-bodied tern in summer. Short, slightly-forked tail. *Spring/summer adult:* Head and underparts primarily *black; back, wings, and tail dark gray;* underwing linings whitish. Midsummer adults become mottled white. *Fall/winter adult and first-year:* Note pied head, with dark smudge from crown to ear coverts and on sides of breast; body and head remain at least partly white in one-year-olds. *Juvenile:* Similar to first-year but with upperpart feathers fringed brown. **VOICE:** Sharp *kik, keek,* or *klea.* **SIMILAR SPECIES:** White-winged Tern (*C. leucopterus*), a rare vagrant in the West, has mostly white upperwing and black underwing lining in spring/summer adult; paler and lacks dark breast mark in first-year and winter plumages. **HABITAT:** *Chlidonias* terns inhabit freshwater marshes, lakes; in migration, also coastal waters, including open ocean.

SOOTY TERN *Onychoprion fuscatus* Accidental vagrant

16 in. (41 cm). *Adult:* Cleanly patterned, black above and white below. Patch on forehead white; bill and feet black. *Juvenile:* Dark brown; back spotted with white; underwing lining and vent grayish. **VOICE:** Nasal *wide-a-wake.* **SIMILAR SPECIES:** Juvenile larger than spring/summer Black Tern and with upperpart feathers tipped white. Bridled Tern (*O. anaethetus;* not shown), also an accidental vagrant to CA, has gray-brown back, white nape collar, white of forehead extending behind eye. **HABITAT:** Warm ocean waters. Sooty Tern a common breeding species in HI (p. 390).

SKIMMERS Subfamily Rynchopinae

Slim, short-legged relatives of gulls and terns. Scissorlike red bill; *lower mandible longer than upper.* **FOOD:** Small fish, crustaceans. **RANGE:** Coasts, ponds, marshes, beaches, rivers of warmer parts of world.

BLACK SKIMMER *Rhynchops niger* Uncommon, local

18–18½ in. (46–47 cm). Very long wings; skims low, with stiff wingbeats, dipping lower mandible in water, snapping shut when it comes in contact with a food item. *Adult:* Black above (nape becomes white in fall/winter); white face and underparts. Bright red bill (tipped with black); *lower mandible juts up to a third beyond upper.* Reddish legs. *Juvenile:* Upperpart feathers paler brown and broadly fringed with whitish; bill smaller, bill and legs duller. *First-year:* Retains white-fringed outer wing coverts, nape whitish in spring/summer. **VOICE:** Soft, short, barking notes. Also *kaup, kaup.* **HABITAT:** Bays, marshes, beaches, protected ocean waters.

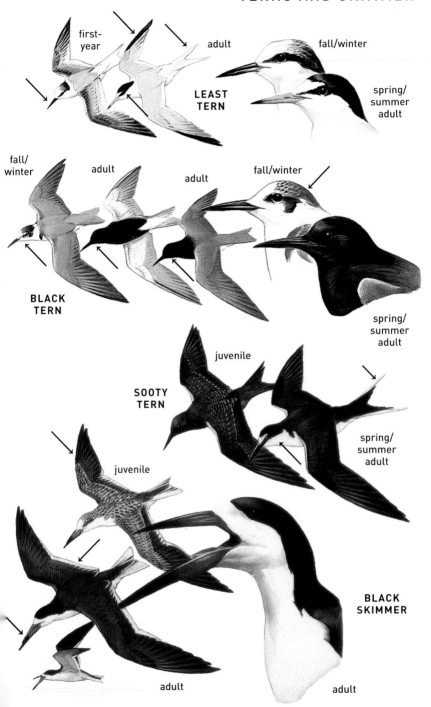

TERNS AND SKIMMER

first-year

adult

LEAST TERN

fall/winter

spring/summer adult

fall/winter

adult

adult

fall/winter

BLACK TERN

spring/summer adult

SOOTY TERN

juvenile

spring/summer adult

juvenile

BLACK SKIMMER

adult

adult

SHOREBIRDS

Many shorebirds (or "waders," as they are called in the Old World) are real puzzlers to the novice, and to many experienced birders as well! There are a dozen plovers in our area, and nearly 60 sandpipers and their allies. Many species have up to four different plumages: spring/summer adult (Apr.–Sept.), winter adult and first-winter (Oct.–Mar.) , first-summer (Apr.–Sept.), and juvenile (July–Sept.). Being able to properly age many species is an important part of correctly identifying them. Noting size, shape, and feeding style is also a critical part of the identification process.

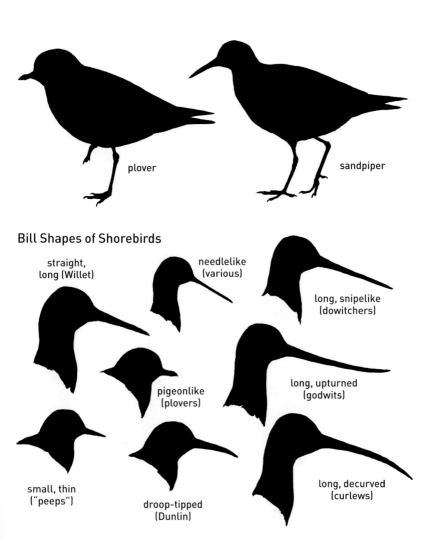

plover

sandpiper

Bill Shapes of Shorebirds

straight,
long (Willet)

needlelike
(various)

long, snipelike
(dowitchers)

pigeonlike
(plovers)

long, upturned
(godwits)

small, thin
("peeps")

droop-tipped
(Dunlin)

long, decurved
(curlews)

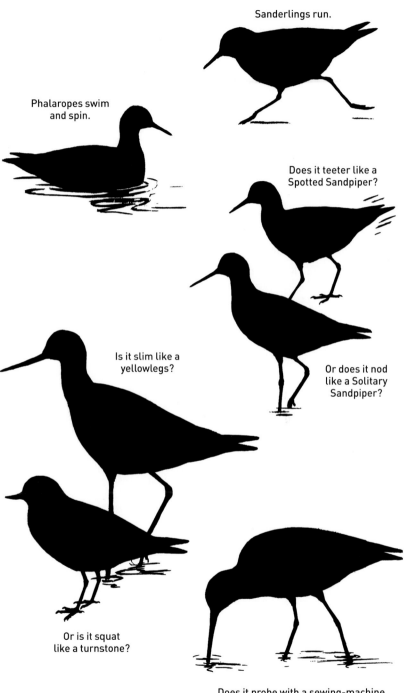

Sanderlings run.

Phalaropes swim and spin.

Does it teeter like a Spotted Sandpiper?

Is it slim like a yellowlegs?

Or does it nod like a Solitary Sandpiper?

Or is it squat like a turnstone?

Does it probe with a sewing-machine motion like a dowitcher?

PLOVERS Family Charadriidae

Plovers are more compactly built and thicker necked than most sandpipers, with shorter, pigeonlike bills and larger eyes. Call assists identification. Unlike most sandpipers, plovers run in short starts and stops, often on dry mud and in fields. Sexes alike or differ slightly. **FOOD:** Small marine life, insects, some vegetable matter. **RANGE:** Nearly worldwide.

BLACK-BELLIED PLOVER Common
Pluvialis squatarola (see also p. 132)

11½ in. (29 cm). A large plover. *Spring/summer adult:* Has *black face and breast* (duller and mottled white in female) and pale speckled back. *Fall/ winter adult, first-winter, and juvenile:* Grayish white (juvenile scalier backed). *First-spring/summer:* Variable between winter and summer. Note *black wingpits* and white rump and tail in flight. **VOICE:** Plaintive slurred whistle, *tlee-oo-eee* or *whee-er-eee*. **SIMILAR SPECIES:** American and Pacific Golden-Plovers slimmer, smaller billed, more golden, and *lack black in underwing and white rump.* **HABITAT:** Mudflats, marshes, beaches; in summer, tundra. Uncommon to rare inland.

AMERICAN GOLDEN-PLOVER Uncommon, local
Pluvialis dominica (see also p. 132)

10¼–10½ in. (26–27 cm). Shows distinct wingtip extension, the primaries extending well beyond tail tip when standing. *Spring/summer adult and first-summer:* Dark, spangled above with *whitish and pale yellow spots;* underparts black (mottled white in female). *Broad white stripe* over eye and down sides of neck and breast. *Winter adult and first-winter:* Gray-brown with distinct pale supercilium, dark brown; back slightly brighter in juvenile, more scaled. **VOICE:** Whistled *queedle* or *que-e-a* (dropping at end). **SIMILAR SPECIES:** Black-bellied Plover, Pacific Golden-Plover. **HABITAT:** Prairies, mudflats, shores, short-grass pastures, sod farms; in summer, tundra. Rare vagrant to W. Coast.

PACIFIC GOLDEN-PLOVER Uncommon, local
Pluvialis fulva (see also p. 132)

10–10¼ in. (25–26 cm). Very similar to American Golden-Plover but wingtip extension beyond tail tip shorter. *Spring/summer adult:* White neck stripe *extends down to flanks* and white present on undertail coverts (but beware molting American Golden-Plovers). Golden spangles on back brighter, bill slightly larger, legs slightly longer. *Winter adult and first-winter:* Slightly *more golden* above than American, substantially so in juvenile. *First-spring/summer:* Variable between winter and summer. See also Eurasian Dotterel (p. 140). **VOICE:** Whistled *chu-wee* or *chu-wee-dle.* **HABITAT:** Same as American, though breeds in wetter tundra. Common in HI (p. 392). Accidental vagrant well inland.

MOUNTAIN PLOVER *Charadrius montanus* Scarce, local

9 in. (23 cm). *Spring/summer adult and first-summer:* White forehead and face, black forecrown and loral stripe, brownish rufous back. *Winter adult and first-winter:* Back uniformly tan-brown; breast whiter; juvenile (not shown) is scalier-backed. Has pale blue-gray legs, light wing stripe, and dark tail band. **VOICE:** Low whistle, variable. **SIMILAR SPECIES:** Black-bellied Plover, golden-plovers, Buff-breasted Sandpiper. **HABITAT:** Plowed fields, short-grass plains, dry sod farms. Rare vagrant east of range and to coast north of s. CA.

PLOVERS

fall/winter

BLACK-BELLIED
PLOVER

fall/
winter

spring/
summer adult

juvenile

juveniles

AMERICAN
GOLDEN-
PLOVER

fall/
winter

spring/summer
adult

PACIFIC
GOLDEN-
PLOVER

MOUNTAIN
PLOVER

fall/
winter

spring/summer

COMMON RINGED PLOVER   *Charadrius hiaticula*   Rare, local

7½ in. (19 cm). A Eurasian species, very similar to Semipalmated Plover; best distinguished by *voice*. Slightly longer bill, darker cheeks. Spring/summer adult male averages bolder supercilium, wider breast-band. Less-extensive basal webbing between toes is difficult to see. **VOICE:** Softer, more minor *poo-eep* or *too-li*. **RANGE:** Breeds on St. Lawrence Is., AK; winters in Old World. Accidental migrant in West. **HABITAT:** Same as Semipalmated Plover.

SEMIPALMATED PLOVER   Common
Charadrius semipalmatus (see also p. 132)

7¼ in. (18 cm). Half the size of Killdeer, with *single dark breast-band. Adult:* Bill orangey with black tip or (in winter) nearly all dark. Male brighter and with more blackish than female; spring/summer brighter than fall/winter. *Juvenile:* Like winter female but back slightly scaly. **VOICE:** Plaintive, upward-slurred *chi-we* or *too-li*. **SIMILAR SPECIES:** Darker above than Piping and Snowy Plovers; the latter also has thinner bill, darker legs. See Lesser Sand-Plover (p. 140). **HABITAT:** Shores, tidal flats; in summer, tundra.

PIPING PLOVER   *Charadrius melodus* (see also p. 132)   Scarce, local

7¼ in. (18 cm). Quite pallid in color, like dry sand. Legs yellow or orange; bill has yellow-orange base, black tip; darker in winter and first-year. Black band on breast occasionally complete. Note tail pattern. **VOICE:** Plaintive whistle: *peep-lo*. **SIMILAR SPECIES:** Snowy and Semipalmated Plovers. **HABITAT:** Sandy beaches, dry mudflats; in summer, also lakeshores and river islands. Casual vagrant in West outside of breeding range; accidental to coast.

SNOWY PLOVER   *Charadrius nivosus* (see also p. 132)   Uncommon

6¼–6½ in. (16–17 cm). A pale flatter-headed plover of beaches and alkaline flats. Note *slim black bill,* dark (sometimes pale) legs. Male has *dark ear patch*, paler and better-marked in summer than winter. *Female and juvenile:* Duller, lack black in winter. **VOICE:** Musical whistle, *pe-wee-ah* or *o-wee-ah;* also a low *prit*. **SIMILAR SPECIES:** Juvenile and winter Piping Plovers are rounder headed, have brighter orange legs, and paler rump and uppertail coverts in flight. **HABITAT:** Beaches, sandy flats, alkaline lakeshores. West Coast populations (subspecies *nivosus*) threatened. Casual vagrant well north of range.

WILSON'S PLOVER   Casual vagrant
Charadrius wilsonia (see also p. 132)

7¾–8 in. (19–20 cm). Larger than Semipalmated Plover, with *wider breast-band* and longer, *heavier black bill*. Legs pinkish gray. Male has black breast-band in summer; female and first-year male browner. **VOICE:** Emphatic *whit!* or *wheet!* **HABITAT:** Open beaches, tidal flats, sandy islands. Casual vagrant to CA.

KILLDEER   *Charadrius vociferus* (see also p. 132)   Common

10½ in. (27 cm). The common plover of fields and pond edges. Note *two black breast-bands* (chick has only one band and might be confused with Wilson's Plover). In flight or distraction display (near nest), shows *rusty orange rump*, longish tail, white wing stripe. Sexes similar. **VOICE:** A loud, insistent *kill-deeah*, repeated. Also a plaintive *dee-ee* (rising), *dee-dee-dee*, etc. **SIMILAR SPECIES:** Other banded plovers smaller, have single breast-band. **HABITAT:** Fields, airports, gravel pits, riverbanks, mudflats.

BANDED PLOVERS

spring/summer adult male

COMMON RINGED PLOVER

fall/winter

fall/winter

spring/summer adult male

SEMIPALMATED PLOVER

spring/summer adult male

spring/summer adult male

PIPING PLOVER

fall/winter

SNOWY PLOVER

spring/summer adult male, breast-band may be unbroken

adult

first-year female

spring/summer adult male

WILSON'S PLOVER

KILLDEER

adult and first-year

chick

Common Ringed

adult males

Piping

Killdeer

Wilson's

Snowy

Semipalmated

OYSTERCATCHERS Family Haematopodidae

Large shorebirds with long, laterally flattened, chisel-tipped, red bills. Sexes alike. **FOOD:** Mollusks, crabs, mussels, marine worms, and other invertebrates. **RANGE:** Widespread on coasts of world; inland in some areas of Europe and Asia.

BLACK OYSTERCATCHER *Haematopus bachmani* **Fairly common**
17–17½ in. (43–44 cm). A large, heavily built, blackish shorebird with straight *orange-red bill,* flattened laterally. Thickish legs are pale pinkish. *Juvenile and first-year:* Bill dark-tipped. **VOICE:** Piercing, sharply repeated, whistled *wheer!* or *kleer!,* often repeated excitedly or in series. **SIMILAR SPECIES:** Second-year Heermann's Gull can resemble Black Oystercatcher when asleep with bill tucked, but has black legs and feet. American Oystercatcher, casual in s. CA, shows white breast, lower underparts, rump, and wing stripe; can have some dark mottling on upper breast and flanks. Also, hybrids between the two oystercatcher species occur in s. CA, which have more extensive dark mottling on underparts and rump. **HABITAT:** Rocky coasts, sea islets.

STILTS and AVOCETS Family Recurvirostridae

Slim waders with very long legs and very slender bills (bent upward in avocets). Sexes fairly similar. **FOOD:** Insects, crustaceans, other aquatic life. **RANGE:** N., Cen., and S. America, Africa, s. Eurasia, Australia, Pacific region.

BLACK-NECKED STILT *Himantopus mexicanus* **Fairly common**
14 in. (36 cm). A large, extremely slim wader; black above (female and juvenile have browner backs), white below. Note *extremely long dark-pinkish legs,* needlelike bill. In flight, black *unpatterned* wings contrast strikingly with white rump, tail, and underparts. **VOICE:** Sharp yipping: *kyip, kyip, kyip.* **SIMILAR SPECIES:** Fall/winter American Avocet. **HABITAT:** Marshes, mudflats, pools, shallow lakes (fresh and alkaline), flooded fields. Scarce to casual vagrant well north and east of range. Resident subspecies occurs in HI (p. 396).

AMERICAN AVOCET *Recurvirostra americana* **Fairly common**
18 in. (46 cm). A large, slim shorebird with very slender, *upturned bill,* more upturned in female. This and striking white-and-black pattern make this bird unique. In spring/summer plumage, head and neck pinkish tan or orangey buff; in fall/winter plumage, this color replaced by pale gray. Avocets feed with scythelike sweep of head and bill. **VOICE:** Sharp *wheek* or *kleet,* excitedly repeated. **HABITAT:** Mudflats, shallow lakes, marshes, prairie ponds. Can occur in large flocks during winter.

BLACK OYSTERCATCHER

BLACK-NECKED STILT

males (female similar but with browner back)

spring/summer

spring/summer

fall/winter

AMERICAN AVOCET

SANDPIPERS, PHALAROPES, and ALLIES
Family Scolopacidae

Small to large shorebirds. Bills more slender than those of plovers. Sexes mostly similar, except in phalaropes. **FOOD:** Insects, crustaceans, mollusks, worms, etc. **RANGE:** Cosmopolitan.

HUDSONIAN GODWIT   Casual vagrant
Limosa haemastica (see also p. 134)
15–15½ in. (38–39 cm). Long, *slightly upturned* bill; *blackish underwing linings*; black tail *ringed broadly with white. Spring/summer:* Male ruddy-breasted, female duller. *Fall/winter:* Gray-backed, pale-breasted; juvenile with more patterned scaly back. **VOICE:** *Tawit!* (or *godwit!*); higher pitched than Marbled Godwit's call. **SIMILAR SPECIES:** Bar-tailed and Black-tailed Godwits (see p. 142). **HABITAT:** Mudflats, prairie pools; in summer, marshy taiga and tundra. Very rare to accidental vagrant in West, south of AK.

MARBLED GODWIT   *Limosa fedoa* (see also p. 134)   Common
17½–18½ in. (44–46 cm). *Buff-brown* with *cinnamon* underwing linings. Spring/summer adults have more barring underneath than fall/winter birds and juveniles. **VOICE:** Accented *kerwhit! (godwit!)*; also *raddica, rad-dica.* **SIMILAR SPECIES:** When head tucked in, difficult to tell from Long-billed Curlew except slightly smaller and thinner, leg color blackish (more blue-gray in the curlew); supercilum averages more distinct. See Bar-tailed Godwit (p. 142). **HABITAT:** Prairies, pools, shores, mudflats, beaches.

LONG-BILLED CURLEW   Fairly common
Numenius americanus (see also p. 134)
22–24 in. (55–60 cm). Note *very long, sickle-shaped bill* (4–8½ in.; 10–21 cm). Larger than Whimbrel and warmer colored overall; lacks distinct dark crown stripes. From below has *cinnamon underwing linings.* Ages and sexes rather similar; female larger with longer bill. **VOICE:** Loud *cur-lee* (rising inflection) or *curlew*; rapid, whistled *kli-li-li-li*; on breeding a longer drawn-out *curleeeeeeeeuuu.* **SIMILAR SPECIES:** See Marbled Godwit. Whimbrel is smaller, grayer (lacks cinnamon tones), and has shorter and blacker bill. **HABITAT:** High plains, rangeland; in winter, cultivated land, mudflats, beaches, salt marshes.

WHIMBREL   *Numenius phaeopus* (see also p. 134)   Fairly common
17–18 in. (43–46 cm). A large gray-brown shorebird with *decurved bill.* Much grayer brown than Long-billed Curlew; bill shorter (2¾–4 in.; 7–10 cm); crown *striped*; in flight, upper surface of outer two primaries has distinct white shafts. Ages and sexes similar through year. Casual vagrant Eurasian subspecies (*variegatus*) have white wedges up lower backs (p. 142). **VOICE:** Five to seven short, rapid whistles: *chee-chee-chee-chee-chee-chee.* **SIMILAR SPECIES:** Long-billed Curlew. In AK and HI, see also Bristle-thighed Curlew (pp. 142 and 392). **HABITAT:** Mudflats, beaches; in summer, tundra. Uncommon to rare inland.

LARGE SANDPIPERS

fall/winter

spring/summer

fall/winter

HUDSONIAN GODWIT

spring/
summer male

MARBLED GODWIT

LONG-BILLED CURLEW

WHIMBREL

WANDERING TATTLER *Tringa incana* Uncommon

11 in. (28 cm). Note *lack of pattern in flight*; solid lead gray above; light line over eye, dark line through it. Legs yellowish. Bobs and teeters like Spotted Sandpiper. *Spring/summer:* Underparts *barred. Fall/winter:* Gray-chested, with no barring. *Juvenile:* Like fall/winter but scaly above. **VOICE:** Clear, distinctive *wheedle-deedle-dee,* all on same pitch. **SIMILAR SPECIES:** In w. AK, see Gray-tailed Tattler (p. 144). **HABITAT:** Rocky coasts, pebbly beaches. Nests on streams above timberline. Common in HI in winter (p. 392). Accidental vagrant in N. America away from Pacific Coast.

SURFBIRD *Calidris virgata* Uncommon

10 in. (25 cm). A stocky sandpiper of wave-washed rocks. Note conspicuous *white rump and tail, the latter tipped with broad black band; legs yellowish.* Bill short, yellow at base. *Spring/summer:* Heavily streaked and spotted with blackish above and below; orangey scapulars. *Fall/winter and juvenile:* Gray above (juvenile slightly scaly) and across breast. **VOICE:** Sharp *pee-weet* or *key-a-weet.* **SIMILAR SPECIES:** Rock Sandpiper smaller, slimmer, with longer curved bill, dark rump. Black Turnstone smaller, darker, with white stripe up back and reddish brown legs. **HABITAT:** Rocky coasts; nests on mountain tundra. Accidental inland.

ROCK SANDPIPER *Calidris ptilocnemis* Uncommon

8¾–9¼ in. (22–24 cm). *Spring/summer:* Suggests a Dunlin, with rusty back, black splotch on breast, but habitats differ completely. *Fall/winter:* Slaty, with white belly, white wing stripe. Legs dull yellow or greenish. **VOICE:** Flickerlike *du-du-du.* When breeding, a trill. **SIMILAR SPECIES:** Black Turnstone and Surfbird are plumper, have shorter bills, and *white across base of tail.* Purple Sandpiper (*C. maritima;* not shown) of East, an accidental vagrant to w. N. America, very similar but has brighter orange legs and bill base, wing stripe slightly less extensive; rufous edging to back feathers in spring broken (solid in Rock Sandpiper). **HABITAT:** Rocky shores; nests on mossy tundra.

RUDDY TURNSTONE *Arenaria interpres* (see also p. 132) Uncommon

9½ in. (24 cm). A squat, robust, *orange-legged* shorebird, with *harlequin pattern. Spring/summer:* Russet back and unique head and upperpart pattern striking in flight. *Fall/winter and juvenile:* Duller. **VOICE:** Staccato *tuk-a-tuk* or *kut-a-kut;* also a single *kewk.* **SIMILAR SPECIES:** Black Turnstone. **HABITAT:** Beaches, mudflats, rocky shores, jetties; in summer, tundra. Uncommon to rare inland. Common in winter in HI (p. 392).

BLACK TURNSTONE Fairly common
Arenaria melanocephala (see also p. 132)

9¼ in. (23 cm). Similar to Ruddy Turnstone but face and breast blacker. Oval white spot before eye and white speckling present in spring/summer. Legs darkish. **VOICE:** Rattling call, higher than that of Ruddy Turnstone. **SIMILAR SPECIES:** Winter and juvenile Ruddy Turnstones have brighter legs, more white in faces, browner backs, and vested breast patches. See also Surfbird. **HABITAT:** Strictly coastal (accidental vagrant inland). Rocky shores, surf-pounded islets, occasionally sandy beaches and mudflats. Nests on coastal tundra.

ROCK-LOVING SHOREBIRDS

WANDERING TATTLER

fall/winter

spring/summer

spring/summer

SURFBIRD

fall/winter

fall/winter

spring/summer

ROCK SANDPIPER

fall/winter

spring/summer male

RUDDY TURNSTONE

fall/winter

BLACK TURNSTONE

spring/summer

RED KNOT *Calidris canutus* (see also p. 138)   Uncommon

10½ in. (27 cm). Larger than Sanderling. Stocky, with medium-length straight bill and short legs. *Spring/summer:* Face and underparts *pale robin red;* back mottled with black, gray, and russet. *Fall/winter:* A dumpy wader with washed-out gray look and mottled flanks; medium-length bill, *pale rump* in flight, greenish legs. *Juvenile:* Has *pale feather edgings* above and pale buff wash on breast. **VOICE:** A low, mellow *tooit-wit* or *wah-quoit;* also a short, low, *tchrrt.* **SIMILAR SPECIES:** Dowitchers. Great Knot (p. 146). **HABITAT:** Tidal flats, sandy beaches, shores; tundra when breeding. Often found with dowitchers, Black-bellied Plovers; occasionally with rocky shorebirds. Uncommon to rare inland.

SANDERLING *Calidris alba* (see also p. 138)   Common

8 in. (20 cm). A plump, active sandpiper of outer beaches, where it chases retreating waves like a wind-up toy. Note bold *white wing stripe* in flight. Hallux (hind toe) absent, unlike other *Calidris* sandpipers. *Spring/summer:* Bright rusty about head, back, and breast (male averages brighter than female). *Fall/winter:* The palest sandpiper; snowy white underparts, plain pale gray back, *black shoulders. Juvenile:* Has salt-and-pepper pattern on back and breast sides. **VOICE:** Short *kip* or *quit.* **SIMILAR SPECIES:** Western Sandpiper and Red-necked Stint (p. 144) smaller, grayer (less white) in winter; hind toe present; beware occasional runty Sanderlings. Dunlin dusky gray in winter, bill longer and drooped. **HABITAT:** Beaches, mudflats, lakeshores; when nesting, stony tundra. Uncommon to rare inland. Common in winter in HI (p. 392).

DUNLIN *Calidris alpina* (see also p. 138)   Common

8½–8¾ in. (22–23 cm). Larger than a peep (p. 120), with *longish, droop-tipped bill.* Black legs. *Spring/summer: Rusty red above,* with *black patch on belly. Fall/winter:* Unpatterned gray or gray-brown above, with *grayish wash across breast. Juvenile* (this plumage rarely seen away from nesting areas): Rusty above, with buffy breast and suggestion of belly patch. Pacific N. American subspecies (*pacifica*) longer-billed than other subspecies, especially those of Asia, rare vagrants to AK and south along the coast; females also larger-billed than males. **VOICE:** Nasal, rasping *cheezp* or *treezp.* **SIMILAR SPECIES:** Winter Sanderling and (smaller) Western Sandpiper have clean white breast; Sanderling also paler above and has straighter bill. See also Rock Sandpiper, Curlew Sandpiper (p. 146). **HABITAT:** Tidal flats, beaches, muddy pools, occasionally rocks and jetties; in summer, moist tundra.

Basic Flight
Patterns of
Sandpipers

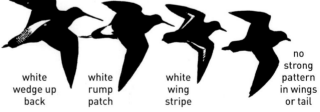

white   white   white   no
wedge up   rump   wing   strong
back   patch   stripe   pattern
                                             in wings
                                             or tail

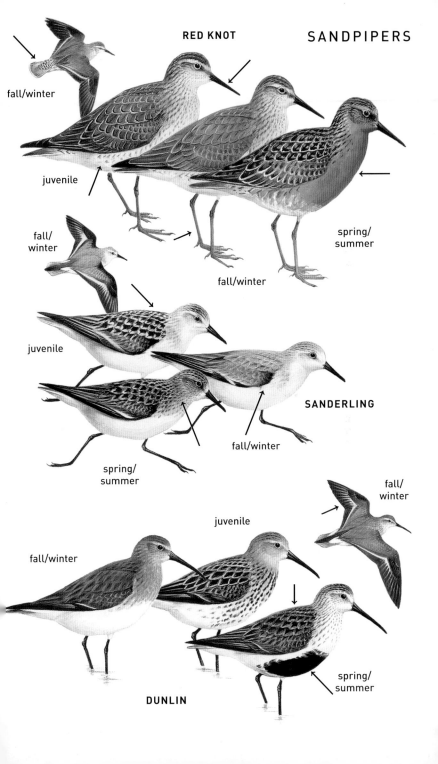

RED KNOT

SANDPIPERS

fall/winter

juvenile

fall/winter

spring/
summer

fall/
winter

juvenile

fall/winter

SANDERLING

spring/
summer

fall/winter

fall/
winter

juvenile

fall/winter

spring/
summer

DUNLIN

PEEPS

Collectively, the three common small sandpipers of N. America are nicknamed "peeps" (other slightly larger *Calidris* sandpipers also referred to sometimes as "peeps"). In Old World, similar small peeps are called "stints."

LEAST SANDPIPER *Calidris minutilla* (see also p. 138) Common

6 in. (15 cm). Distinguished from the other two peeps by its slightly smaller size, *browner* upperparts and breast, and *yellowish or greenish* — not blackish — legs (but which might appear dark if caked in mud). *Bill slighter, finer, and slightly drooped at tip.* Plumage variable. *Adult:* Mostly brownish with some rufous and black in back (spring/summer) or brownish gray (fall/winter). *Juvenile:* Much brighter, with extensive rufous on upperparts and buff wash across breast. **VOICE:** Thin *krreet, kree-eet.* **SIMILAR SPECIES:** Western and Semipalmated Sandpipers have blackish legs, thicker-based bill, paler upperparts, and different voice; whitish breast in fall/winter plumage. See also Temink's and Long-toed Stints (p. 144). **HABITAT:** Mudflats, marshes, rain pools, shores, flooded fields; in summer, taiga wetlands.

SEMIPALMATED SANDPIPER *Calidris pusilla* (see also p. 138) Scarce

6¼ in. (16 cm). Note *straight, somewhat bulbous-tipped bill* of variable but generally short length. *Spring/summer:* Gray-brown above, many birds with a tinge of russet to cheeks and back; dark streaks on breast. *Fall/winter:* Uniformly plain gray across upperparts (rarely seen in our area). *Juvenile:* Breast washed with buff and with fine streaks on sides; scaly upperpart pattern rather uniform, with pale feather edges tinged buff (sometimes reddish) when fresh. **VOICE:** Call *chit* or *chirt* (lacks *ee* sound of Least and Western Sandpipers). **SIMILAR SPECIES:** Most Western Sandpipers have *longer bills, slightly drooped* at tip. Spring/summer Western more rufous above, more heavily streaked below. Juvenile Western has rusty scapulars forming a diagonal bar across grayer back (not found in Semipalmated) and slightly paler face. Not all birds distinguishable in winter plumages. Least Sandpiper smaller, browner, and thinner billed; has *yellowish or greenish* legs. See also Red-necked and Little Stints (p. 144). **HABITAT:** Mudflats, marshes, shores, beaches; in summer, tundra. Scarce vagrant to W. Coast.

WESTERN SANDPIPER *Calidris mauri* Common

6½ in. (17 cm). Legs black. Bill averages thicker at base and longer than Semipalmated Sandpipers and *droops near tip. Spring/summer: Heavily spotted* on breast and flanks; *rusty scapulars, crown, and ear patch. Fall/winter:* Gray or gray-brown above, unmarked whitish below. *Juvenile:* Buffy wash on breast; scaly upperparts, like juvenile Semipalmated but with distinct rusty scapular bar. **VOICE:** Distinct high-pitched *jeet* or *cheet,* unlike lower, soft *chirt* of Semipalmated. **SIMILAR SPECIES:** Semipalmated and Least Sandpipers; Dunlin. Some male Westerns may be particularly difficult to separate from female Semipalmateds; see also voice. Semipalmated rarely winters in our area. **HABITAT:** Shores, beaches, mudflats, marshes; in summer, tundra.

SMALL "PEEP"
SANDPIPERS

fall/winter

juvenile

LEAST
SANDPIPER

spring/summer

fall/winter

juvenile

spring/summer

SEMIPALMATED
SANDPIPER

fall/winter
female

juvenile
male

WESTERN
SANDPIPER

spring/summer
female

Least   Semipalmated   Western

WHITE-RUMPED SANDPIPER　　　　　　　　　Rare to casual
Calidris fuscicollis (see also p. 138)

7½ in. (19 cm). Larger than Semipalmated Sandpiper, smaller than Pectoral Sandpiper. The only peep with completely *white rump*. At rest, this long-winged bird has *tapered* look, with *wingtips extending well beyond tail*. Distinct pale supercilium. *Spring/summer:* Some rusty on crown, face, back. *Dark streaks and chevrons on sides extend to flanks.* Base of lower mandible bright reddish orange. *Juvenile:* Spangled upperparts scalloped rufous and white, fine streaks to buff-washed breast; bold *white eyebrow*. Winter birds are grayer and plainer; not seen in our area. **VOICE:** High, thin, mouselike *jeet,* like two flint pebbles scraping. **SIMILAR SPECIES:** Long wings and very attenuated look shared only by Baird's Sandpiper among other peeps, but Baird's buffier brown overall, has scalier back, and dark center to rump, lacks bold supercilium and dark streaks on flanks, and has much lower-pitched call. **HABITAT:** Prairie pools, shores, mudflats, marshes; in summer, tundra. Scarce vagrant to W. Coast, most being adults in late spring.

BAIRD'S SANDPIPER　　*Calidris bairdii* (see also p. 138)　　Uncommon

7½ in. (19 cm). Larger than Semipalmated and Western Sandpiper, with more *long-winged, tapered look* (wings extend ½ in., 1 cm, beyond tail tip). Legs *black. Spring/summer:* Grayish-white upperparts with black centers to back feathers; white throat; black breast streaking heaviest to sides. *Juvenile:* Head and breast washed buff, throat and breast finely streaked; back feathers with *dark centers and rich buff to buff-orange fringing* creating highly scaled appearance. *Fall/winter:* Browner and duller than Juvenile; not found in our area. **VOICE:** Call a low *kreep* or *kree;* a rolling trill. **SIMILAR SPECIES:** White-rumped and Pectoral Sandpipers. Buff-breasted Sandpiper buffier below, without streaks, and has *yellow* (not *black*) legs. **HABITAT:** Pond margins, grassy mudflats, shores, upper beaches; in summer, tundra. Scarce migrant to W. Coast.

PECTORAL SANDPIPER　　　　　　　　　　Fairly common
Calidris melanotos (see also p. 136)

8¼–8¾ in. (21–23 cm). Medium sized (but variable; male larger than female); plump-bodied but neck longer than in smaller peeps. Note that heavy breast streaks end rather *abruptly,* like a bib. Dark back with two white stripes. Wing stripe faint or lacking; crown variably rusty. Legs usually dull yellowish. Bill may be pale yellow-brown at base. On breeding grounds, males display by expanding breast, exposing black-based feathers. Juvenile similar to adult but brighter rufous on upperparts and crown, buffier wash on breast under streaking. **VOICE:** Low, reedy *churrt* or *trrip, trrip.* **SIMILAR SPECIES:** Sharp-tailed Sandpiper (p. 146). Baird's and Least Sandpipers smaller, usually lack sharp breast-band; legs of Baird's black. **HABITAT:** In migration, prairie pools, sod farms, muddy shores, fresh and tidal marshes; in summer, tundra. Rare in interior West.

SANDPIPERS

juvenile

WHITE-RUMPED
SANDPIPER

spring/
summer

juvenile

spring/
summer

BAIRD'S
SANDPIPER

breeding
male

juvenile

spring/
summer

PECTORAL
SANDPIPER

SPOTTED SANDPIPER
Fairly common

Actitis macularius (see also p. 138)

7½ in. (19 cm). The most widespread sandpiper along shores of small freshwater lakes and streams. Usually solitary. Teeters rear body up and down nervously. Note moderately *long tail. Spring/summer:* Note *round breast spots. Fall/winter and juvenile:* No spots; brown above, with white line over eye (juvenile lightly scaled above), prominent wing stripe. Dusky smudge enclosing white wedge near shoulder is a good aid. Flight distinctive: wings beat in a *shallow arc,* giving a stiff, bowed appearance. **VOICE:** Clear *peet* or *peet-weet!* or *peet-weet-weet-weet-weet.* **SIMILAR SPECIES:** Solitary Sandpiper; see Common Sandpiper. **HABITAT:** Pebbly shores, ponds, streamsides; in winter, also seashores, rock jetties.

STILT SANDPIPER
Uncommon

Calidris himantopus (see also pp. 128 and 136)

8½ in. (22 cm). A tall sandpiper with slight *droop* to tip of bill, legs long and greenish yellow. Feeds like a dowitcher (sewing-machine motion) but *tilts tail up* more than a dowitcher while probing. *Spring/summer:* Heavily marked below with *transverse bars;* back brown with black mottling. Note *rusty cheek patch. Fall/winter:* Yellowlegs-like but unmarked gray above, dark-winged and *white-rumped;* note also more *greenish legs* and *white eyebrow. Juvenile:* Brownish-buff wash to breast; upperpart feathers brown with even pale edgings. **VOICE:** Single *whu* (like Lesser Yellowlegs but lower, hoarser). **SIMILAR SPECIES:** Yellowlegs. Dowitchers pudgier, have longer bills, and show white wedge up back. In winter, Wilson's Phalarope very similar in plumage (see pp. 128 and 130) and structure but has diffent feeding posture and behavior, shorter legs, straighter bill. See also Curlew Sandpiper (p. 146). **HABITAT:** Shallow pools, mudflats, marshes; in summer, tundra. Rare along W. Coast; casual in interior West.

UPLAND SANDPIPER
Scarce, local

Bartramia longicauda (see also p. 136)

12 in. (30–31 cm). A "pigeon-headed" brown sandpiper; larger than Killdeer. Short bill, *small head,* shoe-button eye, thin neck, and *long tail* are helpful points. Often perches with erect posture on fenceposts and poles. Ages and sexes similar through year. **VOICE:** Mellow, whistled *kip-ip-ip-ip,* often heard at night. Song a weird windy whistle: *whoooleeeeee, whee-loooooooooo.* **SIMILAR SPECIES:** Buff-breasted Sandpiper. See also Eskimo and Little Curlews (p. 142). **HABITAT:** Grassy prairies, open meadows, fields, airports, sod farms. Scarce vagrant to W. Coast.

BUFF-BREASTED SANDPIPER
Rare

Calidris subruficollis (see also p. 136)

8¼ in. (21 cm). *Rich buffy* below (paling to whitish on undertail coverts); erect stance, small head, short bill, and yellowish legs. Dark eye stands out on plain face. In flight, white underwing with distinct dark crescent at base of primaries. Ages and sexes similar through year. **VOICE:** Low, trilled *pr-r-r-reet.* Sharp *tik.* **SIMILAR SPECIES:** Baird's, Pectoral, and Upland Sandpipers. Juvenile Ruff (p. 146). **HABITAT:** Dry dirt, sand, and short-grass habitats, including drying lakeshores, pastures, sod farms; in summer, drier tundra ridges. Scarce vagrant to W. Coast.

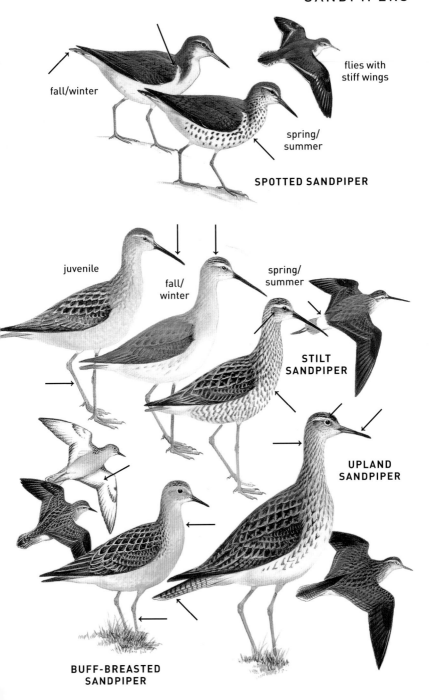

SANDPIPERS

flies with
stiff wings

fall/winter

spring/
summer

SPOTTED SANDPIPER

juvenile

fall/
winter

spring/
summer

**STILT
SANDPIPER**

**UPLAND
SANDPIPER**

**BUFF-BREASTED
SANDPIPER**

WILSON'S SNIPE   *Gallinago delicata* (see also p. 136)   **Fairly common**

10¼–10½ in. (26–27 cm). A tight-sitting marsh and wet-field prober; on nesting grounds may be seen standing on posts. Note *extremely long bill*. Brown, with *buff stripes on back* and a *striped head*. Ages and sexes similar through year. When flushed, flies off in *zigzag,* showing *short rusty orange tail*. **VOICE:** When flushed, a rasping *scaip*. Song a measured *chip-a, chip-a, chip-a,* etc. In high aerial display, a winnowing *huhuhuhuhuhuhu*. **SIMILAR SPECIES:** Dowitchers. See Common Snipe (p. 146). **HABITAT:** Marshes, bogs, ditches, wet fields and meadows.

SHORT-BILLED DOWITCHER   **Fairly common**
Limnodromus griseus (see also p. 138)

11–11¼ in. (27–28 cm). A snipelike bird of open mudflats. Note long bill, sewing-machine feeding motion, and, in flight, *long white wedge up back*. *Spring/summer:* Underparts rich rusty with some barring on flanks. *Fall/winter:* Gray. *Juvenile:* Brighter upperparts, buff wash to neck and breast; *patterned tertial feathers* (fringes broken orange and black) an important distinction from juvenile Long-billed. **VOICE:** Staccato, muted *tu-tu-tu;* pitch of Lesser Yellowlegs. **SIMILAR SPECIES:** Bill length overlaps with that of Long-billed Dowitcher (by about 50 percent) but can be used with caution, especially when assessing variation among groups of birds; shorter bill also results in more angled back when feeding, on average. In fall/winter plumage, differences in call notes and habitat are usually the best way to distinguish the dowitchers; see also Stilt Sandpiper, Red Knot. **HABITAT:** More frequent on large tidal mudflats than Long-billed Dowitcher. In summer, taiga and tundra. Migrates earlier in fall than Long-billed. Uncommon to rare inland.

LONG-BILLED DOWITCHER   **Common**
Limnodromus scolopaceus (see also p. 138)

11½ in. (29 cm). When feeding, shows more round-bodied profile than Short-billed; dark tail bars average wider; bill averages longer (see Short-billed Dowitcher). *Spring/summer:* Underparts *evenly bright rusty to lower belly* (white or very pale lower belly in most Short-billed Dowitchers), with dark spotting on neck and barring on sides. Dark bars on tail broader, giving tail a darker look. *Fall/winter:* Averages darker than Short-billed with smoother gray breast and darker centers to scapulars. *Juvenile:* Gray tertials *with unpatterned solid pale fringe;* Short-billed has *internal rusty markings* similar to "tiger barring." **VOICE:** Single sharp, high *keek,* occasionally given in twos or threes but differs in quality from Short-billed call. **SIMILAR SPECIES:** The two dowitcher species are most easily separated by voice, along with plumage, bill length, habitat. **HABITAT:** Shallow pools, marshes, mudflats during migration; when breeding, tundra. More partial to fresh water than Short-billed, especially in winter, but some overlap.

SNIPELIKE WADERS

winnowing
display
flight

**WILSON'S
SNIPE**

snipe

dowitcher

juvenile

eastern
spring/
summer

**SHORT-BILLED
DOWITCHER**

fall/winter

western
spring/
summer

juvenile

Short-billed
probing

spring/
summer

Long-billed

fall/
winter

**LONG-BILLED
DOWITCHER**

probing

WILLET   *Tringa semipalmata* (see also p. 134)   **Common**

15–16 in. (38–41 cm). Stockier than Greater Yellowlegs; has grayer look, heavier bill, blue-gray legs. In flight, note *striking black-and-white wing pattern*. At rest, this large wader is rather nondescript: gray above, mottled or barred below in spring/summer, unmarked in fall/winter plumage. *Juvenile:* Browner above with light buff spots and bars. **VOICE:** Musical, repetitious *pill-will-willet* (in breeding season); a loud *kay-ee* (second note lower). Also a rapidly repeated *kip-kip-kip*, etc. In flight, *kree-ree-ree*. **SIMILAR SPECIES:** Greater Yellowlegs; see also dowitchers, Wandering Tattler (which is much smaller). **HABITAT:** Marshes, wet meadows, mudflats, beaches. Uncommon to rare inland, away from breeding range.

GREATER YELLOWLEGS   *Tringa melanoleuca* (see also p. 136)   **Common**

14 in. (36 cm). Note *bright yellow legs* (shared with next species). A slim gray sandpiper; back checkered with gray, black, and white. Often teeters body. In flight, appears *dark-winged* (no stripe), with *whitish rump and tail*. Bill long, *slightly upturned, paler at base*. Spring/summer adults blacker above, more barred on breast; fall/winter birds grayer above, whiter below; juveniles pale brownish gray, evenly scaled above. **VOICE:** Three-note strident whistle, *dear! dear! dear!* or *teer-teer-turr* with emphasis on first note. **SIMILAR SPECIES:** Lesser Yellowlegs, Willet; Common Greenshank and Spotted Redshank (p. 140). **HABITAT:** Marshes, mudflats, streams, ponds, flooded fields; in summer, wooded muskeg, spruce bogs.

LESSER YELLOWLEGS   *Tringa flavipes* (see also p. 136)   **Fairly common**

10½ in. (27 cm). Like Greater Yellowlegs, but smaller (obvious when both species are together). Lesser's shorter, slimmer, all-dark bill is *straight* and about *equal to length of head;* Greater's appears slightly uptilted, paler based, and longer than bird's head. Readily separated by voice. Age and seasonal differences similar to Greater. **VOICE:** *Yew* or *yu-yu* (usually one or two notes); less forceful than three-syllable call of Greater. **SIMILAR SPECIES:** Solitary and Stilt Sandpipers, Wilson's Phalarope. Both yellowlegs species may swim briefly, like a phalarope. **HABITAT:** Marshes, mudflats, ponds, flooded fields; in summer, open, moist boreal woods and taiga. Uncommon along Pacific Coast.

SOLITARY SANDPIPER   *Tringa solitaria* (see also p. 136)   **Scarce**

8½ in. (22 cm). Note *dark wings* and conspicuous *white sides of tail* (crossed by bold black bars). A dark-backed sandpiper, whitish below, with *light eye-ring* and greenish legs. Nods like a yellowlegs. Usually alone, seldom in groups. Ages and sexes fairly similar. **VOICE:** *Peet!* or *peet-weet-weet!* (more strident than Spotted Sandpiper's call). **SIMILAR SPECIES:** Lesser Yellowlegs has bright yellow legs, white rump, lacks bold eye-ring. Spotted Sandpiper teeters tail (not head), has different wing and tail patterns. See Wood Sandpiper (p. 140). **HABITAT:** Streamsides, wooded swamps and ponds, ditches, freshwater marshes. Rare west of breeding range and along Pacific Coast.

STILT SANDPIPER   *Calidris himantopus*   **See p. 124**

Fall/winter: Long yellow-green legs, slight droop to bill, white rump; distinct light supercilium.

WILSON'S PHALAROPE   *Phalaropus tricolor*   **See p. 130**

Fall/winter: Straight needle bill, clear white underparts, pale gray back, dull yellow legs.

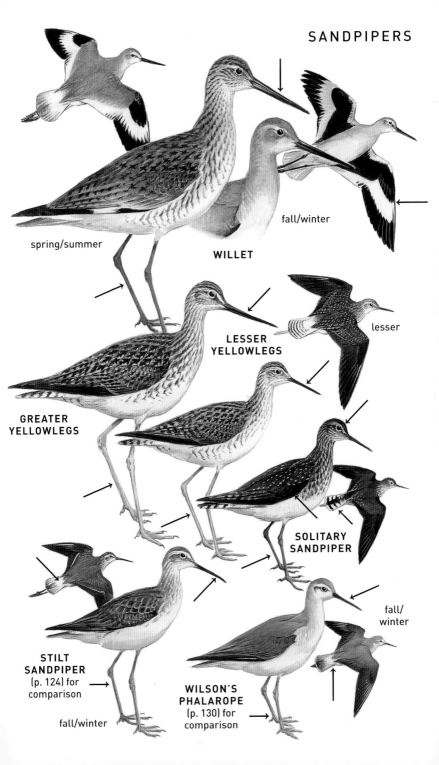

SANDPIPERS

spring/summer

fall/winter

WILLET

LESSER YELLOWLEGS

lesser

GREATER YELLOWLEGS

SOLITARY SANDPIPER

STILT SANDPIPER (p. 124) for comparison

fall/winter

WILSON'S PHALAROPE (p. 130) for comparison

fall/ winter

PHALAROPES

Shorebirds with lobed toes; more at home wading or swimming than on land. Phalaropes often spin like tops, rapidly dabbling for plankton and other marine invertebrates and insects. Female slightly larger and, in spring/summer, more colorful than male. **RANGE:** Circumpolar, with one species confined to Americas.

WILSON'S PHALAROPE
Fairly common

Phalaropus tricolor (see also pp. 128 and 136)

9¼ in. (23½ cm). A trim phalarope, plain-winged (no stripe), with white rump. In addition to spinning in water, also feeds by dashing about on shorelines. *Spring/summer:* Female unique, with *broad black face and neck stripe blending into cinnamon.* Male duller. *Fall/winter:* Whiter below, with no breast streaking (not found in our area). *Juvenile:* Buff and brown pattern above, buffy wash on breast. **VOICE:** Low nasal *wurk;* also *check, check, check.* **SIMILAR SPECIES:** Other two phalaropes in fall have white wing stripe, dark rump, and bold dark patch through eye. See also yellowlegs and Stilt Sandpiper (p. 124), which may swim for brief periods of time. **HABITAT:** Shallow lakes, freshwater marshes, pools, shores, mudflats; in late summer and fall, also large salt lakes (such as Mono Lake, CA, and Great Salt Lake, UT) and marshes.

RED-NECKED PHALAROPE
Common offshore, scarce inland

Phalaropus lobatus (see also p. 138)

7¾ in. (20 cm). Found primarily at sea, although Red-necked is not as pelagic as Red Phalarope. Note dark patch through eye and needlelike black bill. *Spring/summer:* Female gray above, with *rufous chestnut on neck,* white throat and eyebrow. Male duller, but similar in pattern. *Fall/winter:* Both sexes dark gray above with whitish streaks, white below; rare in our area in this plumage. *Juvenile:* Has distinct buff stripes on back. **VOICE:** Sharp *kit* or *whit,* similar to call of Sanderling. **SIMILAR SPECIES:** Red Phalarope. **HABITAT:** In migration, nearshore ocean, bays, ponds; in summer, tundra; in winter, coastal ocean and estuaries (mostly south of the U.S.). Uncommon to rare inland.

RED PHALAROPE
Uncommon offshore, very rare onshore

Phalaropus fulicarius (see also p. 138)

8¼–8½ in. (21–22 cm). Seagoing habits and buoyant swimming at sea. *Spring/summer:* Female has deep *reddish underparts, white face,* and mostly yellow bill. Male duller. *Fall/winter:* Both sexes plain pale gray above, white below; *dark patch* through eye. Bill mostly dark with *yellow base.* *Juvenile:* Has peach-buff wash on neck. **VOICE:** *Whit* or *kit,* higher than Red-necked Phalarope's call. **SIMILAR SPECIES:** Red-necked Phalarope slightly slimmer, has more needlelike bill; juvenile darker gray above with thin pale back stripes. Thicker yellow-based bill of Red Phalarope visible at closer range. In our area, most or all phalaropes observed in winter are Reds. **HABITAT:** More strictly pelagic (less coastal) than Red-necked in migration and winter; sometimes "wrecks" (irruptions of weak or starving birds) to coastal water bodies following winter storms. In summer, tundra. Rare to casual inland.

PHALAROPES

spring/
summer
female

fall/winter

**WILSON'S
PHALAROPE**

fall/winter

juvenile

spring/
summer
male

phalaropes
spin

fall/
winter

**RED-NECKED
PHALAROPE**

spring/
summer
female

juvenile

fall/winter

spring/
summer
male

spring/summer
female

fall/winter

**RED
PHALAROPE**

juvenile

fall/winter

lobed foot of
phalarope

spring/summer male

PLOVERS and TURNSTONE in FLIGHT

Learning their distinctive flight calls can substantially help with identification.

PIPING PLOVER *Charadrius melodus* p. 110

Pale sand colored above, wide black tail spot, whitish rump.
Call a plaintive whistle, *peep-lo* (first note higher).

SNOWY PLOVER *Charadrius nivosus* p. 110

Pale sand color above; tail with dark center, white sides; rump not white.
Call a musical whistle, *pe-wee-ah* or *o-wee-ah.*

SEMIPALMATED PLOVER *Charadrius semipalmatus* p. 110

Mud brown above; dark tail with white borders.
Call a plaintive upward-slurred *chi-we* or *too-li.*

WILSON'S PLOVER *Charadrius wilsonia* p. 110

Similar in pattern to Semipalmated; larger with big bill.
Call an emphatic whistled *whit!* or *wheet!*

KILLDEER *Charadrius vociferus* p. 110

Tawny orange rump, longish tail.
Noisy; a loud *kill-deeah* or *killdeer;* also *dee-dee-dee,* etc.

BLACK-BELLIED PLOVER *Pluvialis squatarola* p. 108

Spring/summer adult: Black below, slivery white above, white undertail coverts.
Fall/wnter, juvenile, and some first-summer birds: Pale grayish above and below.
Year-round: Black wingpits, white in wing, white rump and tail base.
Call a plaintive slurred whistle, *tlee-oo-eee* or *whee-er-ee.*

AMERICAN GOLDEN-PLOVER *Pluvialis dominica* p. 108

Spring/summer adult: Black below, black undertail coverts.
Fall/winter, juvenile, and some first-summer birds: Speckled brown and buff above, grayish below.
Year-round: Underwing grayer than Black-bellied Plover's; no black in wingpits.
Call a querulous whistled *queedle* or *que-e-a.*

PACIFIC GOLDEN-PLOVER *Pluvialis fulva* (not shown) p. 108

Like American, but spring/summer birds have narrower and longer white stripe down sides and some white along flanks and undertail; fall/winter birds and juveniles more gold-washed on upperparts and face; wings shorter proportionally.
Call a loud, whistled *chu-whee* or *chu-wee-dle.*

RUDDY TURNSTONE *Arenaria interpres* p. 116

Harlequin pattern in face distinctive; bold white upperpart patterns.
Call a low chuckling *tuk-a-tuk* or *kut-a-kut.*

BLACK TURNSTONE *Arenaria melanocephala* (not shown) p. 116

Similar to Ruddy but blacker, including head and breast.
Call a short series of rattling notes.

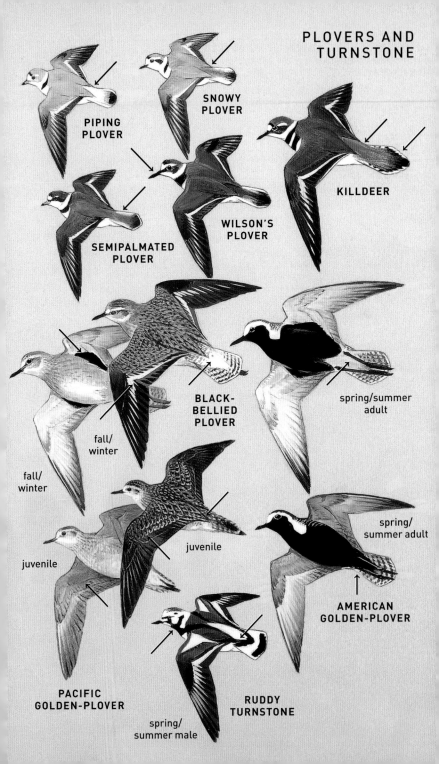

PLOVERS AND TURNSTONE

PIPING PLOVER

SNOWY PLOVER

KILLDEER

SEMIPALMATED PLOVER

WILSON'S PLOVER

BLACK-BELLIED PLOVER

fall/winter

fall/winter

spring/summer adult

juvenile

juvenile

spring/summer adult

PACIFIC GOLDEN-PLOVER

juvenile

RUDDY TURNSTONE

spring/summer male

AMERICAN GOLDEN-PLOVER

LARGE WADERS in FLIGHT

Learn to know their flight calls, which are distinctive.

HUDSONIAN GODWIT   *Limosa haemastica*   p. 114

Upturned bill, white wing stripe, ringed tail. Blackish underwing linings.
Flight call *tawit!,* higher pitched than Marbled Godwit's.

WILLET   *Tringa semipalmata*   p. 128

Contrasty black, gray, and white wing pattern from both above and below.
Flight call a whistled one- to three-note *kree-ree-ree.*

MARBLED GODWIT   *Limosa fedoa*   p. 114

Long upturned bill, tawny brown color. Cinnamon underwing linings.
Flight call an accented *kerwhit!* (or *godwit!*).

WHIMBREL   *Numenius phaeopus*   p. 114

Decurved bill, gray-brown overall color, distinctly striped crown. Grayer
than next species; lacks cinnamon underwing linings; bill darker, to
blackish.
Flight call five to seven short, rapid whistles: c*hee-chee-chee-chee-chee-
chee.*

LONG-BILLED CURLEW   *Numenius americanus*   p. 114

Very long, sicklelike bill (longer in female than male); no head striping.
Bright cinnamon underwing linings. Juvenile's bill shorter but note head
patterns.
Flight call a rapid, whistled *kli-li-li-li.* Also a husky *curr-liew* (the second
note rising).

LARGE SANDPIPERS

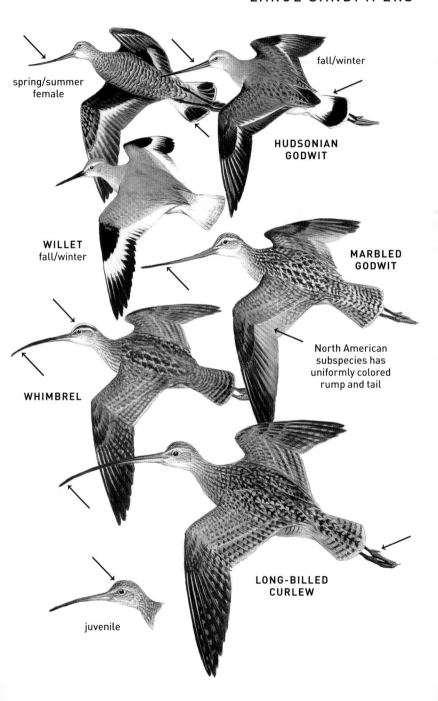

spring/summer female

fall/winter

HUDSONIAN GODWIT

WILLET fall/winter

MARBLED GODWIT

North American subspecies has uniformly colored rump and tail

WHIMBREL

LONG-BILLED CURLEW

juvenile

SNIPELIKE WADERS
and SANDPIPERS in FLIGHT

This plate and the next show the basic flight patterns of these species. Most of these have unpatterned wings, lacking a pale stripe. All are shown in full color on other plates. Learning their distinctive flight calls helps with identifications.

WILSON'S SNIPE *Gallinago delicata* **p. 126**
Long bill, pointed wings, rusty orange tail, zigzag flight.
Flight call, when flushed, a distinctive rasping *scaip*.

SOLITARY SANDPIPER *Tringa solitaria* **p. 128**
Very dark unpatterned wings (underwing dark also — pale in yellowlegs), conspicuous bars on white sides of tail.
Flight call *peet!* or *peet-weet-weet!* (higher than Spotted Sandpiper's).

LESSER YELLOWLEGS *Tringa flavipes* **p. 128**
Similar to Greater Yellowlegs, but smaller, with smaller bill.
Flight call *yew* or *yu-yu* (rarely three), softer than Greater's call.

GREATER YELLOWLEGS *Tringa melanoleuca* **p. 128**
Plain unpatterned wings, whitish rump and tail, long bill.
Flight call a distinctive and forceful three-note whistle, *dear! dear! dear!*

WILSON'S PHALAROPE *Phalaropus tricolor* **p. 128**
Fall/winter: Suggests Lesser Yellowlegs; smaller, whiter, bill needlelike.
Differs in posture and behavior from Stilt Sandpiper.
Flight call a low nasal *wurk*.

BUFF-BREASTED SANDPIPER *Calidris subruficollis* **p. 124**
Buff below; white underwing linings with disinct "comma" marks; plain upperparts.
Flight call a low, trilled *pr-r-r-reet;* usually silent.

STILT SANDPIPER *Calidris himantopus* **p. 124**
Suggests Lesser Yellowlegs, but legs greenish yellow, bill longer and drooped. Differs in posture and behavior from Wilson's Phalarope.
Flight call a single *whu,* lower than Lesser Yellowlegs' call.

UPLAND SANDPIPER *Bartramia longicauda* **p. 124**
Brown; small head, long tail.
Often flies "on tips of wings," like Spotted Sandpiper.
Flight call a mellow whistled *kip-ip-ip-ip*.

PECTORAL SANDPIPER *Calidris melanotos* **p. 122**
Like an oversized Least Sandpiper. Wing stripe faint or lacking.
Flight call a low, reedy *churrt* or *trrip, trrip*.

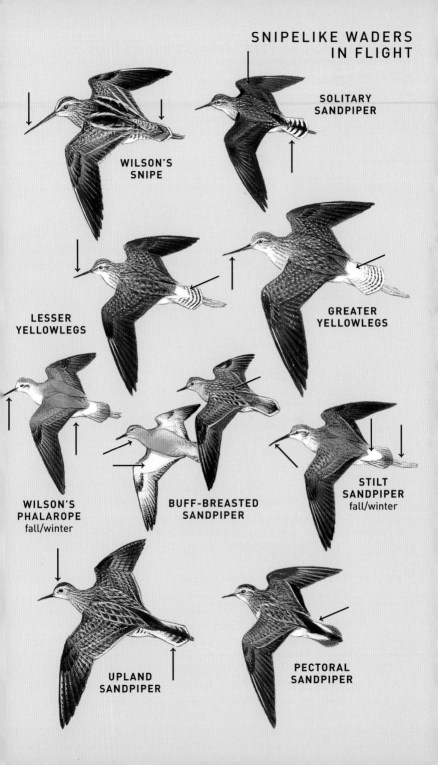

SNIPELIKE WADERS
IN FLIGHT

WILSON'S
SNIPE

SOLITARY
SANDPIPER

LESSER
YELLOWLEGS

GREATER
YELLOWLEGS

WILSON'S
PHALAROPE
fall/winter

BUFF-BREASTED
SANDPIPER

STILT
SANDPIPER
fall/winter

UPLAND
SANDPIPER

PECTORAL
SANDPIPER

SANDPIPERS and PHALAROPES in FLIGHT

DOWITCHERS *Limnodromus* spp. p. 126

Long bill, long wedge of white up back.
Flight call of Short-billed Dowitcher a staccato mellow *tu-tu-tu;* that of Long-billed Dowitcher a single sharp *keek,* often given in twos or threes but not repeatedly or consistently (unlike Short-billed).

DUNLIN *Calidris alpina* p. 118

Fall/winter: Slightly larger than peeps, darker than Sanderling.
Flight call a nasal rasping *cheezp* or *treezp.*

RED KNOT *Calidris canutus* p. 118

Fall/winter: Washed-out gray look, pale rump. Flight call a low *knut.*

WHITE-RUMPED SANDPIPER *Calidris fuscicollis* p. 122

White rump; only smallish peep so marked, but beware partial or poor views of other peeps, all of which have mostly white rumps with narrow dark stripe. Flight call a mouselike squeak, *jeet.*

CURLEW SANDPIPER *Calidris ferruginea* p. 146

Fall/winter: Suggests Dunlin, but rump white.

RUFF *Calidris pugnax* p. 146

If seen well, oval white patch on each side of dark tail distinctive.
Usually silent.

SPOTTED SANDPIPER *Actitis macularius* p. 124

Shallow wing stroke gives stiff, bowed effect; longish tail. Flight call a clear *peet* or *peet-weet.*

SANDERLING *Calidris alba* p. 118

The most contrasting wing stripe of any small shorebird. Flight call a sharp metallic *kip* or *quit.*

RED PHALAROPE *Phalaropus fulicarius* p. 130

Fall/winter: Paler above and plumper than Red-necked Phalarope; bill slightly thicker, yellow based.

RED-NECKED PHALAROPE *Phalaropus lobatus* p. 130

Fall/winter: Sanderling-like, but with dark eye patch, long black needle-like bill. Flight call (both Red-necked and Red Phalaropes) a sharp *kit* or *whit.*

LEAST SANDPIPER *Calidris minutilla* p. 120

Very small, brown with short wings and tail; faint wing stripe.
Flight call a thin *krreet, krreet.*

WESTERN SANDPIPER *Calidris mauri* p. 120

Grayer and slightly larger than Least Sandpiper. Semipalmated Sandpiper (not shown) similar but bill shorter. Flight call of Western jeet, more strident than Least's and unlike Semipalmated's.

BAIRD'S SANDPIPER *Calidris bairdii* p. 122

Larger and longer winged than above two. Size and shape of White-rumped Sandpiper, but rump dark. Flight call a low, raspy *kreep* or *kree.*

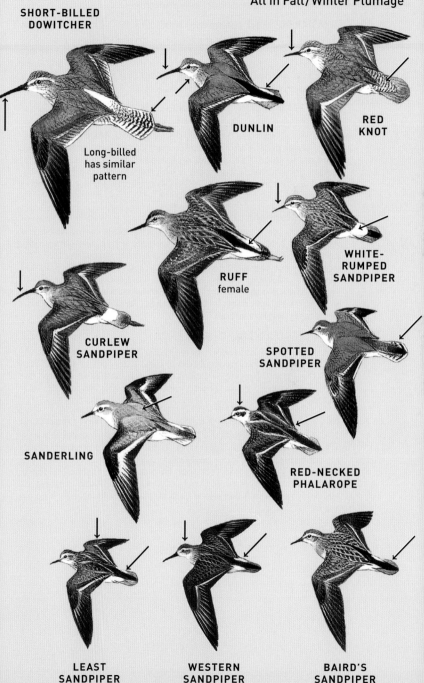

SANDPIPERS AND PHALAROPES
All in Fall/Winter Plumage

SHORT-BILLED DOWITCHER

Long-billed has similar pattern

DUNLIN

RED KNOT

RUFF female

WHITE-RUMPED SANDPIPER

CURLEW SANDPIPER

SPOTTED SANDPIPER

SANDERLING

RED-NECKED PHALAROPE

LEAST SANDPIPER

WESTERN SANDPIPER

BAIRD'S SANDPIPER

RARE SHOREBIRDS from EURASIA

EURASIAN DOTTEREL *Charadrius morinellus* Casual vagrant

8¼–8½ in. (21–22 cm). Narrow white stripe crossing midbreast identifies this dark plover. Broad *white eyebrow stripes* join in V on nape. **VOICE:** Repeated piping, *titi-ri-titi-ri*, running into a trill. **RANGE:** Very rare Asian visitor to w. AK, casual vagrant along Pacific Coast to CA and in HI. A few pairs may breed locally in montane tundra of nw. AK.

LESSER SAND-PLOVER *Charadrius mongolus* Very rare vagrant

7½ in. (19 cm). Asian. Slightly larger and larger-billed than Semipalmated Plover. *Spring/summer:* Very distinctive, with *broad rufous breast-band.* Female duller. *Fall/winter and juvenile:* Breast-band gray-brown; no white collar. **VOICE:** Calls include a ploverlike whistle and a rolling trill. **RANGE:** Rare but regular migrant to Aleutians and Bering Sea islands. Casual vagrant from mainland AK to CA, accidental farther east and in HI.

SPOTTED REDSHANK *Tringa erythropus* Accidental vagrant

12½ in. (32 cm). A slender, long-legged, long-billed shorebird. *Spring/summer: Sooty black,* with small white speckles on back and wings, making bird appear a trifle paler above. Long legs *dark red;* long black bill *reddish basally,* has *slight droop at tip. Fall/winter and juvenile:* Gray and somewhat yellowlegs-like, but legs *orange-red,* bill *orange-red* basally. In flight, shows *long white wedge* on back, white underwing. **VOICE:** Sharp, whistled *tcheet,* with rising inflection. **RANGE:** Casual spring and fall visitor; records widely scattered.

COMMON GREENSHANK *Tringa nebularia* Casual vagrant

13½ in. (34 cm). Slightly larger than Greater Yellowlegs, legs *dull greenish* (not bright yellow). Wedgelike *white rump patch runs up back*, as in a dowitcher. **VOICE:** Ringing, whistled *tew tew tew,* similar to Greater Yellowlegs. **RANGE:** Eurasian species; annual visitor on w. AK islands, accidental elsewhere.

WOOD SANDPIPER *Tringa glareola* Very rare vagrant

8 in. (20 cm). Shape of Solitary Sandpiper, but has pale (not dark) underwings. Pale supercilium. Upperparts slightly paler and browner, *heavily spotted* with pale buff. Rump patch *white* (Solitary has dark rump). Legs dull yellow. Overall, looks very short in rear. **VOICE:** Distinctive, sharp, high *chew-chew-chew* or *chiff-chiff-chiff.* **RANGE:** Regular migrant on Aleutians and Bering Sea islands, accidental elsewhere in N. America and HI.

RARE SHOREBIRDS

EURASIAN DOTTEREL

juvenile

spring/summer male

fall/winter

LESSER SAND-PLOVER

spring/summer male

fall/winter

fall/winter

SPOTTED REDSHANK

spring/summer

COMMON GREENSHANK

fall/winter

spring/summer

WOOD SANDPIPER

RARE SHOREBIRDS

BAR-TAILED GODWIT *Limosa lapponica* Rare, local

16–17 in. (41–44 cm). A smaller godwit than Marbled; bill straighter; legs shorter; underwing plumage distinctive. Alaskan birds (subspecies *baueri*) have *mottled rump* and *whitish tail* crossed by narrow dark bars. *Spring/summer adult:* Male rich *reddish orange,* particularly on head and underparts. Female duller. *Fall/winter and first-year:* Both sexes grayish above, white below, underwing whitish with few markings. *Juvenile:* Underparts washed buffy, back with neat buff-and-black pattern. **VOICE:** Flight call a harsh *kirrick;* alarm a shrill *krick.* **RANGE:** Nests in w. AK; casual to rare vagrant on W. Coast; accidental inland. **HABITAT:** Mudflats, shores, tundra.

BLACK-TAILED GODWIT *Limosa limosa* Casual vagrant

16½ in. (42 cm). Resembles Hudsonian Godwit (white rump, white wing stripe, black tail), but bill is straighter. Best field distinction in all plumages is *white* underwing linings in Black-tailed, *black* in Hudsonian. **VOICE:** Flight call a clear *reeka-reeka-reeka.* **RANGE:** Casual visitor to AK; thus far unrecorded elsewhere in West. **HABITAT:** Lakes, muddy shores.

"EURASIAN" WHIMBREL *Numenius phaeopus* Casual vagrant

Two subspecies of Whimbrel from Eurasia occur as very rare visitors in N. America, with Asian subspecies *variegatus* being a rare but regular migrant in w. AK and casual farther south along Pacific Coast. Differs from N. American Whimbrel by showing mostly *white rump* (mottled grayish in *variegatus*), white wedge up back, paler underwing. **VOICE:** Calls similar to N. American Whimbrel.

BRISTLE-THIGHED CURLEW Rare, local, threatened
Numenius tahitiensis

17½–18 in. (44–46 cm). Very similar to Whimbrel, but buffier to tawnier, back flecking darker, *tail and unbarred rump pale to rich orange.* Breast less streaked. Has unique bristlelike feathers extending from underparts near base of legs. Call very different. **VOICE:** Slurred *chi-u-it* (Inuit name) or *whee-oo-wheep;* suggests call of Black-bellied Plover but louder and slurred. Also a wolf whistle–like *whee-wheeo.* **RANGE:** Nests locally in w. AK; accidental farther south along Pacific Coast. Regular migrant and winter visitor to HI (p. 392). **HABITAT:** In summer, tundra; in winter, reefs, beaches, and fields.

ESKIMO CURLEW *Numenius borealis* Almost certainly extinct

14 in. (36 cm). Last documented record in early 1960s (primarily in e. N. America) and almost assuredly extinct. Much smaller than Whimbrel; bill shorter, thinner, only slightly curved. Underwing linings cinnamon-buff with unbarred primaries (unlike Little Curlew, Upland Sandpiper). Legs slate gray. **HABITAT:** Open grasslands, coastal areas; in summer, tundra.

LITTLE CURLEW *Numenius minutus* Accidental vagrant

12 in. (30 cm). The tiniest curlew. Bill *short and gently decurved.* Breast washed with buff, finely streaked. At rest, wingtips even with tail tip (extend beyond tail in Eskimo Curlew); note difference in *underwing* (pale buff, not cinnamon) and *flanks* (lightly barred, not heavy chevrons). Bill shape differs from Upland Sandpiper's. **RANGE:** Asian species; accidental along W. Coast.

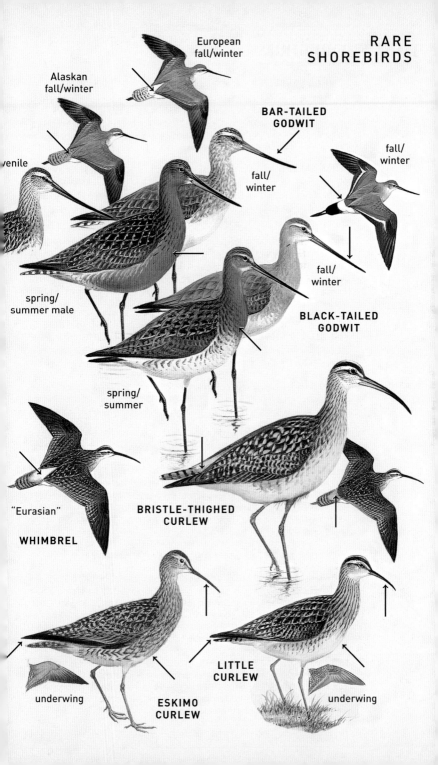

RARE
SHOREBIRDS

European
fall/winter

Alaskan
fall/winter

BAR-TAILED
GODWIT

juvenile

fall/
winter

fall/
winter

fall/
winter

spring/
summer male

BLACK-TAILED
GODWIT

spring/
summer

"Eurasian"

WHIMBREL

BRISTLE-THIGHED
CURLEW

underwing

ESKIMO
CURLEW

LITTLE
CURLEW

underwing

RARE SHOREBIRDS

COMMON SANDPIPER *Actitis hypoleucos*   **Very rare vagrant**

8 in. (20 cm). Resembles fall/winter Spotted Sandpiper (no spots). Note *longer tail*; at rest, wingtips reach only halfway to tail tip. Common has grayer legs and averages more gray on breast. **VOICE:** In flight, *twee-see-see*, thinner than Spotted's call. **RANGE:** Rare vagrant to Aleutians and Bering Sea islands; accidental in HI.

TEREK SANDPIPER *Xenus cinereus*   **Casual vagrant**

9 in. (23 cm). Note *upturned bill* and short *orange-yellow legs, jagged black stripe* along scapulars. In flight, wing has triangular *white trailing edge*. **VOICE:** Fluty *dudududu* or sharp piping *twita-wit-wit-wit*. **RANGE:** Very rare in w. AK islands, accidental farther south and in HI.

LITTLE STINT *Calidris minuta*   **Vary rare vagrant**

6 in. (15 cm). Small peep (stint) with fine bill. *Spring/summer:* Rusty orange above and on breast. Similar to Red-necked Stint, but body less elongated, legs longer, and *dark breast markings washed with orange. Juvenile:* Long wingtip projection, bold white V on mantle, rufous-fringed wing coverts. **VOICE:** Sanderling-like *tit*. **RANGE:** Casual visitor, mostly to coast, and in HI.

RED-NECKED STINT *Calidris ruficollis*   **Rare visitor and breeder, local**

6¼ in. (17 cm). In spring/summer shows *bright rusty head and neck, bordered below by dark streaks. Juvenile:* Has long wingtip projection but plumper body, shorter legs than Little; rusty-fringed scapulars contrast with brown-fringed wing coverts. Bill straight and fine at tip. **VOICE:** Short, clipped *chit,* or *chit chit.* **RANGE:** Rare migrant and very rare breeder in w. AK; casual vagrant to CA, HI, and elsewhere.

GRAY-TAILED TATTLER *Tringa brevipes*   **Rare vagrant, local**

10 in. (25 cm). Very similar to Wandering Tattler; often best told by voice. *Spring/summer:* Upperparts paler, barring on underparts finer and less extensive, and supercilium somewhat bolder than in Wandering Tattler. *Juvenile:* Gray-tailed has more extensive pale markings to scapulars, coverts, and tertials, is slightly paler gray above, and shows whiter flanks (gray usually not extending below folded wings). **VOICE:** Up-slurred whistle, *too-weet?* or *tu-whip?,* with accent on second syllable. Beware: Gray-tailed occasionally gives multinote call and Wandering occasionally gives two-note call, but note quality differs. **RANGE:** Asian species, rare but regular visitor to w. AK islands and HI, accidental elsewhere.

TEMMINCK'S STINT *Calidris temminckii*   **Casual vagrant**

6¼ in. (16 cm). Brownish gray and plainer than Least Sandpiper, with *irregular black spots* on scapulars. Has *elongated,* crouching look; *short dull yellow legs.* In flight, shows *whiter outer tail feathers* but this can be hard to discern. **VOICE:** A dry cricketlike *trree,* often repeated. **RANGE:** Very rare visitor to w. AK, accidental vagrant farther south.

LONG-TOED STINT *Calidris subminuta*   **Casual vagrant**

6 in. (15 cm). Much like Least Sandpiper, but with more erect stance, longer *legs* and *toes,* dark forehead. May suggest miniature Sharp-tailed Sandpiper. **VOICE:** Purring *prrp.* **RANGE:** Rare but regular migrant on w. AK islands; accidental farther south and in HI.

RARE SHOREBIRDS

TEREK SANDPIPER

spring/ summer

juvenile

spring/ summer

COMMON SANDPIPER

fall/winter Spotted Sandpiper (p. 124) for comparison

Wandering Tattler (p. 116) for comparison

spring/ summer **LITTLE STINT**

fall/winter

spring/ summer

spring/ summer

first summer

RED-NECKED STINT

spring/ summer

GRAY-TAILED TATTLER

juvenile

juvenile

TEMMINCK'S STINT

spring/ summer

spring/ summer

LONG-TOED STINT

RARE SHOREBIRDS

SHARP-TAILED SANDPIPER *Calidris acuminate* **Rare to casual visitor**
8½ in. (22 cm). Similar to Pectoral Sandpiper, but shows brighter rusty crown and lacks sharp demarcation between white belly and streaked breast. Most visitors to N. America are juveniles, which have rich *orangey buff breast,* finely streaked on sides only, rather than across breast as in Pectoral. Spring/summer adults have *dark chevrons* extending to flanks. Smaller than Ruff, larger than Long-toed Stint. **VOICE:** Trilled *prreeet* or *trrit-trrit,* sometimes twittered. **RANGE:** Regular fall migrant in w. AK and HI; rare in fall and casual in spring along Pacific Coast; casual to accidental elsewhere. **HABITAT:** Borders of wetlands, muddy shores, wet pastures; in summer, tundra.

GREAT KNOT *Calidris tenuirostris* **Very rare vagrant**
10–11 in. (25–29 cm). Similar to Red Knot but slightly larger and chestier; bill longer and thinner at tip; legs duller, grayish green to olive. *Spring/summer:* Breast conspicuously mottled black; upperpart feathers and some wing coverts fringed bright rufous. *Winter/spring and juvenile:* Similar to Red Knot but upperparts indistinctly streaked; breast gray, usually with indistinct spots. **RANGE:** Very rare visitor to w. AK; accidental vagrant along W. Coast.

CURLEW SANDPIPER **Very rare vagrant**
Calidris ferruginea (see also p. 138)
8½–8¾ in. (21–22 cm). Note slim downcurved bill, blackish legs, and white rump in flight. *Spring/summer:* Male variably rich rufous red; female duller with thin pale barring. *Fall/winter:* Resembles Dunlin, but longer legged, bill curved more evenly throughout rather than drooping at tip; white rump. *Juvenile:* Buff edges on feathers of back give a scaly look; breast washed buff. See also Stilt Sandpiper. **VOICE:** Liquid *chirrip.* **RANGE:** Very rare vagrant along W. Coast and in HI. **HABITAT:** Marshy pools, mudflats; in summer, tundra.

RUFF *Calidris pugnax* (see also p. 138) **Very rare visitor**
Male (Ruff) 12–13 in. (30–32 cm); female (known informally as Reeve) 9 in. (23 cm). *Spring/summer male:* Unique, with erectile *ruffs* and *ear tufts* that may be black, brown, rufous, buff, white, or barred in various combinations. *Spring/summer female:* Smaller than male; lacks ruffs, breast *heavily blotched* with dark. *Fall/winter:* Rather plain, with short bill, small head, thick neck. *Juvenile:* Rich buffy head and breast, very scaly on back. In all plumages, note greenish-yellow to orange legs and rather unique, small-headed, and *erect stance, oval white patches* on sides of tail in flight. **VOICE:** Often silent; flight call a low *too-i* or *tu-whit.* **RANGE:** Very rare but regular migrant or vagrant along W. Coast and in HI; casual vagrant elsewhere inland. **HABITAT:** Mudflats, marshes, coastal pools, wet agricultural fields; in summer, tundra.

COMMON SNIPE *Gallinago gallinago* **Rare, local visitor**
10½ in. (27 cm). Compared with Wilson's Snipe, has paler underwing, bolder white trailing edge to secondaries, weaker flank barring, slightly buffier overall color, and lower-pitched winnowing in flight display. **RANGE:** Regular visitor to w. AK islands; accidental in CA. **HABITAT:** Similar to Wilson's Snipe.

RARE SHOREBIRDS

SHARP-TAILED
SANDPIPER

juvenile

spring/
summer

juvenile

GREAT
KNOT

spring/
summer

breeding
dress of male
variable

male

male

juvenile

CURLEW
SANDPIPER

spring/
summer
male

juvenile
female

fall/
winter

juvenile male

RUFF

spring/
summer
female

COMMON
SNIPE

BITTERNS, HERONS, and ALLIES Family Ardeidae

Medium to large wading birds with long legs and necks, spearlike bills. They hunt with neck erect and roost with head back on shoulders. In flight, neck is folded in an S; legs trail. Plumes develop in winter/spring that are flared when breeding. Sexes similar. Nest colonially in large trees. **FOOD:** Fish, frogs, other aquatic life; mice, gophers, small birds, insects. **RANGE:** Worldwide except colder regions.

GREAT BLUE HERON *Ardea herodias* Common

45–47 in. (115–120 cm). A lean gray bird that stands nearly 4 ft. (122 cm) tall. Long legs, long neck, daggerlike bill, great size and blue-gray color mark this species. *Adult:* Crown white with long head, back, and breast plumes in winter through summer. *Juvenile and first-year:* Duller, crown black or with limited white; plumes absent or shorter. **VOICE:** Deep harsh croaks: *frahnk, frahnk, frahnk.* **SIMILAR SPECIES:** Sandhill Crane, Reddish Egret. **HABITAT:** Marshes, swamps, shores, tidal flats, moist fields.

LITTLE BLUE HERON *Egretta caerulea* Scarce, local

24 in. (61 cm). A small, slender heron. *Adult:* Bluish slate with deep maroon-brown neck; legs dark, bill pale blue with dark tip. *First-year* (see p. 150): All white, often with *grayish wingtips* and sometimes blue tinge to crown. Legs *dull olive;* base of bill pale *blue-gray;* lores dull grayish or gray-green. Molting one-year-olds are boldly pied (p. 150). **VOICE:** Loud, nasal *scaaah.* **SIMILAR SPECIES:** First-year Reddish Egret slightly larger, longer billed, with paler eye, browner, and with pink-based bill. Juvenile and first-year Little Blue like Snowy Egret except bill slightly thicker and grayer based, lores duller, and outer primary tips (if visible) dusky. **HABITAT:** Marshes, ponds, mudflats, swamps, rice fields. Scarce to casual vagrant to W. Coast; casual in interior West.

TRICOLORED HERON *Egretta tricolor* Scarce

26 in. (66 cm). A very slender, dark heron with contrasting *white belly* and white rump. *Long* slender bill. *Adult:* Mostly bluish above; crown and back plumes in spring/summer. *Juvenile:* Neck dull rusty brown; wing coverts tipped rufous. **VOICE:** Series of drawn-out nasal quacks. **SIMILAR SPECIES:** Little Blue Heron, Reddish Egret. **HABITAT:** Marshes, swamps, shores. Scarce to casual vagrant to W. Coast; accidental in interior West.

REDDISH EGRET *Egretta rufescens* Rare. local

30–31 in. (76–79 cm). Note pinkish, black-tipped bill of adult; habitat almost strictly coastal. *Adult:* Neck and back feathers shaggy. Pale eye. Plumage neutral gray with bright rusty head and neck (first-year, not shown, duller grayish brown, with short or no plumes to neck, and with all-dark bill). White morph not found in w. N. America. When feeding, races about with spread wings. **VOICE:** Sometimes a harsh *kraaak!* **SIMILAR SPECIES:** Habitat and feeding behavior differ from other herons and egrets. Dark first-year can resemble adult Little Blue Heron. **HABITAT:** Salt marshes, tidal flats, beaches. Rare visitor to the s. CA coast; accidental in AZ, TX.

DARK HERONS AND EGRET

juvenile

herons' necks may stretch or be looped in when they are standing

herons fly with neck pulled in

adult

GREAT BLUE HERON

adult

LITTLE BLUE HERON

(juvenile and first-year on p. 150)

juvenile

adult

adult

TRICOLORED HERON

adult

REDDISH EGRET

Reddish Egret "dancing" while feeding

GREAT EGRET *Ardea alba* Common

38–39 in. (97–100 cm). A tall, stately, slender white heron with largely *yellow bill.* Legs and feet *black.* In winter through summer, *straight plumes* on back can extend beyond tail; lores greenish. When feeding, assumes an eager, forward-leaning pose, with neck extended. *First-year:* Similar but legs dusky greenish in juvenile; plumes absent or shorter. **VOICE:** Low, hoarse croak. Also *cuk, cuk, cuk.* **SIMILAR SPECIES:** Snowy Egret smaller and with all-black bill, yellow feet. Cattle Egret much smaller. **HABITAT:** Marshes, ponds, shores, mudflats, fields. Rare in interior West; casual vagrant well north of range.

SNOWY EGRET *Egretta thula* Common

24 in. (61 cm). Note the *"golden slippers."* A medium-sized heron, with *slender black bill,* yellow lores, black legs, and distinct *yellow feet. Recurved back plumes* and filamentous head plumes during winter through summer. When feeding, rushes about, shuffling its feet to stir up food. Adults in fall and first-year birds have yellowish or greenish on rear sides of legs; plumes absent or short. **VOICE:** Low croak; in colony, a bubbling *wulla-wulla-wulla.* **SIMILAR SPECIES:** Great Egret has larger yellow bill and black feet. Cattle Egret smaller, squatter, with yellow bill. White first-year Little Blue Heron has blue-gray base to thicker bill, grayer lores, dusky tips to primaries. **HABITAT:** Marshes, swamps, ponds, shores, tidal flats. Rare to casual vagrant well north of range.

LITTLE BLUE HERON *Egretta caerulea* (adult on p. 148)

First-year: White with dusky wingtips, sometimes bluish tinge to crown. Base of bill blue-gray, lores greenish gray, legs dull olive. Less-active feeding style than Snowy Egret. Molting one-year-olds have contrasting blue-and-white feathering.

CATTLE EGRET *Bubulcus ibis* Uncommon to common

19–20 in. (48–51 cm). Smaller, squatter, and thicker necked than Snowy Egret. In spring and summer has variable (topically applied) *buff-orange* plumes on crown, breast, and back; fall/winter adult and first-year have little or no buff. Bill relatively short; bill and legs yellow (can be pinkish when nesting). *Juvenile and first-year:* May have yellow, greenish, or dusky legs; plumes absent or shorter, usually paler buff in spring. **VOICE:** Near breeding colony, a series of nasal grunts. **SIMILAR SPECIES:** Snowy Egret larger and more slender, has black bill and legs, contrasting yellow feet. See first-year Little Blue Heron. Great Egret much larger. **HABITAT:** Farms, marshes, fields, highway edges. Often associates with cattle. Rare to casual vagrant well north of range. Common resident in HI (see p. 396).

WHITE HERON AND EGRETS

SNOWY EGRET

breeding

fall/winter

GREAT EGRET

showy back plumes can be raised during courtship

spring/summer

fall/winter

CATTLE EGRET

molting one-year-old

LITTLE BLUE HERON

juvenile

(adult on p. 148)

BLACK-CROWNED NIGHT-HERON *Nycticorax nycticorax* Uncommon

25 in. (64 cm). This stocky, thick-billed, short-legged heron is usually hunched and inactive; flies to feed at dusk. *Adult: Black back and cap* contrast with pale gray or whitish underparts, two long white head plumes. Eyes red; legs yellowish or greenish (pinkish in high breeding condition). *Juvenile and first-year:* Brown, streaked and spotted with buff and white. Bill with greenish base; eyes small, reddish. Second-year has adultlike plumage but paler, washed brown. **VOICE:** Flat *quok!* or *quark!* Most often heard at dusk. **SIMILAR SPECIES:** Juvenile and first-year may be confused with American Bittern and similar-aged Yellow-crowned Night-Heron. **HABITAT:** Marshes, shores, ponds, marinas; roosts in trees. Common resident in HI (p. 396).

YELLOW-CROWNED NIGHT-HERON *Nyctanassa violacea* Rare, local

24 in. (61 cm). A chunky heron with longer neck and legs than Black-crowned. *Adult:* Gray overall; head black with buffy-white cheek patch and yellowish crown. *Juvenile and first-year:* Similar to Black-crowned Night-Heron, but grayer, underparts more finely streaked; back spotting smaller; wing coverts have pale edges. Bill thicker and lacks greenish-yellow base. Second-year grayer overall, has indistinct adultlike plumage. In flight, entire feet and some of lower legs extend beyond tail. **VOICE:** *Quark,* higher pitched than call of Black-crowned. **HABITAT:** Swamps, marshes, coastal habitats, streams. Often roosts with Black-crowned Night-Herons. Rare breeding visitor to the s. CA coast and accidental vagrant elsewhere in the West.

GREEN HERON *Butorides virescens* Fairly common

17–18 in. (43–46 cm). A small dark heron that looks crowlike in flight (but flies with bowed wingbeats). When alarmed, stretches neck, elevates shaggy crest, and jerks tail. *Adult:* Comparatively *short* legs are *greenish yellow* or *orange* (when breeding). Back has blue-green gloss; neck deep chestnut. *Juvenile and first-year:* Streaked neck and breast, browner above. **VOICE:** Loud *skyow* or *skewk;* series of *kuck* notes. **HABITAT:** Lakes, ponds, marshes, streams. Rare in interior West.

LEAST BITTERN *Ixobrychus exilis* Uncommon, secretive

12–13 in. (31–33 cm). Very small, thin, furtive; straddles reeds. Note large *buff wing patch* (lacking in rails). Back black in adult male, rusty brown in female and juvenile. Dark rufous morph ("Cory's Bittern") extremely rare, primarily in eastern North America. **VOICE:** Song a low, muted *coo-coo-coo;* also gives a raspy, rail-like *khak-khak-khak* series. **SIMILAR SPECIES:** Green Heron. **HABITAT:** Freshwater marshes, reedy ponds. Casual vagrant throughout interior West.

AMERICAN BITTERN *Botaurus lentiginosus* Uncommon

28 in. (71 cm). A stocky brown heron; size of a young night-heron but warmer brown with longer yellowish bill. In flight, *primaries and secondaries blackish to black* and bill held horizontal (slightly downward in night-herons). At rest or when approached, often stands rigid, bill pointing up. *Black stripe shows on sides of neck.* Ages similar. **VOICE:** "Pumping" sound, a low, deep, resonant *oong-ka´ choonk,* etc. Flushing call *kok-kok-kok.* **SIMILAR SPECIES:** First-year night-herons, Green Heron, and (much smaller) Least Bittern. **HABITAT:** Marshes, reedy lakes. Unlike night-herons, seldom sits in trees.

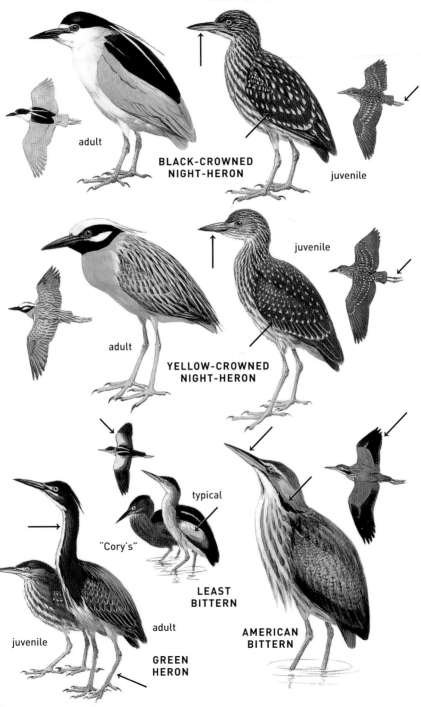

HERONS AND BITTERNS

adult

BLACK-CROWNED NIGHT-HERON

juvenile

juvenile

adult

YELLOW-CROWNED NIGHT-HERON

typical

"Cory's"

LEAST BITTERN

juvenile

adult

GREEN HERON

AMERICAN BITTERN

IBISES and SPOONBILLS Family Threskiornithidae

Ibises are long-legged, heronlike waders with slender, decurved bills. Spoonbills have spatulate bills. Both fly in Vs or lines with necks outstretched. **FOOD:** Small crustaceans, fish, insects, etc. **RANGE:** Tropical and temperate regions.

WHITE-FACED IBIS *Plegadis chihi* Fairly common

23–24 in. (58–62 cm). Dark waders with *long decurved bills.* Flies in lines with neck outstretched, alternately flapping and gliding. *Spring/summer adult:* Chestnut with maroon patch in wing and *white border of feathers* around face, meeting behind eye; pinkish to red facial skin; *red eye. Fall/winter adult:* Head and neck brown, streaked white; less white in face. *First-year:* Less white around browner eye; wings flat olive-green, without maroon. **VOICE:** Deep gooselike quacking. **SIMILAR SPECIES:** Glossy Ibis; hybrids with White-faced known. **HABITAT:** Freshwater marshes, irrigated land. Casual vagrant well north of range.

GLOSSY IBIS *Plegadis falcinellus* Rare to casual

23–24 in. (58–62 cm). Similar to White-faced Ibis, but adult a deeper glossy chestnut, dark facial skin with thin cobalt blue borders, lacking white feathers around eye, and iris brown, without red. Juveniles difficult to identify but by mid-fall iris and facial skin differences develop. **VOICE:** Guttural *ka-onk,* repeated; low *kruk, kruk.* **SIMILAR SPECIES:** See White-faced Ibis. **HABITAT:** Marshes, rice fields, swamps. Casual vagrant to CA; accidental elsewhere in West.

WHITE IBIS *Eudocimus albus* Casual vagrant

24–25 in. (62–64 cm). *Adult:* White, with *restricted black in wingtips,* red *face,* and long *red bill. Juvenile:* Dark brownish, with *white belly, white rump, orangey pink bill.* **VOICE:** Low and nasal *uuhnn!* **SIMILAR SPECIES:** Wood Stork larger, with more black in wing. **HABITAT:** Marshes, lagoons. Casual in AZ and CA; accidental elsewhere in West.

ROSEATE SPOONBILL *Platalea ajaja* Very rare

32 in. (81 cm). Note long, flat, spoonlike bill. In flight, extends neck and often glides between series of wing strokes. Adult: Bright pink, with blood red filamentous feathers on shoulders in spring through fall; tail orange. Crown and face naked, greenish gray. Juvenile: Smooth yellowish bill; head and body feathered white; wing tip brown. **VOICE:** At nesting colony, a low grunting croak. **HABITAT:** Coastal lagoons, mudflats. Casual to rare vagrant to AZ and CA; accidental elsewhere in West.

STORKS Family Ciconiidae

Large and long-legged, with very large, straight, or decurved bills. Sexes alike. Neck and legs extended in flight. **FOOD:** Frogs, crustaceans, lizards, rodents. **RANGE:** S. U.S. to S. America; Africa, Eurasia, E. Indies, Australia.

WOOD STORK *Mycteria Americana* Rare, local

39–41 in. (100–105 cm). Very large; wingspan 5½ ft. (168 cm). *Adult:* White, with *dark naked head* and *much black in wing;* black tail. Bill long, thick, slightly decurved. *First-year:* Bill yellowish; head with downy white feathers slowly lost during first 1–2 years. In flight, alternately flaps and glides or soars very high on thermals. **VOICE:** Hoarse croak. **SIMILAR SPECIES:** In flight, American White Pelican. **HABITAT:** Marshes, lagoons. Rare visitor to AZ, CA; accidental elsewhere in West.

IBISES, SPOONBILL, STORK

WHITE-FACED IBIS

season

Glossy Ibis

facial comparison in breeding

GLOSSY IBIS

first-year

adult

juvenile

WHITE IBIS

adult

adult

ROSEATE SPOONBILL

juvenile

adult

adult

first-year

WOOD STORK

CRANES Family Gruidae

Stately birds, more robust than herons, often with red facial skin. Note arching tufted feathering over rump. In flight, neck extended. Migrate in Vs or lines like geese. Large herons are sometimes wrongly referred to as cranes. **FOOD:** Omnivorous. **RANGE:** Nearly worldwide except Cen. and S. America and Oceania.

WHOOPING CRANE *Grus americana*   Rare, very local, endangered

51–52 in. (130–132 cm); wingspan 7½ ft. (229 cm). The tallest N. American bird and one of the rarest. *Adult:* Large *white* crane with *bare red forehead and lower face.* Primaries *black. Juvenile:* Plumage washed with rust, especially on head, which is feathered; bill dusky. About three years required to develop full adult plumage and head condition. **VOICE:** Shrill, buglelike trumpeting, *ker-loo! ker-lee-oo!* **SIMILAR SPECIES:** Wood Stork has dark head, more black in wing. Egrets and swans lack black in wings. See also American White Pelican and Snow Goose. **HABITAT:** Prairies, fields and pastures, coastal marshes; in summer, muskeg.

COMMON CRANE *Grus grus*   Accidental vagrant

44–50 in. (112–127 cm). Eurasian. *Adult:* Note black neck, white cheek stripe. Feathers arching over rump are blacker than those of Sandhill Crane. *Juvenile:* Entirely gray with yellow bill; develops indistinct adultlike pattern in first year. This vagrant (probably migrating with Sandhill Cranes from Asia) has been recorded in midwestern to w. N. America, most frequently among flocks of Sandhill Cranes.

SANDHILL CRANE *Antigone canadensis*   Fairly common

36–48 in. (90–122 cm); wingspan 6–7 ft. (183–213 cm). *Adult:* Note *bare red crown,* bustlelike rear. A long-legged, long-necked, gray bird, often stained with rust in spring and summer. Juvenile browner, with feathered head, yellowish bill; about three years required to develop full adult plumage and head condition. In flight, neck extended and wings flap with an upward flick. **VOICE:** Rolling, bugled *garoo-a-a-a,* repeated. Younger birds also give a very different, cricketlike call. **SIMILAR SPECIES:** Great Blue Heron is sometimes wrongly called a crane. **HABITAT:** Prairies, fields, marshes, tundra. Smaller "Lesser" Sandhill Crane (subspecies *canadensis*) nests in tundra, larger "Greater" (subspecies *tabida*) nests in grasslands and bogs; both subspecies winter across w. N. America.

CRANES

storks, ibises, and cranes fly with neck outstretched

WHOOPING CRANE

adult

juvenile

COMMON CRANE

adult

Sandhill Crane

SANDHILL CRANE

adult

juvenile

COOTS, GALLINULES, and RAILS Family Rallidae

Rails are rather hen-shaped marsh birds, many of secretive habits and distinctive voices, more often heard than seen. Flight from marshes is brief and reluctant, with legs dangling, although they can also undertake remarkable long-distance migrations at night. Gallinules and coots are much easier to see; they swim and might be confused with small ducks or grebes. They spend most of their time swimming but may also feed on shores. Other than juveniles, ages and sexes generally alike or differ slightly. **FOOD:** Aquatic plants, seeds, insects, frogs, crustaceans, mollusks. **RANGE:** Nearly worldwide.

AMERICAN COOT *Fulica americana*   Common

15–15½ in. (38–39 cm). *Adult:* A slaty, ducklike bird with blackish head and neck, slate gray body, *white bill,* and divided white patch under tail. No side striping. Its big feet are lobed ("scallops" on toes). *Juvenile and first-fall:* Paler, throat whiter, bill duller grayish, without shield; plumage becomes grayer and bill shield develops in first year. Downy chick has bushy *orange-red* feathers on head, a bald crown, and red bill. Gregarious. When swimming, pumps head back and forth. Taking off, it skitters, flight labored, big feet trailing beyond short tail. **VOICE:** Grating *kuk-kuk-kuk-kuk; kakakakakaka;* etc.; also a measured *ka-ha, ha-ha;* various cackles, croaks. **SIMILAR SPECIES:** Juvenile Common Gallinule browner above, has thin white stripe on flanks, and warmer-colored bill; more solitary than coots. **HABITAT:** Ponds, lakes, marshes; in winter, also fields, park ponds, golf courses, lawns, salt bays.

COMMON GALLINULE *Gallinula galeata*   Uncommon

14 in. (36 cm). Also known as Common Moorhen. Note adult's rather chickenlike *red bill with yellow tip, red forehead shield,* and white stripe on flanks. When walking, flicks white undertail coverts; while swimming, pumps head like a coot. *Juvenile and first-fall:* Duller, throat whiter, bill duller brownish, without shield; plumage becomes slatier and bill shield develops in first year. Downy chick with black feathers, a bald crown, and red bill. **VOICE:** Croaking *kr-r-ruk,* repeated; a froglike *kup,* and loud, complaining, henlike *kek, kek, kek* (higher than coot's call). **SIMILAR SPECIES:** American Coot, juvenile and first-year Purple Gallinule. **HABITAT:** Freshwater marshes, reedy ponds. Casual to accidental vagrant in interior West.

PURPLE GALLINULE *Porphyrio martinica*   Casual

13 in. (33 cm). *Adult:* Head and underparts *deep violet-purple,* back bronzy green. Shield on forehead *pale blue;* bill red with yellow tip. Legs *yellow,* conspicuous in flight. *Juvenile and first-fall:* Buffy brown below, dark above tinged greenish; bill dark; sides unstriped; acquires mixed purple feathering and bill develops during first year. **VOICE:** Henlike cackling, *kek, kek, kek;* also guttural notes, sharp reedy cries. **SIMILAR SPECIES:** Common Gallinule lacks greenish plumage, has white side-stripe in all plumages. **RANGE AND HABITAT:** Freshwater swamps, marshes, ponds. Swims, wades, and climbs bushes. Widespread casual vagrant throughout West; accidental to CA.

lobed foot of coot

coots skitter on takeoff

COOT AND GALLINULES

AMERICAN COOT

juvenile

adult

coot chick

adult

gallinule chick

juvenile

adult

juvenile

adult

COMMON GALLINULE

adult

adult

PURPLE GALLINULE

adult

RIDGWAY'S RAIL *Rallus obsoletus* Uncommon, local, endangered

14½–15½ in. (37–39 cm). Recently split from Clapper Rail (*R. crepitans*) of e. N. America. The large "marsh hen" of W. Coast marshes. Sometimes swims. Note henlike appearance; strong legs; long, slightly decurved bill; barred flanks; and white patch under short cocked tail, which it flicks nervously. Juveniles (summer only) are duller grayish with blackish mottled flanks; ages similar, otherwise. **VOICE:** Clattering *kek-kek-kek-kek,* etc., or *cha-cha-cha,* etc. **SIMILAR SPECIES:** Larger than Virginia Rail. King (*R. elegans*) and Clapper Rails of East are similar, but not found within Ridgway's Rail's range. **HABITAT:** Coastal and brackish-water marshes. Populations of coastal CA (subspecies *obsoletus* and *levipes*) and Yuma, AZ (*yumanensis*), endangered. Accidental vagrant inland, away from range.

YELLOW RAIL *Coturnicops noveboracensis* Scarce, local, secretive

7¼ in. (18 cm). Note *white wing patch* (in flight). A small buffy-and-black rail. Bill very short, greenish or yellowish. Back dark, striped, barred, and checkered with buff, white, and black. *Mouselike; very difficult to see.* Ages similar. **VOICE:** Nocturnal ticking notes, often in long series: *tic-tic, tic-tic-tic, tic-tic, tic-tic-tic,* etc., in alternating groups of two and three. Compared to hitting two small stones together. **SIMILAR SPECIES:** Young Sora larger, buffier overall, lacks dark barring and checkering above, has thin pale trailing edge but no white patch in wing. **HABITAT:** Grassy marshes, wet meadows; winters mostly in salt marshes and grain fields. Scarce in winter in coastal CA; casual migrant or vagrant elsewhere throughout West.

VIRGINIA RAIL *Rallus limicola* Fairly common

9½ in. (24 cm). A small rusty rail with gray cheeks, black bars on flanks, and long, slightly decurved, reddish bill with dark tip. Near size of meadowlark; only small rail with *long slender bill.* Juvenile (summer only): Shows much black; otherwise ages similar. **VOICE:** Descending grunt, *wuk-wuk-wuk-wuk,* etc.; also *kidick, kidick,* etc.; various "kicking" and grunting sounds. **SIMILAR SPECIES:** Sora has small stubby bill, unbarred undertail coverts. Ridgway's Rail much larger. **HABITAT:** Fresh and brackish marshes; in winter, also salt marshes.

BLACK RAIL *Laterallus jamaicensis* Scarce, local, secretive

6 in. (15 cm). A tiny blackish rail with small *black* bill; about the size of a young sparrow. Nape deep chestnut. *Very difficult to glimpse.* Ages of full-grown birds similar. *Caution:* All young rails in downy plumage are black. **VOICE:** Male (mostly at night), *kiki-doo* or *kiki-krrr* (or *kitty go*). Also a growl. **HABITAT:** Salt marshes, freshwater marshes, grassy meadows. Rare to casual vagrant to e. CA; accidental elsewhere away from range.

SORA *Porzana carolina* Fairly common

8½ in. (22 cm). Note *short yellow* bill. *Adult:* A small, plump, gray-brown rail with *black patch* on face and throat, more extensive in male than in female. Short, cocked tail reveals white or buff undertail coverts. *Juvenile and first-winter:* Lacks dark throat patch and is browner; acquires duller adult plumage by first spring. **VOICE:** Descending whinny, *whee-ee-ee-ee-ee-ee-e-e-e.* Also a plaintive whistled *keu-wee?* and a sharp *keek.* **SIMILAR SPECIES:** Yellow Rail. Virginia Rail has long slender bill. **HABITAT:** Freshwater marshes; in migration, also wet meadows; in winter, also salt marshes.

RAILS

RIDGWAY'S RAIL

YELLOW RAIL

VIRGINIA RAIL

adult

juvenile

BLACK RAIL

SORA

adult male

juvenile/ first-winter

chick

GALLINACEOUS BIRDS (TURKEYS, PHEASANTS, GROUSE, PARTRIDGES, and OLD WORLD QUAIL) Family Phasianidae

Often called "upland game birds." Turkeys are very large, with wattles and fan-like tail. Pheasants (introduced) have long pointed tail. Grouse are plump, chickenlike birds, without long tail. Partridges (of Old World origin) are intermediate in size between grouse and quail. Quail are the smallest. Ages generally similar, sexes usually differ. **FOOD:** Insects, seeds, buds, berries. **RANGE:** Nearly worldwide.

WILD TURKEY *Meleagris gallopavo*   **Fairly common**

Male 46–47 in. (117–120 cm); female 36–37 in. (91–94 cm). A streamlined version of barnyard turkey, with dark (not white) plumage and rusty instead of white tail tips (southwestern birds have buff-white tail tips). *Adult male:* Head naked, bluish, with red wattles, intensified in display. Tail erected like a fan in display. Bronzy iridescent body; barred primaries and secondaries; prominent "beard" on breast. *Female and first-year male:* Smaller, with smaller and duller head; less iridescent; less likely to have a beard. **VOICE:** "Gobbling" of male like domestic turkey's. Alarm *pit!* or *put-put!* Flock call *keow-keow.* Hen clucks to her chicks. **HABITAT:** Woods, mountain forests, field edges, clearings. Reintroduced in many areas, and such birds are adapting well to being near people. Introduced and fairly common in HI (p. 400).

GREATER SAGE-GROUSE *Centrocercus urophasianus*   **Uncommon**

Male 27–28 in. (69–71 cm); female 22–23 in. (56–58 cm). A large grayish grouse of open sage country, almost as large as a small turkey; identified by its contrasting *black belly patch* and spikelike tail feathers. Male is considerably larger than female, has black throat, and, in communal dancing display, puffs out its white chest, exposing two yellow air sacs on neck, at same time erecting and spreading its pointed tail feathers in a spiky fan. **VOICE:** Flushing call *kuk kuk kuk.* In courtship display, male makes a popping sound. **SIMILAR SPECIES:** Gunnison Sage-Grouse, but these two resident species do not overlap in range. See female Ring-necked Pheasant. **HABITAT:** Sagebrush plains; also foothills and mountain slopes where sagebrush grows.

GUNNISON SAGE-GROUSE   Scarce, very local, endangered
Centrocercus minimus

Male 21–22 in. (53–56 cm); female 18–19 in. (46–49 cm). Recently split from Greater Sage-Grouse, this species is found only in a very geographically restricted region of sw. CO and se. UT. Differs from Greater Sage-Grouse by its slightly smaller size, bushier "crest," and more distinct white barring on tail. Identification by range is most reliable.

GAMEBIRDS

WILD TURKEY

adult male

male display

female

GUNNISON SAGE-GROUSE

male display

GREATER SAGE-GROUSE

male display

female

PTARMIGANS

Hardy Arctic and alpine grouse with feathered feet. They molt three times a year; camouflaging themselves to match the seasons, they change from dark plumage in summer to white in winter; in spring, males are white with darker heads. During spring and fall molting periods they have a patchy look. Ages similar, sexes differ except in winter. A red comb above eye may be erected or concealed. **FOOD:** Buds, leaves, seeds.

WILLOW PTARMIGAN *Lagopus lagopus*   Fairly common

15 in. (39 cm). Willow and Rock Ptarmigans are fairly similar. In breeding season, Willows are variable, but most males are chestnut brown, redder than any plumage or subspecies of Rock Ptarmigan; females are a warm buffy brown that can overlap brown of Rock. White of wings retained all year and, in flight, contrasts with summer body plumage. In winter, white overall with black tail. There is much variation among sexes and between various molts; longest uppertail coverts in summer plumages are barred in females but not males. **VOICE:** Deep raucous calls. Male, a staccato crow, *kwow, kwow, tobacco, tobacco,* etc., or *go-back, go-back.* **SIMILAR SPECIES:** Rock Ptarmigan always has smaller and more slender bill that lacks strong curve on ridge shown by Willow. In winter, male Rock has *black lores* between eye and bill, lacking in both sexes of Willow. Habitats overlap, but Rock tends to prefer higher, more barren hills. See also White-tailed Ptarmigan. **HABITAT:** Tundra, willow scrub, muskeg; in winter, sheltered valleys at slightly lower altitudes.

ROCK PTARMIGAN *Lagopus muta*   Uncommon

14 in. (36 cm). Male in summer and fall is browner or grayer than Willow Ptarmigan, lacking rich chestnut around head and neck. Plumages vary geographically; some Rocks may be paler, grayer, or buffier than shown here, and subspecies *evermanni* of w. Aleutians can be blackish brown or tinged rufous. Females can be similar to female Willow Ptarmigan, but Rock has smaller bill. In winter, white male Rock has *black lores* between eyes and bill, reduced or absent in female, best told from winter female Willow by smaller bill. **VOICE:** Croaks, growls, cackles; usually silent. **SIMILAR SPECIES:** Willow and White-tailed Ptarmigans. **HABITAT:** Tundra, above timberline in mountains (to lower levels in winter); also near sea level in bleak tundra of northern coasts.

WHITE-TAILED PTARMIGAN *Lagopus leucura*   Uncommon

12½–13 in. (31–33 cm). The only ptarmigan normally found south of Canada. Note *white tail,* particularly in flight. In summer, generally browner than other ptarmigans, with blacker sides in male and with white belly, wings, and tail. In winter, pure white except for black eyes and bill. Female similar to male in summer/fall plumages except for barred uppertail coverts. **VOICE:** Cackling notes, clucks, soft hoots. **SIMILAR SPECIES:** The other two ptarmigans have *black* tail in all plumages. **HABITAT:** Alpine tundra, including rocky outcrops and stunted willow thickets.

PTARMIGANS

WILLOW PTARMIGAN

winter

spring/summer male

female

spring/summer male

spring male

ROCK PTARMIGAN

winter

males

western Aleutians male

winter

spring/summer female

male

spring/summer male

WHITE-TAILED PTARMIGAN

winter

early spring molting

spring/summer female

spring/summer male

winter

spring/summer male

RUFFED GROUSE *Bonasa umbellus* — Uncommon

17 in. (43 cm). Note short crest, bold flank bars, and fan-shaped tail with broad black band near tip. Usually not seen until it flushes with a startling whir. Two color morphs, with rufous or gray tail, the former more common in the Pacific Northwest and the latter more common northward. Female smaller and duller than male, with a broken black subterminal tail band. **VOICE:** Low muffled thumping starts slowly, accelerating into a whir: *Bup . . . bup . . . bup . . . bup . . . bup bup up r-rrrrr.* **SIMILAR SPECIES:** Sharp-tailed, Sooty, Dusky, and Spruce Grouse. **HABITAT:** Ground and understory of deciduous and mixed woodlands.

SPRUCE GROUSE *Falcipennis canadensis* — Scarce

16–17 in. (41–43 cm). A *tame,* dark grouse of deep coniferous forests of North. *Male:* Sharply defined *black breast,* with some white spots or bars on sides, and *chestnut band* on tip of tail. Erectile red comb above eye. "Franklin's Grouse" (*franklinii* subspecies group) of Rockies and Cascades lacks chestnut tail tip and has larger white spots on uppertail coverts than "Northern" (*canadensis* group). *Female:* Dark rusty or grayish brown, thickly barred, and with black-and-white spotting below. **VOICE:** Female call is an accelerating, then slowing, series of *wock* notes; also cluck notes. Wing flutter from male's courtship display sounds like distant thunder. **SIMILAR SPECIES:** Sooty and Dusky Grouse larger and grayer, lack bold black-and-white spotting below. **HABITAT:** Coniferous forests.

SOOTY GROUSE *Dendragapus fuliginosus* — Uncommon

20 in. (51 cm). A large dark grouse with long neck and tail, the more coastal of the two species formerly lumped as "Blue Grouse," with distinct gray band on tail tip. *Male:* In courtship display shows yellow eye combs and inflates bright yellow neck sacs with white border. *Female:* Gray-brown, mottled with blackish, belly paler than male's. **VOICE:** Courting male gives a series of five to seven low, muffled booming or hooting notes, usually from perch in a tree; louder than calls of Dusky Grouse. **SIMILAR SPECIES:** Dusky and Spruce Grouse. Female Ruffed Grouse has slight crested look, bold flank bars, and lighter tail with *black band* near tip. **HABITAT:** In summer, all forest types, mountain meadow edges; may move to higher-elevation coniferous forests in winter.

DUSKY GROUSE *Dendragapus obscurus* — Uncommon

20 in. (51 cm). *Male:* In courtship display, eye combs may change from yellow to red. Neck sacs *purplish red* surrounded by broad ring of white feathers. *Female:* See Sooty Grouse. **VOICE:** Courting male gives a series of five to seven low, muffled booming or hooting notes, usually from ground; lower pitched than calls of male Sooty Grouse. **SIMILAR SPECIES:** Sooty Grouse shows no range overlap. See Spruce Grouse. Female with Ruffed Grouse (see Sooty Grouse). **HABITAT:** In summer, all forest types, alpine meadow edges; may move to higher-elevation coniferous forests in winter.

GROUSE

RUFFED GROUSE

gray morph

male display

rusty morph

SPRUCE GROUSE

female

"Franklin's" male

male display

"Northern" male

female Dusky

male

male

male display

male display

SOOTY GROUSE

DUSKY GROUSE

SHARP-TAILED GROUSE *Tympanuchus phasianellus* **Uncommon**

17 in. (43 cm). A pale, speckled-brown grouse of prairies and brushy draws. Note *short pointed tail,* which in display and flight shows *white* at sides. Slight crested look. Marked below by dark bars, spots, and chevrons. Displaying male has yellow eye combs and inflates *purplish* neck sacs; female slightly smaller and duller, has barred crown. **VOICE:** Cackling *cac-cac-cac,* etc. Courting note a single low *coo-oo,* accompanied by quill-rattling, foot-shuffling. **SIMILAR SPECIES:** Prairie-chickens have *rounded, dark* tail and are more barred, rather than spotted, below. Female Ring-necked Pheasant has *long pointed* tail. Ruffed Grouse has banded, *fan-shaped* tail and black neck ruff. **HABITAT:** Prairies, agricultural fields, forest edges, clearings, gullies; open burns and clear-cuts in coniferous and mixed forests.

GREATER PRAIRIE-CHICKEN *Tympanuchus cupido* **Uncommon, local**

17 in. (43 cm). A henlike bird of prairies. Brown, heavily barred. Note *rounded dark tail* (black in male, barred in female). Courting males in communal "dance" inflate orange neck sacs, show off orangey yellow eye combs, and erect black hornlike neck feathers; female slightly smaller and duller, has less-elongated neck plumes and barred crown. **VOICE:** "Booming" male in dance makes a hollow *oo-loo-woo,* suggesting sound made by blowing across a bottle mouth. **SIMILAR SPECIES:** Lesser Prairie-Chicken. Sharp-tailed Grouse, slightly paler overall, has more spots or chevrons on underparts, and has more pointed, white-edged tail. Female Ring-necked Pheasant slightly larger, has long pointed tail. **HABITAT:** Native tallgrass prairie, now very localized; agricultural land.

LESSER PRAIRIE-CHICKEN **Scarce, local, threatened**
Tympanuchus pallidicinctus

16 in. (41 cm). A small, pale brown prairie-chicken; best identified by range. Male's neck sacs are dull *purplish* or *plum colored* (not yellow-orange as in Greater Prairie-Chicken). Breast barring usually paler and thinner than Greater's. **VOICE:** Male's courtship "booming" not as rolling or loud as Greater Prairie-Chicken's. Both sexes give clucking, cackling notes. **SIMILAR SPECIES:** Greater Prairie-Chicken, Sharp-tailed Grouse. **HABITAT:** Sandhill country (sage and bluestem grass, oak shrublands).

GROUSE

SHARP-TAILED GROUSE

female

male display

GREATER PRAIRIE-CHICKEN

female

male display

LESSER PRAIRIE-CHICKEN

female

male display

INTRODUCED GAME BIRDS

RING-NECKED PHEASANT
Phasianus colchicus

Fairly common, introduced

Male 31–33 in. (79–84 cm); female 21–23 in. (53–59 cm). A large chicken-like bird introduced from Eurasia. Note long pointed tail. Runs swiftly; flight strong, takeoff noisy. *Male:* Highly colored and *iridescent,* with *scarlet wattles* on face and *white neck ring* (not always present). *Female:* Mottled brown, with *long pointed tail.* **VOICE:** Crowing male gives loud double squawk, *kork-kok,* followed by brief whir of wings. When flushed, harsh croaks. Roosting call a two-syllable *kutuck-kutuck,* etc. **SIMILAR SPECIES:** Female sage-grouse have black belly patch. Female Sharp-tailed Grouse and prairie-chickens have shorter tails, white (Sharp-tailed) or black (prairie-chickens) outer tail feathers, barred upperparts. **HABITAT:** Farms, fields, marsh edges, brush, grassy roadsides. Periodic local releases for hunting. Introduced and common in HI (p. 400).

GRAY PARTRIDGE *Perdix perdix*

Uncommon, introduced

12½–13 in. (32–34 cm). Introduced from Europe. A rotund gray-brown partridge, smaller than grouse but larger than quail; note short *rufous* tail, *rusty face,* chestnut bars on sides; male also has dark U-shaped splotch on belly; female slightly browner (less gray) above and with buffier lores and eye line. **VOICE:** Loud, hoarse *kar-wit, kar-wit.* **SIMILAR SPECIES:** Chukar (another introduced species, which also has rufous tail) prefers rockier habitat, has red bill and legs, black "necklace." **HABITAT:** Cultivated land, hedgerows, bushy pastures, meadows.

CHUKAR *Alectoris chukar*

Uncommon, introduced

13½–14 in. (34–36 cm). Introduced from Asia. Like a large quail; gray-brown with *bright red legs and bill;* light throat bordered by clean-cut black "necklace." Sides *boldly barred;* tail *rufous.* Sexes similar. **VOICE:** Series of raspy *chuck*s; a sharp *wheet-u.* **SIMILAR SPECIES:** Gray Partridge. Mountain Quail smaller and darker, with duller bill and legs. Red-legged Partridge *(Alectoris rufa),* an occasional escapee, is similar but has streaked breast. **HABITAT:** Rocky, grassy, or brushy slopes; arid mountains, canyons. Birds recently released for hunting may be found well out of range and habitat. Introduced and fairly common in HI (p. 398).

HIMALAYAN SNOWCOCK *Tetraogallus himalayensis* Very local, exotic

28 in. (71 cm). An Asian species, introduced to Ruby Mts. of n. NV from ne. Pakistan. Large, gray-brown body; paler face and neck with rusty brown stripes. Shows white in wing in flight. Flies downslope in the morning to forage and walks upslope during the day. Sexes alike; subspecies in NV (*himalayensis*) has darker upperparts and sides than other subspecies. **VOICE:** Calls include cackles and clucks; display call a loud whistle. **SIMILAR SPECIES:** Chukar. **HABITAT:** Rugged alpine slopes.

INTRODUCED GAME BIRDS

RING-NECKED
PHEASANT

male

female

female

female

male

GRAY
PARTRIDGE

Red-legged Partridge
for comparison

CHUKAR

HIMALAYAN
SNOWCOCK

NEW WORLD QUAIL Family Odontophoridae

Quail are smaller than grouse. Sexes can be alike or unlike. **FOOD:** Insects, seeds, buds, berries. **RANGE:** Nearly worldwide.

CALIFORNIA QUAIL *Callipepla californica* **Common**

10 in. (25 cm). A small, plump, grayish, chickenlike bird, with a *short black plume* curving forward from crown. *Male:* Has *black-and-white face* and throat, *scaled belly pattern*. *Female:* duller. **VOICE:** Three-syllable *qua-quergo*, or *chi-cago*. Also light clucking and sharp *pit* notes. **SIMILAR SPECIES:** Gambel's Quail has rufous crown, different belly pattern; ranges barely overlap. **HABITAT:** Broken chaparral, woodland edges, coastal scrub, parks, farms. Introduced and common in HI (p. 394).

GAMBEL'S QUAIL *Callipepla gambelii* **Common**

10½–11 in. (26–28 cm). Replaces California Quail in desert habitats. *Male:* Has *black patch* on light, *unscaled belly;* flanks and crown more russet. *Female:* Also *unscaled* on belly. **VOICE:** Loud *kaaaa;* also *ka-KAA-ka-ka* and sharp *ut, ut* notes. **HABITAT:** Shrubby desert environments, including parks, suburbs. Uncommon exotic in HI (p. 394).

MOUNTAIN QUAIL *Oreortyx pictus* **Uncommon**

11 in. (28 cm). A gray-and-brown quail of mountains and upland plateaus. *Male:* Distinguished from California Quail by long *straight* head plume and *chestnut* (not black) *throat*, chestnut-and-white sides. *Female:* Similar to male but browner, plume shorter. **VOICE:** Mellow *wook?* or *to-wook?* repeated at intervals by male; loquacious *wew-wew-wew-wew* series. **HABITAT:** Open pine and mixed forests, brushy ravines, montane chaparral.

SCALED QUAIL *Callipepla squamata* **Fairly common**

10 in. (25 cm). A pale grayish quail (sometimes called "Blue Quail") of arid country, with scaly markings on breast and back. *Male:* Note *short bushy white crest*, or "cotton top," a common nickname for this species. Runs; often reluctant to fly. *Female:* Has shorter crest, duller throat finely streaked. **VOICE:** Guinea hen–like *che-kar* (also interpreted as *pay-cos*). **HABITAT:** Shrub-grasslands, brush, arid country.

NORTHERN BOBWHITE **Uncommon local, declining**
Colinus virginianus

9½–10 in. (24–26 cm). Ruddy, barred and striped, with short dark tail. *Male:* Has conspicuous white throat and white eyebrow stripe; in female these are buff. "Masked" Bobwhite (subspecies *ridgewayi*), endangered, with *black throat* and *rusty underparts*, was once found and now locally reintroduced in s. AZ. **VOICE:** Clearly whistled *Bob-white!* or *poor, Bob-whoit!* Covey call *ko-loi-kee?* **SIMILAR SPECIES:** No other N. American quail has white throat. **HABITAT:** Farms, brushy open country, fencerows, roadsides, open woodlands.

MONTEZUMA QUAIL *Cyrtonyx montezumae* **Scarce, local**

8½–9 in. (21–23 cm). A small round quail of Mexican mountains and canyons. *Male:* Note oddly striped *clown's face* (formerly known as "Harlequin Quail"), bushy crest on nape, and *spotted sides*. *Female:* Brown, with less obvious facial striping. Tame. **VOICE:** Male gives a descending whistle; a soft whinnying or quavering cry; ventriloquial. **HABITAT:** Grassy oak canyons, wooded mountain slopes with bunch grass.

QUAIL

CALIFORNIA QUAIL
female
male

GAMBEL'S QUAIL
female
male

MOUNTAIN QUAIL
female
male

SCALED QUAIL

NORTHERN BOBWHITE
female
"Masked" male
Northern male

MONTEZUMA QUAIL
male
female

NEW WORLD VULTURES Family Cathartidae

Blackish; often seen soaring high in wide circles. Their naked heads are relatively smaller than those of hawks and eagles. Vultures are often locally called "buzzards." Silent away from nest site. Ages vary in plumage and head features; sexes alike. **FOOD:** Carrion. **RANGE:** Southern Canada through S. America.

TURKEY VULTURE *Cathartes aura* (see also p. 180)   Common

26–27 in. (66–69 cm); wingspan 6 ft. (183 cm). Nearly eagle-sized. From below, note dark color with *two-toned wings* (flight feathers paler). Soars with *wings in dihedral* (shallow V); rocks and tilts unsteadily. At close range, small, naked *red head* of adult is evident; juvenile has dark bill and grayish head with black mask and bristlelike feathers, head becoming purplish in first year and not fully naked and red until third year. **SIMILAR SPECIES:** Black Vulture; eagles and Zone-tailed Hawk, the latter of which "mimics" Turkey Vulture in flight profile, have larger, feathered heads, shorter tails; eagles also soar with wings held in steady flat plane. **HABITAT:** Usually seen soaring in sky, on ground feeding, or perched on dead trees or posts, often sunning with wings outstretched. Ubiquitous through much of range.

BLACK VULTURE *Coragyps atratus* (see also p. 180)   Uncommon, local

25 in. (64 cm); wingspan less than 5 ft. (152 cm). This dark scavenger is readily identified by short, square tail that barely projects beyond rear edge of wings and by *whitish patch* toward wingtip. Legs longer and whiter than Turkey Vulture's; in flight, feet visible beyond tail. Note distinctive *shallow and quick flapping*, alternating with short glides. **SIMILAR SPECIES:** Turkey Vulture has longer, rounded tail; flapping is slower, less frequent; soars with noticeable dihedral. Beware: juvenile and first-year Turkey Vultures have dark heads but show paler bills and structural and flight-style differences noted above. **HABITAT:** Similar to Turkey Vulture's but avoids higher mountains, prefers wetter lowland areas, sometimes scavenges in dumps. Widespread vagrant well north of breeding range; casual vagrant to CA.

CALIFORNIA CONDOR   Rare, local, endangered
Gymnogyps californianus

46–47 in. (117–120 cm); wingspan 8½–9½ ft. (259–290 cm). Was heading toward extinction; last wild birds captured in 1987. Captive breeding program successful, and some of these birds released to the wild in CA, AZ, and Baja CA. Much larger than Turkey Vulture and has much broader proportions and shorter tail. California Condor also has *flatter wing-plane* when soaring; does not rock or tilt. *Adult:* Extensive *white underwing linings* toward fore edge of wing. Head yellow-orange. *Juvenile and first-year:* Dusky-headed and lacks white underwing linings, size and shape diagnostic; takes up to six or more years to develop full adult plumage and head characteristics. **SIMILAR SPECIES:** Younger Golden and Bald Eagles have some white underwing, but this color is placed differently; size also quite smaller and overall shapes different, proportionally longer-winged. **HABITAT:** Mountains, grassy foothills, coastal bluffs, chaparral. Nests on mountain ledges or in large redwood trees.

VULTURES

adult

TURKEY
VULTURE

juvenile
Turkey

juvenile
Black

adult

BLACK
VULTURE

fourth-/
fifth- year

juvenile

adult

CALIFORNIA
CONDOR

adults

BIRDS of PREY

We tend to call all diurnal raptors with a hooked bill and hooked claws "birds of prey." Actually, they fall into two quite separate families that recently have been shown to be very distantly related:

1. The hawk group (Accipitridae)—kites, harriers, accipiters, buteos, and eagles.
2. The falcon group (Falconidae)—falcons and caracaras. These are more closely related to parrots and songbirds than they are to the hawk group!

The many raptors can be sorted out by their basic shapes and flight styles. When not flapping, they may alternate between soaring, with wings fully extended and tail fanned, and gliding, with wings slightly pulled back and tail folded. These two pages show some basic silhouettes.

glide

full soar

BUTEOS are stocky, with broad wings and a wide, rounded tail.
They often soar and wheel high in the open sky.

glide

full soar

ACCIPITERS have a small head, short rounded wings, and a longish tail.
They typically fly with several rapid beats and a short glide.

HARRIERS are slim, with long, slim, round-tipped wings and a long tail. They fly in open country and glide low, with a vulturelike dihedral.

KITES (except for Snail Kite and Hook-billed Kite) are falcon-shaped, but unlike falcons, they are buoyant gliders, not power fliers.

FALCONS have long pointed wings and a long tail. Their wing strokes are strong and rapid.

OSPREY Family Pandionidae

A monotypic family that forages above water and plunges feet-first for fish. Sexes alike. **FOOD:** Fish. **RANGE:** All continents except Antarctica.

OSPREY *Pandion haliaetus* (see also p. 180) **Fairly common**
23–24½ in. (58–62 cm); wingspan to 6 ft. (183 cm). *Adult:* Blackish brown above, *white below;* head largely white with *broad black mask through eyes.* Flies with distinctive gull-like kink or crook in wings, showing black "wrist" patch to underwing. *Juvenile:* Upperpart feathers fringed whitish or buff, forming scaly pattern. **VOICE:** Series of sharp, annoyed whistles: *cheep, cheep* or *yewk, yewk,* etc. **SIMILAR SPECIES:** First-year Bald Eagle may have dusky "mask." Rough-legged Hawk also has dark wrist mark but lacks wing crook and mask, and usually has dark belly patch. **HABITAT:** Rivers, lakes, marshes, estuaries, coasts.

HAWKS, KITES, EAGLES, and ALLIES
Family Accipitridae

Diurnal birds of prey, with hooked bills and powerful talons. Formerly persecuted but important to the health of ecosystems. **RANGE:** Almost worldwide.

EAGLES

Larger than buteos, with proportionately longer wings. Powerful bills are nearly as long as head. **FOOD:** Bald Eagle, fish, injured waterfowl, carrion; Golden Eagle eats chiefly rabbits, large rodents, snakes, game birds.

BALD EAGLE *Haliaeetus leucocephalus* (see also p. 180) **Fairly common**
31–37 in. (79–94 cm); wingspan 7–8 ft. (213–244 cm). *Adult:* Huge size and dark plumage except *white head* and *white tail* make this bird unmistakable. Bill yellow, massive. Wings held flat when soaring. *Juvenile and first-year:* Mottled dark overall; in second and third year develops variable amounts of *whitish in lower underparts, underwing,* and tail; by fourth and fifth year develops adultlike plumage, some showing a white head with darkish patch through eye, reminiscent of Osprey. **VOICE:** Harsh, high-pitched cackle, *kleek-kik-ik-ik-ik,* or lower *kak-kak-kak.* **SIMILAR SPECIES:** Golden Eagle, Turkey Vulture. **HABITAT:** Coasts, rivers, large lakes; in migration, also mountains, open country.

GOLDEN EAGLE *Aquila chrysaetos* (see also p. 180) **Uncommon**
30–40 in. (76–102 cm); wingspan 7 ft. (213 cm). Glides and soars flat-winged with occasional shallow wingbeats. *Adult:* Uniformly dark below, or with slight paling at base of obscurely banded tail. On hindneck, a *wash of buffy gold. Juvenile and first-year:* In flight, shows *white bases to primaries* and *white tail* with *broad dark terminal band.* Reaches adult plumage (without white in tail) by third or fourth year. **VOICE:** A yelping bark, *kya;* also whistled notes. **SIMILAR SPECIES:** Younger Bald Eagles have larger heads and develop *extensive blotchy white in underwing linings* and lower underparts; tail may be mottled with white at base but is not cleanly banded. Dark-morph buteos are smaller, with more rounded wings and different patterns of whitish in flight feathers. **HABITAT:** Open mountains, foothills, plains, deserts, open country.

OSPREY AND EAGLES

hovering

OSPREY

adult

BALD EAGLE

juvenile

overhead flight
patterns on p. 180

adult

adult

GOLDEN EAGLE

Golden Eagle
juvenile

OSPREY, EAGLES, and VULTURES from Below

OSPREY *Pandion haliaetus* **p. 178**
White body and coverts; black wrist patch; crooked wing.

BALD EAGLE *Haliaeetus leucocephalus* **p. 178**
Adult: White head and tail.
Juvenile: Some white in underwing linings; develops more white on belly and elsewhere in second year.

GOLDEN EAGLE *Aquila chrysaetos* **p. 178**
Adult: Almost uniformly dark; underwing linings dark.
Juvenile: White patch at base of primaries and tail; no white on body.

TURKEY VULTURE *Cathartes aura* **p. 174**
Mostly brownish black. Two-toned wings held in distinct dihedral. Small head, red in adult, blackish to dark pinkish purple in first and second years. Longish tail. Tips and teeters in flight.

BLACK VULTURE *Coragyps atratus* **p. 174**
Blackish overall. Silver patch in outer primaries. Wings held flat or in very slight dihedral. Rapid, shallow wingbeats. Stubby tail. Gray head.

Where the Bald Eagle, Turkey Vulture, and Osprey all are found, they can be separated at a great distance by their manner of soaring: the Bald Eagle with flat wings; the Turkey Vulture with a dihedral; the Osprey often with a gull-like kink or crook in its wings.

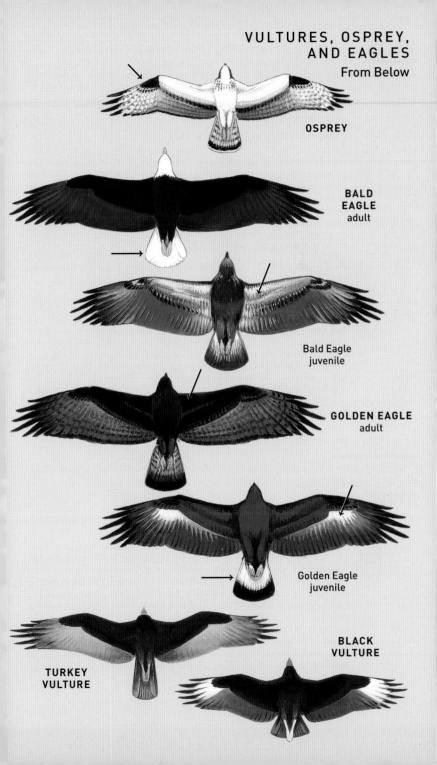

VULTURES, OSPREY, AND EAGLES
From Below

OSPREY

BALD EAGLE
adult

Bald Eagle
juvenile

GOLDEN EAGLE
adult

Golden Eagle
juvenile

TURKEY VULTURE

BLACK VULTURE

KITES

Graceful birds of prey of southern distribution. Somewhat falconlike, with pointed wings. Ages and sexes can be similar or differ. **FOOD:** Large insects, reptiles, rodents. Snail Kite and Hook-billed Kite specialize in snails.

MISSISSIPPI KITE
Uncommon, local

Ictinia mississippiensis (see also p. 192)

14–14½ in. (36–37 cm). Falcon-shaped, graceful, and gray. Gregarious; spends much time soaring. *Adult:* Dark above, lighter below; head *pale gray;* tail and underwing blackish. No other falconlike bird has *black unbarred tail. Whitish secondaries* visible from above. *Juvenile:* Heavily streaked on rusty underparts; assumes adultlike plumage by first spring except retains rusty-mottled underwing. **VOICE:** Usually silent; near nest, a two-syllable *phee-phew.* **SIMILAR SPECIES:** Male Northern Harrier. Falcons. **HABITAT:** Nests in riparian woodlands, residential areas, groves, shelterbelts. Casual vagrant to W. Coast.

WHITE-TAILED KITE *Elanus leucurus* (see also p. 192)
Uncommon

15½–16 in. (39–41 cm). This whitish kite is very buoyant in flight, with pointed wings and *long white tail* that is slightly notched. Soars and glides like a small gull; *often hovers* and drops to ground with wings up. *Adult:* Pale gray above, with white head (male whiter than female), underparts, and tail. *Large black patch* on fore edge of upperwing is obvious on perched birds. From below, shows oval black patch at carpal joint ("wrist") of underwing. *Juvenile:* Like adult, but has *rusty mottling to crown, back, and breast,* and narrow dark band near tip of pale grayish tail; assumes adultlike body plumage in first fall. **VOICE:** Whistled *kew kew kew,* abrupt or drawn out. **HABITAT:** Open groves, river valleys, marshes, grasslands, roadsides. May form communal roosts at night in fall and winter seasons. Widespread vagrant north and east of range.

HARRIERS

Slim raptors with long wings and tail. Flight low, languid, gliding, with wings held in shallow V (dihedral). Sexes not alike. They hunt in open country, often over marshes.

NORTHERN HARRIER
Fairly common

Circus hudsonius (see also p. 192)

18–21 in. (46–54 cm). A slim, long-winged, long-tailed raptor of open country. When hunting, it glides and flies buoyantly and unsteadily low over ground, with wings held slightly above horizontal. Flaps steadily when migrating. In all plumages, distinct *white rump patch* distinguishes Northern Harrier from most other N. American raptors; see juvenile and first-year Gray Hawk and note Cooper's Hawks can flare up white flank patches when courting. *Adult male:* Pale gray, whitish beneath, wingtips black as if "dipped-in-ink." *Adult female:* Brown to grayish brown, streaked below. *Juvenile and first-year:* Russet to warm buff below, with fewer or no streaks. **VOICE:** Weak, nasal whistle, *pee, pee, pee.* **SIMILAR SPECIES:** Gray Hawk, courting Cooper's Hawks, Short-eared Owl. **HABITAT:** Marshes, fields, prairies.

KITES AND HARRIER

juvenile

adult

adult

MISSISSIPPI KITE

juvenile

additional overhead flight patterns on p. 192

juvenile

adult

adult

WHITE-TAILED KITE

juvenile

NORTHERN HARRIER

juvenile

adult male

adult female

ACCIPITERS

Long-tailed woodland raptors with short, rounded wings, adapted for hunting among trees. Typical flight mixes quick beats and a glide. Adult males have bluer upperparts than adult females; females larger. Size distinguishes N. American species within each sex but not always reliably in the field. **FOOD:** Chiefly birds, some small mammals. Sharp-shinned and Cooper's often seen hunting birds at backyard feeders.

SHARP-SHINNED HAWK   Fairly common
Accipiter striatus (see also p. 202)

10–14 in. (25–36 cm). A small, slim woodland hawk, with slim *square-tipped* tail and *short, rounded wings. Adult male:* Dark bluish back, *rusty-barred* breast, red eye; adult female browner and with yellower eye. *Juvenile and first-year:* Dark brown above, *thickly streaked* with rusty brown on underparts; yellow eye. **VOICE:** Like Cooper's Hawk, but shriller; a high *kik, kik, kik* given near nest. **SIMILAR SPECIES:** Cooper's larger, with *larger head* (protruding farther forward past wings in flight), *rounded* tail with broader white tip, thicker legs; male Cooper's and female Sharp-shinned can be close in size. Adult Cooper's has more defined cap. First-year Cooper's *tawnier* on head and has whiter, more *finely streaked* breast. **HABITAT:** Breeds in extensive forests; in migration and winter, open woodlands, wood edges, residential areas.

COOPER'S HAWK   *Accipiter cooperii* (see also p. 202)   Fairly common

14–20 in. (36–51 cm). Very similar to Sharp-shinned Hawk but larger, particularly female. See Sharp-shinned Hawk. **VOICE:** About nest, a rapid *kek, kek, kek;* suggests a flicker. Also a sapsucker-like mewing. **SIMILAR SPECIES:** Sharp-shinned Hawk, Northern Goshawk. **HABITAT:** Like Sharp-shinned but prefers drier and more open areas.

NORTHERN GOSHAWK   *Accipiter gentilis* (see also p. 202)   Scarce

21–26 in. (53–66 cm). Larger, broader-winged, broader-tailed, more buteo-like than Cooper's Hawk. *Adult:* Crown and cheek blackish; *broad white stripe over eye.* Underparts *pale gray, finely barred;* back, bluer in male and grayer in female, is paler than in Cooper's or Sharp-shinned Hawk. *Juvenile and first-year:* Buffier overall than young Cooper's with *bolder eyebrow,* more extensive streaking below, and wavy, irregular tail banding. **VOICE:** *Kak, kak, kak* or *kuk, kuk, kuk,* heavier than Cooper's, given near nest. **SIMILAR SPECIES:** Cooper's Hawk. A soaring goshawk may be initially misidentified as a Red-shouldered Hawk or other buteo. **HABITAT:** Coniferous and mixed forests, especially in mountains; forest edges; winters also in wooded lowlands. Periodic irruptions in fall and winter farther to south.

ACCIPITERS

accipiters have small heads, short rounded wings, long tails

juvenile

adult male

SHARP-SHINNED HAWK

adult

additional overhead flight patterns on p. 202

juvenile

adult male

COOPER'S HAWK

adult

juvenile

adult male

NORTHERN GOSHAWK

adult

BUTEOS and BUTEO-LIKE HAWKS

Large, thickset hawks, with broad wings and wide, rounded tails. Many buteos habitually soar high in wide circles. Much variation; sexes similar, females slightly larger. Young birds usually streaked below. Dark morphs often occur. **FOOD:** Small mammals, sometimes small birds, reptiles, grasshoppers. **RANGE:** Widespread in New and Old Worlds.

HARRIS'S HAWK *Parabuteo unicinctus* (see also p. 196)   Uncommon

20–21 in. (50–53 cm); wingspan 3½ ft. (107 cm). A blackish-brown, buteo-like hawk, with flashing *white rump* and *white band* at tip of tail. Often hunts cooperatively in small groups. *Adult:* Chestnut areas on thighs, shoulders, and underwing; *rusty shoulders;* conspicuous *white* at base of tail. *Juvenile and first-year:* Underparts streaked pale. **VOICE:** Low-pitched, harsh *raaaah!* **SIMILAR SPECIES:** Dark morphs of Ferruginous and Red-tailed Hawks larger, lack bold rusty patches and white tail base. **HABITAT:** Mesquite, cactus deserts. Rare breeding visitor and vagrant to CA.

ZONE-TAILED HAWK *Buteo albonotatus* (see also p. 196)   Uncommon

20 in. (51 cm); wingspan 4 ft. (122 cm). Dull *black,* with more *slender* wings than most other buteos. Often mistaken for Turkey Vulture because of proportions, two-toned underwing, and up-tilted wings — but Zone-tailed has larger feathered head, square-tipped tail, barred underwing, yellow cere and legs. *Adult:* White tail bands (pale gray on topside). *Juvenile and first-year:* Narrower tail bands, *small white spots* on breast. **VOICE:** Nasal, drawn-out *keeeeah.* **SIMILAR SPECIES:** Turkey Vulture, Common Black Hawk, other dark-morph buteos. **HABITAT:** Woodlands, deserts, mountains, canyons. Vagrant north of normal range

GRAY HAWK *Buteo plagiatus* (see also p. 192)   Scarce, local

17 in. (43 cm); wingspan 3 ft. (91 cm). A small buteo. *Adult:* Distinguished by its buteo-like proportions, gray back, *thickly barred gray* breast, white rump band, and *banded* tail (similar to Broad-winged Hawk's). *Juvenile and first-year:* Narrowly barred tail, striped buffy breast, bold face pattern, *white U-shaped bar* across rump. **VOICE:** Drawn-out whistles, *ka-lee-oh* or *kleeeeoo.* **SIMILAR SPECIES:** First-year Broad-winged Hawk has weaker face pattern, lacks white U on rump, has shorter tail, more pointed wings. **HABITAT:** Streamside and subtropical woodlands. Accidental vagrant to CA.

COMMON BLACK HAWK   Scarce, local
Buteogallus anthracinus (see also p. 196)

21 in. (53 cm); wingspan 4 ft. (122 cm). A buteo-like hawk with chunky shape, exceptionally wide wings, and *long* yellow legs. *Adult:* All black with broad white *band* crossing middle of short tail. In flight, whitish spot shows at base of primaries. *Juvenile and first-year:* Dark-backed with heavily striped *buffy* head and underparts; tail white with five or six wavy dark bands. **VOICE:** Series of loud whistles. **SIMILAR SPECIES:** Zone-tailed Hawk. **HABITAT:** Wooded river and stream bottoms. Casual vagrant to CA and elsewhere north of range.

SOUTHWESTERN BUTEOS

adult

juvenile

HARRIS'S
HAWK

adults

juvenile

adult

ZONE-TAILED
HAWK

adults

juvenile

adult

juvenile

GRAY HAWK

juvenile

adults

COMMON
BLACK HAWK

ROUGH-LEGGED HAWK Uncommon
Buteo lagopus (see also pp. 194 and 196)

21–22 in. (53–55 cm). This open-country hawk often *hovers on beating wings* and has *smaller bill* and feet than other buteos. Legs feathered. Many birds have *solid or blotched dark belly* and *black patch* at "wrist" (carpal joint) of underwing. Some adult males have dark bib but lack blackish belly band. Tail *white*, with *broad black band or bands* toward tip. White flash on upperwing. Juvenile and first-year similar but tail with less-distinct band. Dark morph may lack extensive white on tail, but shows broad terminal band and extensive white on underwing. **VOICE:** High-pitched squeal, mostly near nest site. **SIMILAR SPECIES:** Red-tailed Hawk, dark-morph Ferruginous Hawk. **HABITAT:** Nests on tundra escarpments; in winter, open fields, plains, marshes.

RED-SHOULDERED HAWK Fairly common
Buteo lineatus (see also p. 194)

16–20 in. (40–50 cm). In flight, note *translucent patch* or "window" at base of primaries, longish tail. *Adult:* Heavy black-and-white bands on wings and tail, dark *rufous shoulders* and underwing linings, rufous red underparts. *Juvenile and first-year:* Variably streaked and/or barred below; recognized by tail bands and wing "windows." **VOICE:** Two-syllable scream, *kee-yer* (dropping inflection), repeated in series. **SIMILAR SPECIES:** Light-morph Broad-winged Hawk has paler underwing linings, more pointed wing, broader bands on tail, lacks wing "windows." Juvenile Cooper's Hawk can be similar in flight but has longer tail. See also Red-tailed Hawk. **HABITAT:** Woodlands in valleys, canyons, along rivers, marsh edges, residential areas. Vagrant to interior West.

BROAD-WINGED HAWK Uncommon
Buteo platypterus (see also pp. 194 and 196)

15–16 in. (38–41 cm). A small, chunky buteo. *Pale-morph adult:* Note tail banding, with one obvious thick white band often visible from below. Underwing linings whitish, the edge trimmed with black. *Juvenile and first-year:* Heavily streaked along sides of neck, breast, and belly; chest often unmarked. Terminal tail band twice as wide and distinct as other bands. Uncommon dark morph (p. 196), which breeds primarily in Prairie Provinces, similar to dark Short-tailed Hawk but browner (not as black); tail pattern as in light-morph Broad-winged; secondaries paler and less barred underneath. **VOICE:** High-pitched, downward *pwe-eeeeee*. **SIMILAR SPECIES:** Juvenile/first-year Red-shouldered Hawk. See also juvenile Gray and Short-tailed Hawks, accipiters. **HABITAT:** Woods, groves. Rare vagrant to W. Coast.

SHORT-TAILED HAWK Very rare, local
Buteo brachyurus (see also p. 196)

15–16 in. (38–41 cm). A small black or black-and-white buteo. Dark morph has blackish brown body and black underwing linings; light-morph adult blackish above, white below, dark cheeks, *two-toned* underwing pattern, white underwing linings. *Light-morph juvenile and first-year:* Similar to juvenile Broad-winged but less streaked below; secondaries darker on underneath, with more-distinct barring. **VOICE:** Descending, high-pitched scream: *kleeear!* **SIMILAR SPECIES:** Broad-winged Hawk. See also Swainson's Hawk. **HABITAT:** Pines, woodland edges.

BUTEOS

dark morph

light-morph adults

additional overhead flight patterns on pp. 195 and 197

ROUGH-LEGGED HAWK

adult

Western

RED-SHOULDERED HAWK

juvenile

Eastern

dark-morph adult

juvenile light-morphs

adult

adult

juvenile

light-morph juvenile

BROAD-WINGED HAWK

dark-morph adult

dark-morph adult

light-morph adult

light-morph adult

dark-morph adult

SHORT-TAILED HAWK

RED-TAILED HAWK
Common

Buteo jamaicensis (see also pp. 194 and 196)

19–22 in. (48–56 cm). The common conspicuous hawk of roadsides and woodland edges. When soaring, adult has diagnostic *rufous* on topside of tail, paler reddish below. On light-morph birds, note mottled *white patches* on scapulars; *dark patagial bar* on fore edge of wing from below. Otherwise body plumage quite variable. *Juvenile and first-year*: Tail brownish with narrow, dark banding. Underparts typically "zoned" (light breast, dark *belly band*), although some paler birds of sw. TX (subspecies *fuertesi*) can lack belly band. Dark-morph birds variably dark brown to blackish; red tail of adults diagnostic; broad wing shape and tail pattern help identify juvenile and first-year birds. Western Red-tailed Hawks show much variation, with light-, rufous- and dark-morph birds. Dark-morph "Harlan's" Red-tailed Hawk (subspecies *harlani*), an uncommon hawk breeding in AK and wintering to CA and TX, is sootier and tail is usually dirty white, with *longitudinal* mottling and freckling of gray, black, sometimes with red, merging into dark subterminal band. **VOICE:** Asthmatic squeal, *keeer-r-r* (slurring downward). **SIMILAR SPECIES:** Rough-legged, Ferruginous, Swainson's, Red-shouldered, and Broad-winged Hawks. **HABITAT:** Open country, woodlands, prairie groves, mountains, plains, roadsides.

SWAINSON'S HAWK
Common

Buteo swainsoni (see also pp. 194 and 196)

19–21 in. (48–53 cm). A buteo of the plains and CA's Cen. Valley, quite variable in body plumage. Slimmer than Red-tailed Hawk, with narrower, more pointed wings at tips. When gliding, holds wings slightly above horizontal. When perched, *wingtips extend to tail tip.* In light and intermediate morphs, *pale underwing linings contrast with dark flight feathers. Adult:* Light-morph has dark breastband and often a dark-hooded look; tail gray-brown above, often pale toward base. Dark- and rufous-morph birds best identified by shape, shaded flight feathers, and tail pattern. *Juvenile and first-year:* Light morph variably streaked below, usually *more heavily marked on breast than belly*; often best identified by shape and wing pattern. **VOICE:** Shrill, plaintive whistle, *kreeeeeeer.* **SIMILAR SPECIES:** Swainson's wing shape distinctive for a buteo. Lacks white scapular patches and dark patagial marks of bulkier Red-tailed. **HABITAT:** Plains, grasslands, agricultural land, open hills, sparse trees.

FERRUGINOUS HAWK
Uncommon

Buteo regalis (see also pp. 192 and 196)

23–24 in. (58–61 cm). A large buteo of w. states. Note large bill, long gape line, *long tapered wings* with *pale panel* on upper surface of primaries, *mostly white tail. Adult:* Rufous above, especially shoulder, mostly whitish head and breast, rufous wash on tail, rufous thighs form *dark V* on birds from below. Dark morphs are dark rufous to brown with whitish flight feathers and whitish tail. *Juvenile and first-year:* Similar to adult but duller, with fewer rufous tones; tail with indistinct bars or marks. **SIMILAR SPECIES:** Red-tailed Hawk and dark-morph Rough-legged Hawk. Perched dark-morph Ferruginous Hawk can resemble an eagle but is smaller, has paler tail. **HABITAT:** Plains, grasslands, agricultural fields.

BUTEOS

rufous adult

Western juvenile

Eastern juvenile

additional overhead flight patterns on pp. 193 and 195

dark adult

Western adult

Eastern adult

"Harlan's" adult

RED-TAILED HAWK

"Harlan's" adult

dark morph

juvenile

adult

light morph

light morph

adult

SWAINSON'S HAWK

light morph

FERRUGINOUS HAWK

adult

light morph

light morph

dark morph

PALE BUTEOS, HARRIER, and KITES from Below

FERRUGINOUS HAWK *Buteo regalis* (light morph) **p. 190**
Whitish underparts, with dark V formed by reddish thighs in adult. Wings and tail long for a buteo. A bird of western plains and open range.

GRAY HAWK *Buteo plagiatus* **p. 186**
Stocky. Broadly banded tail (suggestive of Broad-winged Hawk); adults have gray-barred underparts. Uncommon resident of se. AZ.

NORTHERN HARRIER *Circus hudsonius* **p. 182**
Male: Whitish wings with black tips and dark trailing edge. Gray hood.
Female: Brown, heavily streaked; note long, slim wings and tail.
Juvenile and first-year (not shown): Warmer brown than adult female, unstreaked body, dark head. From above, all plumages have characteristic white rump.

WHITE-TAILED KITE *Elanus leucurus* **p. 182**
Adult: White body; whitish tail; dark underside to primaries, black mark at primary coverts.

MISSISSIPPI KITE *Ictinia mississippiensis* **p. 182**
Falcon-shaped. *Adult:* Pale gray head, black tail, dark gray and blackish wings, gray body.
Juvenile: Streaked breast; banded square-tipped or notched tail. First spring and summer are adultlike but with underwing mottled brownish.

Kites (except Snail Kite and Hook-billed Kite) are falcon-shaped but, unlike falcons, are buoyant gliders, not power fliers. All are southern.

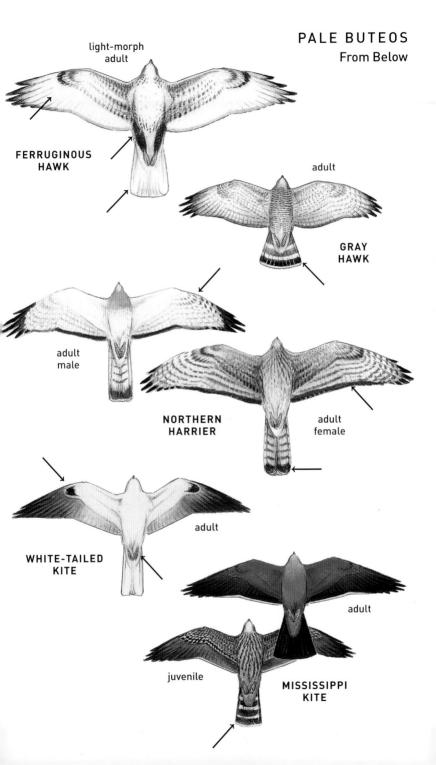

PALE BUTEOS
From Below

light-morph
adult

FERRUGINOUS
HAWK

adult

GRAY
HAWK

adult
male

NORTHERN
HARRIER

adult
female

WHITE-TAILED
KITE

adult

adult

juvenile

MISSISSIPPI
KITE

PALE BUTEOS from Below

RED-TAILED HAWK *Buteo jamaicensis* (light morph) **p. 190**

Reddish tail and dark patagial bar at fore edge of wing are best mark from below. *Adult:* Light chest, streaked belly (often forming belly band); tail plain with little or no banding.
Juvenile and first-year: Streaked below, tail without red and with light banding.

SWAINSON'S HAWK *Buteo swainsoni* (light morph) **p. 190**

Adult: Dark breast-band. Long, pointed, two-toned wings.
Juvenile and first-year: Similar, but has streaks on underbody.

RED-SHOULDERED HAWK *Buteo lineatus* **p. 188**

Adult: Tail strongly banded (white bands narrower than black ones). Body and underwing coverts barred or mottled reddish.
Juvenile and first-year: Chest and belly heavily streaked brown. Both first-year and adult have light crescent "window" on outer wings, longish tail.

BROAD-WINGED HAWK *Buteo platypterus* (light morph) **p. 188**

Smaller and chunkier than Red-shouldered with shorter tail, more pointed wings. *Adult:* Widely banded tail (white bands wider); underwing pale with dark rear margin and tip.
Juvenile and first-year: Body usually streaked, tail narrowly banded, the outermost dark band widest and most distinct.

ROUGH-LEGGED HAWK *Buteo lagopus* (light morph) **p. 188**

Note black primary covert patch at "wrist" contrasting with white primaries and secondaries. Broad, blackish band across belly (blacker and more solid than in Red-tailed) is distinctive. Tail light, with broad, dark subterminal band.

Buteos are chunky, with broad wings and a broad, rounded tail.
They often soar and wheel high in the air.

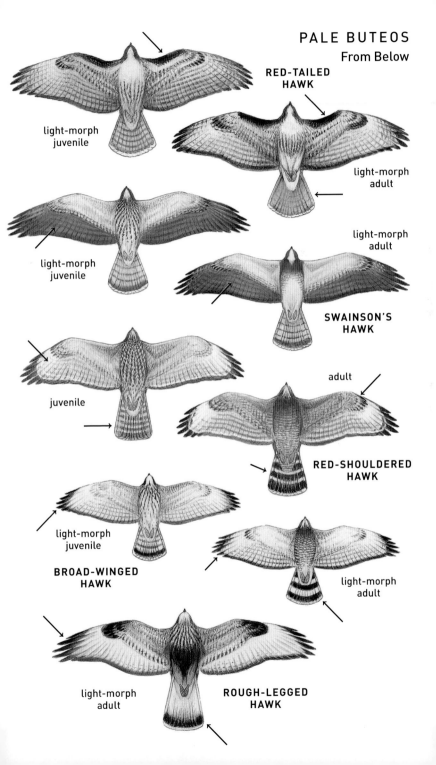

PALE BUTEOS
From Below

RED-TAILED HAWK

light-morph juvenile

light-morph adult

SWAINSON'S HAWK

light-morph adult

light-morph juvenile

RED-SHOULDERED HAWK

juvenile

adult

BROAD-WINGED HAWK

light-morph juvenile

light-morph adult

ROUGH-LEGGED HAWK

light-morph adult

DARK BIRDS of PREY from Below

CRESTED CARACARA *Caracara cheriway* **p. 198**

Whitish chest, black belly, large *pale patches* in primaries, white tail with black band. Elongated neck, stiff-winged flight.

ROUGH-LEGGED HAWK *Buteo lagopus* (dark morph) **p. 188**

Dark body and underwing linings; *whitish flight feathers*; tail light from below, with one broad, *black terminal band* in female; additional bands in male.

FERRUGINOUS HAWK *Buteo regalis* (dark morph) **p. 190**

Similar to dark-morph Rough-legged Hawk, but tail whitish, without dark banding. Note also white wrist marks, or "commas."

SWAINSON'S HAWK *Buteo swainsoni* (dark morph) **p. 190**

In dark morph, pointed wings are usually dark throughout, *including flight feathers;* tail narrowly banded, whitish undertail coverts. Rufous morph may be rustier, with lighter rufous underwing linings.

RED-TAILED HAWK *Buteo jamaicensis* (dark morph) **p. 190**

Typical chunky shape of Red-tailed; tail reddish, brighter above than below; variable. Dark patagial bar on leading edge of wing obscured.

"HARLAN'S" RED-TAILED HAWK *Buteo jamaicensis harlani* **p. 190**

Similar to dark-morph Red-tailed Hawk. Breast mottled white; tail tends to be mottled with gray and whitish and with dusky subterminal band, usually lacks obvious red; primary tips barred dark and light.

BROAD-WINGED HAWK *Buteo platypterus* (dark morph) **p. 188**

Typical small size and broad-winged shape. Tail pattern and flight feathers as in light morph, but body and underwing linings dark brownish to brownish black. Note whiter flight feathers than Short-tailed.

ZONE-TAILED HAWK *Buteo albonotatus* (first-year) **p. 186**

Slim and longish, *two-toned wings* (suggesting Turkey Vulture) with barred flight feathers. Several white bands on slim tail (only one visible on folded tail). Yellow legs. Wings held at slight dihedral.

SHORT-TAILED HAWK *Buteo brachyurus* (dark morph) **p. 188**

Jet-black body and underwing linings. Lightly banded tail; flight feathers more shaded and often more distinctly barred than in dark Broad-winged.

COMMON BLACK HAWK *Buteogallus anthracinus* **p. 186**

Very broad black wings; faint light patches near wingtips. Short, broad tail with broad white band at *midtail* and very broad black subterminal band. Whereas Zone-tailed Hawk seems to mimic Turkey Vulture, a deceptive ploy when it is hunting, chunkier Common Black Hawk may be compared to Black Vulture.

HARRIS'S HAWK *Parabuteo unicinctus* **p. 186**

Chocolate brown body, chestnut underwing linings. Very broad white band at base of black tail, narrow white terminal band. Flies more buoyantly than buteos.

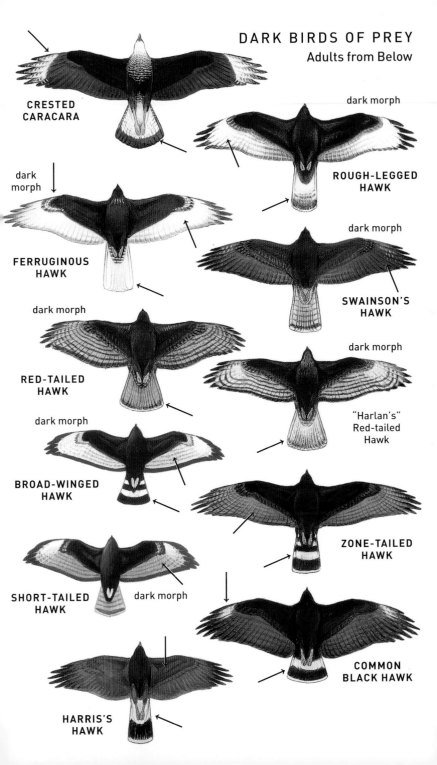

DARK BIRDS OF PREY
Adults from Below

CRESTED CARACARA

dark morph

ROUGH-LEGGED HAWK

dark morph

FERRUGINOUS HAWK

dark morph

SWAINSON'S HAWK

dark morph

RED-TAILED HAWK

dark morph

"Harlan's" Red-tailed Hawk

dark morph

BROAD-WINGED HAWK

ZONE-TAILED HAWK

SHORT-TAILED HAWK

dark morph

COMMON BLACK HAWK

HARRIS'S HAWK

CARACARAS and FALCONS Family Falconidae

Caracaras are large, long-legged birds of prey, and falcons are streamlined with pointed wings, longish tail; recently found to be more closely related to parrots than to other diurnal raptors. Ages and sexes similar or vary in different combinations. **FOOD:** Birds, rodents, reptiles, insects; caracaras scavenge carrion. **RANGE:** Almost worldwide.

CRESTED CARACARA   Uncommon, local
Caracara cheriway (see also p. 196)

23 in. (58 cm). A large, long-legged bird of prey, often seen feeding on roadkill. *Adult:* Black crest and red face distinctive. In flight, underbody presents alternating areas of light and dark: white chest, black belly, and whitish, dark-tipped tail. *Juvenile and first-year:* Browner, streaked on breast; second-year intermediate. Sexes similar. **VOICE:** Weird, guttural series of croaks and rattles. **HABITAT:** Prairies, rangeland, deserts. Casual vagrant well north of range.

PRAIRIE FALCON *Falco mexicanus* (see also p. 202)   Uncommon

16–19 in. (41–50 cm). Like a sandy-colored Peregrine Falcon, with *white eyebrow stripe* and *narrower mustache.* In flight from below, shows *blackish patches* on inner wings. Ages and sexes similar. **VOICE:** Generally silent. Harsh *kak-kak-kak* around nest. **SIMILAR SPECIES:** Juvenile Peregrine darker with bolder face pattern, pale underwing. Female Prairie Merlin *(richardsoni)* much smaller, lacks dark underwing patch. **HABITAT:** Open country, from alpine tundra to grasslands, prairies, agricultural land, deserts, marshes.

GYRFALCON *Falco rusticolus* (see also p. 202)   Scarce

20–25 in. (51–64 cm). A very large Arctic falcon, larger and more robust than Peregrine Falcon; *tail broader and longer.* On perched birds, *wingtips do not reach near tail tip.* Wingbeats slower. Thinner mustache. Occur as brown, gray, and white color morphs. Juvenile and first-year duller; sexes similar. **VOICE:** Harsh *kak-kak-kak* series. **SIMILAR SPECIES:** Peregrine Falcon smaller, slimmer, with darker hood and mustache, and shorter tail. Prairie Falcon slimmer, pale brown. See also Northern Goshawk. **HABITAT:** Arctic barrens, seacoasts, open mountains; in winter, open country, coastlines. Vagrant south of normal winter range.

PEREGRINE FALCON *Falco peregrinus* (see also p. 202) Fairly common

16–20 in. (41–51 cm). A robust, medium-large falcon with pointed wings, narrow tail, and quick, powerful wingbeats. Note *wide black mustache.* *Adult:* In widespread "N. American" subspecies (*anatum*), upperparts slaty blue, breast washed rose, barred and spotted black below breast. *Juvenile and first-year:* Brown, heavily streaked below. Northwestern "Peale's" *(subspecies pealei)*, breeding off s. AK and BC, larger, adults more heavily marked on breast, juveniles much darker (blackish in some). Smaller "Tundra" Peregrine (subspecies *tundrius*), which migrates through the U.S., is slimmer, adult is paler, and juvenile has pale crown. **VOICE:** A rapid *kek kek kek kek* or repeated *we'chew.* **SIMILAR SPECIES:** Merlin, Gyrfalcon. **HABITAT:** Nests on cliffs and ledges; open country, from mountains to coasts. Now breeds (on building ledges and bridges) in many major cities. Regular migrant and winter visitor to small numbers in HI (p. 404).

CARACARA AND LARGE FALCONS

juvenile

CRESTED CARACARA

adults

gray morph

brown morph

GYRFALCON

white morph

gray morph

Tundra juvenile

PRAIRIE FALCON

brown morph

PEREGRINE FALCON

Pacific ("Peale's") juvenile

Pacific ("Peale's") adult

Tundra adult

North American adults

AMERICAN KESTREL *Falco sparverius* (see also p. 202) **Fairly common**
9½–10½ in. (24–27 cm). No other N. American *small* hawk has *rufous back or tail.* Male has blue-gray wings. Both sexes have black-and-white face with double mustache. *Hovers* for prey on rapidly beating wings. Ages similar. **VOICE:** Rapid, high *klee klee klee* or *killy killy killy.* **SIMILAR SPECIES:** Merlin lacks rufous and is more compact, flies much quicker; never hovers. **HABITAT:** Open country, farmland, wood edges, residential areas, dead trees, wires, roadsides.

MERLIN *Falco columbarius* (see also p. 202)　　　　　　**Uncommon**
11–12 in. (28–31 cm). A small and compact falcon; suggests a miniature Peregrine Falcon, but with less distinct mustache. *Adult male:* In most common N. American subspecies (*columbarius*, "Taiga" Merlin), upperparts darkish blue-gray, tail *gray* with broad black bands, underparts streaked reddish brown. *Female, juvenile, and first-year:* Dark brown above, with banded tail; boldly streaked below. "Prairie" subspecies *(richardsonii)* paler gray or brown (color of a Prairie Falcon), lacks or has indistinct mustache. Coastal northwestern "Black" subspecies *(suckleyi),* very dark, lacks light eyebrow stripe. Females are browner above and with less distinct tail bands; first-year males are like females but white as opposed to buff tail tips. **VOICE:** High, rapid *kee-kee-kee-kee.* **SIMILAR SPECIES:** Sharp-shinned Hawk has rounded (not pointed) wings. See American Kestrel, Peregrine and Prairie Falcons. **HABITAT:** Open woods, cliffs, grasslands, tundra; in migration and winter, also marshes, beaches, locally in cities and neighborhoods.

EURASIAN KESTREL *Falco tinnunculus*　　　　**Accidental vagrant**
13½–14 in. (34–36 cm). Similar to American Kestrel, but slightly larger. *Adult male:* Duskier mustache on grayish head, spotted upperparts and wing coverts; gray tail ending in black subterminal band and white tip. *Female and juvenile:* Rusty brown crown, upperparts, and secondaries; duskier primaries; underparts barred on breast, spotted on belly. **RANGE:** Eurasian species. Casual to accidental vagrant to W. Coast from w. AK to CA.

EURASIAN HOBBY *Falco subbuteo*　　　　　　**Casual vagrant**
12½–13 in. (31–33 cm). Most aerial of the falcons; sickle-shaped wings and short tail produce a swiftlike outline. Flight dashing, with rapid, clipped wingbeats, recalling Peregrine Falcon; never hovers. *Adult:* Distinctly patterned, with dark slate mustache, cap, and upperparts, cream throat, heavily streaked underparts, chestnut thighs and vent, and darkly barred underwing. *Juvenile and first-year:* Lacks chestnut areas. **SIMILAR SPECIES:** Peregrine Falcon. **RANGE:** Eurasian species. Casual vagrant to w. AK; accidental elsewhere.

APLOMADO FALCON *Falco femoralis* (see also p. 202)　　**Rare, local**
15–16½ in. (38–42 cm). A little smaller than Peregrine Falcon. *Long wings and tail.* Note *dark underwing* and *black belly,* contrasting with white or pale cinnamon breast. Thighs and undertail coverts orange-brown. Juveniles have scalier brown backs and adult females have less-distinct breast bands than males. **VOICE:** High-pitched whistled scream: *klee-klee-klee-klee!* **SIMILAR SPECIES:** Peregrine Falcon. **RANGE:** Formerly a very rare visitor from Mex., reintroduced to s. NM; northern populations endangered. **HABITAT:** Arid brushy deserts and grasslands, yucca flats.

SMALL FALCONS

AMERICAN KESTREL

female

male

female

male

"Taiga" juvenile female

"Taiga" male

"Pacific" (Black) male

"Prairie" male

MERLIN

"Taiga" adults

RARE FALCONS

EURASIAN HOBBY

EURASIAN KESTREL

juvenile

male

male

female

adult

adult male

APLOMADO FALCON

ACCIPITERS and FALCONS from Below

COOPER'S HAWK *Accipiter cooperii* p. 184

Underparts rusty (adult). Tail rounded and tipped with broad white terminal band. Note head and neck projecting noticeably beyond leading edge of wing.

NORTHERN GOSHAWK *Accipiter gentilis* p. 184

Adult with bold facial pattern, underbody heavily barred with pale gray. Tail and wings broad.

SHARP-SHINNED HAWK *Accipiter striatus* p. 184

Small. When folded, tail square or notched, with narrow pale tip. Fanned tail slightly rounded. Note small head and short neck barely projecting beyond wing.

PEREGRINE FALCON *Falco peregrinus* p. 198

Falcon shape; large; bold face pattern; longer wings than Merlin or Kestrel.

AMERICAN KESTREL *Falco sparverius* p. 200

Small; banded rufous tail. Paler underwing and less heavily marked underparts than Merlin.

MERLIN *Falco columbarius* p. 200

Small; heavily marked underparts and dark underwing; heavily banded tail.

GYRFALCON *Falco rusticolus* p. 198

Larger than Peregrine Falcon; without that bird's contrasting facial pattern, and with broader wings and tail. Varies in color from brown to gray to white.

APLOMADO FALCON *Falco femoralis* p. 200

Black belly band or vest, light chest, orange undertail. Tail barred with black.

PRAIRIE FALCON *Falco mexicanus* p. 198

Size of Peregrine Falcon. *Dark axillars* ("wingpits") and inner coverts.

Accipiters (bird hawks) have short rounded wings and a long tail. They fly with several rapid beats and a short glide. They are better adapted to hunting in the woodlands than most other hawks. Females are larger than males. Juveniles (not shown) have a streaked breast.

Falcons have long, pointed wings and a relatively long tail. Wing strokes are typically rapid and continuous.

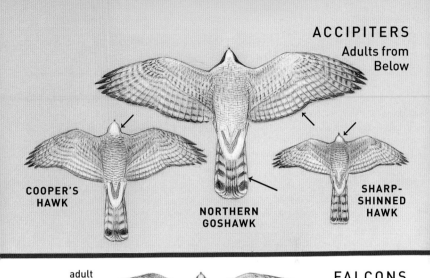

ACCIPITERS
Adults from Below

COOPER'S HAWK

NORTHERN GOSHAWK

SHARP-SHINNED HAWK

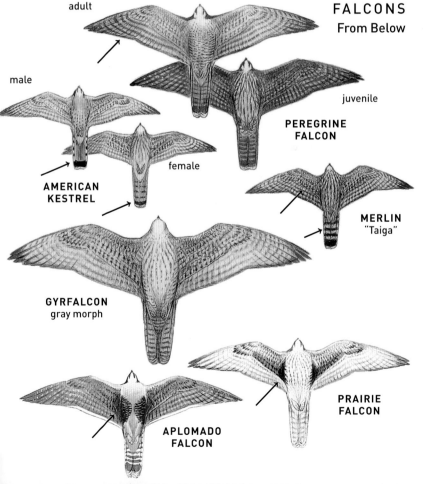

FALCONS
From Below

adult

male

female

PEREGRINE FALCON

juvenile

AMERICAN KESTREL

MERLIN "Taiga"

GYRFALCON gray morph

APLOMADO FALCON

PRAIRIE FALCON

OWLS Families Tytonidae (Barn Owls) and Strigidae (Typical Owls)

Chiefly nocturnal birds of prey, with large heads and flattened faces forming facial disks; large, forward-facing eyes; hooked bill and claws; usually feathered feet. Flight noiseless, mothlike. Some species have "horns," or ear tufts. Ages and sexes largely similar. **FOOD:** Rodents, birds, reptiles, fish, large insects. **RANGE:** Nearly worldwide.

BARN OWL *Tyto alba*   Uncommon

16 in. (41 cm). A long-legged, pale, monkey-faced owl. *White heart-shaped face and dark eyes;* no ear tufts. Distinguished in flight by unstreaked whitish, buff, or pale cinnamon underparts (ghostly at night) and warm tawny-brown back. **VOICE:** Shrill, rasping hiss or screech: *kschh* or *shiiish.* **SIMILAR SPECIES:** Short-eared Owl streaked, has darker face and underparts, *yellow* eyes. **HABITAT:** Open country, groves, dry washes, barns, towns, cliffs, marshes.

SHORT-EARED OWL *Asio flammeus*   Uncommon

15 in. (38 cm). An owl of open country; often foraging at dawn and dusk or during cloudy days. Sometimes tussles with Northern Harrier, with which it shares habitats and prey resources. Streaked, tawny brown color and diagnostic, irregular flopping flight identify it. Buff wing patches with *black carpal ("wrist") marks* and pale trailing edge to secondaries. Dark facial disk emphasizes yellow eyes. Females average darker than males. **VOICE:** Emphatic, sneezy bark: *kee-yow!, wow!,* or *waow!* **SIMILAR SPECIES:** Long-eared Owl similar in flight, but with jerkier wing action, more-orange eyes, darker feathering without white trailing edge to secondaries. **HABITAT:** Grasslands, fresh and salt marshes, dunes, tundra. Roosts on ground, rarely in trees. Indigenous resident in HI (p. 402).

LONG-EARED OWL *Asio otus*   Uncommon

15 in. (38 cm). A slender, medium sized owl with long ear tufts. Usually seen "frozen" close to trunk of a tree. Much smaller and slimmer than Great Horned Owl; underparts streaked *lengthwise,* not barred crosswise. Ears *closer together, erectile;* much black around eyes. **VOICE:** Occasionally one or two long *hooo*s, a catlike whine, or a doglike bark. **SIMILAR SPECIES:** Short-eared Owl in flight. See Great Horned Owl. **HABITAT:** Coniferous and deciduous woodlands, desert groves, riparian thickets. Often roosts in groups. Hunts over open country.

GREAT HORNED OWL *Bubo virginianus*   Common

21–22 in. (54–56 cm). A *very large* owl with ear tufts, or "horns." Heavily *barred* beneath; conspicuous *white throat bib.* In flight, as large as a buteo; looks neckless, large-headed, broad-winged. Varies geographically and individually from very dark to rather pale. Often active just before dark. **VOICE:** Male usually utters five or six resonant hoots: *hoo hu-hu-hu, hoo! hoo!* Female's hoots slightly higher pitched, one note less. Young birds make catlike screams, especially when begging in late summer. **SIMILAR SPECIES:** Long-eared Owl smaller with lengthwise streaking rather than crosswise barring beneath; ears closer together; lacks white bib. **HABITAT:** Forests, woodlots, deserts, residential areas, open country.

OWLS

SHORT-EARED OWL

female (male is whiter below)

female

BARN OWL

male

female

LONG-EARED OWL

fly on awkward stiff wings, often at dusk

flies like Short-eared but not as often seen at dusk

typical

subarctic

GREAT HORNED OWL

SPOTTED OWL *Strix occidentalis* Scarce, threatened

17½–18 in. (45–46 cm). A large, dark-brown forest owl with puffy round head. Large *dark eyes* and *heavily spotted chest and barred belly* identify this bird, which in northern parts of range is being displaced by Barred Owl; populations here (subspecies *caurina*) and in the sw. U.S. (*lucida*) are considered threatened. **VOICE:** High-pitched hoots, like barking of a small dog; usually in groups of three (*hoo, hoo-hoo*) or four (*hoo, who-who-whooo*). Also a longer series of rapid hoots in crescendo; female gives a rising whistle. **SIMILAR SPECIES:** See Barred Owl. **HABITAT:** In North, mature old-growth coniferous and mixed coniferous forests; in South, more varied habitats, including conifers, mixed woods, wooded canyons.

BARRED OWL *Strix varia* Uncommon

20–21 in. (51–53 cm). A large, brown, puffy-headed woodland owl with large, moist *brown* eyes. Barred *across* chest and streaked *lengthwise* on belly; this combination separates it from Spotted Owl. **VOICE:** Usually eight accented hoots, in two groups of four: *hoohoo-hoohoo, hoohoohooHOOaaw*. Sometimes rendered as *who cooks for you, who cooks for you-all.* The *aaw* at end is characteristic and sometimes uttered singly or as *hoo-aww.* **SIMILAR SPECIES:** Other large owls, except Barn and Spotted, have ear tufts and/or yellow eyes. **HABITAT:** Woodlands, wooded river bottoms, wooded swamps. Recent colonizer in West; increasing in CA.

GREAT GRAY OWL *Strix nebulosa* Scarce

26–28 in. (67–73 cm). Our largest N. American owl; very tame. Plumage soft, dusky gray, heavily striped *lengthwise* on underparts. Round-headed, without ear tufts; large, *strongly lined facial disk* dwarfs *yellow* eyes. Note *black chin spot* bordered by two broad *white mustaches.* Tail long for an owl. An irruptive species in eastern parts of range; invades well to the south one year, then may be rare for several years. **VOICE:** Deep *whoo-hoo-hoo.* Also deep single *whoo*s. **SIMILAR SPECIES:** Barred and Spotted Owls much smaller, browner. **HABITAT:** Coniferous forests, adjacent meadows, bogs. Often hunts by day, particularly in winter.

SNOWY OWL *Bubo scandiacus* Scarce

22–24 in. (56–61 cm). An irruptive, large, mostly *white*, Arctic, day-flying owl. Round head, *yellow eyes.* Variably flecked or barred with black to dusky, adult males less so than females and young birds. **VOICE:** Usually silent. Flight call when breeding a loud, repeated *krow-ow;* also a repeated *rick.* **SIMILAR SPECIES:** Barn Owl whitish on underparts only; much smaller and has dark eyes. Many downy young owls are whitish. See Gyrfalcon (white morph). **HABITAT:** Prairies, fields, marshes, beaches; in summer, Arctic tundra. Perches on dunes, posts, haystacks, ground in open country, sometimes buildings. Has cyclic winter irruptions southward into U.S., with vagrants as far as cen. CA, TX, and HI.

LARGE OWLS
Without Ear Tufts

SPOTTED OWL

BARRED OWL

Barred

Spotted

first-year female

SNOWY OWL

GREAT GRAY OWL

adult male

WESTERN SCREECH-OWL *Megascops kennicottii* Fairly common

8½ in. (22 cm). A widespread small owl with conspicuous ear tufts. Yellow eyes. Usually *gray* overall, but n. Great Basin population has two color morphs, *gray* and *brown*. Birds in northwestern humid regions are *usually* darker brown; those in arid regions paler, grayer. Bill dark with pale tip. **VOICE:** Series of hollow whistles on one pitch, running into a tremolo (rhythm of a small ball bouncing to a standstill). **SIMILAR SPECIES:** Eastern Screech-Owl has paler bill but best told by voice and ranges, which barely overlap. See Whiskered Screech-Owl. Flammulated Owl smaller, plumage darker and tinged rusty, has dark eyes. **HABITAT:** Wooded canyons, oak groves, shade trees, well-vegetated residential areas, pinyon-juniper and cactus woodlands.

WHISKERED SCREECH-OWL *Megascops trichopsis* Uncommon, local

7¼–7½ in. (18–19 cm). Very similar to Western Screech-Owl. Has large white spots on scapulars, coarser black spots on underparts, longer facial bristles, *yellow-green bill, smaller legs and feet.* Readily identified by voice. **VOICE:** *Boo-boo, booboo-boo-boo, booboo-boo-boo,* etc.; arrangement of this "code" may vary. At times a repeated, four-syllable *chooyoo-coo-cooo,* vaguely suggestive of White-winged Dove. **SIMILAR SPECIES:** Western Screech-Owl. **HABITAT:** Canyons, pine-oak woods, sycamores; typically at higher elevation than Western Screech-Owl.

FLAMMULATED OWL *Psiloscops flammeolus* Uncommon

6–7 in. (15–18 cm). Smaller than a screech-owl and less conspicuous. Our only small owl north of Arizona *with dark eyes.* Dark, largely gray, with *tawny scapulars* and inconspicuous ear tufts. Southern birds rustier. **VOICE:** Mellow *hoot* (also *hoo-hoot* or *hu-hu, hoot*), low in pitch for so small an owl; repeated steadily at intervals of two or three seconds. Ventriloquial. **SIMILAR SPECIES:** Screech-owls. **HABITAT:** Open pine and fir forests in mountains and canyons. Migratory habits poorly known.

EASTERN SCREECH-OWL *Megascops asio* Uncommon

8½ in. (22 cm). Two color morphs: red and gray. No other owl is bright foxy red. Juvenile fluffy and may lack conspicuous ear tufts. **VOICE:** Mournful whinny or wail; tremulous, *descending* in pitch. Sometimes a series of notes on one pitch. **SIMILAR SPECIES:** Like Western Screech-Owl, but separated by voice and, usually, range. Bill paler (greenish, versus gray-black in Western). Also differs in having bright *red* morph. **HABITAT:** Deciduous woodlands, shade trees.

BURROWING OWL *Athene cunicularia* Fairly cncommon

9½ in. (24 cm). A medium-small owl of open country, often seen by day standing erect on ground or low perches near nesting or wintering burrows, culverts, or drain-pipe entrances. Note *long legs.* Barred and spotted, with white chin stripe, round head. Bobs and bows when agitated. **VOICE:** Rapid, chattering *quick-quick-quick.* At night, a mellow *co-hoo,* higher than Mourning Dove's *coo.* Also a Barn-Owl-like screech. Juvenile in burrow rattles like rattlesnake to deter predators. **HABITAT:** Open grasslands, unplowed prairies, farmland, airfields, golf courses.

SMALL OWLS

WESTERN SCREECH-OWL

Northwest

gray morph

Great Basin

FLAMMULATED OWL

dark morph

WHISKERED SCREECH-OWL

gray morph

EASTERN SCREECH-OWL

red morph

BURROWING OWL

NORTHERN HAWK OWL *Surnia ulula* Scarce

16 in. (41 cm). A medium-sized, slender, day-flying owl, with *long, rounded tail* and *barred underparts*. Often *perches at tip of tree* and jerks tail like a kestrel. **VOICE:** Falconlike chattering *kikikiki* and *illy-illy-illy-illy.* Also a harsh scream. **HABITAT:** Open coniferous forests, birch scrub, tamarack bogs, muskeg, field edges. Accidental vagrant well south of range.

NORTHERN SAW-WHET OWL *Aegolius acadicus* Uncommon

8 in. (20 cm). Smaller than a screech-owl, without ear tufts. Underparts have blotchy, reddish brown streaks. Bill black. Forehead streaked white. *Juvenile:* Chocolate brown with conspicuous white eyebrows; belly *tawny ocher.* **VOICE:** A mellow, whistled note repeated in endless succession: *too, too, too, too,* etc., more than 100 times per minute. Longer, faster, and more regular than in Northern Pygmy-Owl. Also raspy, squirrel-like yelps. **SIMILAR SPECIES:** Boreal Owl. **HABITAT:** Coniferous and mixed woods, swamps.

BOREAL OWL *Aegolius funereus* Scarce

10 in. (25 cm). A small earless owl of northern and high-elevation coniferous forests. Similar to Northern Saw-whet Owl, but a bit larger; facial disk pale grayish white, *framed with black;* bill pale horn color or *yellowish;* forehead *thickly spotted* with white. *Juvenile:* Similar to juvenile Northern Saw-whet, but duskier; eyebrows grayish; belly obscurely blotched. **VOICE:** An accelerating series of hoots, similar to a winnowing snipe; call includes a raspy *skew.* **SIMILAR SPECIES:** Northern Saw-whet Owl. **HABITAT:** Spruce, fir, and lodgepole-pine forests; muskeg. Sporadically appears south of normal range, in East.

NORTHERN PYGMY-OWL *Glaucidium gnoma* Uncommon

6¾–7 in. (17–18 cm). *Black patches* on each side of hindneck suggest "eyes on back of the head." A very small, earless owl; warm or gray brown, with *sharply streaked underparts* and *rather long tail barred with white.* Frequently heard calling in daytime. Often mobbed by birds. **VOICE:** Single mellow whistle, *hoo,* repeated in well-spaced series, once every two or three seconds. Also a rolling series, ending with two or three deliberate notes: *too-too too-too-too-too-too-too-took-took-took.* Birds in se. AZ mountain canyons double the *hoos.* **SIMILAR SPECIES:** Ferruginous Pygmy-Owl, Northern Saw-whet Owl. **HABITAT:** Open coniferous and mixed woods, wooded canyons.

FERRUGINOUS PYGMY-OWL *Glaucidium brasilianum* Rare, local

6½–6¾ in. (16–17 cm). Hunts and calls by both day and night. Often mobbed by birds. Streaking on breast *brownish* rather than black; crown has fine pale streaks (not dots). Tail *rusty, barred with black.* **VOICE:** *Chook* or *puip;* sometimes repeated monotonously two or three times per second. **SIMILAR SPECIES:** Northern Pygmy-Owl (note habitat). **HABITAT:** In s. AZ, saguaro desert.

ELF OWL *Micrathene whitneyi* Uncommon

5¾ in. (15 cm). A tiny, short-tailed, earless owl. Underparts softly striped rusty; eyebrows white. Favors woodpecker holes in saguaros, telephone poles, or trees. Found at night by call. **VOICE:** Rapid, high-pitched *whi-whi-whi-whi-whi-whi* or *chewk-chewk-chewk-chewk,* etc., puppylike, with chattering in middle of series. **SIMILAR SPECIES:** Western Screech-Owl. **HABITAT:** Saguaro and mesquite woodlands and deserts, wooded canyons.

SMALL OWLS

NORTHERN HAWK OWL

juvenile

NORTHERN SAW-WHET OWL

adult

BOREAL OWL

Northern Pygmy-Owl note "eye pattern" on nape

FERRUGINOUS PYGMY-OWL

ELF OWL

gray morph

typical

NORTHERN PYGMY-OWL

GOATSUCKERS (NIGHTJARS)
Family Caprimulgidae

Nocturnal birds with ample tails, large eyes, tiny bills, large bristled gapes, and very short legs. At rest they are camouflaged by their "dead-leaf" patterns. Ages similar; sexes can differ in wing and tail patterns. Most species best identified by voice. **FOOD:** Nocturnal insects. **RANGE:** Nearly worldwide.

COMMON NIGHTHAWK *Chordeiles minor* Uncommon to fairly common

9½ in. (24 cm). Slim-winged; flies high in air with erratic strokes. Prefers dusk. Note *broad white bar* across pointed wing. Male has white bar across tail and larger white bars in wings than female. At rest, *tertials extend well past white wing patch* and wingtips extend to or beyond tail tip; in flight, white bars occur about halfway out primaries. Darker northwestern subspecies shown; interior western subspecies paler and tawnier; more similar to Lesser. **VOICE:** Nasal *peer* or *pee-ik*. **SIMILAR SPECIES:** Lesser Nighthawk has white bar closer to wing tip and tertials shorter. **HABITAT:** Open country throughout western range; often seen in air over cities, towns. Sits on ground, roofs, limbs.

LESSER NIGHTHAWK *Chordeiles acutipennis* Fairly common

8½–9 in. (21–23 cm). Slightly smaller than Common Nighthawk; white bar (*buffy* in female) *closer to tip of wing*; at rest, this bar even with or slightly beyond tips of tertials. More extensive brown spotting on inner primaries. Undertail coverts browner, less sharply barred. Readily identified by odd calls. **VOICE:** Low *chuck chuck* and soft purring or whinnying sound, much like trilling of a toad. **HABITAT:** Lowlands; grasslands, deserts, dirt roads. Sits on branches and ground. Vagrant well north of range.

COMMON POORWILL *Phalaenoptilus nuttallii* Uncommon

7½–7¾ in. (19–20 cm). Smaller and shorter-winged than a nighthawk, *without white bar in wings*; tail *short, rounded, and with white corners* (slightly buffier in female). Short wings and tail give it a *compact look* at rest, usually on ground. **VOICE:** At night, a loud, repeated *poor-will* or *poor-jill.* **SIMILAR SPECIES:** Mexican Whip-poor-will. **HABITAT:** Dry or rocky hills, including open pine forests and chaparral; roadsides.

BUFF-COLLARED NIGHTJAR *Antrostomus ridgwayi* Rare, local

8¾–9 in. (22–23 cm). Similar to Mexican Whip-poor-will but with *buff or tawny collar* across hindneck. Outer tail feathers with white tips in male but not in female. Best told by calls. **VOICE:** Staccato, cricketlike notes, terminating with longer, strongly accented phrase, *cuk-cuk-cuk-cuk-cuk-cuk-cuk-cukacheea.* **RANGE:** Annual in se. AZ; accidental to CA. **HABITAT:** Rocky slopes and washes near mesquite or junipers.

MEXICAN WHIP-POOR-WILL *Antrostomus arizonae* Uncommon

9¾–10 in. (25–26 cm). Recently split from Eastern Whip-poor-will (*A. vociferus*; not shown), which breeds west into SK and is accidental in CA. More often heard than seen; when flushed, flits away mothlike on rounded wings. Male has large *white tail patches;* smaller and buffier in female. At rest, tail extends beyond wings, unlike nighthawk's. Note *black throat.* **VOICE:** A rolling, repeated *WHIP poor-WEEL,* burry in quality. **SIMILAR SPECIES:** Common Poorwill. Eastern Whip-poor-will slightly smaller, extent of white in male's tail greater, call not burry. **HABITAT:** Drier second-growth montane pine-oak woodlands.

COMMON NIGHTHAWK

NIGHTHAWKS

male

female

Lesser male

female

male

COMMON POORWILL

male

female

male

LESSER NIGHTHAWK

BUFF-COLLARED NIGHTJAR

male

MEXICAN WHIP-POOR-WILL

female

PIGEONS and DOVES Family Columbidae

Plump, fast-flying birds with small heads and low, cooing voices; nod their heads as they walk. Some have fanlike tails (such as Rock Pigeon) and others have pointed tails (such as Mourning Dove). Ages and sexes mostly similar; juveniles are scaled above. **FOOD:** Seeds, waste grain, fruit, insects. **RANGE:** Nearly worldwide in tropical and temperate regions.

BAND-TAILED PIGEON *Patagioenas fasciata* Fairly common

14½–15 in. (37–38 cm). Heavily built; might be mistaken for Rock Pigeon except for its woodland habitat and tendency to alight in trees. Note *broad pale band* across end of tail; *white band* on nape. Feet *yellow*. Bill *yellow* with *dark tip*. **VOICE:** Hollow owl-like *oo-whoo* or *whoo-oo-whoo,* repeated. **SIMILAR SPECIES:** Rock Pigeon. **HABITAT:** Oak canyons, foothills, chaparral, mountain forests; also some residential areas, parks. Often flies high over trees in flocks.

AFRICAN COLLARED-DOVE *Streptopelia roseogrisea* Exotic

12 in. (30 cm). Escaped cage bird, also known as Ringed Turtle-Dove (*S. risoria*), formerly occurring in small urban populations and as escapees but has declined with arrival of Eurasian Collared-Dove. Paler than Eurasian Collared-Dove, especially undertail coverts and underside of flight feathers. Voice a series of two-syllable cooing notes rather than three as in Eurasian. Hybrids with Eurasians and paler (leucisitic?) Eurasian Collared-Doves complicate identification.

EURASIAN COLLARED-DOVE *Streptopelia decaocto* Common

12½–13 in. (32–33 cm). Recent colonizer of N. America from Eurasia via the Caribbean; has rapidly increased throughout our area. Slightly chunkier than Mourning Dove, *paler beige,* and with *square-cut tail*. Note *narrow black ring on hindneck. Grayish undertail coverts.* Three-toned wing pattern in flight. **VOICE:** *Three*-noted *coo-COOO-cup.* **SIMILAR SPECIES:** African Collared-Dove. White-winged Dove smaller, lacks neck collar, white in wing obvious. **HABITAT:** Towns, field edges, cultivated land.

SPOTTED DOVE *Streptopelia chinensis* Uncommon, local, exotic

12 in. (30–31 cm). Introduced from Asia. Note *broad collar of black and white spots* on hindneck. A bit larger than Mourning Dove; tail rounded with much white in corners. *Juvenile:* Upperparts scaled; lacks collar, but can be told by shape of spread tail. **VOICE:** *Coo-who-coo;* resembles cooing of White-winged Dove. **SIMILAR SPECIES:** Mourning Dove. Populations in s. CA, now much reduced but this is a common introduced species in HI (p. 402). **HABITAT:** Residential areas, parks.

ROCK PIGEON (ROCK DOVE, DOMESTIC PIGEON)
Columba livia Fairly common, introduced

12½ in. (32 cm). Typical birds are silvery gray with iridescent purple and green head and breast, *whitish rump, two black wing bars,* and broad, dark tail band. Domestic stock or feral birds may have many color variants ranging from blackish to dark reddish with variable white patterns, to entirely white. **VOICE:** Soft, gurgling *coo-roo-coo.* **SIMILAR SPECIES:** Band-tailed Pigeon. **HABITAT:** Cities, farms, cliffs, bridges. Introduced and common in HI (p. 402).

PIGEONS AND DOVES

BAND-TAILED PIGEON

AFRICAN COLLARED-DOVE

EURASIAN COLLARED-DOVE

SPOTTED DOVE

plumages variable

ROCK PIGEON

typical form

WHITE-WINGED DOVE *Zenaida asiatica* Common

11½–12 in. (29–30 cm). A dove of desert, readily known by *white wing patches, large when bird is in flight, narrow when at rest.* Otherwise similar to Mourning Dove, but tail *rounded* and tipped with broad white corners, bill slightly longer, eye orangey red. **VOICE:** Harsh cooing, *ooo-uh-CUCK oo (who cooks for you?).* Sounds vaguely like crowing of a young rooster. **SIMILAR SPECIES:** Mourning Dove, Eurasian Collared-Dove. **HABITAT:** Open areas: river woods, mesquite, saguaros, desert oases, groves, towns, feeders. Widespread vagrant north of range.

MOURNING DOVE *Zenaida macroura* Common

12 in. (30–31 cm). The common widespread wild dove. Brown; smaller and slimmer than Rock Pigeon and Eurasian Collared-Dove. Note *pointed tail* with large white spots. *Male* with slightly bluer crown and rosier breast than *female;* juvenile scaled above. **VOICE:** Hollow, mournful *coah, cooo, coo, cooo.* At a distance, only the three *coos* are audible. **SIMILAR SPECIES:** White-winged Dove, Eurasian Collared-Dove. **HABITAT:** Farms, towns, open woods, fields, scrub, roadsides, grasslands, feeders. Introduced and uncommon in HI (p. 402).

RUDDY GROUND-DOVE *Columbina talpacoti* Rare

6½–6¾ in. (16–17 cm). This rare but regular visitor (and very rare breeder) from Mex. is similar to Common Ground-Dove but is slightly larger, longer tailed, and longer billed; has *dark, grayish base* to bill, *lacks all scaliness,* and *has dark underwing lining* (rufous in Common Ground-Dove). Blackish spots or streaks on wing coverts *extend to scapulars.* *Male:* Washed rufous, crown pale blue; easily identified. *Female and juvenile:* Similar to female Common Ground-Dove but plainer brown and gray. **VOICE:** Cooing similar to Common Ground-Dove's, but faster and more repetitive: *pity-you pity-you pity you.* **SIMILAR SPECIES:** Inca Dove, Common Ground-Dove. **HABITAT:** Farms, livestock pens, fields, brushy areas. Often found with Inca Dove and Common Ground-Dove.

COMMON GROUND-DOVE *Columbina passerina* Uncommon

6¼–6½ in. (15–16 cm). A very small dove. Note *stubby black tail,* scaly breast, pinkish or orangey base of bill. Rounded wings flash *rufous* in flight; *bronzy* spots on wing coverts *but not scapulars;* underwing coverts rufous. Feet yellow or pink. *Male:* Body tinged pinkish. *Female:* Browner; *scapulars lack marks* found on female Ruddy. **VOICE:** Soft, monotonously repeated *woo-oo, woo-oo,* etc. May sound monosyllabic — *wooo,* with rising inflection. **SIMILAR SPECIES:** Inca Dove, Ruddy Ground-Dove. **HABITAT:** Farms, orchards, brushy areas, roadsides. Casual vagrant north of range.

INCA DOVE *Columbina inca* Fairly common

8¼–8½ in. (21–22 cm). A very small, slim dove with *scaly* look. *Rufous* in primaries (as in ground-doves), but has *longer tail* with *white sides and corners,* noticeable in flight. **VOICE:** Monotonous *coo-hoo* or *no-hope.* **SIMILAR SPECIES:** Common Ground-Dove has short tail without obvious white, lacks scaling on back. **HABITAT:** Towns, parks, farms.

DOVES

WHITE-WINGED DOVE

MOURNING DOVE

male

female

RUDDY GROUND DOVE

male

female

COMMON GROUND DOVE

male

female

INCA DOVE

CUCKOOS, ROADRUNNERS, and ANIS
Family Cuculidae

Slender, long-tailed birds; feet zygodactyl (two toes forward, two backward). Sexes alike. **FOOD:** Cuckoos eat caterpillars, other insects; roadrunners eat reptiles, rodents, large insects, small birds; anis eat seeds, fruit. **RANGE:** Warm and temperate regions of world; some cuckoos (but not ours) are parasitic.

BLACK-BILLED CUCKOO *Coccyzus erythropthalmus* Scarce

11½–12 in. (29–30 cm). *Adult:* Similar to Yellow-billed Cuckoo, but *bill dark gray to blackish;* adult has narrow *red orbital ring. No rufous in wing;* undertail spots small. *Juvenile and first-fall:* Has greenish to yellowish orbital ring and often small amount of rufous in wing; thus more like Yellow-billed Cuckoo, but has *all-dark bill.* **VOICE:** Fast, rhythmic *cucucu, cucucu, cucucu,* etc. The grouped rhythm (three or four) is typical, but often employs irregular cadences. May sing at night. **HABITAT:** Wood edges, groves, thickets. Accidental vagrant to W. Coast.

YELLOW-BILLED CUCKOO *Coccyzus americanus* Scarce

12 in. (30–31 cm). Slim and sinuous with brown back and white underparts. *Rufous* in wings, *large white* spots at tips of dark undertail feathers, *yellow* lower mandible on slightly curved bill, and dusky orbital ring; juvenile and first-fall birds have less-distinct tail spots and yellowish orbital rings. **VOICE:** Song a distinctive, rapid, throaty *ka-ka-ka-ka-ka-ka-ka-ka-ka-ka-ka-ka-kow-kow-kowlp-kowlp — kowlp — kowlp* (slowing toward end). Often heard during hot afternoons. **SIMILAR SPECIES:** Black-billed Cuckoo. **HABITAT:** Riparian woodlands, cottonwood groves. Western populations restricted in range and considered threatened. Casual vagrant north of range.

GREATER ROADRUNNER *Geococcyx californianus* Fairly common

22–23 in. (56–58 cm). Roadrunners are peculiar cuckoos that run on ground. A large, slender, streaked bird, with long, white-edged tail; shaggy crest; long legs. White crescent on wing (visible when spread). **VOICE:** Six to eight low, dovelike *coos,* descending in pitch. **SIMILAR SPECIES:** Thrashers are much smaller. **HABITAT:** Deserts, open country with scattered cover, chaparral, brush. Often seen running alongside or across road, usually singly.

GROOVE-BILLED ANI *Crotophaga sulcirostris* Casual

13–13½ in. (33–34 cm). A coal black, grackle-sized bird with long loose-jointed tail, short wings, and *large bill with high curved ridge* and noticeable angle to lower mandible (giving it puffinlike profile), with distinct bill grooves or ridges, more prominent in older adults. Flight weak; alternately flaps and sails. Often moves in groups. **VOICE:** Repeated *whee-o* or *tee-ho,* first note slurring up. **SIMILAR SPECIES:** Grackles. **HABITAT:** Thickets, open woodlands. Widespread vagrant north of range.

CUCKOOS, ETC.

YELLOW-BILLED
CUCKOO

BLACK-BILLED
CUCKOO

first-
fall

adults

adult

GREATER
ROADRUNNER

GROOVE-BILLED
ANI

PARAKEETS and PARROTS Family Psittacidae

Noisy, compact birds with stout, hooked bills. Parakeets smaller, with long, pointed tail. **RANGE:** Worldwide. Carolina Parakeet (*Conuropsis carolinensis*) formerly occurred in e. U.S. and west to CO; now extinct.

WHITE-WINGED PARAKEET
Brotogeris versicolurus

Locally uncommon, exotic

YELLOW-CHEVRONED PARAKEET
Brotogeris chiriri

Locally fairly common, exotic

9 in. (23 cm). Native to S. America, these two similar *Brotogeris* parakeets are locally established in Los Angeles areas. Note yellow primary coverts, white secondaries in White-winged. White-winged formerly more common but recently outnumbered by Yellow-chevroned.

RED-CROWNED PARROT
Amazona viridigenalis

Locally fairly common, exotic

12 in. (30 cm). Large, with red crown (reduced in first-year), blue nape, red wing panels. **VOICE:** Loud, raucous notes and squeals. **RANGE AND HABITAT:** Native to ne. Mex. Exotic populations in s. CA and Honolulu (p. 404).

THICK-BILLED PARROT
Rhynchopsitta pachyrhyncha

Rare, local, endangered

16–17 in. (40–43 cm). Large, with red forehead, eyebrow, and bend of wing; underwing patterned with black, yellow, and red. Tail longer than in Amazon parrots. **VOICE:** Loud, laughinglike *ca-ca-ca-ca* calls. **RANGE AND HABITAT:** Native to n. Mex. and formerly se. AZ. Reintroduction program in 1980–90s not successful but individuals since reported.

ROSY-FACED LOVEBIRD
Agapornis roseicollis

Locally fairly common, exotic

6–6½ in. (15–16 cm). A small, short-tailed parakeet, adult male with distinctive peach-colored to red face; female and first-year greener. Found in large tight flocks. **VOICE:** High-pitched, twittering *cheep* calls. **RANGE AND HABITAT:** Native to Africa; established locally in Phoenix area and on Maui (p. 404).

NANDAY PARAKEET *Nandayus nenday*
Unestablished, exotic

(S. America) 12 in. (30 cm). Populations in n. Los Angeles, CA. Also known as "Black-hooded" Parakeet.

ROSE-RINGED PARAKEET *Psittacula krameri*
Unestablished exotic

(Africa, India) 16 in. (41 cm). Small populations in Los Angeles; larger population in Bakersfield, CA. Introduced and common in HI (p. 404).

MITRED PARAKEET *Psittacara mitratus*
Unestablished exotic

(S. America) 15 in. (38 cm). Moderate populations in Los Angeles; found occasionally elsewhere in N. America and on Maui.

RED-MASKED PARAKEET
Psittacara erythrogenys

Unestablished exotic

(S. America) 12½–13½ in. (30–34 cm). Moderate populations in Los Angeles and San Francisco areas; established on Oahu and Hawaii I. (p. 404).

LILAC-CROWNED PARROT *Amazona finschi*
Unestablished exotic

(Mex.) 12½–13½ in. (30–34 cm). Populations in Los Angeles and San Diego.

PARAKEETS AND PARROTS

WHITE-WINGED PARAKEET

Established

RED-CROWNED PARROT

YELLOW-CHEVRONED PARAKEET

ROSY-FACED LOVEBIRD

adult

adult male

THICK-BILLED PARROT

Non-established

NANDAY PARAKEET

ROSE-RINGED PARAKEET

MITRED PARAKEET

RED-MASKED PARAKEET

LILAC-CROWNED PARROT

KINGFISHERS Family Alcedinidae

Chiefly solitary birds with large heads and strong bills. Perch above water and hover and plunge for fish; some species eat insects, lizards. **RANGE:** Almost worldwide.

BELTED KINGFISHER *Megaceryle alcyon*   **Fairly common**

13 in. (33 cm). Our common widespread kingfisher. Hovers on rapidly beating wings while fishing and frequently rattles as it flies: the Belted Kingfisher is easily recognized. *Adult male:* Blue-gray above, with ragged bushy crest and broad gray chest-band. *Adult female:* Has an additional rusty breast-band. *First-year:* Similar in both sexes but blue chest-band mottled with rusty feathers. **VOICE:** Distinctive, loud dry rattle. **HABITAT:** Streams, lakes, coasts; nests in banks, perches on wires.

GREEN KINGFISHER *Chloroceryle americana*   **Scarce, local**

8½–8¾ in. (22 cm). Kingfisher shape, small size; flight buzzy, direct. Upperparts deep green with white spots; collar and underparts white, sides spotted. *Adult male:* Has *rusty* breast-band. *Adult female:* Has one or two greenish bands. *First-year:* Birds of both sexes have mixed rufous and green feathers in breast. **VOICE:** Sharp clicking, *tick tick tick;* also a sharp squeak. **HABITAT:** Small rivers and ponds with clear water. Accidental vagrant north of range.

WOODPECKERS Family Picidae

Chisel-billed, wood-boring birds with strong zygodactyl feet (two toes front, two rear), long tongues, and stiff spiny tails that act as props for climbing. Flight usually undulating. **FOOD:** Tree-boring insects and grubs; some species eat ants, flying insects, acorns. **RANGE:** Most wooded parts of world.

PILEATED WOODPECKER *Dryocopus pileatus*   **Uncommon**

16½–17 in. (42–44 cm). A spectacular, *crow-sized* woodpecker, black with flaming red *crest*. Female has blackish forehead, lacks red on mustache. Size, sweeping wingbeats, and flashing white underwing in flight are distinctive. Creates large *oval* or *oblong* foraging pits in dead or dying trees. **VOICE:** Call resembles that of a flicker, but louder, deeper, irregular: *kik-kik-kikkik-kik-kik,* etc. Also a more ringing, double-note call. **HABITAT:** Coniferous and hardwood forests with large mature trees; woodlots.

ARIZONA WOODPECKER *Dryobates arizonae*   **Uncommon, local**

7½ in. (19 cm). A *brown-backed* woodpecker with *white-striped face;* spotted and barred below. Male has red nape patch. The only U.S. woodpecker with *solid brown* back. **VOICE:** Sharp *spik;* a hoarse whinny. Fairly similar to Hairy Woodpecker's calls. **SIMILAR SPECIES:** Ladder-backed, Downy, and Hairy Woodpeckers all blacker, underparts not as spotted. **HABITAT:** Canyon woodlands of oak, juniper, and pine-oak.

WHITE-HEADED WOODPECKER *Dryobates albolarvatus*   **Uncommon**

9¼ in. (23 cm). Our only woodpecker with *white head.* Male (but not female) has red patch on nape; otherwise black overall, with large white patch in primaries. No white on rump (as in Acorn Woodpecker). **VOICE:** Sharp, *doubled ki-dik,* sometimes rapidly repeated, *chick-ik-ik-ik;* also a rattle similar to Downy's. **SIMILAR SPECIES:** Downy and Hairy Woodpecker calls are *single, not double,* notes. **HABITAT:** Mountain pine forests, particularly ponderosa, Jeffrey, and sugar pines.

KINGFISHERS AND WOODPECKERS

hovering

BELTED KINGFISHER

adult male

GREEN KINGFISHER

first-year female

plunging

adult female

adult male

ARIZONA WOODPECKER

female

male

female

male

male

female

PILEATED WOODPECKER

WHITE-HEADED WOODPECKER

RED-HEADED WOODPECKER
Uncommon, local

Melanerpes erythrocephalus

9¼ in. (24 cm). *Adult:* A black-backed woodpecker with *entirely red* head (other woodpeckers may have patch of red). Back *solid black*, rump white. Large, square *white patches* conspicuous on wing, including when sitting on a tree. Sexes similar. *Juvenile:* Dusky-headed; wing patches mottled with dark through first year. **VOICE:** Loud *queer* or *queeah*. **SIMILAR SPECIES:** Red-bellied Woodpecker has only partially red head. **HABITAT:** Farm country, shade trees in towns. Casual vagrant west of range, accidentally to CA.

LEWIS'S WOODPECKER   *Melanerpes lewis*
Uncommon

10¾–11 in. (27–28 cm). A large, dark woodpecker with *crowlike flight*, flycatching habits. *Adult:* Has extensive *pinkish red belly*, *wide gray collar*, and dark red face patch. Sexes similar. *Juvenile:* Duller. **VOICE:** Usually silent. Occasionally a harsh *churr* or *chee-ur.* **SIMILAR SPECIES:** Red-headed and Acorn Woodpeckers. American Crow. **HABITAT:** Open, burned, or logged forests, usually of ponderosa pine or oak; river groves, oak savanna.

ACORN WOODPECKER   *Melanerpes formicivorus*
Common

9 in. (23 cm). Social, usually found in clans. A black-backed woodpecker with conspicuous white rump, *white wing patches* in flight, and whitish eyes. Note *clownish black, white, and red head pattern*, female with an extra black band on crown. Ages similar. Stores acorns in holes drilled in bark and wooden building sides. **VOICE:** *Whack-up, whack-up, whack-up,* or *ja-cob, ja-cob.* Also raspy noises and calls. **HABITAT:** Oak woods, mixed oak-pine forests, foothills. Casual vagrant north and east of range.

RED-BELLIED WOODPECKER   *Melanerpes carolinus*
Uncommon

9¼ in. (24 cm). *Adult:* A *zebra-backed* woodpecker with *red cap, white rump.* Red covers both crown and nape in male, *only nape in female. Juvenile:* Also zebra-backed, but head devoid of red. **VOICE:** Call *kwirr, churr,* or *chaw;* also *chiv, chiv* and a muffled flickerlike series. **SIMILAR SPECIES:** Golden-fronted Woodpecker. **HABITAT:** Woodlands, groves, orchards, towns, feeders. Casual vagrant west of range.

GILA WOODPECKER   *Melanerpes uropygialis*
Fairly common

9¼ in. (24 cm). A zebra-backed woodpecker; in flight, shows *white wing patch.* Head and underparts gray-brown; male but not female has red cap. **VOICE:** Rolling *churr* and a sharp *pit* or *yip.* **SIMILAR SPECIES:** Ladder-backed Woodpecker, found in same habitats, blackish with striped face, lacks white wing patch. See also female Williamson's Sapsucker. **HABITAT:** Desert washes, saguaros, riparian woodlands, towns.

GOLDEN-FRONTED WOODPECKER
Fairly common

Melanerpes aurifrons

9½ in. (25 cm). A zebra-backed woodpecker with light underparts and white rump. Has white wing patch in flight. *Male:* Note *multicolored head* (yellow near bill, poppy red on crown, orange nape). *Female:* Lacks red crown patch (juvenile has tan head and nape, lacking color). **VOICE:** Tremulous *churrrr;* flickerlike *kek-kek-kek-kek.* **SIMILAR SPECIES:** Note aberrant Red-bellied Woodpecker can have yellow lores. **HABITAT:** Mesquite, woodlands, groves.

WOODPECKERS

juvenile

adult

**RED-HEADED
WOODPECKER**

juvenile

**LEWIS'S
WOODPECKER**

adult

male

female

**ACORN
WOODPECKER**

male

female

**RED-BELLIED
WOODPECKER**

male

female

**GILA
WOODPECKER**

male

female

**GOLDEN-FRONTED
WOODPECKER**

NORTHERN FLICKER   *Colaptes auratus*   Common

12–12½ in. (30–32 cm). Note conspicuous *white rump* in flight, barred *brown back*, and *black patch* across chest. Often hops awkwardly on ground, feeding on ants. "Yellow-shafted" Flicker, of the North and East, has *golden yellow* underwings and tail, *red crescent* on nape; *gray crown*; *tan-brown cheeks*; male has *black* mustache. "Red-shafted" Flicker of the West has *salmon red* underwing and undertail, lack red crescent on nape; has *brownish crown* and *gray cheeks*; male has *red* mustache. Intergrades are fairly common in western edge of plains; these and Yellow-shafteds are uncommon in winter throughout West. **VOICE:** Loud *wick wick wick wick wick*, etc. Also a loud *klee-yer* and a squeaky *flick-a, flick-a*, etc. (See Pileated Woodpecker.) **SIMILAR SPECIES:** Gilded Flicker. **HABITAT:** Open coniferous forests, woodlots, towns.

GILDED FLICKER   *Colaptes chrysoides*   Uncommon, local

11–11½ in. (28–29 cm). Similar to Yellow-shafted Flicker but crown mustard brown, male has *red* mustache, black breast patch slightly thicker, dark barring on back narrower. **VOICE:** Same as Northern Flicker's, but slightly higher pitched. **HABITAT:** Cactus deserts, riparian woodland corridors; Northern Flicker rarely found in same habitat.

WILLIAMSON'S SAPSUCKER   *Sphyrapicus thyroideus*   Uncommon

9 in. (23 cm). Characteristic *sapsucker white wing patches*. *Male:* Black with white facial stripes and rump, *red throat, yellow belly*. *Female:* Very different looking: brownish and *zebra-backed* with white rump, *barred sides, brown head*, yellow belly. **VOICE:** Nasal *cheeer*. Drum is several rapid thumps followed by three or four slower thumps. **SIMILAR SPECIES:** Other sapsuckers. **HABITAT:** High-elevation coniferous forests, in winter, to lower elevations and occasionally in other types of trees. Casual vagrant east of range.

RED-BREASTED SAPSUCKER   *Sphyrapicus ruber*   Uncommon

8½ in. (22 cm). Sapsuckers drill orderly rows of small holes in trees for sap and the insects it attracts. Note *longish sapsucker wing patch*. Red-breasted has *entirely red head and breast*. Sexes similar; northern subspecies (*ruber*) brighter than southern subspecies (*daggettii*). *Juvenile:* Head and body mottled brown in summer. Hybridizes with Red-naped Sapsucker. **VOICE:** Nasal mewing note, *cheerrrr;* drum in this and other sapsuckers several rapid thumps followed by several slow, rhythmic thumps. **SIMILAR SPECIES:** Hybrid Red-naped × Red-breasted Sapsuckers usually have more black and white on face and mix of black and red on breast. **HABITAT:** Coniferous and mixed woods, groves, fruit trees.

RED-NAPED SAPSUCKER   *Sphyrapicus nuchalis*   Fairly common

8½ in. (22 cm). Very similar to Yellow-bellied Sapsucker but note *red nape*. Black frame around throat *broken* toward rear. Female has white chin. **SIMILAR SPECIES:** Yellow-bellied and Red-breasted Sapsuckers; beware hybrids. **HABITAT:** Coniferous, mixed, and deciduous woodlands; aspen groves. Casual vagrant east of range.

YELLOW-BELLIED SAPSUCKER   *Sphyrapicus varius*   Uncommon

8½ in. (22 cm). *Adult:* Male has all-red throat, female white. *Juvenile:* Unlike other sapsuckers, retains brown plumage through winter. **VOICE:** Similar to Red-breasted Sapsucker. **SIMILAR SPECIES:** Red-naped Sapsucker. **HABITAT:** Coniferous, mixed, and deciduous woods, shade trees. Scarce vagrant to W. Coast in fall and winter.

WOODPECKERS
Flickers and Sapsuckers

NORTHERN FLICKER

"Red-shafted"

"Yellow-shafted"

"Red-shafted" female

"Red-shafted" male

"Yellow-shafted" male

males

Gilded Flicker

GILDED FLICKER

"Red-shafted"

WILLIAMSON'S SAPSUCKER

juvenile male

male

female

juvenile

southern

RED-BREASTED SAPSUCKER

northern

female

female

juvenile

RED-NAPED SAPSUCKER

male

male

YELLOW-BELLIED SAPSUCKER

NUTTALL'S WOODPECKER *Dryobates nuttallii* Fairly common

7½ in. (19 cm). A black-and-white zebra-backed woodpecker of the far West. Male has red crown. Juvenile *Dryobates* and *Picoides* woodpeckers have sparse red flecking to crown in both sexes (more red in males). **VOICE:** Descending rattle, sharper than in Downy. Call a low *pa-tick*. **SIMILAR SPECIES:** Ladder-backed Woodpecker range barely overlaps (hybrids are known), has thicker white stripes on face and back. Downy Woodpecker. **HABITAT:** Oak woodlands; recently expanding to other habitats.

LADDER-BACKED WOODPECKER *Dryobates scalaris* Fairly common

7¼ in. (18 cm). The black-and-white zebra-backed woodpecker found in more arid country *east of Sierra Nevada.* Male has red crown. **VOICE:** Rattling series, *chikikikikikikikikik,* diminishing. Call a sharp *pick* or *chik* (like Downy Woodpecker). **SIMILAR SPECIES:** Nuttall's Woodpecker. **HABITAT:** Deserts, canyons, pinyon-juniper, riparian woodlands, arid brush.

HAIRY WOODPECKER *Dryobates villosus* Common

9–9¼ in. (23–24 cm). Note *white* back and *large* bill. Downy and Hairy Woodpeckers both checkered and spotted with black and white; male has small red patch on back of head, female does not. *Juvenile:* May have red to yellowish crown patch, more extensive in male. **VOICE:** Kingfisher-like rattle, quicker than that of Downy. Call a sharp *peek!* (Downy says *pick.*) **SIMILAR SPECIES:** Downy Woodpecker. American Three-toed Woodpecker. **HABITAT:** Coniferous forests, deciduous woods, shade trees.

DOWNY WOODPECKER *Dryobates pubescens* Fairly common

6½–6¾ in. (17 cm). Note *white back* and *small bill.* Outer tail feathers spotted, red nape patch of male in unbroken square. Coloration varies regionally in both Downy and Hairy. **VOICE:** Rapid whinny of notes, descending in pitch. Call a flat *pick,* not as sharp as Hairy's *peek!* **SIMILAR SPECIES:** Hairy Woodpecker larger, has larger bill and clean white outer tail feathers. **HABITAT:** Woods, riparian thickets, residential areas.

AMERICAN THREE-TOED WOODPECKER *Picoides dorsalis* Scarce

8½–8¾ in. (22 cm). Males of this and the next species have three toes, a *yellow cap* (note some juvenile Hairys have sparse yellow in crown), *barred sides* in both sexes. Both species inhabit boreal and montane forests. American Three-toed is distinguished by irregular white patch on back (Rockies) or *bars* (farther north). Female lacks yellow cap. **VOICE:** A level-pitched whinny and a flat *pyik.* **SIMILAR SPECIES:** Black-backed Woodpecker, Hairy Woodpecker. **HABITAT:** Coniferous forests, particularly in burned areas and where deadwood is present.

BLACK-BACKED WOODPECKER *Picoides arcticus* Scarce

9½ in. (24 cm). Note combination of *solid black back* and *barred sides.* Male has *yellow cap.* **VOICE:** Low flat *kuk* or *puk* and a short buzzy call. **SIMILAR SPECIES:** American Three-toed and Hairy Woodpeckers. **HABITAT:** Coniferous forests, particularly in burned areas and where deadwood is present.

NUTTALL'S WOODPECKER

male

female

WOODPECKERS

male

female

LADDER-BACKED WOODPECKER

northern and eastern male

northwestern male

HAIRY WOODPECKER

Rockies male

female

northwestern male

Rockies and eastern male

female

DOWNY WOODPECKER

female

Rockies male

AMERICAN THREE-TOED WOODPECKER

northern male

male

female

BLACK-BACKED WOODPECKER

TROGONS Family Trogonidae

Brightly colored forest birds with short necks, stubby bills, and long tails. Remain motionless for long periods, then explode in a flutter to pluck berries. **FOOD:** Small fruit, insects. **RANGE:** Mainly tropical parts of world.

EARED QUETZAL *Euptilotis neoxenus* Very rare

13½–14 in. (35–36 cm). Note *black bill, lack of white breast-band,* and mostly *white* underside of blue tail. "Ears" of male inconspicuous. **VOICE:** High-pitched, rising squeal; series of whistled notes. **RANGE AND HABITAT:** Very rare visitor from Mex. to mountains and canyons in AZ.

ELEGANT TROGON *Trogon elegans* Uncommon, local

12–12½ in. (31–32 cm). *Adult male:* Note *geranium red belly, white breast-band,* yellow bill, and *finely barred underside of tail* (coppery above). *Female:* Brown head with *white mark* on cheek. First-year male mottled red and green. **VOICE:** Series of low, coarse notes: *kowm kowm kowm kowm kowm kowm* or *koa, koa, koa,* etc. **HABITAT:** Mountain forests, pine-oak and sycamore canyons.

SWIFTS Family Apodidae

Structurally distinct from swallows, with shorter forewings. Flight very rapid, "twinkling," sailing, narrow wings often stiffly bowed. Ages and sexes similar. **FOOD:** Flying insects. **RANGE:** Nearly worldwide.

VAUX'S SWIFT *Chaetura vauxi* Fairly common

4¾ in. (12 cm). Our smallest swift. Between spurts of rapid wingbeats, glides with wings *bowed* in a *crescent.* **VOICE:** High-pitched, rapid ticking or chippering notes, insectlike trills. **SIMILAR SPECIES:** Chimney Swift is similar but slightly larger and longer winged, has darker throat and rump, and louder and chippier calls. **HABITAT:** Open sky over woodlands, water; nests in tree cavities, can roost in chimneys during migration.

CHIMNEY SWIFT *Chaetura pelagica* Uncommon

5¼ in. (13 cm). Like a cigar with wings. Dark, with long, slightly curved, stiff wings and stubby tail. Rapid, twinkling wingbeats interspersed with bowed-winged glides. **VOICE:** Loud, rapid ticking or twittering notes. **SIMILAR SPECIES:** Vaux's and Black Swifts. **HABITAT:** Open sky; nests and roosts in chimneys. Casual vagrant to W. Coast.

BLACK SWIFT *Cypseloides niger* Uncommon, local

7¼ in. (18 cm). A large *blackish* swift with noticeable notched tail (sometimes fanned), deeper in adult male. At close range, a touch of white on forehead. Slower wingbeats than in other U.S. swifts. **VOICE:** Sharp *plik-plik-plik-plik-plik,* etc., at nest site. **SIMILAR SPECIES:** Vaux's and Chimney Swifts much smaller, Vaux's with paler throat. **HABITAT:** Open sky; favors mountains, coastal cliffs; nests behind waterfalls.

WHITE-THROATED SWIFT *Aeronautes saxatalis* Uncommon

6½ in. (17 cm). Note contrasting *black-and-white pattern.* In poor light look for long slim tail. **VOICE:** Shrill, excited *jejejejeje,* in descending scale, similar to Canyon Wren song. **SIMILAR SPECIES:** Other swifts; Violet-green Swallow. **HABITAT:** Open sky. Breeds mainly in dry mountains, canyons, cliffs; locally on sea cliffs and man-made structures.

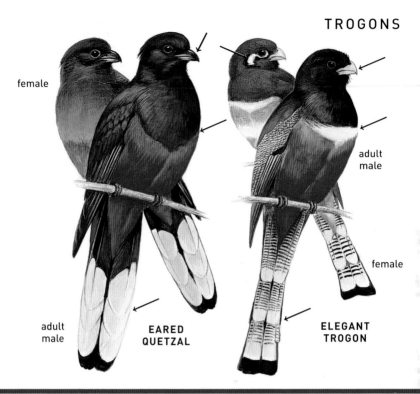

TROGONS

female

adult male

EARED QUETZAL

adult male

female

ELEGANT TROGON

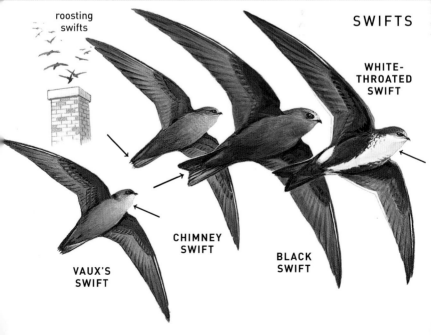

SWIFTS

roosting swifts

WHITE-THROATED SWIFT

VAUX'S SWIFT

CHIMNEY SWIFT

BLACK SWIFT

HUMMINGBIRDS Family Trochilidae

The smallest of birds, with needlelike bills for sipping nectar. Adult males of most species with iridescent gorget throat and sometimes crown feathers; in poor light, these feathers can appear dark. Hummingbirds hover when feeding and can fly backward; their wingbeats are so rapid that they appear as a blur. Pugnacious. Vocal differences can be important identification aids. **FOOD:** Nectar (red flowers favored), small insects, spiders. **RANGE:** W. Hemisphere; majority in Tropics.

ANNA'S HUMMINGBIRD *Calypte anna* Common

4 in. (10 cm). *Adult male:* The only U.S. hummer with *rose red crown;* throat also rose red. *Female and first-summer male:* Slightly larger than other hummers, grayer below, with *green sides* and more heavily spotted throat than female Costa's or Black-chinned Hummingbird; adult female has small, red, central throat patch. The only common winter hummingbird along Pacific Coast. **VOICE:** Raspy chatters; song squeaking, grating notes, and when diving in aerial display male makes *sharp popping sound* with tail. **SIMILAR SPECIES:** Black-chinned and Costa's Hummingbirds. **HABITAT:** Gardens, parks, feeders, chaparral, open woods.

COSTA'S HUMMINGBIRD *Calypte costae* Uncommon

3½ in. (9 cm). *Adult male:* Note *purple* or *amethyst* throat and crown. Feathers of gorget *project* markedly rearwards at sides. *Female and first-fall male:* Similar to other hummingbirds but whiter, especially on throat. The inner six primaries of *Calypte* are the same width as the outer primaries, whereas those of *Archilochus* are thinner. **VOICE:** Series of pipping notes. Male in display, a rising *zing.* **SIMILAR SPECIES:** Females and first-fall males duller green above than those of Black-chinned Hummingbird, bill and tail shorter, inner primaries broader, *voices differ.* Female Anna's larger, mottled, gray and green on sides. **HABITAT:** Deserts, coastal sage scrub, chaparral, arid hillsides, feeders.

BLACK-CHINNED HUMMINGBIRD Fairly common
Archilochus alexandri

3¾ in. (10 cm). *Adult male:* Note *black throat* and conspicuous white collar; iridescent blue-violet of lower throat shows only in certain lights. *Female and first-fall male:* Similar to these plumages in other hummingbirds but crown often grayish, back dull, bill longer. The outermost primary is *more curved and club-shaped* in Black-chinned than in Ruby-throated Hummingbird. **VOICE:** Male's wings hum in courtship display. Chase calls high, squeaky. Other call a soft *chew.* **SIMILAR SPECIES:** Ruby-throated, Costa's, and Anna's Hummingbirds. **HABITAT:** Riparian woodlands, wooded canyons, semiarid country, chaparral, suburbs, feeders.

RUBY-THROATED HUMMINGBIRD Uncommon, local
Archilochus colubris

3¾ in. (10 cm). *Adult male: Fiery red throat,* iridescent green back, forked tail. *Female:* Lacks red throat; tail blunt, with white spots. *First-fall male:* Like female but tail slightly forked, a few scattered ruby feathers molt in during fall. **VOICE:** Like Black-chinned Hummingbird's. **SIMILAR SPECIES:** Male Broad-tailed Hummingbird lacks forked tail, typically makes wing-trill sound. See Black-chinned Hummingbird. **HABITAT:** Flowers, gardens, wood edges, over streams. Casual fall vagrant to CA.

HUMMINGBIRDS

ANNA'S HUMMINGBIRD

adult male

adult female

COSTA'S HUMMINGBIRD

adult male

female

BLACK-CHINNED HUMMINGBIRD

adult male

female

RUBY-THROATED HUMMINGBIRD

adult male

adult male

female

sphinx moths resemble hummingbirds

BROAD-TAILED HUMMINGBIRD   Fairly common
Selasphorus platycercus

4 in. (10 cm). Tail long, the central feathers broad relative to other hummers in our area. *Adult male:* Crown and back green; throat bright *rose red*; greenish on sides. *Female and first-fall male:* Sides tinged with buff; touch of rufous at basal corners of tail. Male known by *shrill trilling* sound of wings. **VOICE:** A variety of vocal sounds. *Chi-chewee chi-chewee* often given in flight. Call a sharp *chit!* **SIMILAR SPECIES:** Female and first-fall male Calliope Hummingbirds smaller, with smaller bill; at rest *wingtips extend beyond short, square-cut tail.* Female and first-fall male Rufous Hummingbirds have smaller tail, usually richer rufous on sides and more rufous in tail. Male Ruby-throated Hummingbird smaller with forked tail. **HABITAT:** Mountains and canyons; common at feeders.

RUFOUS HUMMINGBIRD   *Selasphorus rufus*   Common

3¾ in. (9–10 cm). *Adult male:* Note bright *rufous or red-brown upperparts*, sometimes mottled green but rufous predominates; throat flaming orange-red. Aerial display is a closed ellipse, slowing on return climb. *Female and first-fall male:* Green-backed; dull *rufous on sides and at base of outer tail feathers*. Adult females and first-fall birds show iridescent orange-red feathers on throat. **VOICE:** Aggressive flight call a buzzy *zap* followed by sputtering notes, or *zeee chippity chippity.* Male's wings make high trill in flight. **SIMILAR SPECIES:** Allen's, Calliope, and Broad-tailed Hummingbirds. **HABITAT:** Coniferous forests, wooded or brushy areas, feeders; mountain meadows.

ALLEN'S HUMMINGBIRD   *Selasphorus sasin*   Fairly common

3¾ in. (9–10 cm). *Adult male:* Like Rufous Hummingbird but back *green*, sometimes mottled orange but green predominates. *Female and first-fall male:* Very difficult to distinguish in field from those of Rufous, especially in Mar.–May and July–Aug. when both species co-occur in CA; Allen's has narrower rectrices, and these can sometimes be used with experience to separate birds of known age and sex to species. **VOICE:** Flight call similar to that of Rufous but aerial display of male differs, starting "pendulum display" in shallow arcs followed by a steep climb and swoop back with an air-splitting *vrrrip.* **SIMILAR SPECIES:** Rufous Hummingbird. See also female Broad-tailed and Calliope Hummingbirds. **HABITAT:** Scrubby or brushy slopes, riparian areas, gardens, feeders.

CALLIOPE HUMMINGBIRD   *Selasphorus calliope*   Uncommon

3¼ in. (8 cm). The smallest hummer found in U.S. and Canada. *Adult male:* Throat with purple-red rays on white background, which may be folded like a dark inverted V. *Female and first-fall male:* Similar to female Broad-tailed and Rufous Hummingbirds (which have buffy sides, some rufous at base of tail), but Calliope has a *shorter wedge-shaped tail (wingtips extend beyond tail at rest)*, is slightly smaller and shorter billed; rust on sides paler, face pattern has dark and pale spots in front of eye, weak pale line over base of bill. **VOICE:** High-pitched chips and buzzes in series. **HABITAT:** Mountains and canyons, feeders; in migration, also foothills and occasionally lowlands.

HUMMINGBIRDS

adult male

BROAD-TAILED HUMMINGBIRD

RUFOUS HUMMINGBIRD

adult male

female

female

ALLEN'S HUMMINGBIRD

adult male

adult male

female

CALLIOPE HUMMINGBIRD

BROAD-BILLED HUMMINGBIRD

Uncommon, local

Cynanthus latirostris

4 in. (10 cm). *Adult male:* Dark green above and below, with *blue throat* (bird may look all black at a distance or in poor light). Bill *reddish* with black tip. Tail notched and *bluish black,* often flicked when hovering. *Female:* Identified by combination of *dull orange-red base to bill* (often restricted to lower mandible), *dark tail,* and *unmarked, pearly gray* throat; thin white line behind eye. *First-year male:* Femalelike as juvenile but mottled male coloration increases though year. **VOICE:** Distinctive rough, dry chattering, like that of Ruby-crowned Kinglet, diagnostic among hummingbirds in our area. **SIMILAR SPECIES:** White-eared Hummingbird. **HABITAT:** Desert canyons, mountain slopes, riparian woodlands, agaves, mesquite, feeders. Casual vagrant to CA coast.

WHITE-EARED HUMMINGBIRD *Hylocharis leucotis*

Rare, local

3¾ in. (10 cm). A rare but regular summer visitor to s. AZ mountains. *Adult male: Bill short, orangey red,* with black tip; *broad white stripe behind eye.* Underparts dark greenish, throat blue and green, crown purple. *Female:* Orangey red bill, bold white stripe behind eye. Note small *green spots* on throat. *First-year male:* Femalelike but gradually acquires blue-green in breast, purple crown. **VOICE:** Makes a variety of thin chips, sometimes in rapid series. **SIMILAR SPECIES:** Female Broad-billed Hummingbird often mistaken for rarer White-eared (reddish-based bill and pronounced white eye stripe), but note *vocal differences* and Broad-billed's slightly longer bill, slightly shorter white eyebrow, more forked tail, and evenly gray throat and underparts. **HABITAT:** Montane pine-oak woods near streams; feeders.

BLUE-THROATED MOUNTAIN-GEM

Uncommon, local

Lampornis clemenciae 5 in. (13 cm). Note large tail with *large white patches. Male:* A very large hummingbird, with black and white stripes about eye and *blue throat;* big black tail with large white patches at corners. First-year male has duller and more-restricted blue in throat. *Female:* Large, with *evenly gray* throat and underparts, white marks on face, and tail with *large white corners,* as in male. **VOICE:** Call a distinctive squeaking *seek.* **SIMILAR SPECIES:** Rivoli's Hummingbird, Plain-capped Starthroat. **HABITAT:** Near wooded streams in mountain canyons; feeders. Casual vagrant north of range.

RIVOLI'S HUMMINGBIRD *Eugenes fulgens*

Uncommon

5¼ in. (13 cm). Recently split from Magnificent Hummingbird. *Adult male:* A very large hummingbird with *blackish belly, bright green throat,* and *purple crown.* Can look all black at a distance. Sometimes the bird briefly glides on set wings. *Female:* Large; greenish above, washed with greenish or dusky below. First-year male is femalelike but mottled male coloration increases though year. **VOICE:** Call a thin, sharp *chip;* distinctive. **SIMILAR SPECIES:** Female distinguished from female Blue-throated Mountain-Gem by voice, more mottled underparts, short eye stripe, and tail with greenish and more obscure pale corners. **HABITAT:** Mountain glades, pine-oak woods, canyons, feeders. Rare vagrant north and east of range; accidental to CA.

HUMMINGBIRDS

BROAD-BILLED HUMMINGBIRD

adult male

female

WHITE-EARED HUMMINGBIRD

adult male

female

BLUE-THROATED MOUNTAIN-GEM

male

female

RIVOLI'S HUMMINGBIRD

adult male

female

MEXICAN VIOLETEAR *Colibri thalassinus*   Accidental vagrant

4¾ in. (12 cm). Recently split from Green Violetear. Stray from Mex., most records in summer from TX but records as far west as CA. A large, dark hummingbird. Sexes mostly similar. Green with violet ear patch, bluish tail. Bill long and slightly decurved. **VOICE:** Song and call a series of dry *chip*s. **SIMILAR SPECIES:** Broad-billed and Rivoli's Hummingbirds. **RANGE AND HABITAT:** Mountains, canyons; in U.S., often seen at feeders.

VIOLET-CROWNED HUMMINGBIRD *Amazilia violiceps*   Scarce, local

4½ in. (11 cm). A medium-sized hummer with *immaculate white underparts, including throat;* bill *red* with dark tip. Crown *violet-blue* in adult, *dull greenish blue* in first-year birds; sexes similar although adult males average brighter crowns. No iridescent gorget on male. **VOICE:** Aggressive call a series of squeaky notes. Call note *chak*. **SIMILAR SPECIES:** Costa's Hummingbird white below but smaller, bill without red. **HABITAT:** Riparian woodlands, lower canyons, sycamores, agaves, feeders. Accidental vagrant to CA.

BERYLLINE HUMMINGBIRD *Amazilia beryllina*   Rare

4¼ in. (11 cm). Mexican species; rare visitor and casual breeder in se. AZ. *Male: Glittering green* on underparts; *deep rich rufous in wings,* rump, and tail. Bill partly red. *Female:* Duller; throat and belly mottled gray. **VOICE:** All vocal sounds very scratchy and buzzy. **HABITAT:** Oak-clad mountain canyons; often at feeders.

LUCIFER HUMMINGBIRD *Calothorax lucifer*   Scarce, local

3½ in. (9 cm). A small hummingbird. Note pronounced *decurved bill. Adult male: Purple throat, rusty or buffy sides. No* purple on crown (as in Costa's Hummingbird); tail *deeply forked,* often folded. *Female: Decurved bill, underparts extensively buff,* rufous at base of outer tail feathers; older birds sometimes have purple in throat. First-year male is like female but tail shallowly forked, gradually acquires purple in throat. **VOICE:** Series of dry twitters. Male in courtship display makes "playing-card shuffle" sound. **SIMILAR SPECIES:** Black-chinned Hummingbird's long bill may also have slight curve. **HABITAT:** Arid slopes, agaves, feeders.

PLAIN-CAPPED STARTHROAT *Heliomaster constantii*   Scarce vagrant

5 in. (13 cm). Mexican species, casual visitor at lower elevations in s. AZ. Sexes similar. A large, *long-billed* hummer, adult with red throat, *white facial stripes, white rump. Juvenile:* Throat gray, gradually acquires red throat feathers through first year. Often hawks insects. **VOICE:** Variety of strong *chips* given singly or in series. **SIMILAR SPECIES:** Blue-throated, Rivoli's, and Anna's Hummingbirds. **HABITAT:** Creek beds, dry washes, often at feeders.

RARE OR LOCAL HUMMINGBIRDS

VIOLET-CROWNED HUMMINGBIRD

female

adult male

MEXICAN VIOLETEAR

male

adult male

tail may fold in a spikelike point

female

BERYLLINE HUMMINGBIRD

female

LUCIFER HUMMINGBIRD

PLAIN-CAPPED STARTHROAT

adult

PASSERINES Order Passeriformes

Passerines, also known as "perching birds" or "songbirds," comprise the rest of the species in this book. They are distinguished from other birds by having one toe back and three forward, ideal for perching.

TYRANT FLYCATCHERS Family Tyrannidae

New World Flycatchers, or Tyrant Flycatchers, make up the largest family of birds in the world, with approximately 425 known species. A large number are very similar and require attention to details to separate them. Most species perch quietly, sitting upright on exposed branches, from which they sally forth to snap up insects. Bill flattened, with bristles at base. Ages and sexes similar in most but not all species. **FOOD:** Mainly flying insects. Some species also eat fruit in winter. **RANGE:** New World; the vast majority in the Neotropics.

OLIVE-SIDED FLYCATCHER *Contopus cooperi* Uncommon

7½ in. (19 cm). A stout, large-headed flycatcher; often perches on dead snags at tops of trees. Note large bill and *dark chest patches* separated by narrow strip of white (like unbuttoned vest). A *cottony tuft* may poke from behind wing. **VOICE:** Call a two- or three-note *pip-pip-pip.* Song a spirited whistle, *I SAY there* or *Quick three beers!,* middle note highest, last one sliding. **SIMILAR SPECIES:** Wood-pewees, Greater Pewee. **HABITAT:** Coniferous forests, burns.

GREATER PEWEE *Contopus pertinax* Uncommon, local

7¾ in. (20 cm). Resembles Olive-sided Flycatcher, but more obvious crest, breast more uniformly gray with *no white stripe* down center. *Lower mandible brighter and more extensively orangey.* **VOICE:** Thin, plaintive whistle, *ho-say, ma-re-ah.* Call *pip-pip.* **SIMILAR SPECIES:** Olive-sided Flycatcher, Western Wood-Pewee. **HABITAT:** High in trees of pine and pine-oak forests of mountains, canyons. Casual winter vagrant to s. CA.

WESTERN WOOD-PEWEE *Contopus sordidulus* Fairly common

6¼ in. (16 cm). A dusky, medium-small flycatcher with two narrow wing bars but *no eye-ring.* Often appears "vested" below (with "top button buttoned"). Some fresh fall birds tinged yellow on belly. Black bill usually has small amount of pale at base of lower mandible. **VOICE:** Nasal *peeeer* (less commonly, *pee-yee*), more guttural (less clear) than in Eastern Wood-Pewee. **SIMILAR SPECIES:** Eastern Wood-Pewee. Olive-sided Flycatcher larger, more strongly "vested," different voice. Distinguished from *Empidonax* flycatchers by lack of any tail flicking, longer primaries, and calls; most *Empidonax* also have eye-rings. **HABITAT:** Pine-oak forests, open conifers, canyon and riparian woodlands. Prefers mid-canopy.

EASTERN WOOD-PEWEE *Contopus virens* Uncommon, local

6¼ in. (16 cm). Note *two narrow wing bars, no eye-ring,* and variably pale orangish lower mandible. *Slightly larger* than *Empidonax* flycatchers, but with no eye-ring; wings extend farther down tail; *does not flick tail.* Very similar to Western Wood-Pewee, but slightly greener or paler gray above and clearer below (vest "not buttoned"); best distinguished by voice, range. **VOICE:** Sweet plaintive whistle, *pee-a-wee,* slurring down then up (less commonly, *pee-ur*), and a *chip.* **SIMILAR SPECIES:** Western Wood-Pewee. Eastern Phoebe lacks wing bars; bobs tail downward. **HABITAT:** Woodlands, groves. Mid-canopy. Casual vagrant to W. Coast.

FLYCATCHERS

GREATER
PEWEE

OLIVE-SIDED
FLYCATCHER

EASTERN
WOOD-PEWEE

WESTERN
WOOD-PEWEE

EMPIDONAX FLYCATCHERS

Flycatchers of this genus share the characteristics of light eye-ring and two pale wing bars. Species are notoriously difficult to separate, especially cross-continental vagrants. When breeding, they can often be identified by habitat and manner of nesting, while songs and calls are also useful. For silent birds, including migrants, distinguishing physical characteristics are subtle and include size and shape of bill, color of lower mandible, shape and boldness of eye-ring, color of wings and wing-feather edging, pattern of underparts, primary (wingtip) projection, tail length, and direction of tail wag.

LEAST FLYCATCHER *Empidonax minimus*　　　　**Uncommon**

5¼ in. (13 cm). A small *Empidonax*, plumage variable but usually *grayish* above and *pale* below with *bold white eye-ring*, medium-short wingtip projection, and short, wide-based bill. Whitish wing bars on mostly blackish wing. First-fall birds (p. 246) fresher, greener and yellower. Actively flicks tail. **VOICE:** Song an emphatic, sharply snapped *che-bek!* Call a sharp, dry *whit.* **SIMILAR SPECIES:** Willow and Alder Flycatchers are browner above with bigger bill, longer wingtips, and weaker eye-ring. Hammond's and Dusky Flycatchers have darker throat and underparts, duller wings. Hammond's also has *thinner, darker bill,* more teardrop-shaped eye-ring, and longer wingtips. **HABITAT:** Mixed woodlands, poplars, aspens. Rare vagrant to W. Coast.

YELLOW-BELLIED FLYCATCHER *Empidonax flaviventris*　　**Uncommon**

5½ in. (14 cm). Back green, rounded yellowish eye-ring, dusky breast band, wings blackish with bold whitish edging. First-fall birds (p. 246) much yellower below, including chin and throat. **VOICE:** Song a simple, spiritless *chi-lek;* also a rising *chu-wee;* call an explosive *peeyup,* distinct among *Empidonax.* **SIMILAR SPECIES:** Cordilleran and Pacific-slope Flycatchers very similar but slightly browner, with peaked head; *teardrop-shaped eye-ring;* duller wings and wing-feather edging. See Acadian Flycatcher (p. 246). **HABITAT:** In summer, boreal forests, muskeg. Casual vagrant to W. Coast.

WILLOW FLYCATCHER *Empidonax traillii*　　　　**Uncommon**

5¾ in. (15 cm). Alder and Willow Flycatchers are nearly identical in appearance, a bit larger, longer billed, and often browner than Least Flycatcher. They may be separated from each other mainly by voice and breeding habitat. Willow averages paler and browner (less olive) and has grayer head than Alder, has a slightly weaker or no eye-ring, and duller wing-feather edging on average. First-fall birds (p. 246) fresher, greener. **VOICE:** Song a sneezy *fitz-bew,* unlike the *fee-BE-o* of Alder. Call a soft *whit.* **HABITAT:** Bushes, willow thickets, mountain meadows, etc. Subspecies of Southwest (*estimus*) endangered.

ALDER FLYCATCHER *Empidonax alnorum*　　　　**Fairly common**

5¾ in. (15 cm). The northern counterpart of Willow Flycatcher, with which it was formerly lumped as "Traill's Flycatcher." Greener, smaller-billed, and with brighter wing-feather edging than Willow but best distinguished by voice and range. **VOICE:** Song an accented *fee-BE-o* or *rree-BE-o.* Call *kep* or *pit,* sharper than in Willow. **HABITAT:** Willows, alders, brushy swamps, swales. Casual vagrant to W. Coast.

Adults on Breeding Grounds

EMPIDONAX FLYCATCHERS

— — — *che-BEK* or *chebek*

Empidonax flycatchers are often best identified by voice. Breeding habitat is also a helpful clue.

chi-lek

farms, orchards, groves, open woods; n. U.S. and Canada

LEAST FLYCATCHER

grayest of eastern species

coniferous woods, bogs; Canada, n. edge of U.S.

YELLOW-BELLIED FLYCATCHER

throat and breast washed with yellow

WESTERN WOOD-PEWEE

comparison of pewee and Empidonax flycatcher

WILLOW FLYCATCHER

fitz-bew

fee-bee'-o

wet and dry thickets, brushy pastures, old orchards, willows; mostly in U.S.

WILLOW FLYCATCHER

alder swamps, wet thickets, usually near water; n. U.S., Canada

ALDER FLYCATCHER

BUFF-BREASTED FLYCATCHER *Empidonax fulvifrons*   Scarce, local

5 in. (13 cm). Distinguished from the other *Empidonax* by its small size and *rich buffy breast*. **VOICE:** Accented *chee-lik*. Call a dry *pit* or *whit*. **SIMILAR SPECIES:** Northern Beardless-Tyrannulet. **HABITAT:** High-elevation canyons, open pine forests. Accidental vagrant to CA.

PACIFIC-SLOPE FLYCATCHER *Empidonax difficilis*   Common

5½ in. (14 cm). This and Cordilleran formerly considered conspecific, as "Western Flycatcher." Voice and range are only identification clues. Pacific-slope Flycatcher slightly less colorful than Cordilleran but much overlap. Note greenish to olive upperparts and *yellowish* underparts, *including throat*. Eye-ring of Pacific-slope and Cordilleran is *teardrop-shaped and broken above*. First-fall birds duller olive above, dingier below. **VOICE:** Song of both species a thin, squeaky *pit-PEET SWEEE;* variable. Call a thin upslurred *tsueet*. **SIMILAR SPECIES:** Cordilleran and Yellow-bellied Flycatchers. See Acadian Flycatcher (p. 246). **HABITAT:** Riparian, mixed, or coniferous woodlands.

CORDILLERAN FLYCATCHER *Empidonax occidentalis*   Uncommon

5½ in. (14 cm). Separated from Pacific-slope Flycatcher only by range and voice. **VOICE:** Song similar to that of Pacific-slope but call on breeding ground differs, a two-noted *soo-seet*. **SIMILAR SPECIES:** Pacific-slope and Yellow-bellied Flycatchers. **HABITAT:** Riparian, mixed, or coniferous woodlands; shaded canyons, often with rock walls.

HAMMOND'S FLYCATCHER *Empidonax hammondii*   Fairly common

5½ in. (14 cm). Both Hammond's and Dusky Flycatchers breed in coniferous and mixed woods, with Hammond's preferring a more closed canopy. Hammond's has more *teardrop-shaped eye-ring; shorter and thinner bill* (almost kingletlike); is more prone to flick wings; has slightly shorter tail and longer wings. Molts *before* migrating, after which both age groups (see p. 246) more greenish above and yellowish below with grayer throat. **VOICE:** Similar to that of Dusky Flycatcher but lower pitched. Also, abrupt *tse-beek*; in migration, a sharp, thin *peep* or *peek*. **SIMILAR SPECIES:** Dusky Flycatcher. Least Flycatcher has blacker wings with brighter edging, wider and thicker bill, shorter wingtips, and lacks pale edges to tail. **HABITAT:** Woodlands (see above); in migration, also riparian thickets.

DUSKY FLYCATCHER *Empidonax oberholseri*   Uncommon

5¾ in. (15 cm). Very similar to Hammond's Flycatcher; see that account for differences. First-fall birds (p. 246) fresher, greener and yellower. **VOICE:** Three-part song ends in a high *preet*. Call a dry *whit*. **SIMILAR SPECIES:** Least, Hammond's, and Gray Flycatchers. **HABITAT:** Breeds in open pine forests, montane chaparral with scattering of trees, brushy meadow and stream edges.

GRAY FLYCATCHER *Empidonax wrightii*   Uncommon

6 in. (15 cm). Similar to Dusky and Hammond's Flycatchers, but in spring and summer paler and grayer overall; bill larger, and lower mandible mostly pinkish with a distinct black tip. In fall and early winter (see p. 246), trace of yellow below, olive above, more similar to Dusky Flycatcher. Has habit of *first wagging tail downward* (all other *Empidonax* flick tail upward); *best noted immediately after bird lands*. **VOICE:** Two-syllable *chewip* or *cheh-we*. Call a dry *whit*. **SIMILAR SPECIES:** Other western *Empidonax*. **HABITAT:** Dry pine forests with sagebrush, pinyon-juniper; in winter, willows, mesquite. Often drops to ground to grab prey.

Adults on Breeding Grounds

WESTERN *EMPIDONAX* FLYCATCHERS

Empidonax flycatchers are often best identified by voice. Breeding habitat is also a helpful clue.

PACIFIC-SLOPE FLYCATCHER and CORDILLERAN FLYCATCHER

moist woods, groves, shady canyons; generally not separable except by breeding range

pit-PEET *swEEE*

PIT-ik

BUFF-BREASTED FLYCATCHER

oak-pine canyons; AZ, NM

heeLIK *CHEWW*

zvREET

RI-drt *PRRDT*

chVREE

SEE-pik

HAMMOND'S FLYCATCHER

closed-canopy coniferous forests

chwEEP *CHI-wik*

DUSKY FLYCATCHER

montane chaparral, open coniferous woodlands

GRAY FLYCATCHER

sagebrush, pinyon-juniper

FIRST-FALL *EMPIDONAX* FLYCATCHERS

First-fall *Empidonax* flycatchers differ in appearance from worn breeding adults, averaging brighter. Vagrants of most species can occur across N. America, making identification of first-fall migrants challenging.

ACADIAN FLYCATCHER   Accidental vagrant in West
Empidonax virescens (adult not shown)
5¾ in. (15 cm). Note long wings and tail. Chin and throat white and wings bolder vs. "Western" Flycatchers.

YELLOW-BELLIED FLYCATCHER   Casual vagrant in West
Empidonax flaviventris (see also p. 242)
5½ in. (14 cm). Separate from "Western" Flycatchers by brighter green back; wings brighter edging; eye-ring rounded behind eye, usually yellowish; olive-streaked breast-band usually present.

"WESTERN" FLYCATCHERS   Common in West
Empidonax difficilis/occidentalis (adult not shown)
5½ in. (14 cm). Back dull olive, wings brownish with dull edging, eye-ring almond shaped, breast usually lacks banded effect.

ALDER FLYCATCHER   Casual vagrant in West
Empidonax alnorum (see also p. 242)
5¾ in. (15 cm). Greener (less olive, grayish, or brownish) than in western Willow Flycatchers; wing-feather edging brighter; bill smaller.

WILLOW FLYCATCHER   Uncommon in West
Empidonax traillii (see also p. 242)
5¾ in. (15 cm). See Alder Flycatcher. Eastern Willows (subspecies *traillii* and *campestris*, casual vagrants to West) are greener and can be more difficult to separate; head often grayer, wing edging duller.

LEAST FLYCATCHER   Rare vagrant in West
Empidonax minimus (see also p. 242)
First-fall birds variable, generally grayish, sometimes tinged olive above, and washed lemon below. Bill triangular, broad based, and wings blackish with bold lemon edging; outer edges of tail not whitish. Wing-tip projection intermediate but not as long as in Hammond's.

GRAY FLYCATCHER   Uncommon in West
Empidonax wrightii (see also p. 244)
Plumage pale grayish, although note first-fall birds can be tinged olive above and yellow below. Bill long, straight, pinkish-yellow with distinct black tip from below; outer edges of tail white. Wags tail downward.

DUSKY FLYCATCHER   Uncommon in West
Empidonax oberholseri (see also p. 244)
Grayish, washed olive when fresh; underparts tinged yellow; outer edges of tail pale to whitish. Bill long and thin, dark below; lores often pale. Wing projection shortish, wings duller and tail longer than in Least.

HAMMOND'S FLYCATCHER   Fairly common in West
Empidonax hammondii (see also p. 244)
Bill very small, almost warblerlike; thinner than in Least. Wing projection long. Grayish to bright greenish above and yellow below. Outer edges of tail whitish; wings duller than in Least.

FIRST-FALL *EMPIDONAX* FLYCATCHERS

ACADIAN FLYCATCHER

YELLOW-BELLIED FLYCATCHER

"WESTERN" FLYCATCHER

ALDER FLYCATCHER

WILLOW FLYCATCHER

LEAST FLYCATCHER

GRAY FLYCATCHER

DUSKY FLYCATCHER

HAMMOND'S FLYCATCHER

MISCELLANEOUS FLYCATCHERS

BLACK PHOEBE *Sayornis nigricans* Common
6¾–7 in. (17–18 cm). Our only *black-breasted* flycatcher; belly white. Has typical phoebe tail-bobbing habit. *Juvenile:* Wing bars cinnamon-buff. **VOICE:** Thin, strident *fi-bee, fi-bee,* rising then dropping; also a sharp slurred *chip.* **SIMILAR SPECIES:** Eastern Phoebe, juncos (which are ground-loving birds and show very different behaviors). **HABITAT:** Streams, walled canyons, farmyards, towns, parks; usually near water. Vagrant well north of range.

EASTERN PHOEBE *Sayornis phoebe* Scarce
7 in. (18 cm). Note *downward tail-bobbing.* A grayish, medium-sized flycatcher *without eye-ring or strong wing bars* (thin buff wing bars on juvenile); small, *all-dark bill* and dark head; yellowish belly in fall. **VOICE:** Song a well-enunciated *phoe-be* or *fi-bree* (second note alternately higher or lower). Call a sharp *chip.* **SIMILAR SPECIES:** Western Wood-Pewee and smaller *Empidonax* flycatchers have conspicuous wing bars; bills partly yellowish or horn colored on lower mandible. All *Empidonax* except Gray Flycatcher flick tail *upward.* **HABITAT:** Streamsides, bridges, farms, roadsides, towns. Rare vagrant in fall and winter to W. Coast.

SAY'S PHOEBE *Sayornis saya* Fairly common
7½ in. (19 cm). A midsized, pale brownish flycatcher with contrasty black tail and *orange-buff belly.* Sits in open, often on low fence-lines or on rocks in dry open fields. **VOICE:** Plaintive, down-slurred *pweer* or *pee-ee.* **SIMILAR SPECIES:** Ash-throated and Dusky-capped Flycatchers, Eastern Phoebe. **HABITAT:** Open country, dry scrub, canyons, ranches.

NORTHERN BEARDLESS-TYRANNULET Uncommon, local
Camptostoma imberbe
4¼ in. (11 cm). A very small, nondescript flycatcher that may suggest a kinglet, Bell's Vireo, or juvenile Verdin. Grayish olive, with *slight crested* look. *Dull wing bars* and indistinct pale supercilium. Smaller and smaller-headed than *Empidonax* flycatchers, with stubbier bill and different voice. **VOICE:** Thin *peeee-yuk.* A gentle, descending *ee, ee, ee, ee, ee.* **SIMILAR SPECIES:** Buff-breasted and other *Empidonax* flycatchers. **HABITAT:** Lowland woods, mesquite, stream thickets, lower canyons. Builds a globular nest with entrance on side.

BLACK
PHOEBE

EASTERN
PHOEBE

SAY'S PHOEBE

NORTHERN
BEARDLESS-
TYRANNULET

MYIARCHUS and SIMILAR FLYCATCHERS

BROWN-CRESTED FLYCATCHER *Myiarchus tyrannulus* Uncommon

8¾ in. (22 cm). A kingbird-sized flycatcher. Similar to Ash-throated Fly-catcher, but larger, with noticeably larger bill. Underparts brighter yellow. Tail rusty, a bit less so than in Ash-throated. Voice important. **VOICE:** Sharp *whit* and rolling, throaty *purreeer.* Voice much more vigorous and raucous than Ash-throated's. **SIMILAR SPECIES:** Great Crested Fly-catcher. **HABITAT:** Sycamore-dominated canyons, cottonwood groves, saguaros.

GREAT CRESTED FLYCATCHER *Myiarchus crinitus* Uncommon, local

8½–8¾ in. (21–22 cm). Similar to western *Myiarchus* but note cinnamon wings and tail, dark olive back, *mouse gray breast,* bright yellow belly, *strongly contrasting tertial pattern* and pink-based bill. **VOICE:** Loud whistled *wheeep!* Also a rolling *prrrrreet!* **SIMILAR SPECIES:** Brown-crested and Ash-throated Flycatchers have dark lower mandibles, paler gray breasts, paler yellow bellies, and duller wings with less contrasting tertials. Vocal differences important. **HABITAT:** Woodlands, groves. Very rare vagrant to W. Coast.

DUSKY-CAPPED FLYCATCHER Uncommon, local
Myiarchus tuberculifer

7 in. (18 cm). Similar to Ash-throated Flycatcher, but slightly smaller overall with proportionately larger bill; cap and throat darker, belly brighter yellow, and *almost no rusty* in tail. Voice distinctive. **VOICE:** Distinctive, mournful, down-slurred whistle, *pweeeur.* **HABITAT:** Pine-oak and deciduous canyons. Very rare vagrant in winter north along Pacific Coast.

ASH-THROATED FLYCATCHER *Myiarchus cinerascens* Fairly common

8–8¼ in. (20–21 cm). Except for prairie and desert Southwest border areas, this is normally the only flycatcher in West with rusty tail. Smaller than a kingbird, grayish brown above with two pale wing bars, *whitish* throat, *pale* gray breast, *pale yellowish belly,* and *rufous tail.* Head slightly bushy. **VOICE:** *Prrt* (likened to a police whistle); also a rolling *chi-queer* or *prit-wheer.* **SIMILAR SPECIES:** Great Crested, Brown-crested, and Dusky-capped Flycatchers; Say's Phoebe. **HABITAT:** Semiarid country, deserts, brush, mesquite, pinyon-juniper, chaparral, open woods.

SULPHUR-BELLIED FLYCATCHER Uncommon, local
Myiodynastes luteiventris

8½ in. (22 cm). A large flycatcher with *bright rufous tail* and dark patch through eye; underparts *pale yellowish, with black streaks.* No other U.S. flycatcher is streaked *above and below.* **VOICE:** High, penetrating *kee-ZEE ick! kee-ZEE ick!* (like squeezing a bathroom rubber duckie). **HABITAT:** Midelevation canyons, often with sycamores. Accidental vagrant north of range.

BROWN-CRESTED
FLYCATCHER

MYIARCHUS
FLYCATCHERS
Most Have Extensively
Rusty Tails

GREAT
CRESTED
FLYCATCHER

DUSKY-CAPPED
FLYCATCHER

ASH-THROATED
FLYCATCHER

SULPHUR-BELLIED
FLYCATCHER

KINGBIRDS

WESTERN KINGBIRD *Tyrannus verticalis*   Common

8¾ in. (22 cm). The most widespread kingbird in West. Note *pale gray head and breast,* white throat, *yellowish belly,* smaller bill. Western's *black tail* has *narrow white edges.* **VOICE:** Shrill, bickering calls; a sharp *kip* or *whit-ker-whit;* dawn song *pit-PEE-tu-whee.* **SIMILAR SPECIES:** Cassin's and Tropical Kingbirds. **HABITAT:** Farms, shelterbelts, semiopen country, roadsides, fences, wires.

EASTERN KINGBIRD *Tyrannus tyrannus*   Common

8½ in. (22 cm). Lack of yellow underparts and the *white band* across tail tip marks Eastern Kingbird. Red crown mark is concealed and rarely seen. Often seems to fly quiveringly on tips of wings. Harasses crows, hawks. **VOICE:** Rapid sputter of high, bickering electric-shock notes: *dzee-dzee-dzee,* etc., and *kit-kit-kitter-kitter,* etc. Also a nasal *dzeep.* **SIMILAR SPECIES:** Thick-billed Kingbird. **HABITAT:** River groves, farms, roadsides, fences, wires. Rare vagrant to W. Coast.

CASSIN'S KINGBIRD   Uncommon to fairly common
Tyrannus vociferans

9 in. (23 cm). Like Western Kingbird, but *darker head and chest contrast with whitish chin and upper throat,* darker olive-gray back; *no distinct white sides* on dark brown (not truly black) tail, which may be *lightly tipped with gray-buff.* Wing coverts often edged pale gray. **VOICE:** Low, nasal *queer, chi-queer,* or *chi-beer;* also an excited *ki-ki-ki-dear, ki-dear, ki-dear.* **SIMILAR SPECIES:** Worn Western Kingbirds may lack white sides on tail, but head, breast, and back *paler, lack contrasty pale chin* and pale edges to wing coverts, and have *different call.* In much of interior, Cassin's prefers higher elevations. **HABITAT:** Semiopen country, pine-oak mountains, pinyon-juniper; in winter, ranch groves, eucalyptus, olive orchards.

THICK-BILLED KINGBIRD *Tyrannus crassirostris*   Scarce, local

9½ in. (24 cm). A large kingbird with *oversized bill;* differs from similar kingbirds in having extensive *dark cap.* Entirely dark tail. *Adult:* Upperparts *brownish,* underparts *whitish* with pale yellow wash on belly. *Fall adult and first-fall:* May be washed quite yellow below, first-fall with cinnamon wing-feather edging. **VOICE:** Quick, shrill *brrr-zee* or *kut'r-eet.* **SIMILAR SPECIES:** Eastern Kingbird. Bright, fresh fall birds are larger billed, darker headed than Tropical Kingbird. **HABITAT:** Riverbed woodlands, particularly sycamores. Casual winter vagrant to s. CA.

TROPICAL KINGBIRD *Tyrannus melancholicus*   Uncommon, local

9¼ in. (23 cm). Similar to Western and Cassin's Kingbirds, but note *larger and longer bill ,* notched and *brownish* tail; bright yellow on underparts *includes breast.* **VOICE:** Repeated twittery *kip-kip-kip* calls. **SIMILAR SPECIES:** Couch's Kingbird (*T. couchii*) of s. TX and accidental vagrant to West, very similar but bill smaller, calls a nasal *queer* or *beeer.* **HABITAT:** Groves along streams and ponds, open areas with scattered trees, phone wires. Scarce fall vagrant well north along Pacific Coast; accidental elsewhere in West.

KINGBIRDS

EASTERN
KINGBIRD

WESTERN
KINGBIRD

CASSIN'S
KINGBIRD

THICK-
BILLED
KINGBIRD

fall

TROPICAL KINGBIRD

Couch's
Kingbird for
comparison

Tropical

More TYRANT FLYCATCHERS and BECARD

FORK-TAILED FLYCATCHER *Tyrannus savana*   Accidental vagrant

14½–16 in. (37–41 cm). Vagrant from Tropics. Told from Scissor-tailed Flycatcher by *black cap*, white flanks and underwing. Black tail not rigid in flight. *First-year:* Much shorter tail; might be confused with Eastern Kingbird but note paler gray back. **VOICE:** Mechanical-sounding *tik-tik-tik.* **SIMILAR SPECIES:** Scissor-tailed Flycatcher. **RANGE:** Normal range from Mex. to S. America. Vagrant to U.S. and Canada; records widespread, predominantly from the Plains eastward during summer through fall, but also occurring accidentally to W. Coast. **HABITAT:** Open fields, pastures with scattered trees, wires.

SCISSOR-TAILED FLYCATCHER *Tyrannus forficatus*   Uncommon

13–15 in. (33–38 cm). A beautiful bird, pale pearly gray, adult male with *extremely long, scissorlike tail* that is usually folded. Flanks orange-buff, underwing linings salmon pink. *Female and first-year male:* Shorter tail and duller sides may suggest Western Kingbird. Hybrids are known. **VOICE:** Harsh *keck* or *kew;* a repeated *ka-leep;* also shrill, kingbirdlike bickerings and stutterings. **SIMILAR SPECIES:** Western Kingbird, Fork-tailed Flycatcher. **HABITAT:** Semiopen country, ranches, farms, roadsides, fences, wires. Widespread vagrant north and west of range, casually to W. Coast.

ROSE-THROATED BECARD *Pachyramphus aglaiae*   Rare, local

7¼ in. (18 cm). Big-headed and thick-billed. *Adult male:* Dark gray above, pale to dusky below, with *blackish cap and cheeks* and lovely *rose-colored throat* (lacking or reduced in some males). *Female:* Brown above, with *dark cap* and *light buffy collar* around nape. Underparts strong buff. *First-year male*: Like female but with rose feathers in throat, grayish feathers in back. **VOICE:** Thin, slurred whistle, *seeoo.* **SIMILAR SPECIES:** Kingbirds, Say's Phoebe. **HABITAT:** Riparian woodlands, particularly cottonwoods and sycamores.

VERMILION FLYCATCHER *Pyrocephalus rubinus*   Uncommon

6 in. (15 cm). *Adult male:* Crown (often raised in slight bushy crest) and underparts *flaming vermilion;* upperparts brown and tail blackish. *First-year male:* Femalelike but lower belly washed pinkish, variably gains red mottling throughout body feathering during first year. *Female:* Breast whitish, narrowly streaked; belly washed with pinkish to salmon (adult) or pale lemon (first-year). **VOICE:** *P-p-pit-zee* or *pit-a-zee.* **SIMILAR SPECIES:** Female told from Say's Phoebe by shorter tail, pale supercilium, dusky streaks on breast. **HABITAT:** Moist areas in arid country, such as streams, ponds, pastures, golf courses, ranches. Casual year-round vagrant well north of range.

FLYCATCHERS

**FORK-TAILED
FLYCATCHER**

adult

**SCISSOR-TAILED
FLYCATCHER**

adult
male

first-year
female

adult

female

**ROSE-THROATED
BECARD**

adult
male

first-year
male

first-year
female

adult female

adult
male

**VERMILION
FLYCATCHER**

SWALLOWS and MARTINS Family Hirundinidae

Slim, streamlined form and graceful flight characterize swallows and martins. Pointed wings; short bill with very wide gape; tiny feet. **FOOD:** Mostly flying insects. **RANGE:** Worldwide except for polar regions, remote islands.

TREE SWALLOW *Tachycineta bicolor*　　　　　Common

5¾ in. (15 cm). *Adult:* Male *steely blue,* tinged green above; *white below.* Female varies from slightly duller than male to largely brown. *Juvenile:* Dusky gray-brown back and smudgy band across breast. Tree Swallows have distinctly notched tail; glides followed by quick flaps and short climbs. **VOICE:** Rich *cheet* or *chi-veet;* a liquid twitter, *weet, trit, weet,* etc. **SIMILAR SPECIES:** Violet-green Swallow smaller, paler above eye, obvious white patches on sides of rump, male green and purple above. Northern Rough-winged Swallow has dingier throat, different flight style, and Bank Swallow smaller, browner and has bolder dark breast-band than juvenile Tree. All N. American swallows also have different calls. **HABITAT:** Open country near water, marshes, meadows, lakes. Nests in holes, in trees, and birdhouses.

BANK SWALLOW *Riparia riparia*　　　　Uncommon to fairly common

5 in. (12 cm). *Our smallest* swallow. *Brown-backed with slightly darker wings and paler rump.* Note distinct *dark breast-band* in all plumages. White of throat *curls up behind ear. Wingbeats rapid and shallow.* Ages and sexes similar. **VOICE:** Dry, trilled chitter or rattle, *brrt* or *trr-tri-tri.* **SIMILAR SPECIES:** Northern Rough-winged Swallow and juvenile Tree Swallow. Bank's smaller size stands out in mixed flock. **HABITAT:** Near water; marshes, lakes, coasts. Nests colonially in sandbanks.

NORTHERN ROUGH-WINGED SWALLOW　　　　Fairly common
Stelgidopteryx serripennis

5¼ in. (12 cm). *Adult:* Brown-backed and rumped; *throat and upper breast brownish to dusky;* no breast-band. Flight more languid; wings pulled back at end of stroke. Juvenile has cinnamon-rusty wing bars. **VOICE:** Call a low, liquid *trrit,* lower and less grating than Bank Swallow's. **SIMILAR SPECIES:** Plainer than Bank Swallow and juvenile Tree Swallow. **HABITAT:** Near lakes, rivers, coasts. Nests in banks, pipes, and crevices, but not colonially as Bank Swallow does.

VIOLET-GREEN SWALLOW *Tachycineta thalassina*　　Fairly common

5¼ in. (13 cm). Note *white patches that almost meet* over base of tail. *Adult male:* Dark and shiny above; glossed with beautiful *green on back and purple on rump and uppertail;* clear white below. *White of face partially encircles eye.* Female and first-winter male are duller above, white above eye tinged grayish or brownish; juveniles are brown above, with little or no green. **VOICE:** A twitter; a thin *ch-lip* or *chew-chit;* rapid *chit-chit-chit wheet, wheet.* **SIMILAR SPECIES:** Tree Swallow lacks white patches on sides of rump or pale feathering above eye, has bluer back, slightly larger size and longer wings. See also White-throated Swift. **HABITAT:** Widespread but more often in mountains than other swallows. Nests in holes in trees, sometimes in birdhouses, in open coniferous woods, canyons, towns.

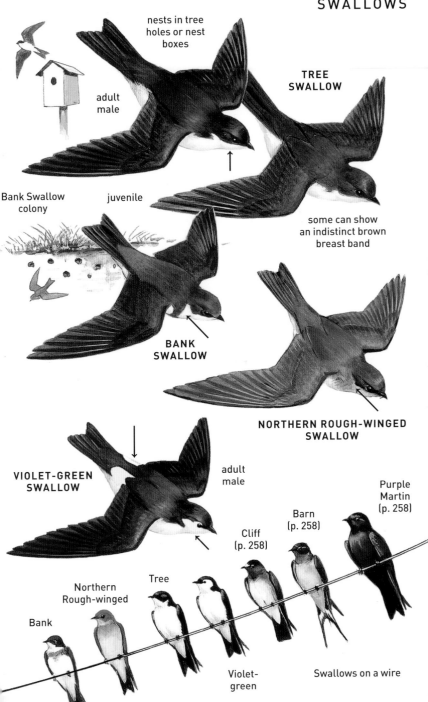

SWALLOWS

nests in tree
holes or nest
boxes

adult
male

**TREE
SWALLOW**

some can show
an indistinct brown
breast band

Bank Swallow
colony

juvenile

**BANK
SWALLOW**

**NORTHERN ROUGH-WINGED
SWALLOW**

**VIOLET-GREEN
SWALLOW**

adult
male

Purple
Martin
(p. 258)

Barn
(p. 258)

Cliff
(p. 258)

Northern
Rough-winged

Tree

Bank

Violet-
green

Swallows on a wire

PURPLE MARTIN *Progne subis* Uncommon, local

8 in. (20 cm). The largest N. American swallow. *Adult male:* Uniformly blue-black *above and below. Female and first-fall male:* Light-bellied; throat and breast grayish, often with faint gray collar; first-spring male mottled dark. **VOICE:** Throaty and rich *tchew-wew*, etc., or *pew, pew*. Song gurgling, ending in a succession of rich, low guttural notes. **SIMILAR SPECIES:** Tree and other swallows much smaller than female Purple Martin, cleaner white below. **HABITAT:** Towns, farms, open or semiopen country, often near water. Nests in cavities in trees (such as sycamores and ponderosa pines), posts, and, in s. AZ, saguaros; rarely martin houses as in East.

CAVE SWALLOW *Petrochelidon fulva* Uncommon

5½ in. (14 cm). *Adult:* Similar to Cliff Swallow (rusty rump, square-cut tail), but face colors reversed: *throat and cheeks buffy* (not dark), forehead *dark chestnut* (not pale, although Cliff Swallows in Southwest have chestnut forehead). *Buff color sets off dark mask and cap.* Juvenile is brown overall, including *pale brown to whitish throat* and breast. **VOICE:** Clear, sweet *weet* or *cheweet;* a loud, accented *chu, chu.* **SIMILAR SPECIES:** Cliff Swallow. **HABITAT:** Open country. Cuplike nest placed in caves, culverts, and under bridges; nests colonially. Casual to accidental vagrant to s. CA.

CLIFF SWALLOW *Petrochelidon pyrrhonota* Common

5½ in. (14 cm). *Adult:* Note *rusty, orange,* or *buffy rump,* steely blue upperparts, pale hind collar. From below, appears square-tailed, with red face and dark throat patch. Birds of se. AZ to sw. TX (subspecies *swainsoni*) have cinnamon to rufous foreheads, more like Cave Swallow. Juvenile is dusky above with muted head pattern; breast buff; *throat mixed with some dark.* **VOICE:** *Zayrp;* a low *chur.* Alarm call *keer!* Song consists of creaking notes and guttural gratings. **SIMILAR SPECIES:** Barn and Cave Swallows. **HABITAT:** Open to semiopen land, farms, cliffs, lakes, where it breeds colonially in mud-jug or gourdlike nests under eaves and bridges.

BARN SWALLOW *Hirundo rustica* Common

6¾ in. (17 cm). Our only swallow that is truly *swallow-tailed;* also the only one with *white tail spots. Adult:* Blue-black above; cinnamon-buff below, with darker throat; male brighter and longer-tailed than female. *Juvenile and first-fall:* Duller overall and paler, more whitish below. Flight direct, close to ground; wingtips pulled back at end of stroke; not much gliding. **VOICE:** Soft *vit* or *kvik-kvik, vit-vit.* Also *szee-szah* or *szee.* Anxiety call a harsh, irritated *ee-tee* or *keet.* Song a musical twitter interspersed with guttural notes. **SIMILAR SPECIES:** Other N. American swallows have notched (not deeply forked) tail. **HABITAT:** Open or semiopen land; farms, fields, marshes, lakes; often perches on wires; usually near habitation. Builds *cuplike nest inside* barns or under eaves, not in tight colonies like Cliff Swallow.

SWALLOWS

martin house

adult male

PURPLE
MARTIN

female and
first-year
male

CAVE
SWALLOW

adult

adult

CLIFF
SWALLOW

juglike nests under eaves
or on cliffs; colonial

Southwest

nests on
beams
inside
barns

adult male

female

BARN
SWALLOW

LEAF WARBLERS Family Phylloscopidae

Large family of similar, small green birds resembling some wood-warblers in size, habits, and habitats. Have short outer primaries. **RANGE:** Eurasia and Africa; one species breeds in Alaska.

DUSKY WARBLER *Phylloscopus fuscatus* Very rare vagrant

5¼ in. (13 cm). A small, plain Old World warbler; *brown above, no wing bars.* Whitish below, with *buffy eyebrow,* flanks, and undertail coverts. **VOICE:** Call a hard *tik* or *tik-tik.* **SIMILAR SPECIES:** Arctic Warbler. **RANGE:** Asian species; vagrant to AK and CA. **HABITAT:** Thick scrub.

ARCTIC WARBLER *Phylloscopus borealis* Uncommon, local

5 in. (13 cm). A small, greenish, Old World warbler. Dull greenish above, whitish below; light eyebrow; *narrow whitish wing bar* and sometimes short upper bar. Fresh birds in fall are brighter green above, yellowish below. Sexes similar. **VOICE:** Song a monotonous series of buzzy notes; call a buzzy *tsik* or *dzrit.* **SIMILAR SPECIES:** Orange-crowned and Tennessee Warblers have different bill shapes, lack prominent wing bars and short outer primary, have different calls. Recently split Kamchatka Leaf-Warbler (*P. examinandus*), a casual vagrant to AK and possibly nw. Canada and CA, averages slightly greener by age and a slightly longer outer primary; perhaps best identified by call notes, a drier and faster *trrt* or *trr-trrt.* **HABITAT:** Willow and alder scrub. Artic Warbler possibly an accidental vagrant to nw. Canada, CA.

OLD WORLD FLYCATCHERS Family Muscicapidae

Large and varied, primarily Old World family. Delicate sparrow-sized birds, often flicking wings and wagging tails near ground level. **FOOD:** Insects, fruit. **RANGE:** Eurasia and Africa; two species breed in Arctic N. America.

BLUETHROAT *Cyanecula svecica* Scarce, local

5½ in. (14 cm). A small, sprightly bird; often cocks tail which, when slightly spread, shows *chestnut base.* Distinct pale supercilium. *Male: Blue throat* (mottled buff in fall/winter plumage) with *reddish patches.* *Female:* Whitish throat with *dark necklace.* **VOICE:** Call a sharp *tac* and soft *wheet;* cricketlike notes. Song of repetitious notes, musical and varied. **SIMILAR SPECIES:** Siberian Rubythroat. **HABITAT:** Dwarf willows and alders, thick brush. Accidental vagrant to CA.

SIBERIAN RUBYTHROAT *Calliope calliope* Casual vagrant

6 in. (15 cm). Brown above; white eyebrow and whiskers. *Male: Ruby red throat,* gray breast. *Female:* White throat, light brown sides. **VOICE:** Series of chattering notes. Call a sharp *chak.* **SIMILAR SPECIES:** Bluethroat. **RANGE:** Asian species; casual vagrant to w. AK.

NORTHERN WHEATEAR *Oenanthe oenanthe* Uncommon, local

5¾ in. (15 cm). A small, dapper bird of Arctic barrens, particularly rocky areas and roadsides, fanning its tail and bobbing. Note *white rump and sides of tail.* Black on tail forms *broad inverted T. Spring/summer male:* Pale gray back, black wings, and *black ear patch. Female and fall/winter male:* Variably buffier, with brown back, reduced black in face. **VOICE:** Call a hard *chak-chak* or *chack-weet, weet-chack.* **HABITAT:** Open, stony areas; in summer, rocky tundra. Casual vagrant to CA.

ALASKA AND ARCTIC NESTERS AND VAGRANTS

DUSKY WARBLER

ARCTIC WARBLER

adult male

female

BLUETHROAT

female

male

SIBERIAN RUBYTHROAT

fall/winter

spring/ summer male

NORTHERN WHEATEAR

ACCENTORS Family Prunellidae

Eurasian family, thrushlike but more closely related to pipits; bills warblerlike. One vagrant species in N. America. **FOOD:** Insects, seeds. **RANGE:** Palearctic.

SIBERIAN ACCENTOR *Prunella montanella*   Very rare vagrant

5½ in. (14 cm). *Dark cheeks; bright ocher-buff eyebrow; bright ocher-buff throat and underparts;* plum brown upperparts. **VOICE:** Call a thin, high-pitched *sree* given in series. **RANGE:** Very rare fall visitor to w. AK islands; accidental elsewhere in nw. Canada and the U.S., often in winter at feeders. **HABITAT:** Thickets, feeders.

THRUSHES Family Turdidae

Large-eyed, slender-billed, usually strong-legged songbirds. Thrushes are often fine singers, making up for their generally drab plumages. **FOOD:** Insects, worms, snails, berries, fruit. **RANGE:** Nearly worldwide.

EASTERN BLUEBIRD *Sialia sialis*   Uncommon, local

7 in. (18 cm). Similar to Western Bluebird but slightly paler blue, *throat reddish,* lower underparts whiter. *Juvenile:* Grayish with some telltale blue in wings and tail; *back and breast speckled.* **VOICE:** Call a musical *chur-wi.* Song three or four gurgling notes. **SIMILAR SPECIES:** Western Bluebird. Fresh female Mountain Bluebirds have whitish flanks, longer wings. **HABITAT:** Open country with scattered trees; farms, roadsides. Bluebirds often nest in boxes.

WESTERN BLUEBIRD *Sialia mexicana*   Fairly common

7 in. (18 cm). A blue-backed bird that appears round-shouldered when perched. *Male:* Head, wings, and tail *blue;* breast and back *rusty red. Throat blue. Female:* Paler, duller, with rusty breast, *grayish* throat and belly. Juvenile similar to juvenile Eastern Bluebird but belly darker; found only in breeding range, accompanied by parents. **VOICE:** Short *pew* or *mew.* Also a hard, chattering note. **SIMILAR SPECIES:** Eastern and Mountain Bluebirds. **HABITAT:** Open pine forests, oak savannas, farms; in winter, semiopen habitats.

MOUNTAIN BLUEBIRD *Sialia currucoides*   Fairly common

7¼–7½ in. (18–19 cm). *Adult male: Turquoise blue,* paler below; belly whitish. No rusty; first-year male duller blue with some brown. *Female:* Dull brownish gray, with touch of pale blue on rump, tail, and wings; shows pale rusty breast and sides in fresher fall/winter plumages. **VOICE:** Low *chur* or *vhew.* Song a short, subdued warble. **SIMILAR SPECIES:** Posture straighter and slimmer than other bluebirds. Warmer-colored birds in fresh plumage lack rusty-colored flanks. **HABITAT:** Open country often with some trees. Usually found in flocks or small groups in winter.

TOWNSEND'S SOLITAIRE *Myadestes townsendi*   Uncommon

8½ in. (22 cm). A slim gray bird with *white eye-ring, white sides on tail,* and *buffy wing patches. Juvenile:* Dark overall with light spots and scaly belly. **VOICE:** Song a rich warbling. Call a high-pitched *eek,* like a squeaky bicycle wheel. **SIMILAR SPECIES:** Northern Mockingbird, but Townsend's eye-ring, darker breast, and especially buff wing patches diagnostic. **HABITAT:** Variety of coniferous forests almost to tree line, rocky cliffs; in winter, particularly fond of junipers, also chaparral, open woods.

ACCENTOR, BLUEBIRDS, AND SOLITAIRE

SIBERIAN ACCENTOR

EASTERN BLUEBIRD

male

juvenile

WESTERN BLUEBIRD

male

female

MOUNTAIN BLUEBIRD

female

adult male

juvenile

TOWNSEND'S SOLITAIRE

VEERY *Catharus fuscescens*   **Fairly common**

7 in. (18 cm). *Catharus* thrushes are all brownish to reddish above, spotted below, and can be difficult to separate; ages are similar (except juvenile plumage, briefly held, is spotted above) and sexes alike. In Veery, note *uniform rusty brown* cast above and pale grayish flanks (often looking whitish). Grayish face with little or no eye-ring; the *Catharus* with least-distinct spotting on breast. **VOICE:** Song liquid, breezy, ethereal, wheeling downward: *vee-ur, vee-ur, veer, veer.* Call a down-slurred *phew* or *view.* **SIMILAR SPECIES:** Out-of-range vagrants can be confused with western subspecies of Swainson's Thrush, but these have distinct buffy eye-ring or spectacles, browner sides and flanks, and different vocalizations. **HABITAT:** Moist riparian woods, willow and alder thickets, meadows in pine forests. Casual vagrant to CA coast.

SWAINSON'S THRUSH *Catharus ustulatus*   **Fairly common**

7 in. (18 cm). This thrush is marked by its conspicuous *buffy eye-ring* or *spectacles,* buff on cheeks and upper breast, and tail the same color as the back. Interior mountain subspecies (*swainsoni* group) dull *olivey brown* above, coastal western subspecies (*ustulatus* group) warmer brown, sometimes approaching russet. **VOICE:** Song is breezy, flutelike phrases, each phrase sliding *upward.* Call a liquid *whit* or *foot.* **SIMILAR SPECIES:** Veery, Gray-cheeked Thrush. Hermit Thrush may have indistinct eye-ring, but is smaller, more upright in posture, and has *contrasty rufous tail, little or no buff* on breast, more-distinct and blackish breast spotting; regularly *flicks wings and raises tail,* and *vocalizations differ.* **HABITAT:** Moist spruce and fir forests, riparian woodlands; in migration, other woods. Often skulks in thick vegetation.

GRAY-CHEEKED THRUSH *Catharus minimus*   **Uncommon**

7–7¼ in. (17–18 cm). A dull, "cold-colored," *gray-brown,* furtive thrush, distinguished from Swainson's by its *grayish* cheeks and *grayish,* less conspicuous, often broken eye-ring. *Little or no buff on breast.* **VOICE:** Song thin and nasal, downward, *whee-wheeoo-titi-wheew.* Call a downward *pheu.* **SIMILAR SPECIES:** Other thrushes. **HABITAT:** Boreal forests, tundra willow and alder scrub; in migration, woodlands. Casual vagrant to CA.

HERMIT THRUSH *Catharus guttatus*   **Fairly common**

6¾ in. (17 cm). A smallish spot-breasted brown thrush with *rufous tail.* When perched, it has habit of *flicking wings* and of *cocking tail and dropping it slowly.* Different subspecies groups vary in exact color of back and flanks, eastern and Pacific coastal birds generally being warmer, interior western birds grayer. **VOICE:** Call a low *chuck;* also a scolding *tuk-tuk-tuk* and a rising, whiny *pay.* Song clear, ethereal, flutelike; three or four phrases at *different pitches,* each with a *long introductory note.* **SIMILAR SPECIES:** Swainson's and Gray-cheeked Thrushes. **HABITAT:** Coniferous or mixed woods; in winter, woods, thickets, chaparral, parks, gardens.

SPOTTED
THRUSHES

VEERY

SWAINSON'S
THRUSH

East and
interior West

Pacific
Coast

GRAY-CHEEKED
THRUSH

tail-lifting

interior
West

HERMIT
THRUSH

Pacific Coast
and East

AMERICAN ROBIN *Turdus migratorius*   Common

10 in. (25 cm). A very familiar bird; often seen on lawns, with an erect stance, giving short runs then pauses. Recognized by dark gray back and brick red breast. Dark stripes on white throat. Subspecies vary in plumage brightness (birds in CA are paler than shown here), but within subspecies adult males have head and tail blacker and underparts solid deep reddish; these colors are duller in females, and first-year birds of each sex are slightly duller than adults. *Juvenile:* Has dark-speckled, pale rusty breast. **VOICE:** Song a clear caroling; short phrases, rising and falling, often prolonged. Calls *tyeep* and *tut-tut-tut.* **SIMILAR SPECIES:** Varied Thrush and Rufous-backed Robin. **HABITAT:** Wide variety of habitats, including towns, parks, lawns, farmland, shade trees, many types of forests and woodlands; in winter, often found in berry-producing trees. Eyebrowed Thrush (*T. obscurus,* not shown), a rare vagrant to AK and CA, is robinlike but slimmer and with distinct white or buff eyebrow.

VARIED THRUSH *Ixoreus naevius*   Uncommon

9½ in. (24 cm). Similar to American Robin, but with *orangish eye stripe, orange wing bars,* and *orange bar on underwing* visible in flight. *Male: Blue-gray above,* with wide *black breast-band. Female:* Duller gray above, with *gray breast-band.* First-year birds within each sex are duller than adults. *Juvenile:* Dull brown; breast-band imperfect or speckled. **VOICE:** Song a long, eerie, quavering, whistled note, followed, after a pause, by one on a lower or higher pitch. Call a quivering low-pitched *zzzew* or *zzzeee,* and a liquid *chup.* **SIMILAR SPECIES:** Orangey wing bars and eye stripe, and a breast-band, distinguish it from a robin, with which it only rarely mingles. **HABITAT:** Thick, wet coniferous and mixed forests; in winter, also other moist, dense woods, ravines, thickets, roadsides at dawn.

RUFOUS-BACKED ROBIN *Turdus rufopalliatus*   Very rare visitor

9¼ in. (24 cm). Like a pale American Robin, but with orangier tinge below, *rufous back,* and *no white around eye.* More heavily streaked throat. *Orangier bill.* Female and first-year male duller. A timid skulker. **VOICE:** Call a soft whistled *teeww.* **SIMILAR SPECIES:** American Robin. **RANGE AND HABITAT:** Most records from AZ, but also recorded as casual vagrant west to CA, north to UT, and east to TX. Woods and thickets, often near water.

AZTEC THRUSH *Ridgwayia pinicola*   Casual visitor

9¼ in. (24 cm). Resembles Varied Thrush but with *dark hood,* white belly, white rump. Wings strikingly *patched with white. Male:* Blackish on head, breast, and back. *Female:* Brownish. First-year birds duller within each sex. Often sits still for long periods. **VOICE:** Nasal, wheezy *wheeeah.* Usually silent. **SIMILAR SPECIES:** Northern Mockingbird, juvenile Spotted Towhee. **RANGE AND HABITAT:** Casual late-summer visitor from Mex. to se. AZ and w. TX. Mixed montane woodlands, especially pine-oak forests. Furtive in dense vegetation.

THRUSHES

male

female

juvenile

AMERICAN
ROBIN

adult
male

juvenile

female

VARIED
THRUSH

male

male

female

AZTEC
THRUSH

male

RUFOUS-BACKED
ROBIN

MOCKINGBIRDS and THRASHERS
Family Mimidae

Excellent songsters; some mimic other birds. Strong-legged; usually longer tailed than true thrushes, bill usually longer and more decurved. Ages and sexes similar. **FOOD:** Insects, fruit. **RANGE:** New World.

LONG-BILLED THRASHER *Toxostoma longirostre*   Rare, local

11½ in. (29 cm). *Duller brown* above than Brown Thrasher, breast stripes *blacker, cheeks grayer;* bill longer, slightly more curved, and all dark. **VOICE:** Song similar to Brown Thrasher's, but more jumbled. Call a harsh *tchuk.* **SIMILAR SPECIES:** Brown Thrasher. **HABITAT:** Brush, mesquite. Casual vagrant to NM, CO.

BROWN THRASHER *Toxostoma rufum*   Uncommon

11½ in. (29 cm). Slimmer but longer tailed than a robin; *bright rufous* above, *heavily streaked* below. Note *wing bars,* slightly curved bill, long tail, and yellow eyes. **VOICE:** Song a succession of deliberate notes and phrases resembling Gray Catbird's song, but each phrase usually *in pairs.* Call a harsh *chack!* **SIMILAR SPECIES:** *Catharus* thrushes have shorter tails, lack wing bars, are spotted (not striped) below, and have brown (not yellow) eyes. See Long-billed Thrasher. **HABITAT:** Thickets, brush. Very rare vagrant to W. Coast.

SAGE THRASHER *Oreoscoptes montanus*   Uncommon

8½ in. (22 cm). Smaller than other thrashers. Gray-backed, with heavily streaked breast, white wing bars, and *white tail corners.* Eyes pale yellow, duller in juvenile and first-fall. Small size, shorter tail, *shorter bill,* and *striped breast* distinguish it from other western thrashers (but see Bendire's Thrasher). Streaking may be muted in worn plumage in late summer. **VOICE:** Song is clear, ecstatic warbled phrases, sometimes repeated in thrasher fashion; more often continuous, suggestive of Black-headed Grosbeak. Call a blackbirdlike *chuck.* **SIMILAR SPECIES:** Cactus Wren, Bendire's Thrasher. **HABITAT:** Sagebrush, mesas; in winter, also deserts. Rare visitor to W. Coast.

GRAY CATBIRD *Dumetella carolinensis*   Common

8¾ in. (23 cm). Slate gray; slim. Note *black cap. Chestnut undertail coverts* (may not be noticeable). Flips tail jauntily. **VOICE:** *Catlike mewing;* distinctive. Also a grating *tcheck-tcheck.* Song is disjointed notes and phrases; not repetitious, compared with other mimids. **HABITAT:** Riparian undergrowth, brush. More often heard than seen. Rare vagrant to W. Coast.

NORTHERN MOCKINGBIRD *Mimus polyglottos*   Common

10 in. (25 cm). A familiar and conspicuous species. Gray; slimmer, longer tailed than a robin. Note *large white patches* on wings and tail, prominent in flight. **VOICE:** Song a varied, prolonged succession of notes and phrases, may be repeated a half-dozen times or more before changing. Often heard at night. Mockingbirds are excellent mimics of other species. Call a loud *tchack;* also *chair.* **SIMILAR SPECIES:** Shrikes have dark facial masks. Juvenile mockingbird might be similar to Sage Thrasher but latter shows streaks rather than spots below and lacks white in wings. **HABITAT:** Towns, parks, gardens, farms, roadsides, thickets. More common in drier habitats. Introduced and uncommon in HI (p. 408).

THRASHERS AND
MOCKINGBIRDS

LONG-BILLED
THRASHER

BROWN
THRASHER

SAGE
THRASHER

GRAY
CATBIRD

NORTHERN
MOCKINGBIRD

wing-flashing

juvenile

CALIFORNIA THRASHER *Toxostoma redivivum* Fairly common

12 in. (31 cm). Note *pale cinnamon belly and undertail coverts;* tail long; bill long and *sickle-shaped.* Eyes dark brown. The only thrasher of coastal CA. **VOICE:** Call a dry *chak,* also a sharp *g-leek.* Song a sustained series of notes and phrases, some musical, some harsh, *repeated once or twice.* **SIMILAR SPECIES:** Crissal Thrasher very similar but has deeper chestnut undertail coverts; ranges do not overlap. **HABITAT:** Chaparral, coastal sage scrub, thickets, parks, gardens.

CRISSAL THRASHER *Toxostoma crissale* Uncommon

11½ in. (29 cm). A *rather dark* thrasher of desert habitats, with long, *deeply curved bill.* Note dark *chestnut undertail coverts,* darker than in other thrashers. No breast spots. Eyes dull yellowish. **VOICE:** Song sweeter and less spasmodic than in other thrashers. Call *pichoory* or *chideary,* repeated two or three times. **SIMILAR SPECIES:** California Thrasher does not overlap in range. **HABITAT:** Dense brush along desert streams, mesquite thickets, willows, locally at higher elevations in manzanita, scrub oak.

LECONTE'S THRASHER *Toxostoma lecontei* Uncommon to scarce

11 in. (28 cm). A *very pale* thrasher of driest deserts. Has contrastingly *darker tail.* Salmon-rust undertail coverts. Dark eyes stand out on plain face. Rather shy. Runs long distances on ground. **VOICE:** Song (Jan.–Apr.) similar to songs of most other thrashers. Call *ti-reep,* rising on second syllable. **SIMILAR SPECIES:** Crissal and California Thrashers much darker. **HABITAT:** Desert flats with sparse bushes, mostly saltbush or creosote bush.

CURVE-BILLED THRASHER *Toxostoma curvirostre* Fairly common

11 in. (28 cm). The most common desert thrasher, can be told from other western thrashers by *well-curved* bill and *mottled breast,* which is less distinct in subspecies *palmeri* of AZ than in subspecies *oberholseri* of TX and NM. Eyes pale orange. Juvenile shows yellower eyes, somewhat straighter bill. **VOICE:** Call a sharp, liquid *whit-wheet!* Song a musical series of notes and phrases, almost grosbeaklike in quality but faster. Not much repetition. **SIMILAR SPECIES:** Bendire's Thrasher has *shorter, straighter bill, with slight paling at base,* is slightly browner overall, breast spots more triangular (except when worn), different call. **HABITAT:** Deserts, arid brush, lower canyons, ranch yards.

BENDIRE'S THRASHER *Toxostoma bendirei* Uncommon, local

9¾ in. (25 cm). Note *shorter, more robinlike bill* (lower mandible quite straight), with paler (horn-colored or pale gray) base. Breast lightly spotted. Eyes usually *yellow.* **VOICE:** Song a *continuous,* clear, double-note warble, not broken into phrases. Call a soft *tirup.* **SIMILAR SPECIES:** Juvenile Curve-billed may have a bill as short as Bendire's, and yellow eyes, but plumage fluffy and fresh versus worn in adult Bendire's. Worn Sage Thrashers' bills are much shorter and straighter, backs usually darker and wing bars more distinct, even in worn plumage. **HABITAT:** Deserts, yuccas, dry brushy farmland. Accidental vagrant to north of range.

THRASHERS

CALIFORNIA
THRASHER

CRISSAL
THRASHER

LECONTE'S
THRASHER

CURVE-
BILLED
THRASHER

AZ

TX and NM

BENDIRE'S
THRASHER

DIPPERS Family Cinclidae

Plump, stub-tailed; like very large wrens. Solitary or in family groups. Dippers dive and swim underwater, where they walk on bottom. **FOOD:** Insects, larvae, aquatic invertebrates, small fish. **RANGE:** Eurasia, w. N. and S. America.

AMERICAN DIPPER *Cinclus mexicanus*   Uncommon

7½ in. (19 cm). A chunky, *slate-colored* bird of rushing mountain streams. *Tail stubby.* Legs pale, *eyelids white.* Note bobbing motions. *Juvenile:* Has paler underparts and bill. **VOICE:** Call a sharp, buzzy *zeet*, heard above rushing water. Song clear and ringing, wrenlike. **HABITAT:** Fast-flowing streams in mountains and canyons; more rarely pond edges. Nests under bridges, behind waterfalls. Some birds move to lower elevations in winter. Casual vagrant east and south of range.

WAXWINGS Family Bombycillidae

Pointed crests; waxy red tips on secondaries in adult and some first-year individuals. Gregarious. **FOOD:** Berries, insects. **RANGE:** N. Hemisphere.

BOHEMIAN WAXWING *Bombycilla garrulus*   Uncommon, irregular

8¼ in. (21 cm). Similar to Cedar Waxwing, but larger and grayer, with *no yellow on belly;* wings with strong white or *white and yellow* markings, undertail coverts *deep rusty.* Juvenile like Cedar but larger, grayer. Often travels in large flocks; shape in flight very starlinglike. **VOICE:** *Zrreee,* rougher than thin note of Cedar Waxwing. **HABITAT:** Boreal forests; in winter, widespread, irruptive, in search of berries, often in towns. Vagrants occur well south of range in some years.

CEDAR WAXWING *Bombycilla cedrorum*   Common

7¼ in. (18 cm). Note *yellow band* at tip of tail. A sleek, crested, brown bird, larger than House Sparrow. *Juvenile:* Grayish olive-brown, with blurry streaks below. Waxwings are gregarious and nomadic in fall/winter season, flying and feeding in compact flocks. Primarily berry eaters but also flycatch. **VOICE:** High, thin lisp or *zeee* or *zreee*; rather constantly given while feeding and in flight. **SIMILAR SPECIES:** Bohemian Waxwing. Juvenile Cedars (which can be seen in migration) smaller, browner. **HABITAT:** Open woodlands, streamside willows and alders, orchards; in winter, towns, fruiting trees, and bushes.

SILKY-FLYCATCHERS Family Ptiliogonatidae

Slim, crested, waxwinglike birds. **FOOD:** Berries, insects. **RANGE:** Southwestern U.S. to Panama.

PHAINOPEPLA *Phainopepla nitens*   Uncommon

7¾ in. (20 cm). Both sexes are sleek, crested, with red eye. *Adult male:* Glossy black with conspicuous *white wing patches* in flight. *Female:* Dark gray; wing patches light, not as conspicuous as male's. First-year male is gray, mottled black. **VOICE:** Call a soft, rising *wurp* and harsher *churrrr.* Song a weak, wheezy, and disconnected warble. **SIMILAR SPECIES:** Cedar Waxwing. Northern Mockingbird also has white wing patches but lacks crest and has much white in tail. **HABITAT:** Desert scrub, mesquite, oak foothills, pepper trees; fond of misltetoe berries. Casual vagrant west, north, and east of breeding range.

DIPPER, WAXWINGS, AND PHAINOPEPLA

adult

AMERICAN
DIPPER

juvenile

BOHEMIAN
WAXWING

CEDAR
WAXWING

juvenile

female

female
shows
similar but
smaller
white wing
patch

adult
male

PHAINOPEPLA

JAYS, CROWS, and ALLIES Family Corvidae

Large perching birds with strong, longish bill, nostrils covered by forward-pointing bristles. Jays are often blue. Magpies are black and white, with long tails. Crows and ravens are large and black. Sexes alike. First-year birds of most species resemble adults. **FOOD:** Almost anything edible. **RANGE:** Worldwide except s. S. America, Antarctica, Oceana.

CALIFORNIA SCRUB-JAY *Aphelocoma californica*　　　**Common**

11–11¼ in. (29 cm). A noisy familiar bird in CA. *Crestless* with blue head, wings, and tail, *brownish* back, white throat with *necklace*. **VOICE:** Rough, rasping *kwesh . . . kwesh*. Also a harsh *shreck-shreck-shreck-shreck*. **SIMILAR SPECIES:** Woodhouse's Jay does not overlap in range. **HABITAT:** Oaks, pine-oak, oak-chaparral of foothills, riparian woodlands, residential areas, parks.

ISLAND SCRUB-JAY *Aphelocoma insularis* (not shown)　　　**Very local**

12½–13 in. (31–33 cm). Found only on Santa Cruz I. off coast of s. CA, most restricted range of any species in N. America. **VOICE:** Same as California Scrub-Jay. **SIMILAR SPECIES:** Similar to California Scrub-Jay (no range overlap) but slightly longer and larger billed; deeper blue, darker cheek. **HABITAT:** Woodlands and scrubby habitat.

WOODHOUSE'S SCRUB-JAY *Aphelocoma woodhouseii*　　　**Common**

11–11¼ in. (29 cm). Similar to California Scrub-Jay (from which it was recently split) but duller; throat and sides grayer, not contrasting as much with back; face plainer; sides of breast lack blue. **VOICE:** Similar to California Scrub-Jay but higher pitched, rasping *kwesh* call more often double-noted. **SIMILAR SPECIES:** Mexican Jay. **HABITAT:** Riparian and oak woodlands, pinyon-juniper, residential areas, parks.

MEXICAN JAY *Aphelocoma wollweberi*　　　**Fairly common, local**

11½ in. (29 cm). A blue crestless jay of the Southwest. Resembles Woodhouse's Scrub-Jay, but *more uniform;* back and breast grayer. *No strong contrast* between throat and breast. Also *lacks narrow whitish line over eye.* In AZ, juvenile has partly yellow bill. **VOICE:** Querulous *wink? wink?* or *zhenk?* **SIMILAR SPECIES:** Woodhouse's Scrub-Jay brighter and more contrasting; calls differ. **HABITAT:** Pine-oak and oak-juniper woodlands.

BLUE JAY *Cyanocitta cristata*　　　**Fairly common**

11 in. (28 cm). A showy, noisy, *crested jay*. Bold *white spots on wings and tail;* whitish and dull gray underparts; *black necklace.* **VOICE:** Harsh slurring *jeeah* or *jay;* a musical *queedle, queedle;* many other notes. Mimics calls of Red-shouldered and Red-tailed Hawks. **SIMILAR SPECIES:** Steller's Jay. **HABITAT:** Woodlands, suburban gardens, groves, towns, feeders. Casual vagrant to W. Coast.

STELLER'S JAY *Cyanocitta stelleri*　　　**Common**

11½ in. (29 cm). Foreparts *blackish;* rear parts (wings, tail, belly) *deep blue.* Some interior birds have white eyebrow. **VOICE:** Loud *shook-shook-shook* or *shack-shack-shack* or *wheck-wek-wek-wek-wek* or *kwesh kwesh kwesh;* harsh *jjaairr* and many other notes: very familiar sounds throughout western coniferous forests. Frequently mimics hawks. **SIMILAR SPECIES:** Other "blue jays" have white below. **HABITAT:** Montane coniferous and pine-oak forests; also some residential areas, feeders; in winter, lowlands. Rare vagrant or visitor east of range.

JAYS

CALIFORNIA
SCRUB-JAY

WOODHOUSE'S
SCRUB-JAY

AZ juvenile

MEXICAN
JAY

BLUE JAY

STELLER'S JAY

PINYON JAY *Gymnorhinus cyanocephalus*　　　　　**UNCOMMON**

10½ in. (27 cm). Looks *like a small dull blue crow*, though chunkier, with long, sharp bill. Readily told from other jays by its short tail, uniform pale blue coloration (can look grayish in certain lighting), and crowlike flight. Pinyon Jays are gregarious, often gathering in large noisy flocks and walking about like small crows. **VOICE:** Nuthatchlike *nasal* cawing, *kaa-ah* or *karn-ah* (descending inflection); has mewing effect. Also jaylike notes; chattering. **SIMILAR SPECIES:** Other western jays. **HABITAT:** Primarily pinyon-juniper; also dry, open ponderosa and Jeffrey pine woodlands; ranges into sagebrush. Casual vagrant to W. Coast.

CLARK'S NUTCRACKER *Nucifraga columbiana*　　　**Fairly common**

12 in. (30–31 cm). Built like a small crow, with *light gray* or tan-gray body and large *white patches* in trailing edge of black wings and outer tail feathers, a diagnostic pattern among birds of high mountains of the West. Long bill. Tame birds often can be fed by hand. **VOICE:** Flat, drawn-out, grating *caw, khaaa* or *khraaa*. **SIMILAR SPECIES:** Canada Jay has shorter bill, lacks white patches. **HABITAT:** Coniferous forests in mountains as high as near tree line; mountain resorts. Occasionally disperses to lowlands; vagrants as far as the W. Coast and Prairie states in fall and winter.

CANADA JAY *Perisoreus canadensis*　　　　　　**Uncommon**

11¼–11½ in. (28–29 cm). A large, fluffy, gray bird of cool northern forests; larger than a robin. Formerly known as Gray Jay and called "Whiskey Jack" by woodsmen. *Adult: Black* patch or partial cap across back of head and *white forehead* (or crown); suggests a huge overgrown chickadee. *Juvenile: Dark sooty*, almost blackish; only distinguishing mark is *whitish whisker.* Pacific Coast and far northern birds have more dark on heads; Rocky Mt. birds have mostly white heads. **VOICE:** Soft *whee-ah;* also many other notes, some harsh. **SIMILAR SPECIES:** Clark's Nutcracker. **HABITAT:** Spruce and fir forests. Becomes tame around campgrounds, picnic areas.

YELLOW-BILLED MAGPIE *Pica nuttalli*　　　**Fairly common, local**

16½–17 in. (42–43 cm). Very similar to Black-billed Magpie, but smaller, *bill yellow.* At close range, crescent of bare yellow skin below eye is visible. Except for rare vagrants or escapees, ranges of our two magpies do not overlap. **VOICE:** Similar to Black-billed Magpie's *maag?*, etc. **HABITAT:** Oak savanna, riparian groves, ranches, farms. Usually in small to medium-sized flocks.

BLACK-BILLED MAGPIE *Pica hudsonia*　　　　**Fairly common**

18½–19½ in. (47–49 cm); tail 9½–12 in. (24–30 cm). A large, slender, *black-and-white bird*, with *long, graduated tail.* In flight, iridescent greenish black tail streams behind and large *white patches flash in wings.* **VOICE:** Harsh, rapid *queg queg queg queg* or *wah-wah-wah.* Also a querulous, nasal *maag?* or *aag-aag?* **SIMILAR SPECIES:** Yellow-billed Magpie. **HABITAT:** Rangeland, brushy country, conifers, streamsides, forest edges, farms. Often in flocks. Casual vagrant to W. Coast.

JAYS AND MAGPIES

PINYON JAY

CLARK'S NUTCRACKER

adult

CANADA JAY

North and Pacific

Rockies

Canada Jay juvenile

YELLOW-BILLED MAGPIE

BLACK-BILLED MAGPIE

NORTHWESTERN CROW *Corvus caurinus* Uncommon, local

16 in. (41 cm). This small beachcombing crow of the Pacific Northwest is very similar to American Crow but is slightly smaller and has slightly quicker wingbeats. It replaces the latter on the narrow northwestern coastal strip. There is apparently integration with American Crow in Puget Sound area; hence some believe they may be conspecific. **VOICE:** *Khaaa* or *khaaw.* Usually more resonant than American Crow's *caw.* Also, *cowp-cowp-cowp.* **SIMILAR SPECIES:** American Crow. **HABITAT:** Near tidewater, shores, coastal towns.

AMERICAN CROW *Corvus brachyrhynchos* Common

17–17½ in. (43–45 cm). A large, familiar, chunky, ebony bird. Completely black; slightly glossed with purplish in strong sunlight. Bill and feet strong and black. Often gregarious. American Crows in CA smaller than elsewhere in the U.S. **VOICE:** Loud *caw, caw, caw* or *cah* or *kahr.* **SIMILAR SPECIES:** Common Raven larger, has longer wedge-shaped tail (shorter and more rounded in American Crow), more swept-back wings, different call. See also Chihuahuan Raven, Northwestern Crow. **HABITAT:** Woodlands, farms, fields, river groves, shores, towns, dumps. Rare in Southwest border region.

CHIHUAHUAN RAVEN *Corvus cryptoleucus* Fairly common

19–19½ in. (48–50 cm). Slightly larger than American Crow; a small raven of arid plains and deserts. Flies with typical flat-winged glide of a raven; has somewhat wedge-shaped tail. White feather bases on neck and breast sometimes show when feathers are ruffled by the wind, hence former name "White-necked" Raven. **VOICE:** Hoarse *kraak,* flatter and higher than Common Raven's. **SIMILAR SPECIES:** Difficult to tell from Common Raven, particularly when separate, but slightly smaller and tail slightly less wedge-shaped, calls higher pitched, and bristles extend farther down upper mandible. Bases to Common Raven's feathers are grayish. **HABITAT:** Arid and semiarid scrub and grasslands, deserts, yucca, mesquite, towns, dumps.

COMMON RAVEN *Corvus corax* Common

23½–24 in. (59–61 cm). Note longer *wedge-shaped tail.* Much larger than American Crow. More hawklike in flight, it alternates flapping and sailing, gliding on flat, somewhat swept-back wings (crow glides much less and with slight upward dihedral). When bird is perched and not too distant, note "goiter" look created by shaggy throat feathers and heavier "Roman-nose" bill. **VOICE:** Croaking *cr-r-ruck* or *prruk;* also a metallic *tok.* **SIMILAR SPECIES:** American Crow, Chihuahuan Raven. **HABITAT:** Boreal and mountain forests, desert lowlands (particularly in winter), cliffs, tundra, towns, dumps. Has been increasing in West; flocks of nonbreeding birds now found along the coast.

CROWS AND
RAVENS

NORTHWESTERN
CROW

AMERICAN
CROW

crows
have
rounded
tails

CHIHUAHUAN
RAVEN

may show white
on nape when
feathers are
ruffled

ravens have
wedge-shaped
tails

COMMON
RAVEN

CHICKADEES and TITMICE Family Paridae

Small, plump, small-billed birds. Acrobatic when feeding. Ages and sexes similar. Often found in mixed-species flocks during fall/winter season with other parids, kinglets, warblers, etc. **FOOD:** Insects, seeds, acorn mast, berries; at feeders, suet, sunflower seeds. **RANGE:** Widespread in N. America, Eurasia, Africa.

BLACK-CAPPED CHICKADEE *Poecile atricapillus* Common

5–5¼ in. (12–13 cm). This small, tame acrobat can be separated from other widespread chickadees except Carolina by its *solid black cap* in conjunction with *gray back* and buffy-pink sides. **VOICE:** Clearly enunciated *chick-a-dee-dee-dee.* Song a clear whistle, *fee-bee-ee* or *fee-bee,* first note higher. **SIMILAR SPECIES:** Carolina Chickadee. **HABITAT:** Mixed and deciduous woods; riparian thickets, shade trees, residential areas, feeders.

CHESTNUT-BACKED CHICKADEE *Poecile rufescens* Fairly common

4¾ in. (12 cm). The cap, bib, and white cheeks indicate a chickadee; the *chestnut back and rump,* this species. Sides *chestnut* (or *gray* in subspecies *neglectus* found along coast of cen. CA). **VOICE:** Hoarser and more rapid than Black-capped Chickadee: *sick-a-see-see.* No whistled song. **HABITAT:** Moist coniferous forests, oaks, willows, shade trees, parks.

MOUNTAIN CHICKADEE *Poecile gambeli* Fairly common

5¼ in. (13 cm). Similar to Black-capped Chickadee, but black of cap interrupted by *white line over eye.* **VOICE:** Song a clear whistled *fee-bee-bee* or *fee-ee-bee-bee,* first note or two usually higher; also *tsick-a-zee-zee-zee,* huskier than Black-capped's, and a rolling *deedleedleoo.* **SIMILAR SPECIES:** Other chickadees, Black-crested Titmouse. **HABITAT:** Mountain forests, conifers; irregularly moves to lower elevations in winter. Casual vagrant east of range and to W. Coast.

GRAY-HEADED CHICKADEE *Poecile cinctus* Rare, local

5½ in. (14 cm). This subarctic chickadee can be separated from Boreal Chickadee by its *grayer cap* and *more extensive white cheek.* **VOICE:** Peevish *dee-deer* or *chee-ee.* **HABITAT:** Spruce forests, particularly at border with streamside willow and alder thickets and cottonwoods.

MEXICAN CHICKADEE *Poecile sclateri* Uncommon, local

5 in. (13 cm). Similar to Black-capped Chickadee, but *black of throat more extensive,* spreading across upper breast. Note *dark gray sides.* Lacks whitish supercilium of Mountain Chickadee. The only chickadee in its local U.S. range. **VOICE:** Nasal and husky for a chickadee: a low *dzay-dzee.* **HABITAT:** Montane coniferous forests; sometimes moves to lower canyons in winter.

BOREAL CHICKADEE *Poecile hudsonicus* Uncommon

5½ in. (14 cm). Note *dull brown cap,* rich brown to pinkish brown flanks, extensively *grayish cheeks.* **VOICE:** Wheezy *chick-che-day-day;* notes slower, more raspy and drawling than lively *chick-a-dee-dee-dee* of Black-capped Chickadee. **SIMILAR SPECIES:** Gray-headed Chickadee. **HABITAT:** Coniferous forests, evergreen plantations; somewhat irruptive, occasionally moving south of normal range in winter.

CHICKADEES

BLACK-CAPPED CHICKADEE

cen. CA coast

CHESTNUT-BACKED CHICKADEE

MOUNTAIN CHICKADEE

GRAY-HEADED CHICKADEE

MEXICAN CHICKADEE

BOREAL CHICKADEE

BLACK-CRESTED TITMOUSE *Baeolophus atricristatus* **Fairly common**

6¼ in. (16 cm). Birds bearing the name "titmouse" are our only *small* gray-backed birds with pointed crest. Black-crested is a small gray bird with *black crown and crest*. Forehead and underparts pale, sides rusty. Juveniles, found only in spring/summer and usually with their parents, have mostly gray crest. **VOICE:** Chickadee-like calls. Song a whistled *peter peter peter peter* or *hear hear hear hear.* Varied. **SIMILAR SPECIES:** Tufted Titmouse has plain gray crest and black forehead. Bridled Titmouse has harlequin face pattern. **HABITAT:** Woodlands, canyons, towns, feeders.

OAK TITMOUSE *Baeolophus inornatus* **Fairly common**

5¾ in. (15 cm). This is the sole titmouse west of Sierra Nevada. Very like Juniper Titmouse (formerly considered subspecies of one species, "Plain Titmouse") but slightly browner. **VOICE:** Call a scratchy *sissi-chee*. Song a whistled *weety weety* or *tee-wit tee-wit tee-wit;* highly variable but huskier than Chestnut-backed Chickadee. **SIMILAR SPECIES:** Other titmice, but separated by range. **HABITAT:** Oak and oak-pine woods; locally in riparian woodlands, shade trees, residential areas.

JUNIPER TITMOUSE *Baeolophus ridgwayi* **Uncommon**

5¾ in. (15 cm). Very similar to Oak Titmouse, although Juniper is slightly grayer. **VOICE:** Call more rapid than Oak's, *si-dee-dee-dee-dee.* **SIMILAR SPECIES:** Juvenile Black-crested Titmice with gray crests, especially at Big Bend and Edwards Plateau areas of TX, where Juniper Titmice do not occur. **HABITAT:** Pinyon-juniper and oak-juniper woodlands.

BRIDLED TITMOUSE *Baeolophus wollweberi* **Fairly common**

5¼ in. (13 cm). Crest and black-and-white *"bridled"* face identify this small gray titmouse of Southwest. **VOICE:** Similar to other titmice and chickadees, but higher and faster. Song a repeated two-syllable phrase. **SIMILAR SPECIES:** Black-crested Titmouse. Mountan Chickadee has a different face pattern, lacks crest. **HABITAT:** Oak, pine-oak, and sycamore canyons, riparian woodlands, feeders.

TITMICE

BLACK CRESTED
TITMOUSE

OAK
TITMOUSE

JUNIPER
TITMOUSE

BRIDLED
TITMOUSE

Mountain
Chickadee (p. 280)
for comparison

NUTHATCHES Family Sittidae

Small, stubby tree climbers with strong bills and feet; often go down trees headfirst. **FOOD:** Bark insects, seeds, nuts. **RANGE:** Most of N. Hemisphere.

WHITE-BREASTED NUTHATCH *Sitta carolinensis*   Fairly common
5¾ in. (15 cm). Note the *black cap* (gray in female) and beady black eye on white face. Undertail coverts chestnut. **VOICE:** Song a series of low, nasal notes on one pitch, higher in interior West. Call a distinctive nasal *yank, yank, yank.* **SIMILAR SPECIES:** Red-breasted Nuthatch. **HABITAT:** Forests, primarily in oaks or mixed pine-oak.

RED-BREASTED NUTHATCH *Sitta canadensis*   Common
4½ in. (11 cm). A small nuthatch with *broad black line* through eye and white line above it. Crown black in male, gray in female; underparts washed rusty in male, paler in female. First-year birds of each sex duller. **VOICE:** A distinctive *ank* or *enk.* **SIMILAR SPECIES:** Pygmy Nuthatch. **HABITAT:** Coniferous forests; in winter, also other trees, feeders. Irruptive, sometimes moving well south of range in winter.

PYGMY NUTHATCH *Sitta pygmaea*   Fairly common
4¼ in. (11 cm). A very small, pine-loving nuthatch, with *gray-brown cap coming down to eye* and a whitish spot on nape. Usually in flocks. Ages and sexes similar. **VOICE:** High, piping *peep-peep* or *pit-pi-dit-pi-dit.* Often heard before it is seen. **SIMILAR SPECIES:** Red-breasted Nuthatch. **HABITAT:** Favors ponderosa, Jeffrey, and Monterey pines, Douglas-fir.

TREE CREEPERS Family Certhiidae

Small, slim, stiff-tailed birds, with slender, slightly curved bill used to probe tree trunks. **FOOD:** Bark insects. **RANGE:** Temperate N. Hemisphere.

BROWN CREEPER *Certhia americana*   Uncommon
5¼ in. (13 cm). Brown above, whitish below, with *slender decurved bill* and *stiff* tail, which is used as a brace during climbing. **VOICE:** Call a single high, thin *seee.* Song a high, thin, sibilant *see-ti-wee-tu-wee* or *trees, trees, trees, see the trees.* **HABITAT:** Nests in coniferous and mixed woodlands; in winter, also in groves, shade trees.

PARROTBILLS and WRENTITS
Family Paradoxornithidae

Small, long-tailed denizens of brushy cover. This Old World family includes one species in N. America. **FOOD:** Insects, fruit. **RANGE:** Temperate Asia.

WRENTIT *Chamaea fasciata*   Fairly common
6½ in. (17 cm). Heard far more often than seen. Note *long,* rounded, slightly cocked tail and obscurely streaked breast. *Eye distinctly pale.* Bill short. Northern birds brighter and more pinkish. Behavior wrenlike; rarely flies more than 30 feet. Ages and sexes alike. **VOICE:** Song of staccato ringing notes on one pitch; starting deliberately, running into a trill like a bouncing ball. Female gives slower, double-noted version. Call a soft *prr.* **SIMILAR SPECIES:** Wrens have shorter tails. **HABITAT:** Chaparral, coastal sage scrub, brush, garden shrubs.

NUTHATCHES, CREEPER, AND WRENTIT

female

RED-BREASTED NUTHATCH

female

male

male

WHITE-BREASTED NUTHATCH

PYGMY NUTHATCH

BROWN CREEPER

southern

northern

WRENTIT

LONG-TAILED TITS Family Aegithalidae

Very small birds with long tail, usually found in flocks. **FOOD:** Insects. **RANGE:** Primarily Asia with single species each in Europe and N. America.

BUSHTIT *Psaltriparus minimus*   Common

4½ in. (11 cm). A very small, plain bird that moves in *straggling, twittering flocks*. Grayish and brownish with stubby bill, longish tail. Adult male and juvenile have dark eyes, female yellow eyes; juvenile male of "Black-eared Bushtit" (subspecies *dimorphicus*) of s. NM and w. TX can have black or black-marked cheeks. **VOICE:** Insistent twittering given constantly as flocks move. **SIMILAR SPECIES:** Verdin. **HABITAT:** Oak scrub, chaparral, pinyon-juniper, parks, residential areas.

PENDULINE TITS Family Remizidae

Smal birds with short tails and tiny pointed bills. Not found in flocks. **FOOD:** Insects, berries. **RANGE:** Old World; single species in N. America.

VERDIN *Auriparus flaviceps*   Fairly common

4½ in. (11 cm). Tiny. *Adult:* Gray, with *yellowish head, rufous bend of wing* (often hidden). Sexes similar. *Juvenile:* Just plain gray. **VOICE:** Insistent *see-lip*. Rapid chipping. Song a three-note whistle, *tsee see-see*. **SIMILAR SPECIES:** Bushtit differs in bill shape. See also Lucy's Warbler. **HABITAT:** Arid brush, mesquite.

WRENS Family Troglodytidae

Small brown birds with slim, slightly curved bill; tail often cocked. Songs often pleasing, making up for the drab plumage. Ages and sexes alike. **FOOD:** Insects, spiders. **RANGE:** Throughout Americas; one species in Eurasia.

HOUSE WREN *Troglodytes aedon*   Common

4½–4¾ in. (11–12 cm). A small, energetic, gray-brown wren with long tail, light eye-ring, and no strong eyebrow stripe. **VOICE:** Stuttering, gurgling song rises in a musical burst, then falls at end; calls a rolled *prrrrr* and harsh *cheh, cheh*. **SIMILAR SPECIES:** Winter and Pacific Wrens. **HABITAT:** Open woods, thickets, towns, gardens; often nests in bird boxes.

WINTER WREN *Troglodytes hiemalis*   Uncommon

4 in. (10 cm). Similar to House Wren but smaller, *much stubbier tail*, stronger eyebrow, and *dark, heavily barred belly*. Mouselike, staying close to ground. **VOICE:** Song a rapid succession of high tinkling warbles, trills. Call a soft, two-syllable *chemp-chemp* (suggests Song Sparrow). **SIMILAR SPECIES:** House Wren. Difficult to separate from Pacific Wren where co-occuring on migration or in winter. **HABITAT:** Dense woodlands underbrush, fallen trees. Casual winter vagrant to W. Coast.

PACIFIC WREN *Troglodytes pacificus*   Fairly common

4 in. (10 cm). Recently split from Winter Wren. Slightly darker and warmer, with less distinct barring to wings and tail, but best identified by voice. **VOICE:** Song similar to Winter Wren but with fewer trailing segments. Call a harder *timp-timp* (suggests Wilson's Warbler). **SIMILAR SPECIES:** House Wren, Winter Wren. **HABITAT:** Deep canyons; ferns; streambeds, coniferous forests. Casual vagrant east of normal range.

BUSHTIT, VERDIN, SMALL WRENS

VERDIN

adult

Pacific
Coast

interior

juvenile

females have
yellow eyes

juvenile
male
"Black-eared"

BUSHTIT

WINTER
WREN

HOUSE
WREN

PACIFIC
WREN

BEWICK'S WREN *Thryomanes bewickii* **Common**

5¼ in. (13 cm). Note longish tail with *white corners* and bold *white eyebrow stripe*. Mouse brown above, white below. **VOICE:** Song suggests Song Sparrow's, but thinner, starting on two or three high notes, dropping, ending in a trill; calls sharp *vit, vit* and buzzy *dzzzzzt*. **SIMILAR SPECIES:** Carolina Wren. Habitats of Marsh and Bewick's Wrens do not overlap. **HABITAT:** Thickets, underbrush, gardens, coastal chapparal, sagebrush.

CAROLINA WREN *Thryothorus ludovicianus* **Scarce, local**

5½ in. (14 cm). *Warm rusty brown* above, variably buff below; conspicuous *white eyebrow stripe*. **VOICE:** Two- or three-syllable chant: *tea-kettle, tea-kettle, tea kettle*, or *chirpity, chirpity, chirpity, chirp*. Chips and churrs. **SIMILAR SPECIES:** Bewick's Wren grayer, tail longer. **HABITAT:** Tangles, undergrowth, woods, gardens. Casual vagrant west of range.

SEDGE WREN *Cistothorus platensis* **Uncommon, secretive**

4½ in. (11 cm). Stubbier than Marsh Wren; buffier, with *buffy* undertail coverts, *barred wings*, and *finely streaked* crown. **VOICE:** Song a dry staccato chattering: *chap chap chap chap chap chap chap chapper-rrrrr*. Call a single or double warblerlike *chap*. **SIMILAR SPECIES:** Smaller than Marsh Wren, crown streaked; supercilium indistinct. **HABITAT:** Grassy and sedgy marshes and meadows. Casual vagrant to W. Coast.

MARSH WREN *Cistothorus palustris* **Fairly common**

5 in. (13 cm). Note *white stripes on back* and white eyebrow stripe, unstreaked dark crown. **VOICE:** Song reedy, gurgling, *cut-cut-turrrrrrrrr-ur*, often ending in rattle; can sing at night. Call a low *tsuck-tsuck*. **SIMILAR SPECIES:** Sedge Wren. **HABITAT:** Fresh and brackish cattail, tule, and bulrush marshes; in winter, also salt marshes. Rare outside of marsh habitats during migration.

CANYON WREN *Catherpes mexicanus* **Fairly common**

5¾–6 in. (15 cm). Note *white bib*. Rusty, with dark rufous brown belly contrasting with white breast and throat. Long, slightly decurved bill. Often climbs vertically on rocks, exploring cracks and crevices. **VOICE:** Gushing cadence of clear, curved notes tripping down scale; *tee tee tee tee tew tew tew tew*. Call a shrill *beet*. **HABITAT:** Drier habitats: cliffs, canyons, rockslides, stone buildings. Casual vagrant east of range.

ROCK WREN *Salpinctes obsoletus* **Fairly common**

6 in. (15 cm). A gray western wren with *finely streaked breast*, rusty rump, and *buffy terminal tail band*. Frequently bobs. **VOICE:** Song consists of thrasherlike phrases and buzzy trills, repeated at lazy intervals. Also a loud call *ti-keer*. **SIMILAR SPECIES:** Canyon Wren. **HABITAT:** Rocky slopes, canyons, rubble. Rare vagrant east of range.

CACTUS WREN *Campylorhynchus brunneicapillus* **Fairly common**

8½ in. (22 cm). A very large wren of arid country. Distinguished from our other wrens by *much larger size and heavy spotting, clustered on upper breast*. White supercilium, chestnut cap. Spotted outer tail feathers. **VOICE:** Monotonous *chu-chu-chu-chu* or *chug-chug-chug-chug*, on one pitch, gaining speed. **SIMILAR SPECIES:** Sage Thrasher. **HABITAT:** Arid areas of cactus, mesquite, yucca.

WRENS

BEWICK'S
WREN

CAROLINA
WREN

SEDGE
WREN

MARSH
WREN

CANYON
WREN

ROCK
WREN

juvenile

CACTUS
WREN

KINGLETS Family Regulidae

Tiny active birds with small slender bills, short tails, bright red crowns in males. Often found with chickadees, nuthatches, and creepers. Ages alike, sexes differ. **FOOD:** Insects, larvae. **RANGE:** Eurasia, N. America.

RUBY-CROWNED KINGLET *Regulus calendula* Common

4¼ in. (11 cm). Tiny, olive-gray, smaller than warblers, *flicks wings constantly.* Note broken white eye-ring, bold wing bars bordered behind by *black bar.* Male has *scarlet crown patch* (stands out when crest erect in excitement); female lacks red. **VOICE:** Husky *ji-dit.* Song is chattering *tee tee tee-tew tew tew—ti-didee, ti-didee, ti-didee.* **SIMILAR SPECIES:** Golden-crowned Kinglet. See Hutton's Vireo. **HABITAT:** In summer, coniferous forests; in winter, variety of other habitats, residential areas.

GOLDEN-CROWNED KINGLET *Regulus satrapa* Fairly common

4 in. (10 cm). Note tiny size, *boldly striped face,* wing bars. Male but not female has red in crown. **VOICE:** High, wiry *see-see-see.* Song a series of high thin notes, ascending, then dropping into a little chatter. **SIMILAR SPECIES:** Ruby-crowned Kinglet. **HABITAT:** Conifers; in winter, sometimes other trees.

GNATCATCHERS Family Polioptilidae

Active birds with slender bill. Gnatcatchers have long, mobile tail, often flipped and cocked. **FOOD:** Insects, larvae. **RANGE:** Throughout Americas.

BLUE-GRAY GNATCATCHER Uncommon to fairly common
Polioptila caerulea

4½ in. (11 cm). Tiny, slim, blue-gray above, whitish below, with narrow *white eye-ring. Long tail* is *mostly white underneath.* Adults and males average brighter than first-year birds and females; males acquire black line above eye in spring/summer. **VOICE:** Call a thin, peevish *zpee;* often doubled, *zpee-zee.* Song thin and squeaky, easily overlooked. **SIMILAR SPECIES:** Other gnatcatchers. **HABITAT:** Dry, open woods and scrub.

BLACK-CAPPED GNATCATCHER *Polioptila nigriceps* Rare, local

4¼ in. (11 cm). Rare visitor and local breeder to se. AZ. Note *largely white undertail* and *long bill.* Spring/summer male has *black cap;* brown tinge to plumage, winter male with black mark above eye. **VOICE:** Rough *meeeer.* **SIMILAR SPECIES:** Blue-gray Gnatcatcher. **HABITAT:** Brushy washes.

BLACK-TAILED GNATCATCHER *Polioptila melanura* Uncommon

4½ in. (11 cm). Similar to Blue-gray Gnatcatcher, but underside of tail *largely black.* Spring/summer male has *black cap,* winter male has black mark above eye. **VOICE:** Call a thin harsh *chee,* repeated two or three times; soft *chip-chip-chip* series. **SIMILAR SPECIES:** California Gnatcatcher. **HABITAT:** Desert brush, ravines, dry washes, mesquite.

CALIFORNIA GNATCATCHER *Polioptila californica* Scarce, local

4½ in. (11 cm). No range overlap with Black-tailed Gnatcatcher. Dull *gray below,* tinged buff-brown on wings and flanks, less white on undertail than Black-tailed Gnatcatcher. **VOICE:** Kittenlike *meew,* rising then falling; harsher *jih-jih-jih.* **SIMILAR SPECIES:** Blue-gray Gnatcatcher. **HABITAT:** Restricted to coastal sage scrub. CA populations endangered.

KINGLETS AND GNATCATCHERS

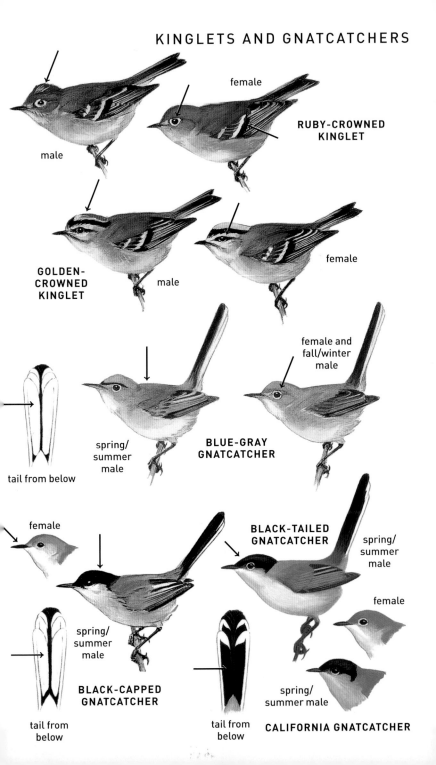

RUBY-CROWNED KINGLET

female

male

GOLDEN-CROWNED KINGLET

male

female

tail from below

BLUE-GRAY GNATCATCHER

spring/summer male

female and fall/winter male

BLACK-TAILED GNATCATCHER

spring/summer male

female

female

spring/summer male

tail from below

BLACK-CAPPED GNATCATCHER

tail from below

spring/summer male

CALIFORNIA GNATCATCHER

SHRIKES Family Laniidae

Fierce songbirds, with hook-tipped bills, that perch watchfully on bush tops, treetops, wires; often impale prey on thorns, barbed wire. **FOOD:** Insects, lizards, small rodents, and birds. **RANGE:** Old World; two species in N. America.

NORTHERN SHRIKE *Lanius borealis*   Scarce

10–10¼ in. (25–26 cm). Similar to Loggerhead Shrike, but larger, adults paler; note *faintly barred* breast, larger bill with *pale base. Juvenile: Brown*, with weak mask and *fine barring* below; becomes mottled gray in first year. **VOICE:** Song a disjointed, thrasherlike succession of harsh and musical notes. Call *shek-shek;* a grating *jaaeg.* **SIMILAR SPECIES:** Loggerhead Shrike, Northern Mockingbird. **HABITAT:** Semiopen country, taiga. Vagrants can occur south of normal range.

LOGGERHEAD SHRIKE *Lanius ludovicianus*   Uncommon

9 in. (23 cm). Big head, slim tail; gray, black, and white, with *black mask, short hooked bill.* Flies low with flickering shallow flight showing white patches. *Juvenile:* Has faint barring below *briefly in late summer.* **VOICE:** Song of repeated, deliberate phrases; *queedle, queedle, tsurp-see, tsurp-see,* etc. Call *shack shack* or *jeeer jeeer.* **SIMILAR SPECIES:** Northern Shrike, Northern Mockingbird. **HABITAT:** Semiopen country, wires, fences, trees, shrubs. Populations on San Clemente I., CA (subspecies *mearnsi*), endangered.

VIREOS Family Vireonidae

Small, rather plain birds, less-active than wood-warblers; bills thicker, more curved, and with small hook to tip. Ages and sexes usually similar. **FOOD:** Insects, fruit in winter. **RANGE:** Canada to Argentina.

BELL'S VIREO *Vireo bellii*   Uncommon

4¾ in. (12 cm). Small, nondescript. Thin, pale, broken eye-ring and loral stripe. One or two weak wing bars. Endangered,southwestern "Least Bell's Vireo" (subspecies *pusillus*) is grayer, flips tail like gnatcatcher. **VOICE:** Husky phrases short: *cheedle cheedle chee? cheedle cheedle chew!* **SIMILAR SPECIES:** Warbling Vireo has plain wings, bold eyebrow. White-eyed Vireo has bolder wing bars, yellow lores. Gray Vireo slightly larger with complete eye-ring; note voice and habitat. **HABITAT:** Willows, streamsides, mesquite. Casual vagrant to CA coast.

BLACK-CAPPED VIREO *Vireo atricapilla*   Scarce, local, endangered

4½ in. (11 cm). Small and sprightly; cap *glossy black* in adult male, slate gray in first-fall male and female; first-spring male acquires mottled black-and-gray cap. Note wing bars, white spectacles, *red* eyes. **VOICE:** Song hurried, angry, restless phrases. Call a harsh *chit-ah.* **SIMILAR SPECIES:** Blue-headed Vireo larger with dark eyes. **HABITAT:** Oak scrub, brushy hills, canyons. Accidental west and north of range.

WHITE-EYED VIREO *Vireo griseus*   Uncommon, local

5 in. (13 cm). Note *yellow spectacles, whitish throat,* wing bars, yellowish sides, white eye (dark through first fall). Somewhat skulking. **VOICE:** Song a sharp *CHICK-a-per-weeoo-CHICK;* variable. **SIMILAR SPECIES:** Bell's Vireo. **HABITAT:** Wood edges, brush, brambles, dense undergrowth. Very rare vagrant to W. Coast.

adult

juvenile

NORTHERN SHRIKE

LOGGERHEAD SHRIKE

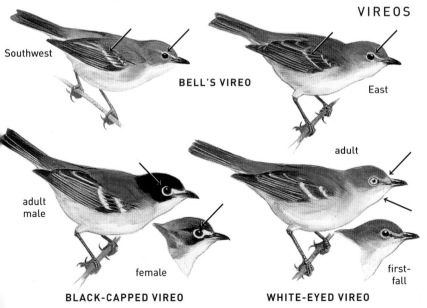

VIREOS

Southwest

BELL'S VIREO

East

adult male

female

BLACK-CAPPED VIREO

adult

first-fall

WHITE-EYED VIREO

BLUE-HEADED VIREO *Vireo solitarius* Uncommon

5¼ in. (14 cm). The northern/eastern representative of the spectacled "Solitary Vireo" complex, also including Cassin's and Plumbeous Vireos. Note *sharply demarcated* blue-gray cap, *bright white* spectacles and throat, *bright green* back, yellowish wash to side. **VOICE:** Song of burry but sweet phrases with deliberate pauses between: *wee-ay, chweeo, chuweep* (slower than Red-eyed Vireo with fewer notes per phrase). All three species also give a whiny chatter. **SIMILAR SPECIES:** Cassin's Vireo. **HABITAT:** Coniferous, mixed, and deciduous woods. Rare vagrant to W. Coast.

CASSIN'S VIREO *Vireo cassinii* Uncommon

5¼ in. (14 cm). Back greener and sides more yellowish than Plumbeous but duller overall with less contrasting face pattern than Blue-headed Vireo. Bill averages smaller. **VOICE:** Song like Blue-headed's but slurred, less sweet: *wee-ay, chweeo, chuweep.* **SIMILAR SPECIES:** Dull first-year female Blue-headeds can be difficult to separate from bright adult male Cassin's, and dull Cassin's can approach bright Plumbeous. See also Gray and Bell's Vireos. **HABITAT:** Coniferous, mixed, and deciduous woods.

PLUMBEOUS VIREO *Vireo plumbeus* Uncommon

5½ in. (15 cm). Although their nesting ranges barely overlap, all three "Solitary Vireo" species may occur together on migration and winter grounds. Plumbeous is mostly gray above, whitish below, with grayish or grayish-olive wash to sides of breast and variable wash of gray or yellow on flanks. **VOICE:** Song similar to Cassin's but Plumbeous is slowest, burriest. **SIMILAR SPECIES:** Blue-headed and Cassin's Vireos. See also Gray Vireo. **HABITAT:** Coniferous, mixed, and deciduous woods.

YELLOW-THROATED VIREO *Vireo flavifrons* Uncommon

5½ in. (14 cm). Bright yellow throat, yellow spectacles, and white wing bars. Olive back contrasts with gray rump. **VOICE:** Song similar to Blue-headed Vireo's, but lower pitched with *burry quality;* swings back and forth with phrases that sound like *ee-yay, three-eight.* **SIMILAR SPECIES:** Pine Warbler has some dusky streaks below, white tail spots, smaller bill. **HABITAT:** Deciduous woodlands, shade trees, particularly oaks. Rare vagrant to W. Coast.

GRAY VIREO *Vireo vicinior* Scarce

5½ in. (14 cm). This plain, gray-backed vireo of arid mountains has *complete, narrow, white eye-ring* and only *one faint wing bar.* Though drab, it has a feisty character, flipping tail like a gnatcatcher. **VOICE:** Song similar to Plumbeous Vireo's, but sweeter, more rapid, in regular series. **SIMILAR SPECIES:** Plumbeous Vireo stockier, has shorter tail that is not flipped, bold spectacles rather than just eye-ring, and two, thicker wing bars. See Bell's Vireo. **HABITAT:** Pinyon-juniper woodlands, brushy slopes, chamise-dominated chaparral, scrub oak.

HUTTON'S VIREO *Vireo huttoni* Fairly common

5 in. (13 cm). A chunky olive-brown vireo with bold wing bars. Note *incomplete eye-ring,* broken *above,* and large light loral spot. **VOICE:** Buzzy, rising *zu-weep* or falling *zee-ur,* oft-repeated; a hoarse, deliberate *day dee dee.* **SIMILAR SPECIES:** Ruby-crowned Kinglet very similar in plumage but smaller with skinny black legs, smaller bill, quicker movements, black "highlight bar" below lower wing bar. **HABITAT:** Woodlands, parks, particularly with oaks.

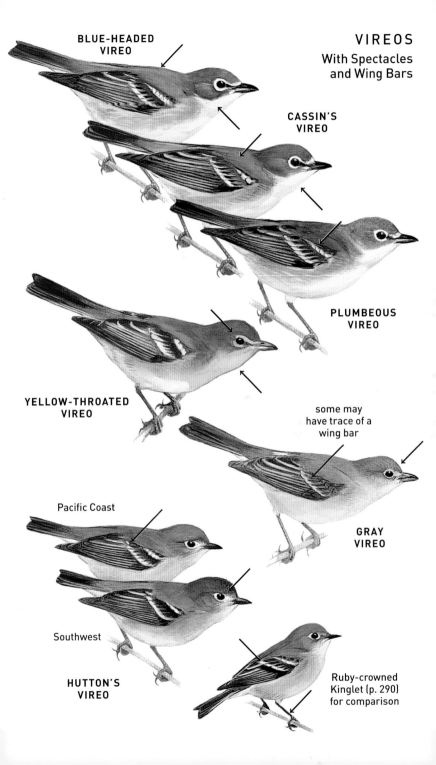

BLUE-HEADED VIREO

VIREOS
With Spectacles and Wing Bars

CASSIN'S VIREO

PLUMBEOUS VIREO

YELLOW-THROATED VIREO

some may have trace of a wing bar

GRAY VIREO

Pacific Coast

Southwest

HUTTON'S VIREO

Ruby-crowned Kinglet (p. 290) for comparison

RED-EYED VIREO *Vireo olivaceus* Uncommon

6 in. (15 cm). Note *gray cap* contrasting with olive back, and strong, *black-bordered white eyebrow stripe (supercilium)*. Red iris may not be obvious at a distance and is brown in first-fall birds of this and Yellow-green Vireo. **VOICE:** Song is abrupt, robinlike phrases, monotonous. Call a nasal, whining *chway*. **SIMILAR SPECIES:** Warbling Vireo slightly smaller, duller and less contrasty above, with pale lores, arching supercilium, and dark brown eyes at all ages. See Yellow-green Vireo, which is scarce and local. **HABITAT:** Deciduous woodlands, shade trees, groves. Very rare vagrant to W. Coast.

YELLOW-GREEN VIREO *Vireo flavoviridis* Casual

6–6¼ in. (15–16 cm). This tropical species is very similar to Red-eyed Vireo, but has *strong yellow tones* on sides, flanks, and undertail coverts; back *yellower* green; head stripes *less distinct;* bill slightly *longer* and paler. **SIMILAR SPECIES:**Note first-fall Red-eyed Vireos may have yellow on flanks and undertail coverts. **VOICE:** Song slower than Red-eyed's, suggestive of House Sparrow. **RANGE:** Casual in TX and in s. AZ; very rare (and increasing) fall vagrant to coastal CA. **HABITAT:** Deciduous woods, riparian thickets.

WARBLING VIREO *Vireo gilvus* Fairly common

5½ in. (14 cm). One of the widespread vireos that lack wing bars. In this *very plain* species, note *whitish breast, pale lores,* and *lack of black borders* on eyebrow stripe, that also arches slightly above dark eye. Back tinged dull greenish. First-fall birds have more yellow on sides. **VOICE:** Song distinctive: a languid warble, unlike broken phrases of other vireos; suggests Purple Finch's song, but less spirited, with burry undertone. Call a wheezy querulous *twee* and short *vit*. **SIMILAR SPECIES:** Philadelphia Vireo rounder headed, smaller billed, and has "cuter" look; yellowish on throat and breast is as bright in middle as on sides; has slate gray line through lores. Red-eyed Vireo larger, greener above, and has bolder eyebrow stripe. **HABITAT:** Deciduous and mixed woods, aspen groves, cottonwoods, riparian woodlands, shade trees.

PHILADELPHIA VIREO *Vireo philadelphicus* Uncommon

5¼ in. (13 cm). This smallish vireo has a face pattern reminiscent of Warbling Vireo, but with more distinct dark eye line (including lores) imparting "cuter" look, slightly greener back, and single faint wing bar. Underparts pale and vary from a small wash of pale yellow on lower throat and upper breast in duller adults to more extensive yellow in bright first-fall birds. **VOICE:** Song very similar to Red-eyed Vireo's; higher, slower. Call a quick, husky *niff-niff-niff-niff*. **SIMILAR SPECIES:** Bright Warbling Vireos in fall tinged green above and have yellow on sides, but that yellow is *dull or lacking in center of breast and throat;* also *lack Philadelphia's dark line through lores.* Different song. See also Tennessee Warbler. **HABITAT:** Second-growth woodlands, poplars, willows, alders. Very rare vagrant to W. Coast.

VIREOS
With Eyelines and
Wing Bars

RED-EYED
VIREO

adult

first-fall

YELLOW-GREEN
VIREO

adult

first-fall

WARBLING
VIREO

adult

spring/summer

PHILADELPHIA
VIREO

first-fall
female

fall/
winter

spring/
summer
male

Tennessee
Warbler
(p. 300) for
comparison

OLIVE WARBLER Family Peucedramidae

Single species. Closely resembles a wood-warbler but now placed in its own family. Longer winged than wood-warblers, tail deeply notched; short, tenth outer primary present. **FOOD:** Insects. **RANGE:** Pine and oak forests in mts. of AZ and NM to Nicaragua.

OLIVE WARBLER *Peucedramus taeniatus*   Uncommon, local

5¼ in. (13 cm). All plumages have *deeply notched tail* and bold wing bars with *white patch at base of primaries. Adult male:* Note *orange-brown head and chest* and *black ear patch. Female:* Duller, crown tinged olive, breast yellowish; ear patch dusky. *First-year male:* Like female, but brighter, some orange-brown mottling often present in crown and breast. **VOICE:** Song a ringing *peter peter peter peter,* variable. Call a rich *kew.* **SIMILAR SPECIES:** Grace's Warbler has grayer back and crown, black streaking on flanks. **HABITAT:** Pine and fir forests of high mountains. Forages high in trees.

WOOD-WARBLERS Family Parulidae

Popular, active, brightly colored birds, smaller than sparrows, with thin bills. The majority have some yellow in plumage. Ages and sexes usually differ. **FOOD:** Mainly insects though several species also eat fruit in fall and winter. **RANGE:** N. America to n. Argentina. Many N. American wood-warblers breed in boreal and eastern deciduous forests and are rare vagrants to the W. Coast.

GOLDEN-WINGED WARBLER *Vermivora chrysoptera* Very rare vagrant

4¾ in. (12 cm). *Male:* Note *yellow wing patch* and *black throat.* Yellow fore-crown, black *ear patch,* whitish underparts. *Female:* Ear and throat patches grayer. First-year birds of each sex duller. **VOICE:** Song a buzzy *bee-bz-bz-bz.* Call like Blue-winged's. **SIMILAR SPECIES:** See "Brewster's," "Lawrence's," and Blue-winged Warblers. **RANGE AND HABITAT:** Very rare vagrant to W. Coast from e. N. America. In migration, found in open woodlands, undergrowth.

"BREWSTER'S" AND "LAWRENCE'S" WARBLERS   Casual vagrants

Golden-winged and Blue-winged Warblers hybridize where their ranges overlap, producing two basic types, "Brewster's" and "Lawrence's" War-blers. Brewster's is more variable, typically showing whitish underparts; some can have white or yellow wing bars and some are tinged yellow below. Lawrence's is typically bright yellow below but with black head pattern of Golden-winged. Hybrid combinations can also resemble par-ent species with hints of the other species. Females and first-year males duller. **VOICE:** May sing like either parent. **RANGE AND HABITAT:** See Blue-winged and Golden-winged Warblers. Accidental to W. Coast.

BLUE-WINGED WARBLER *Vermivora cyanoptera*   Very rare vagrant

4¾ in. (12 cm). Note *narrow black line through eye.* Face and underparts yellow; wings *have two white bars.* Female averages duller than male, especially in crown, and first-year birds average duller within each sex. **VOICE:** Song a buzzy *beeee-bzzz.* Call a sharp *tsik.* **SIMILAR SPECIES:** "Brewster's," "Lawrence's," Prothonotary, Golden-winged, and Yellow Warblers. **RANGE AND HABITAT:** Very rare vagrant to W. Coast from e. N. America. In migration, found in field edges, undergrowth, woodland openings.

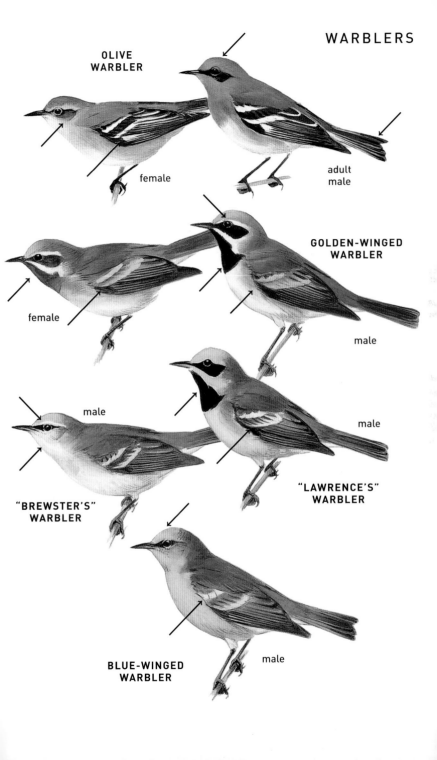

WARBLERS

OLIVE WARBLER

female

adult male

GOLDEN-WINGED WARBLER

female

male

"BREWSTER'S" WARBLER

male

male

"LAWRENCE'S" WARBLER

BLUE-WINGED WARBLER

male

TENNESSEE WARBLER *Oreothlypis peregrina*   **Fairly common**

4¾ in. (12 cm). Note short tail, *bold eyebrow, white undertail coverts. Spring/summer male:* Pale bluish gray head. *Female and first-fall male:* Duller, greenish on head, yellow on breast. *First-fall female:* Duller still (p. 320). **VOICE:** Song staccato: *ticka ticka ticka ticka, swit swit, chew-chew-chew-chew-chew.* Call a sweet *chip.* **SIMILAR SPECIES:** Arctic Warbler, Orange-crowned Warbler, Philadelphia Vireo. **HABITAT:** Boreal forests; in migration, a variety of woodlands. Rare vagrant to W. Coast.

ORANGE-CROWNED WARBLER *Oreothlypis celata*   **Common**

5 in. (13 cm). Generally drab *olive green* to dull yellowish, with *yellow undertail coverts* and *blurry breast streaking.* Northern (*celata*) and Great Basin (*orestera*) birds gray-headed, those of Pacific Coast (*lutescens*) brighter yellow-green. Within each subspecies, adult males brighter than first-year males and females, with first-year females dullest (p. 320). Orange crown-patch seldom visible. **VOICE:** Song a colorless trill, becoming weaker toward end. Call a sharp *stik.* **SIMILAR SPECIES:** Dull Tennessee Warbler greener with white undertail coverts. **HABITAT:** Open woodlands, brushy clearings, willows, chaparral, parks, gardens.

COLIMA WARBLER *Oreothlypis crissalis*   **Scarce, local**

5¾ in. (15 cm). Drab, with *yellow rump* and undertail coverts. Larger than Virginia's Warbler; sides *brownish;* lacks yellow on breast. **VOICE:** Song a trill, like Chipping Sparrow but more musical and ending in two lower notes. **SIMILAR SPECIES:** Lucy's and Virginia's Warblers. **HABITAT:** Oak-pine canyons.

NASHVILLE WARBLER *Oreothlypis ruficapilla*   **Uncommon**

4¾ in. (12 cm). Note *white eye-ring* in combination with *yellow* throat. *Head gray,* back olive-green, no wing bars, underparts bright yellow with white vest. Adults and males brighter than first-year birds and females (see p. 320). **VOICE:** Song two-part: *seebit, seebit, seebit, seebit, titititi* (ends like Chipping Sparrow's song). Call a sharp *pink.* **SIMILAR SPECIES:** Some dull first-year female Nashvilles almost as dull as Virginia's, but always have *yellow on throat.* **HABITAT:** Open mixed woods with under-growth, forest edges, bogs; in migration, also brushy areas.

VIRGINIA'S WARBLER *Oreothlypis virginiae*   **Uncommon**

4¾ in. (12 cm). *Male:* A slim *gray* warbler with *yellowish rump* and *bright yellow undertail coverts, white eye-ring,* rufous patch in crown (usually concealed), and touch of yellow on breast. Flicks or jerks tail. *Female and first-year male:* Duller. First-year female can lack yellow on breast, but has *yellow undertail coverts.* **VOICE:** Song loose, colorless notes on nearly the same pitch: *chlip-chlip-chlip-chlip-chlip-wick-wick.* Call a sharp *pink,* like Nashville and Lucy's Warblers' calls. **SIMILAR SPECIES:** Nashville and Lucy's Warblers. **HABITAT:** Oak canyons, brushy slopes, pinyon-juniper. Scarce vagrant to W. Coast.

LUCY'S WARBLER *Oreothlypis luciae*   **Uncommon**

4¼ in. (11 cm). A small desert warbler; known by its *chestnut rump patch.* Dull white eye-ring, small patch of chestnut on crown (difficult to see). Ages and sexes similar though females slightly duller. **VOICE:** High *weeta weeta weeta che che che che,* on two pitches. Call a sharp *pink.* **SIMILAR SPECIES:** Virginia's Warbler. **HABITAT:** Mesquite along desert streams and washes; willows, cottonwoods. Casual vagrant north along W. Coast.

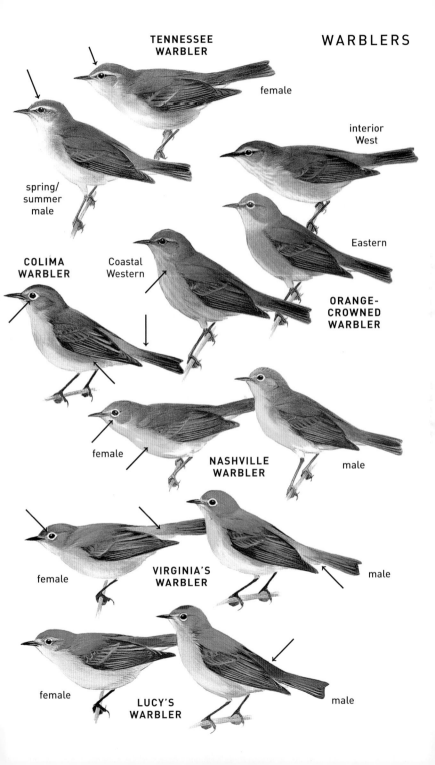

TENNESSEE
WARBLER

WARBLERS

female

interior
West

spring/
summer
male

Eastern

COLIMA
WARBLER

Coastal
Western

ORANGE-
CROWNED
WARBLER

female

NASHVILLE
WARBLER

male

female

VIRGINIA'S
WARBLER

male

female

LUCY'S
WARBLER

male

NORTHERN PARULA *Setophaga americana* Rare

4½ in. (11 cm). A small warbler, *bluish above,* with yellow throat and breast and two white wing bars. *Greenish patch* on back; *broken white eye-ring.* Bright adult male has *dark breast-band*; first-year female lacks breast-band, washed greenish on head (p. 318). **VOICE:** Song a buzzy trill: *zeeeeeeeee-up.* Also *zh-zh-zh-zheeeeee.* **SIMILAR SPECIES:** Tropical Parula has dark face mask, no eye-ring. **RANGE AND HABITAT:** Rare vagrant to W. Coast; breeds very rarely in CA, where found in riparian woodlands.

TROPICAL PARULA *Setophaga pitiayumi* Rare, local

4½ in. (11 cm). Similar to Northern Parula, but darker, with *black face, lacks white eye-ring.* Two bold white wing bars. Lacks color bands across chest of male Northern Parula. Adult and male slightly brighter than first-year birds and female. **VOICE:** Like Northern Parula's. **SIMILAR SPECIES:** Northern Parula. **RANGE AND HABITAT:** Oaks, dry forests; very rare breeder in w. TX; accidental vagrant to AZ, CA.

YELLOW WARBLER *Setophaga petechia* Common

5 in. (13 cm). Extensively yellow; the only warbler with *yellow tail spots,* and all ages/sexes also have *yellow edgings to wing and tail.* Male has *rusty breast streaks* (fainter or lacking in female and first-fall male). Note dark beady eye. *First-fall female:* Lacks breast streaks; some individuals may be quite dull, with noticeable eye-ring, and brighter yellow restricted to lower vent and undertail coverts (p. 318). **VOICE:** Song a bright cheerful *tsee-tsee-tsee-tsee-titi-wee* or *weet weet weet weet tsee-tsee wew.* Variable. Call a soft, rich *chip.* **SIMILAR SPECIES:** Wilson's Warblers and brighter Orange-crowned Warblers lack yellow tail spots. Note vocal differences. **HABITAT:** Riparian woodlands and understory, particularly alders and willows; also parks, gardens.

CHESTNUT-SIDED WARBLER *Setophaga pensylvanica* Rare

5 in. (13 cm). Usually holds tail cocked up at an angle. *Spring/summer:* Note *yellow crown, chestnut sides*; males brighter than females. In fall, chestnut in sides lacking or reduced, upperparts plainer lime greenish with narrow white eye-ring and *two pale yellow* wing bars (p. 318). **VOICE:** Song and call similar to Yellow Warbler's. **HABITAT:** Undergrowth, overgrown edges, small trees. Rare vagrant to W. Coast.

MAGNOLIA WARBLER *Setophaga magnolia* Uncommon

5 in. (13 cm). *Spring/summer male:* Upperparts blackish, with large white patches on wings and tail; underparts yellow, with heavy black stripes. *Female and fall/winter male:* Duller. *First-fall female:* Has weak stripes on sides, weak grayish band across upper breast (p. 318). All ages and sexes show distinctive tail pattern, black crossed midway by *broad white band.* **VOICE:** Song suggests Yellow Warbler's but is shorter: *weeta weeta weet-see* (last note rising) or *weeta weeta wit-chew.* Call an odd nasal note. **SIMILAR SPECIES:** Yellow-rumped Warbler. **HABITAT:** Low conifers; in migration, a variety of woodlands. Rare vagrant to W. Coast.

WARBLERS

female

male

NORTHERN
PARULA

male

TROPICAL
PARULA

spring/
summer
female

YELLOW
WARBLER

spring/
summer
male

spring/
summer
female

CHESTNUT-SIDED
WARBLER

spring/
summer
male

spring/
summer
female

MAGNOLIA
WARBLER

spring/
summer
male

CAPE MAY WARBLER *Setophaga tigrina* Scarce

5 in. (13 cm). *Spring/summer male:* Note *chestnut* cheeks. Yellow below, striped with black; rump yellow, crown black. *Female and fall/winter male:* Lack chestnut cheeks; duller, breast paler, dull *patch of yellow behind ear, yellowish rump. First-fall female:* Distinctly *gray*, can lack yellow (p. 318). **VOICE:** Song a very high, thin *seet seet seet seet.* **SIMILAR SPECIES:** Dull fall/winter females may be confused with Yellow-rumped Warbler but are plainer; have small pale patch behind ear; duller, greenish-yellow rump; and shorter tail. **HABITAT:** Boreal spruce forests; in migration, broadleaf trees. Very rare vagrant to W. Coast.

BLACK-THROATED BLUE WARBLER Very rare vagrant
Setophaga caerulescens

5¼ in. (13 cm). *Male:* Clean-cut; upperparts *deep blue;* throat and sides *black,* belly white; wing with large white spot at base of primaries. First-year male similar but slightly duller, greener. *Female:* Olive–backed, with light line over eye and smaller *white wing spot* (may be obscured in first-year female); see p. 320. **VOICE:** Song a husky, lazy *zur, zur, zur, zreee* or *beer, beer, bree* (ending higher). Call a hard *thip,* similar to call of Dark-eyed Junco. **RANGE AND HABITAT:** Very rare vagrant to W. Coast from e. N. America. In migration, found in mixed woodlands.

YELLOW-RUMPED WARBLER *Setophaga coronata* Common

5½ in. (14 cm). Includes "Audubon's" (*auduboni*) and "Myrtle" (*coronata*) Warblers, two subspecies groups formerly considered separate species. Note bright *yellow rump* in all subspecies, ages, and sexes. *Spring/summer male:* Blue-gray above; heavy black breast patch; crown and side patches yellow. Audubon's (breeds in w. U.S., sw. Canada) differs from Myrtle (breeds in AK, much of Canada, e. U.S, and fairly common in winter to W. Coast) in having *yellow throat* not extending to neck (as white does in Myrtle), larger white wing patches, no white supercilium, plainer face. *Spring/summer female:* Similar but duller overall. *Fall/winter:* Duller, more brownish above; whitish below (see also p. 318); throat often lacks yellow in first-fall Audubon's; *rump yellow.* **VOICE:** Variable song, juncolike but two-part, rising or dropping in pitch, *seet-seet-seet-seet-seet, trrrrrrrr.* Call a loud *check* or *chip* (Myrtle) or more nasal *tchenp* (Audubon's). **SIMILAR SPECIES:** Cape May and Magnolia Warblers. **HABITAT:** Coniferous forests. In migration and winter, varied; open woods, coastal bushes, brush, thickets, parks, gardens, upper beaches.

BLACK-THROATED GRAY WARBLER Fairly common
Setophaga nigrescens

5 in. (13 cm). *Spring/summer and adult male:* Gray above, with black throat, cheek, and crown separated by *white. Small yellow spot in lores. Female:* Slaty crown and cheek; dusky or light throat; loral spot duller yellow. *First-fall:* Male like adult female but throat mottled black; female duller, may be tinged brownish above; cheeks dull gray; loral spot pale. **VOICE:** Song a buzzy chant, "full of Zs," *zeedle zeedle zeedle ZEETche* (next-to-last or last note higher). Call a dull *tup.* **SIMILAR SPECIES:** See Black-and-white Warbler. **HABITAT:** Nests in oaks, pinyon-juniper, mixed woods.

WARBLERS

spring/
summer
male

spring/
summer
female

**CAPE MAY
WARBLER**

female

**BLACK-
THROATED BLUE
WARBLER**

male

first-fall

spring/summer
male

"Myrtle"
Warbler

**YELLOW-RUMPED
WARBLER**

spring/summer
female

**BLACK-
THROATED GRAY
WARBLER**

spring/
summer male

spring/
summer
male

"Audubon's"
Warbler

female and
fall/winter
male

first-fall male

female

GOLDEN-CHEEKED WARBLER
Setophaga chrysoparia

Scarce, local, endangered

5¼ in. (14 cm). Like Black-throated Green Warbler but back *black to darker olive with black streaks;* blacker line through eye; flanks lack yellow. **VOICE:** Song a hurried *tweeah, tweeah, tweesy* or *bzzzz, laysee, daysee.* Call a flat *tip.* **RANGE AND HABITAT:** Breeds in junipers, oaks, and streamside trees of Edwards Plateau, TX. Accidental vagrant to CA.

HERMIT WARBLER *Setophaga occidentalis*

Uncommon

5 in. (13 cm). *Spring/summer and adult male:* Note bright *yellow face* set off by *black throat and nape* and gray back. *Female and first-fall male:* Black of throat much reduced or wanting, but plain-looking yellow face, gray back, and *unstreaked* underparts identify it. **VOICE:** Song three high lisping notes followed by two abrupt lower ones: *seedle, seedle, seedle, CHUP CHUP.* Call a flat *tip* (like Townsend's Warbler's). **SIMILAR SPECIES:** Black-throated Green Warbler, Townsend's Warbler. Hybrid Townsend's × Hermit Warblers occur, have various combinations of characteristics. **HABITAT:** Coniferous forests; in migration, coniferous and deciduous woods.

TOWNSEND'S WARBLER *Setophaga townsendi*

Fairly common

5 in. (13 cm). *Spring/summer and adult male:* Easily distinguished by *black-and-yellow pattern of head,* with *blackish cheek patch; underparts yellow;* heavily striped sides. *Adult female and first-fall male:* Throat largely yellow, with no or mottled black; *well-defined dark cheek patch. First-fall female:* Duller, with grayish cheeks. **VOICE:** Song higher than Black-throated Gray Warbler's: *dzeer dzeer dzeer tseetsee* or *weazy, weazy, seesee.* Call a soft, flat *tip.* **SIMILAR SPECIES:** See Hermit Warbler. Black-throated Green Warbler, dull Blackburnian Warblers. **HABITAT:** Tall conifers, cool fir forests; in migration and winter, also oaks, riparian woodlands, parks, gardens.

BLACK-THROATED GREEN WARBLER *Setophaga virens*

Uncommon

5 in. (13 cm). Yellow face in all plumages. *Spring/summer and adult male:* Black throat and olive-green crown. *Female and first-fall male:* Much less black on throat; unmarked olive green back, *black mottling on sides of upper breast. First-fall female:* dullest (p. 318). **VOICE:** Buzzy *zoo zee zoo zoo zee* or *zee zee zee zee zoo zee.* Call a flat *tip* or *tup.* **SIMILAR SPECIES:** Golden-cheeked and Townsend's Warblers. Hermit Warbler has yellow on crown, lacks eye stripe; back gray; no black stripes on sides. **HABITAT:** Mainly coniferous or mixed woods; in migration, variety of woodlands. Very rare vagrant to W. Coast.

BLACKBURNIAN WARBLER *Setophaga fusca*

Fairly common

5 in. (13 cm). *Spring/summer and adult male:* Black and white, with *flame orange* on head and throat. *Female and first-fall male:* Paler orange on throat; dark cheek patch. First-fall female dullest with yellow throat (p. 318). Note *pale back stripes.* **VOICE:** Song *zip zip zip titi tseeeeeee.* Call a rich *chip.* **SIMILAR SPECIES:** Dull Townsend's Warbler yellower in head, back greener. **HABITAT:** Breeds in conifers. Rare vagrant to W. Coast.

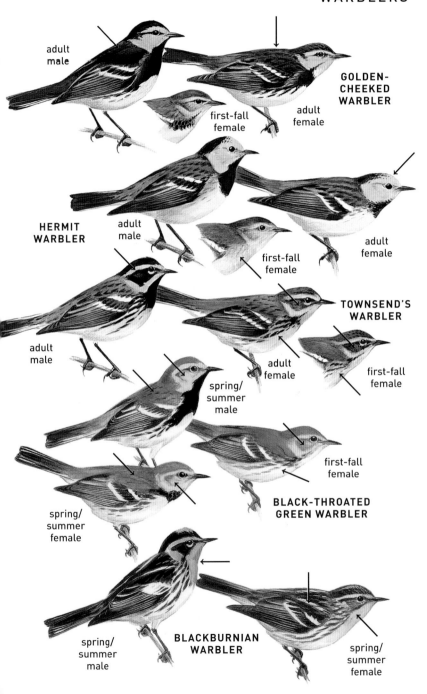

WARBLERS

adult male

first-fall female

adult female

GOLDEN-CHEEKED WARBLER

HERMIT WARBLER

adult male

first-fall female

adult female

adult male

TOWNSEND'S WARBLER

adult female

first-fall female

spring/summer male

first-fall female

spring/summer female

BLACK-THROATED GREEN WARBLER

spring/summer male

BLACKBURNIAN WARBLER

spring/summer female

PINE WARBLER *Setophaga pinus* Casual vagrant

5½ in. (14 cm). Note dark cheeks, blurry streaking at breast-sides, unstreaked back, white tail spots, and dark feet. *Adult male:* Yellow-breasted, with olive-green back, *white wing bars.* Adult female and first-year male duller; brownish olive above (p. 318). *First-fall female:* Often obscure, can lack yellow (see also p. 318). **VOICE:** Song a trill like Chipping Sparrow's. Call a sweet *chip.* **SIMILAR SPECIES:** Fall/winter Blackpoll and Bay-breasted Warblers have more black streaking in back, less prominent dark cheeks. **RANGE AND HABITAT:** Casual vagrant and winter visitor from e. N. America to W. Coast, where found almost exclusively in pines.

PRAIRIE WARBLER *Setophaga discolor* Very rare vagrant

4¾ in. (12 cm). *Bobs tail;* underparts yellow, paling on undertail coverts; black stripes *confined to sides; two black face marks,* one through eye, one below. At close range, chestnut marks may be seen on back of male (reduced in female). *First-fall:* Duller, male with gray cheeks, female with olive cheeks (p. 318). **VOICE:** Song a thin *zee zee zee zee zee zee zee zee.* Call a sharp *tschip.* **SIMILAR SPECIES:** Pine, Palm, and Yellow Warblers. **RANGE AND HABITAT:** Very rare vagrant to W. Coast from e. N. America. During migration, found in brushy areas.

PALM WARBLER *Setophaga palmarum* Uncommon

5¼ in. (14 cm). Note constant *bobbing* of tail. Both sexes brownish or olive above; yellowish or dirty white below, narrowly streaked; *bright yellow* undertail coverts, white spots in tail corners. In spring/summer has *chestnut cap;* ages and sexes rather similar. Two subspecies: Eastern breeders (casual vagrant to W. Coast) have more yellow below and on eyebrow; western breeders (scarce vagrant to W. Coast) duller, may have yellow restricted to undertail coverts in fall. First-fall birds slightly duller (see also p. 318). **VOICE:** Song weak, repetitious notes: *zhe-zhe-zhe-zhe-zhe-zhe.* Call a distinctive sharp *tsup.* **SIMILAR SPECIES:** Yellow-rumped and Prairie Warblers. **HABITAT:** In summer, wooded borders of boreal foreest, muskeg. In migration and winter, bushes, weedy fields. A ground-loving warbler.

YELLOW-THROATED WARBLER *Setophaga dominica* Very rare vagrant

5½ in. (14 cm). A gray-backed warbler with *yellow throat. Black eye mask,* white wing bars, black stripes on sides. Ages and sexes similar; first-fall female slightly duller. Creeps about branches of trees. **VOICE:** Song slurred notes dropping slightly in pitch: *tee-ew, tew, tew, tew, tew, tew wi* (last note rising). Call a rich *chip.* **SIMILAR SPECIES:** Grace's and female Blackburnian Warblers. **RANGE AND HABITAT:** Very rare vagrant and winter visitor from e. N. America to W. Coast. On migration and in winter, often found in palms.

GRACE'S WARBLER *Setophaga graciae* Uncommon

5 in. (13 cm). *Gray-backed, with yellow throat and upper breast,* two wing bars, *yellowish eyebrow stripe,* dark streaks on sides. First-year birds and female slightly duller than adults and males. **VOICE:** *Cheedle cheedle che che che che* (ends in a trill). Call a soft, sweet *chip.* **SIMILAR SPECIES:** Yellow-rumped ("Audubon's") Warbler lacks yellow on breast, has yellow rump. Yellow-throated Warbler has white patch behind ear, blacker facial pattern. **HABITAT:** Pine-oak forests of canyons and mountains. Very rare vagrant to CA.

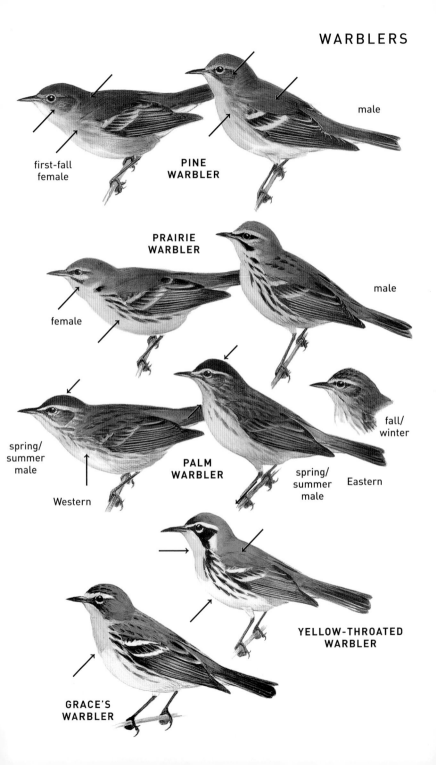

WARBLERS

PINE WARBLER

first-fall female

male

PRAIRIE WARBLER

female

male

PALM WARBLER

spring/
summer
male

Western

fall/
winter

spring/
summer
male

Eastern

YELLOW-THROATED WARBLER

GRACE'S WARBLER

BAY-BREASTED WARBLER *Setophaga castanea* Scarce

5½ in. (14 cm). *Spring/summer male:* Note *chestnut throat, upper breast, and sides; buff patch* on neck. *Spring/summer female:* Paler, with whitish throat. *Fall/winter:* Olive green above; two white wing bars; pale *buff or chestnut flanks, dark feet; no streaks on back or breast* (p. 318). **VOICE:** High, thin, sibilant *tees teesi teesi,* all on one pitch. Call a sharp *chip,* like Blackpoll Warbler's. **SIMILAR SPECIES:** See fall/winter Blackpoll and Pine Warblers. **HABITAT:** Woodlands; in summer, conifers. Very rare vagrant to W. Coast.

BLACKPOLL WARBLER *Setophaga striata* Uncommon

5½ in. (14 cm). *Spring/summer male:* A striped gray warbler with *black cap, white cheeks, distinct pale legs. Spring/summer female: Greenish gray above,* whitish below, *streaked. Fall/winter:* Olive above, greenish yellow below, *faintly streaked* on back and on breast; two wing bars; *whitish undertail coverts* (p. 318); usually bright *yellow legs* (or at least *feet*). **VOICE:** Song a thin, very high-pitched *zi-zi-zi-zi-zi-zi-zi-zi-zi,* becoming stronger then diminishing. Call a sharp *chip.* **SIMILAR SPECIES:** Black-and-white Warbler has white stripe through crown and on back, different behavior. Fall/winter Bay-breasted Warbler has buff wash on flanks and undertail coverts and dark feet. See also Pine Warbler. **HABITAT:** Conifers; in migration, broadleaf trees. Rare vagrant to W. Coast.

BLACK-AND-WHITE WARBLER *Mniotilta varia* Uncommon

5¼ in. (13 cm). *Creeping along trunks* and branches of trees, this warbler is *striped lengthwise with black and white* and has striped crown, white stripes on back. *Spring/summer and adult male:* Black throat partly or mostly lost in winter. *Female and first-fall male:* Paler cheeks, fainter streaks below, and buffy wash on flanks. **VOICE:** Song a thin *weesee weesee weesee weesee;* sometimes can drop in pitch midway. Call a sharp *chip.* **SIMILAR SPECIES:** Blackpoll and Black-throated Gray Warblers. **HABITAT:** Woods. Rare vagrant and winter visitor to W. Coast.

AMERICAN REDSTART *Setophaga ruticilla* Uncommon

5¼ in. (13 cm). Butterfly-like; actively flitting, with drooping wings and spread tail. *Adult male:* Black; *bright orange patches* on wings and tail. *Female:* Gray-olive above; *yellow flash patches* on wings and tail. *First-year male:* Like female, but tinged with orange on chest patches, acquires black splotches on face in spring. **VOICE:** Songs (often alternated) *zee zee zee zee zwee* (last note higher), *tsee tsee tsee tsee tsee-o* (last syllable dropping), and *teetsa teetsa teetsa teetsa teet* (notes paired). Call a slurred, rich *chip.* **HABITAT:** Second-growth woods, riparian woodlands. Scarce spring and fall vagrant to W. Coast.

WARBLERS

BAY-BREASTED
WARBLER

spring/
summer female

spring/
summer
male

spring/
summer
female

spring/
summer male

BLACKPOLL
WARBLER

female and
first-fall
male

adult and
spring male

BLACK-AND-
WHITE
WARBLER

adult
male

female

AMERICAN
REDSTART

first-year
male

OVENBIRD *Seiurus aurocapilla*   Uncommon

6 in. (15 cm). More often seen than heard on breeding grounds. When seen, usually walking on leafy floor of woods. Suggests a small thrush, but *striped* rather than spotted beneath. *Orangish patch on crown bordered by blackish stripes. White eye-ring.* Ages and sexes similar. **VOICE:** Song an emphatic *TEACHer, TEACHer, TEACHer,* etc., in crescendo. Call a loud, sharp *tshuk.* **SIMILAR SPECIES:** Waterthrushes. See also spotted thrushes (p. 264). **HABITAT:** Near or on ground in leafy and pine-oak woods; in migration, also thickets. Rare vagrant to W. Coast.

NORTHERN WATERTHRUSH *Parkesia noveboracensis*   Fairly common

5¾ in. (15 cm). Suggests a small thrush. *Walks* along water's edge and *teeters* like a Spotted Sandpiper. Brown-backed, often tinged olive, with *striped* underparts, strong eyebrow stripe; both eyebrow and underparts vary from whitish to pale yellow. *Throat striped.* Ages and sexes similar. **VOICE:** Call a sharp *chink.* Song a vigorous, rapid *twit twit twit sweet sweet sweet chew chew chew* (*chew*s drop in pitch). **SIMILAR SPECIES:** Louisiana Waterthrush, Ovenbird. **HABITAT:** Wet boreal woods with standing water; in migration, wet riparian thickets, marsh edges. Rare vagrant and winter visitor to W. Coast.

LOUISIANA WATERTHRUSH *Parkesia motacilla*   Very rare

6 in. (15 cm). Similar to Northern Waterthrush, but underparts *white on breast, pinkish buff on flanks and undertail coverts.* Bill slightly larger. *Eyebrow stripe pure white and flares noticeably behind eye.* Throat usually *lacks stripes.* Legs pinkish. Ages and sexes similar. **VOICE:** Song of three clear slurred whistles, followed by a jumble of twittering notes dropping in pitch. **SIMILAR SPECIES:** Northern Waterthrush. **HABITAT:** Streams, brooks, ravines. Bobs when walking, more exaggerated than in Northern. Casual vagrant and winter visitor to W. Coast.

WORM-EATING WARBLER   Very rare vagrant
Helmitheros vermivorum

5¼ in. (13 cm). *Dull olive,* with *black stripes on buffy head.* Breast *rich buff.* Ages and sexes similar. **VOICE:** Song a series of thin dry notes, thinner and more insectlike than trill of Chipping Sparrow. Call a flat *chip,* or *zeet-zeet* in flight. **SIMILAR SPECIES:** Ovenbird, Swainson's Warbler, waterthrushes. **RANGE AND HABITAT:** Rare vagrant and winter visitor to W. Coast from e. N. America. On migration and winter, found primarily in thickets where it probes dead-leaf clusters.

PROTHONOTARY WARBLER *Protonotaria citrea*   Casual vagrant

5½ in. (14 cm). *Male:* Entire head and breast deep *yellow to orangey.* Wings blue-gray *with no bars.* Adult female and first-year male intermediate. *First-year female:* Duller yellow, forehead and crown washed green, tail spots fewer and smaller (see also p. 320). **VOICE:** Song *zweet zweet zweet zweet zweet zweet,* on one pitch. Call a loud *seep.* **SIMILAR SPECIES:** Yellow and Blue-winged Warblers. **RANGE AND HABITAT:** Very rare vagrant to W. Coast from e. N. America. In migration, riparian woodlands, stream edges.

OVENBIRD

fresh fall

NORTHERN WATERTHRUSH

LOUISIANA WATERTHRUSH

worn spring

WORM-EATING WARBLER

first-year female

PROTHONOTARY WARBLER

adult male

fall female

KENTUCKY WARBLER *Geothlypis formosa* Casual vagrant

5¼ in. (13 cm). Note *broad black sideburns* extending down from eye and *yellow spectacles.* Female and first-year male duller but retain distinctive mask pattern. **VOICE:** Song a rapid rolling chant, *tory-tory-tory-tory* or *churry-churry-churry-churry.* Call a rich, low *tup.* **SIMILAR SPECIES:** Common Yellowthroat lacks spectacles. See also Hooded Warbler. **RANGE AND HABITAT:** Very rare vagrant from e. N. America, most often in spring. In migration, woodlands undergrowth.

CONNECTICUT WARBLER *Oporornis agilis* Scarce

5¾–6 in. (15 cm). Similar to MacGillivray's and Mourning Warblers, but slightly larger and plumper; note *walking behavior* — on limbs and ground — and *complete white eye-ring, long undertail coverts* reaching almost to tail tip. *Spring/summer and adult:* Hood gray in male, gray-brown in female. *First-fall:* Duller, with brownish hood, paler throat (see also p. 320). **VOICE:** Repetitious *chip-chup-ee, chip-chup-ee, chip-chup-ee, chip* or *sugar-tweet, sugar-tweet, sugar-tweet.* **SIMILAR SPECIES:** First-fall Mourning Warbler has broken eye-ring (rarely looking complete); yellow throat. Also, Mourning is faster and twitchier, hops rather than walks. Nashville Warbler also has eye-ring, but is smaller, has yellow throat, and actively feeds in trees. See also MacGillivray's Warbler. **HABITAT:** Poplar bluffs, muskeg, boreal woods; in migration, undergrowth. Feeds mostly on ground. Very rare vagrant to W. Coast.

MOURNING WARBLER *Geothlypis philadelphia* Uncommon

5¼ in. (13 cm). Shy and skulking. Olive above, yellow below, with slate-gray hood encircling head and neck. *Spring/summer and adult male:* Has irregular black bib. *Female and first-fall male:* May have thin eye-ring that is barely broken, typically not thicker eye-arcs of MacGillivray's Warbler. Some spring/summer females and all first-fall birds have yellow throats (see also p. 320). Yellow undertail coverts of medium length between Connecticut and MacGillivray's Warblers. **VOICE:** Song *chirry, chirry, chorry, chorry* (*chorry* lower). Considerable variation. Call a hard, buzzy, wrenlike *chack.* **SIMILAR SPECIES:** MacGillivray's and Connecticut Warblers. **HABITAT:** Thickets, undergrowth. Very rare vagrant to W. Coast.

MACGILLIVRAY'S WARBLER *Geothlypis tolmiei* Uncommon

5¼ in. (13 cm). *Spring/summer and adult male:* Olive above, yellow below, with *slate gray hood* (blackish lores and upper breast) completely encircling head and neck. *Thick, partial white eye-ring is broken fore and aft, forming crescents.* *Female:* Similar, but hood paler, washed out on throat. *First-fall:* Like female but duller; throat buff. **VOICE:** Song a rolling *chiddle-chiddle-chiddle, turtle-turtle,* last notes dropping; or *sweeter-sweeter-sweeter, sugar-sugar.* Call a low, hard *chik,* given often. **SIMILAR SPECIES:** First-fall birds told from those of Mourning Warbler by *buff to grayish white throat,* without yellow. Orange-crowned Warbler has grayish head, olive-yellow body, and pale, broken eye-ring; but is smaller, has a sharper bill, and feeds more actively, higher up in bushes and trees. See also voice. **HABITAT:** Low dense undergrowth; shady thickets.

female
similar but
duller

**KENTUCKY
WARBLER**

male

spring/
summer
male

first-fall
female

female

**CONNECTICUT
WARBLER**

first-fall
female

spring/
summer
female

**MOURNING
WARBLER**

spring/
summer male

first-fall
female

spring/
summer
female

**MACGILLIVRAY'S
WARBLER**

spring/
summer male

COMMON YELLOWTHROAT *Geothlypis trichas* Common

5 in. (13 cm). Wrenlike. *Spring/summer and adult male:* Distinctive *black mask*, yellow throat and upper breast; first-fall male has reduced and duller dusky mask. *Female:* Olive-brown, with yellow throat, duller below, but brighter yellow undertail coverts; lacks black mask, cap sometimes slightly reddish. First-fall female can be very dull, with buff rather than yellow throat (see also p. 320). **VOICE:** Bright rapid chant, *witchity-witchity-witchity-witch;* sometimes *witchy-witchy-witchy-witch*. Call a husky *tchep.* **SIMILAR SPECIES:** Duller females distinguished from first-fall and female Mourning and MacGillivray's Warblers by whitish belly, smaller size. **HABITAT:** Marshes, wet riparian thickets, woodland edges.

WILSON'S WARBLER *Cardellina pusilla* Common

4¾ in. (12 cm). *Male:* Golden yellow with *round black cap*; ages similar. Adult female has smaller cap, located closer to forecrown. *First-year female:* Can have very small cap in W. Coast populations or no cap in interior West populations. Otherwise, in all ages/sexes, back is olive, underparts yellow, supercilium indistinct yellow, *lores yellow*, tinged orange on Pacific Coast. Constantly moving and flitting about. **VOICE:** Song a thin, rapid little chatter, dropping in pitch at end: *chi chi chi chi chi chet chet.* Call a flat *timp.* **SIMILAR SPECIES:** Female Hooded Warbler has white spots in tail, dark lores. Yellow Warbler has yellow spots in shorter tail, yellow edging in wings. See also Orange-crowned Warbler. Note vocal differences. **HABITAT:** Thickets and trees along streams, moist riparian tangles, low shrubs, willows, alders.

HOODED WARBLER *Setophaga citrina* Rare vagrant

5¼ in. (13 cm). *Male:* Black *hood* or cowl encircles yellow face and forehead; ages similar. *Female:* Has variable amount of black in head, from a partial hood in adults to none in most first-year females (p. 320); yellow face is usually distinctively outlined, and note *white tail spots.* **VOICE:** Song a loud whistled *weeta wee-tee-o.* Call a sharp *chink,* like waterthrushes. **SIMILAR SPECIES:** Female Wilson's Warblers without black cap lack tail spots and any suggestion of Hooded's face pattern. **HABITAT:** Rare vagrant to W. Coast from e. N. America, most often in spring; in migration, wooded areas, tangles.

CANADA WARBLER *Cardellina canadensis* Scarce

5¼ in. (13 cm). Note "necklace" across breast. *Male:* Solid gray above; bright yellow below, with *necklace of short black stripes;* white vent; first-year males duller, more femalelike. *Adult female:* Similar but necklace fainter, upperparts may be washed with brownish. *First-fall female:* may have only hint of necklace (p. 320). All have *spectacles of white eye-ring and yellow loral stripe.* No white in wings or tail. **VOICE:** Song a staccato burst, irregularly arranged. *Chip, chupety swee-ditchety.* Call *tchip.* **SIMILAR SPECIES:** Magnolia and Grace's Warblers. **HABITAT:** Forest undergrowth, shady thickets. Very rare vagrant to W. Coast.

WARBLERS

COMMON
YELLOWTHROAT

adult
male

adult
female

female

Interior West
first-fall
female

WILSON'S
WARBLER

male

HOODED
WARBLER

adult
female

male

adult
female

CANADA
WARBLER

male

FALL WARBLERS

Most of these have streaks or wing bars.

RUBY-CROWNED KINGLET *Regulus calendula* p. 290
(Not a warbler.) Broken eye-ring, pale wing bars, wing-flicking behavior.

CHESTNUT-SIDED WARBLER *Setophaga pensylvanica* p. 302
First-fall: Green above, grayish white below; eye-ring; tail cocked at angle. Sexes overlap in plumage.

PINE WARBLER *Setophaga pinus* p. 308
Differs from Blackpoll and Bay-breasted in heavier bill, unstreaked back, dark legs. First-fall female can lack yellow.

BAY-BREASTED WARBLER *Setophaga castanea* p. 310
Note dark legs and feet, buff flanks and undertail coverts, unstreaked breast. First-fall males can have some richer bay on flanks.

BLACKPOLL WARBLER *Setophaga striata* p. 310
Very similar to Bay-breasted Warbler but slimmer. Note streaked back and breast, yellowish legs and especially feet.

NORTHERN PARULA *Setophaga americana* p. 302
First-fall: Small and short-tailed. Bluish head, broken eye-ring, and yellow throat; wing bars. Female lacks marks on breast.

MAGNOLIA WARBLER *Setophaga magnolia* p. 302
First-fall: Broad white band at midtail. Note yellow rump. Faint dusky band across yellow breast. Side streaking. Sexes similar in first fall.

PRAIRIE WARBLER *Setophaga discolor* p. 308
First-fall: Jaw stripe, side streaks. Bobs tail. Female duller than male.

YELLOW WARBLER *Setophaga petechia* p. 302
Yellow edging on wings and tail. Beady dark eye. Some drab females may resemble Orange-crowned Warbler, but note lack of face pattern.

BLACKBURNIAN WARBLER *Setophaga fusca* p. 306
First-fall: Yellow or yellow-orange throat, dark cheek; broad supercilium, dark blackish back with pale stripes, upper wing bar triangular.

BLACK-THROATED GREEN WARBLER *Setophaga virens* p. 306
First-fall: Yellow cheek framed by olive. Note black on sides of upper breast, plain greenish back.

PALM WARBLER *Setophaga palmarum* p. 308
Brownish back, yellowish undertail coverts. Bobs tail.

YELLOW-RUMPED WARBLER *Setophaga coronata* p. 304
First-fall: Bright yellow rump, streaked back; brownish above. Flightier behavior than most other warblers; hawks insects; eats berries in winter.

CAPE MAY WARBLER *Setophaga tigrina* p. 304
First-fall: Streaked breast, greenish yellow rump. Female grayer than dull Yellow-rumped Warbler.

RUBY-CROWNED KINGLET

female

not a warbler

CHESTNUT-SIDED WARBLER

first-fall

SELECTED FALL WARBLERS

With Streaks or Wing Bars

fall male

PINE WARBLER

BLACKPOLL WARBLER

first-fall

PINE WARBLER

first-fall female

BAY-BREASTED WARBLER

first-fall

first-fall

first-fall male

NORTHERN PARULA

MAGNOLIA WARBLER

PRAIRIE WARBLER

YELLOW WARBLER

first-fall female

first-fall male

first-fall

first-fall female

BLACK-THROATED GREEN WARBLER

BLACKBURNIAN WARBLER

PALM WARBLER

western first-fall

first-fall female

YELLOW-RUMPED WARBLER

"Audubon's" (plainer face)

CAPE MAY WARBLER

first-fall female

FALL WARBLERS

Most of these lack streaks or wing bars.

ORANGE-CROWNED WARBLER *Oreothlypis celata* **p. 300**
First-year: Dingy breast with faint dusky streaks, yellow undertail coverts, faint eye line. First-fall birds of drab greenish with gray head.

TENNESSEE WARBLER *Oreothlypis peregrina* **p. 300**
First-fall: Similar to Orange-crowned Warbler but has white undertail coverts; more conspicuous eyebrow stripe; greener above; trace of a pale yellowish wing bar; shorter tail. Note also needle-thin bill.

PHILADELPHIA VIREO *Vireo philadelphicus* **p. 296**
(Not a warbler.) "Vireo" song and actions. Note also thicker vireo bill. Compare with female Tennessee Warbler.

HOODED WARBLER *Setophaga citrina* **p. 316**
First-year female: Yellow eyebrow stripe, mostly yellow face, dark lores, bold white tail spots. (First-fall male resembles adult male.)

WILSON'S WARBLER *Cardellina pusilla* **p. 316**
First-year: Smaller and slimmer than Hooded Warbler with yellow lores, mostly olive cheeks, slimmer tail with no white. First-fall male has partial black cap; many first-fall females lack black.

BLACK-THROATED BLUE WARBLER *Setophaga caerulescens* **p. 304**
Female: Dark cheek, white wing spot. In some first-fall females this white spot is obscured, but note dark cheek and dull olive back. (First-fall male resembles adult male.)

CONNECTICUT WARBLER *Oporornis agilis* **p. 314**
First-fall: Large size. Plump. Brownish hood; complete, bold eye-ring. Walks.

MOURNING WARBLER *Geothlypis philadelphia* **p. 314**
First-fall female: Suggestion of hood; broken eye-ring. Brighter yellow below than Connecticut Warbler, including throat, contrary to grayish white throat of MacGillivray's Warbler.

NASHVILLE WARBLER *Oreothlypis ruficapilla* **p. 300**
First-fall: Yellowish (male) to buff (female) throat; sides of breast and undertail coverts tinged yellow, dull in females; eye-ring white to dingy pale; crown and nape grayish. Short tail, which it can bob.

COMMON YELLOWTHROAT *Geothlypis trichas* **p. 316**
First-fall female: Yellowish to buff throat, dull yellow breast and undertail coverts; brownish sides; white belly. Large bill and behavior help separate this from similar dull warblers.

PROTHONOTARY WARBLER *Protonotaria citrea* **p. 312**
First-year: Golden head tinged greenish on crown; dark eye stands out on plain face. Gray wings, white undertail, long bill.

CANADA WARBLER *Cardellina canadensis* **p. 316**
First-fall: Lores yellow, eye-ring white. Grayish to brownish gray above, yellow below, trace of necklace (nearly absent on duller females).

SELECTED FALL WARBLERS

Without Streaks or Wing Bars

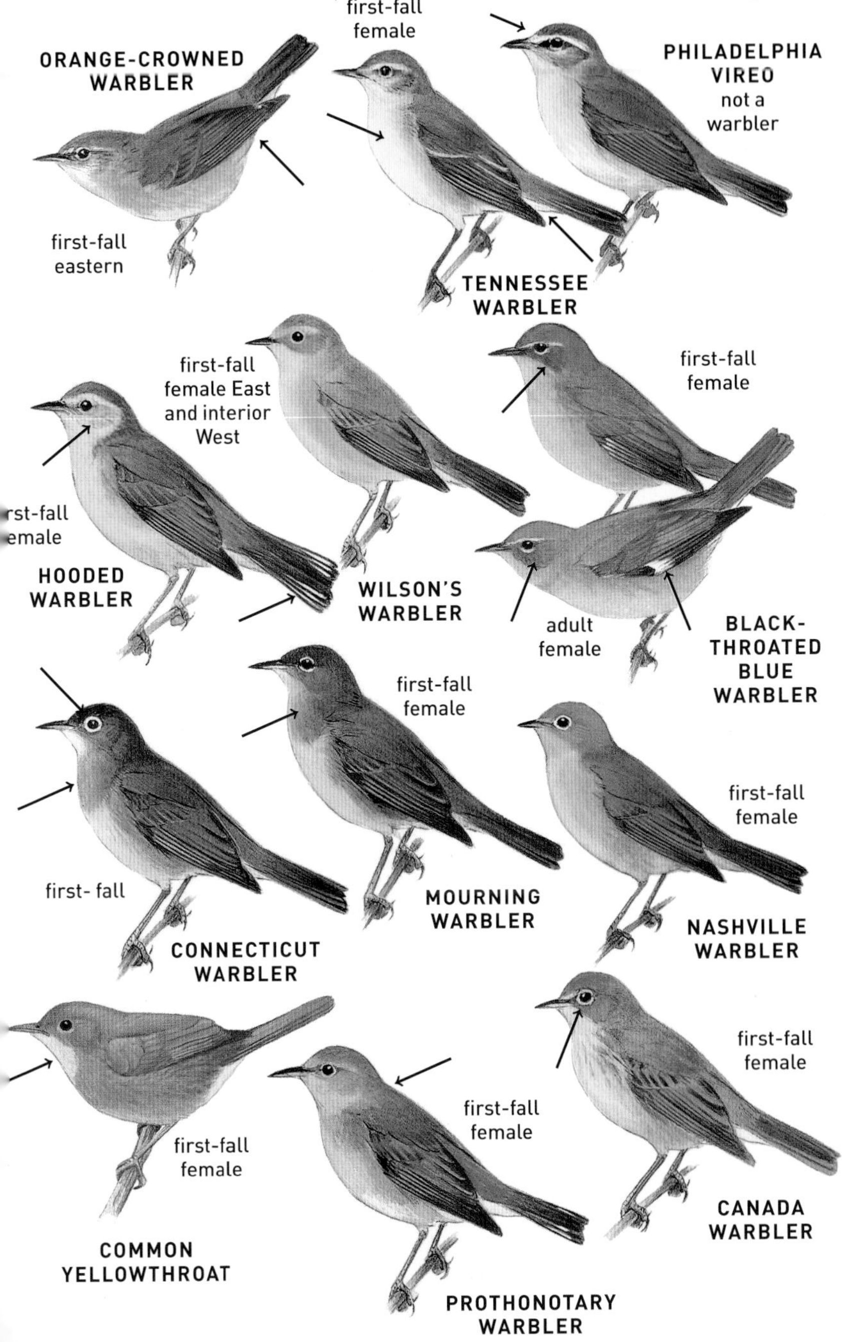
ORANGE-CROWNED WARBLER
first-fall eastern
first-fall female
TENNESSEE WARBLER
PHILADELPHIA VIREO
not a warbler
rst-fall
emale
HOODED WARBLER
first-fall female East and interior West
WILSON'S WARBLER
first-fall female
adult female
BLACK-THROATED BLUE WARBLER
first- fall
CONNECTICUT WARBLER
first-fall female
MOURNING WARBLER
first-fall female
NASHVILLE WARBLER
first-fall female
COMMON YELLOWTHROAT
first-fall female
PROTHONOTARY WARBLER
first-fall female
CANADA WARBLER

PAINTED REDSTART *Myioborus pictus* Uncommon

5¾ in. (15 cm). Elegant bird with half-spread wings and tail, showing off *large white patches*. Black head and upperparts; *large bright red patch* on lower breast and belly. White crescent under eye. *Juvenile:* Lacks red; otherwise ages and sexes similar. **VOICE:** Song a repetitious *weeta weeta weeta wee* or *weeta weeta chilp chilp chilp.* Call *clee-ip,* suggesting a siskin. **SIMILAR SPECIES:** Red-faced Warbler, American Redstart. **HABITAT:** Pine-oak canyons and mountains; comes to sugar-water feeders. Rare vagrant north of range and to Coastal cen. CA.

RED-FACED WARBLER *Cardellina rubrifrons* Uncommon, local

5½ in. (14 cm). The only U.S. warbler with *bright red face and throat.* Note black patch on head, and white nape and rump. Ages and sexes similar. **VOICE:** Clear, sweet song, similar to Yellow Warbler. Call a sharp *chip* or *chup.* **SIMILAR SPECIES:** Painted Redstart overlaps in range and habitat. **HABITAT:** Open fir and pine-oak forests in upper canyons, mountains. Casual vagrant north of range and to coastal cen. CA.

RUFOUS-CAPPED WARBLER *Basileuterus rufifrons* Very rare, local

5 in. (13 cm). *Rufous cap and cheek* separated by white eyebrow stripe. Long, spindly tail often held cocked up at angle. Ages and sexes similar. **VOICE:** Accelerating series of whistled, musical chips and warbles. Call *tick.* **SIMILAR SPECIES:** Common Yellowthroat. **RANGE:** Very rare visitor from Mex. to s. AZ (where it has bred) and TX. **HABITAT:** Thick brush, oak woodlands near water.

NORTH AMERICAN CHATS Family Icteriidae

Traditionally placed with wood warblers but was recently afforded its own family because of its larger body and bill size and other factors.

YELLOW-BREASTED CHAT *Icteria virens* Uncommon

7½ in. (19 cm). Larger than our warblers, with *heavy bill* and *long tail.* Note *white* spectacles, *bright yellow* throat and breast. No wing bars. **VOICE:** Repeated whistles, alternating with harsh notes and soft *caws*; often in awkward courtship display flight. Single notes: *whoit, kook, zhairr,* etc. **SIMILAR SPECIES:** Common Yellowthroat (much smaller). **HABITAT:** Brushy tangles, briars, stream thickets, where it skulks.

STARLINGS Family Sturnidae

A large and varied family; sharp-billed, usually short-tailed. Gregarious and adaptable. **FOOD:** Insects, seeds, berries. **RANGE:** Widespread in Old World.

EUROPEAN STARLING *Sturnus vulgaris* Common, introduced

8½ in. (22 cm). Note *short tail* and *sharply pointed bill.* In flight, has *triangular wings;* flies swiftly and directly. *Spring/summer:* Plumage iridescent, bill *yellow,* blue-based in male, pink-based in female. *Fall/winter:* Heavily speckled with white, bill dark. *Juvenile:* Dusky gray-brown, a bit like a female cowbird, but stockier, tail shorter, bill longer. **VOICE:** Harsh, wheezy *tseeeer;* a whistled *whooee.* Mimics other birds. **SIMILAR SPECIES:** Cedar Waxwing, in flight. **HABITAT:** Cities, suburbs, parks, feeders, farms. Competes for nesting holes with native cavity-nesting species.

WARBLERS, CHAT, STARLING

PAINTED REDSTART

juvenile

adult

RED-FACED WARBLER

RUFOUS-CAPPED WARBLER

male

Common Yellowthroat (p. 316 for comparison)

YELLOW-BREASTED CHAT

spring/ summer

EUROPEAN STARLING

juvenile

fall/winter

PIPITS and WAGTAILS Family Motacillidae

Pipits and wagtails are found in open areas, walking on the ground. Pipits are streaked birds with white outer tail feathers and thin bills; two species of wagtails breed in AK are widespread in the Old World, with two species breeding eastward into AK. **FOOD:** Insects, seeds. **RANGE:** Nearly worldwide.

AMERICAN PIPIT *Anthus rubescens* Fairly common

6½ in. (17 cm). A *slim-billed, sparrowlike* bird of open country. *Bobs tail* as it *walks.* Underparts buff; *outer tail feathers white;* legs blackish to dusky pinkish. Spring/summer birds grayer above, pinker and less streaked below; fall/winter birds washed olive and buff. Ages and sexes alike. Asian subspecies (*japonicus*) rare but regular vagrant along Pacific Coast, grayer above, more boldly streaked below, legs pinkish. **VOICE:** Call a distinctive, thin *jeet* or *jee-eet.* In aerial song flight, *chwee chwee chwee chwee chwee chwee chwee.* **SIMILAR SPECIES:** Red-throated and Sprague's Pipits. **HABITAT:** In summer, Arctic and alpine tundra; in migration and winter, fields, short-grass habitats, shores.

SPRAGUE'S PIPIT *Anthus spragueii* Uncommon, secretive

6½ in. (17 cm). A furtive species. Note *pinkish legs.* Buffy below, with *striped back* and white outer tail feathers. *Plain buffy face with beady dark eye.* Ages and sexes alike. More solitary than American Pipit. When flushed, often towers high, then drops like a rock. Does *not* wag tail. **VOICE:** Sings high in air; a sweet, thin jingling *shiing-a-ring-a-ring-a-ring-a.* When flushed, a distinctive *squeet* or *squeet-squeet* call. **SIMILAR SPECIES:** American Pipit differs in facial pattern and voice, has darker legs, wags tail. See juvenile Horned Lark. **HABITAT:** Short- to medium-grass prairies and fields. Very rare vagrant and winter visitor to CA.

RED-THROATED PIPIT *Anthus cervinus* Rare, local

6 in. (15 cm). Rare Pacific Coast visitor, almost exclusively in fall; very rarely in spring in w. AK, where a few nest. *Adult:* Spring/summer male has *pinkish red face and breast;* duller in female. In fall/winter, *heavily streaked below; bold striping on back,* pinkish legs. **VOICE:** Call a distinctive, high, thin *speeee* or *speeuh* and a hoarse *tzeez.* **SIMILAR SPECIES:** American Pipit is less streaked and has different call, darker legs. **HABITAT:** In summer, hillside tundra. Rare vagrant along Pacific Coast in migration, often found with American Pipits.

WHITE WAGTAIL *Motacilla alba* Rare, local

7¼ in. (18 cm). Note bold head pattern, gray back, and white wing patches. "Black-backed" Wagtail (subspecies *lugens*), has *black back* in spring/summer plumage, *more white in wings.* Males bolder than females, first-fall birds duller than adults, sex by sex. **VOICE:** Call a lively *tchizzik,* also an abrupt *tchik.* **SIMILAR SPECIES:** Duller fall Eastern Yellow Wagtails have less white in face and wings, different call. **HABITAT:** Tundra, open country, shorelines. Casual vagrant along Pacific Coast.

EASTERN YELLOW WAGTAIL Uncommon, local
Motacilla tschutschensis

6½ in. (17 cm). *Adult:* Grayish to brownish above, *yellow below;* male brighter than female. *First-fall:* Dull whitish or tinged yellow below; throat outlined in dark. **VOICE:** Call a buzzy *tsoueep.* Song *tsip-tsip-tsipsi.* **SIMILAR SPECIES:** White Wagtail. **HABITAT:** Willow scrub on tundra, marshy country, shorelines. Casual vagrant along Pacific Coast.

PIPITS AND WAGTAILS

AMERICAN PIPIT

fall/winter
North American
spring/summer
Asian

SPRAGUE'S PIPIT

Sprague's overhead

American and Red-throated pipits wag their tails

towering flight

RED-THROATED PIPIT

spring/summer female

spring/summer male

fall/winter

WHITE WAGTAIL

spring/summer male

fall/winter

EASTERN YELLOW WAGTAIL

first-fall female

spring/summer male

"Black-backed"

spring/summer male

LARKS Family Alaudidae

Brown terrestrial birds with long hind claws. Often joined by longspurs and Snow Buntings during winter. Larks sing in high display flights. **FOOD:** Seeds, insects. **RANGE:** Mainly Old World.

EURASIAN SKYLARK
Alauda arvensis

Scarce, local, introduced and vagrant

7¼ in. (19 cm). Slightly larger than a sparrow, with *short crest*; brown, strongly streaked; breast streaked; *trailing edge of wing and sides of tail white*. Ages and sexes similar. **VOICE:** Call a clear, liquid *chir-r-up*. Song, in hovering flight, musical, with long-sustained runs and trills. **SIMILAR SPECIES:** Juvenile Horned Lark, pipits. **RANGE:** Introduced birds are resident on s. Vancouver I., BC, and in HI (p. 408). Also casual vagrant to w. AK islands, WA, OR, and HI. **HABITAT:** Open country, airports.

HORNED LARK *Eremophila alpestris*

Uncommon to common

7–7¼ in. (18–19 cm). *Male:* Note head pattern. Larger than a sparrow, with *black mustache,* two small *black "horns,"* and black breast splotch. *Walks* on short legs. From below, white with *black* tail. *Female:* Similar but duller. *Juvenile:* Very different, *streaked below*. **VOICE:** Song tinkling, often prolonged; from ground or in air. Call a clear *tsee-titi*. **SIMILAR SPECIES:** Juvenile can be misidentified as Sprague's Pipit, longspurs, or sparrows. **HABITAT:** Prairies, short-grass and dirt fields, shores, tundra. Populations of w. WA–OR (subspecies *strigata*) threatened.

LONGSPURS and SNOW BUNTINGS
Family Calcariidae

Recently split family that now consists of six species, all of which occur in our area. Legs are short such that birds appear to feed on their bellies. Longspurs are birds of open country; in fall/winter season, often found in flocks with pipits and larks. **FOOD:** Seeds, insects on breeding grounds.

SNOW BUNTING *Plectrophenax nivalis*

Uncommon

6¾ in. (17 cm). Note extensive amount of white. Browner in fall and winter, but flashing *white wing patches* in flight diagnostic. *Spring/summer male:* Black back contrasting with white head and underparts; bill black. Females and first-fall birds duller, less white, bill dull yellowish brown; all ages and sexes become whiter in spring due to plumage wear (not molt). **VOICE:** Call a sharp, whistled *teer* or *tew*; also a rough, purring *brrt*, similar to Lapland Longspur's calls. Song a musical *ti-ti-chu-ree*, repeated. **SIMILAR SPECIES:** McKay's Bunting. Leucistic juncos, House Sparrows, etc., sometimes mistaken for Snow Buntings. **HABITAT:** Prairies, fields, dunes, shores; in summer, tundra. Vagrant well south of normal winter range, including to HI.

MCKAY'S BUNTING *Plectrophenax hyperboreus*

Scarce, local

7 in. (18 cm). Breeds regularly only on St. Matthew and Hall Is., AK. Similar to Snow Bunting but all age/sex classes whiter, the spring/summer male almost pure white, except for ends of primaries and scapulars and near tips of central tail feathers. **VOICE:** Song of male suggests American Goldfinch. **SIMILAR SPECIES:** Snow Bunting. **HABITAT:** Tundra, barrens, shores; in fall/winter mixes with Snow Buntings. Vagrant to WA.

LARKS AND BUNTINGS

overhead

towering flight

juvenile

prairie

EURASIAN SKYLARK

HORNED LARK

adult males

northern

SNOW BUNTING

winter female

winter male

Snow Bunting summer male

summer male

winter

summer female

summer

Snow Bunting males

winter female

McKay's Bunting male

MCKAY'S BUNTING

LAPLAND LONGSPUR
Calcarius lapponicus

Uncommon to fairly common

6¼ in. (16 cm). The most widespread N. American longspur. *Spring/summer male: Black face outlined with white* is distinctive. Rusty collar. *Fall/winter male:* Sparse black streaks on sides, dull rusty nape, and smudge across breast help identify it. *Female:* Resembles fall/winter male, first-year duller. In all fall/winter plumages note *dark frame to rear cheek, rufous-brown edging to wing coverts*, tail pattern. **VOICE:** In flight, a dry rattle, also a musical *teew;* when perched, a soft *pee-dle.* Song in display flight is vigorous, musical. **SIMILAR SPECIES:** Smith's Longspur has similar tail pattern but buffier below; note face pattern, white checks in wings. Other longspurs have more white in tail. **HABITAT:** In summer, tundra; in winter, open fields, short-grass prairies, shores.

CHESTNUT-COLLARED LONGSPUR *Calcarius ornatus*

Uncommon

6 in. (15 cm). *Spring/summer male:* Solid *black* below, except on throat and lower belly; nape *chestnut. Fall/winter male:* Colors muted by brown feather edging. *Female:* Very plain; best field marks are tail pattern (dark triangle on white tail), dark bill, and flight call. **VOICE:** Song short, feeble, but musical; suggests Western Meadowlark. Call a finchlike or turnstonelike *ji-jiv* or *kittle-kittle*, unique among longspurs. **SIMILAR SPECIES:** McCown's Longspur. **HABITAT:** Plains, native-grass prairies; generally prefers some cover. Winter flocks may disappear in grass until flushed. Rare vagrant to W. Coast.

MCCOWN'S LONGSPUR *Rhynchophanes mccownii*

Uncommon, local

6 in. (15 cm). *Spring/summer male:* Crown and patch on breast black, tail largely white. Hindneck *gray* (brown or chestnut in other longspurs). *Female and fall/winter male:* Rather plain; note tail pattern (inverted T of black on white) and *swollen-looking, pinkish, fleshy bill.* Some birds are especially *plain looking*, reminiscent of female House Sparrow. **VOICE:** Song in display flight is clear sweet warbles, suggestive of Lark Bunting. Call a dry rattle, softer than Lapland Longspur's. Also a soft *pink.* **SIMILAR SPECIES:** Female Chestnut-collared Longspur is darker, usually more heavily marked below, has slightly smaller and *darker (not pinkish)* bill, different call. **HABITAT:** Plains, prairies, short-grass and dirt fields. Very rare vagrant to W. Coast.

SMITH'S LONGSPUR *Calcarius pictus*

Scarce, local

6¼ in. (16 cm). This secretive longspur prefers enough grassy cover to disappear. It is *warm buff on entire underparts.* Tail edged with white, as in Vesper Sparrow and Lapland Longspur. *Spring/summer male: Deep buff;* ear patch with *white spot*, strikingly outlined by *black triangle. Female and fall/winter:* Less distinctive; *buffy breast* lightly streaked; small pale spot on side of neck; most have white patch in wing coverts (absent or obscure in some females). **VOICE:** Rattling or clicking notes in flight (likened to winding a cheap watch). Song sweet, warblerlike, terminating in *WEchew.* Does not sing in flight. **SIMILAR SPECIES:** Lapland and Chestnut-collared Longspurs, Vesper Sparrow, Sprague's Pipit. **HABITAT:** Prairies, fields, airports; in summer, tundra with scattered bushes. Casual vagrant to W. Coast.

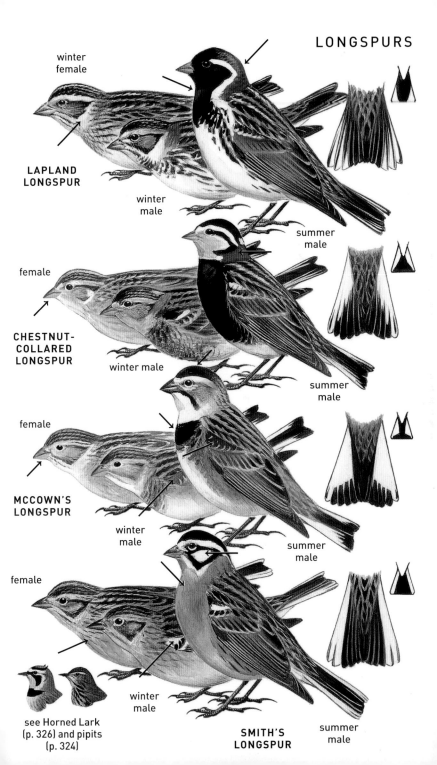

LONGSPURS

winter
female

LAPLAND
LONGSPUR

winter
male

summer
male

female

CHESTNUT-
COLLARED
LONGSPUR

winter male

summer
male

female

MCCOWN'S
LONGSPUR

winter
male

summer
male

female

see Horned Lark
(p. 326) and pipits
(p. 324)

winter
male

SMITH'S
LONGSPUR

summer
male

NORTH AMERICAN TOWHEES, SPARROWS, and JUNCOS Family Passerellidae

Formerly lumped with Old World seed-eating birds. Juveniles more heavily streaked; otherwise, ages and sexes mostly similar. **FOOD:** Seeds, insects, fruit. **RANGE:** Throughout Americas.

GREEN-TAILED TOWHEE
Pipilo chlorurus

Uncommon to fairly common

7¼ in. (18 cm). Note *rufous cap,* conspicuous *white throat,* black mustache, gray chest, and plain *olive green upperparts* (sexes similar). Juvenile plainer, breast streaked. **VOICE:** Call a catlike mewing note. Song variable, often: *weet-churr-cheeeeee-churr.* **HABITAT:** Brushy montane slopes, meadows; in winter, brushy and riparian woods. Rare to coast.

EASTERN TOWHEE *Pipilo erythrophthalmus*
Casual vagrant

8 in. (20–21 cm). Smilar to Spotted Towhee but back and wings *lack spots;* has white patch at base of primaries; female's head browner. **VOICE:** Call a loud *chewink!* **SIMILAR SPECIES:** Northwestern Spotted Towhees have fewer spots but lack white in primaries. **RANGE:** Casual visitor from East to Plains states. **HABITAT:** Open woods, brushy undergrowth, feeders.

SPOTTED TOWHEE *Pipilo maculatus*
Common

8 in. (20–21 cm). Note *rufous sides. Male:* Head and chest black; sides rufous red, belly white, *back heavily spotted with white* (amount varying geographically; see Eastern Towhee). Flashes *white patches* in tail corners. Eye fiery red. *Female:* Similar, but black replaced by dusky grayish black to brownish black. *Juvenile:* Streaked, with flash pattern in tail; browner iris. **VOICE:** Song a drawn-out, buzzy *chweeeeee* or *chup chup chup zeeeeeeee;* variable. Call a catlike *gu-eeee?* or (Southwest mountains) rising and falling *chreeeer.* **SIMILAR SPECIES:** Eastern Towhee. **HABITAT:** Open woods, undergrowth, chaparral, brushy edges, gardens.

CANYON TOWHEE *Melozone fusca*
Uncommon

8¾ in. (22 cm). Slightly paler and grayer than California Towhee, crown washed rufous, more distinct dusky necklace and spot on breast (sexes similar). **VOICE:** Call an odd *shed-lp* or *kedlp.* Song an accelerating string of call notes, different from California Towhee. **SIMILAR SPECIES:** Abert's Towhee. **HABITAT:** Brushy canyons, deserts, residential areas, feeders.

CALIFORNIA TOWHEE *Melozone crissalis*
Common

9 in. (23 cm). A familiar, dull brown, ground-loving bird, with moderately long, dark tail. Note pale *rusty undertail coverts* and streaked necklace. Juvenile lightly streaked overall, has cinnamon wing bars. **VOICE:** Call a metallic *chink.* Song a rapid *chink-chink-ink-ink-ink-ink-ink-ink,* often ending in trill. **SIMILAR SPECIES:** Canyon and Abert's Towhees (ranges do not overlap). **HABITAT:** Brushy areas, coastal scrub, canyons, gardens. Birds of Inyo Co., CA (subspecies *eremophila*) threatened.

ABERT'S TOWHEE *Melozone aberti*
Fairly common

9½ in. (24 cm). Similar to Canyon Towhee, but note *blackish facial patch embracing base of bill;* rest of underparts uniform, sometimes washed cinnamon or pinkish buff; rustier undertail coverts. Juvenile streaked but has darker face. **VOICE:** Call a sharp *peek* and high squeal. Song a rapid series of high *peek* and lower *tuk* notes. **SIMILAR SPECIES:** Canyon Towhee. **HABITAT:** Riparian scrub, desert brush, mesquite, parks.

TOWHEES

GREEN-TAILED
TOWHEE

female

juvenile

EASTERN
TOWHEE

male

male

juvenile

SPOTTED
TOWHEE

female

CANYON
TOWHEE

CALIFORNIA
TOWHEE

ABERT'S
TOWHEE

RUFOUS-WINGED SPARROW *Peucaea carpalis* Scarce, local

5¾ in. (15 cm). An AZ specialty. Suggests Chipping Sparrow, but plumper bodied, tail not notched. *Double black "whiskers,"* rufous eye line, gray stripe through rufous crown. *Rufous shoulder* not easily seen. Juvenile has streaked breast. **VOICE:** Song musical, one or two notes followed by rapid series of chips. **SIMILAR SPECIES:** Rufous-crowned Sparrow. **HABITAT:** Desert grasslands, thorn brush, desert hackberry, mesquite.

RUFOUS-CROWNED SPARROW *Aimophila ruficeps* Uncommon

6 in. (15 cm). Dark, with plain dusky breast, rufous cap and line behind eye, rounded tail. Note *black whiskers* bordering throat and *distinct circular whitish eye-ring.* Juvenile has streaked breast. Seen singly or in pairs. **VOICE:** Song stuttering, gurgling, suggesting a thin House Wren song. Call *dear, dear, dear.* **SIMILAR SPECIES:** Rufous-winged and Chipping Sparrows paler, more slender, smaller billed, lack or have less-distinct whiskers. **HABITAT:** Grassy or rocky slopes with sparse low bushes; open pine-oak woods.

BOTTERI'S SPARROW *Peucaea botterii* Uncommon, local

6 in. (15 cm). Nondescript. Buffy breast, plain brown tail lacking white corners. Juvenile has sparse streaks on breast. *Best identified by voice.* Bill culmen slightly curved. **VOICE:** Song a constant tinkling and "pitting," sometimes running into a dry trill on same pitch. Very unlike Cassin's song. **SIMILAR SPECIES:** Cassin's Sparrow, breeding in same habitat, is very similar, but usually grayer, has faint dusky streaks on flanks, small white corners to tail, straighter bill culmen; upperparts often more patterned, less streaked; "skylarks" when singing (which Botteri's doesn't do). **HABITAT:** Desert grasslands and bunch grass (particularly sacaton grass).

CASSIN'S SPARROW *Peucaea cassinii* Fairly common

6 in. (15 cm). A large, drab sparrow of open arid country; underparts dingy, unmarked or with faint streaking on flanks. Upperparts appear patterned, with anchor-shaped markings on individual feathers. Individuals can be either more rufous or grayer than shown. *Pale or whitish corners* on *rounded,* gray-brown tail. Juvenile has dark breast streaking. **VOICE:** Song one or two short notes, a high sweet trill, and two lower notes: *ti ti tseeeeeee tay tay.* Often "skylarks" in air, giving trill at climax; also flicks wings and tail in flight. **SIMILAR SPECIES:** Botteri's Sparrow. Savannah Sparrow smaller, streakier overall, and shorter tailed than Cassin's. **HABITAT:** Desert grasslands and semiarid prairies, bushes. Casual fall vagrant to coastal n. CA.

VESPER SPARROW *Pooecetes gramineus* Uncommon

6¼ in. (16 cm). *White outer tail feathers* are conspicuous when bird flies. Otherwise suggests slightly largish Savannah Sparrow but has prominent *whitish eye-ring, chestnut* bend of wing. Note white malar stripe and lack of central crown stripe. **VOICE:** Song similar to Song Sparrow's but throatier; two clear minor notes followed by two higher ones. Call a brief *tseet.* **SIMILAR SPECIES:** Savannah Sparrow lacks bright white outer tail feathers and distinct eye-ring. **HABITAT:** Meadows and prairies with scattered trees or bushes (such as sage), roadsides, farm fields.

SPARROWS

RUFOUS-WINGED
SPARROW

RUFOUS-
CROWNED
SPARROW

BOTTERI'S
SPARROW

CASSIN'S
SPARROW

VESPER
SPARROW

LARK SPARROW *Chondestes grammacus* **Fairly common**

6½ in. (17 cm). *Adult:* Note *distinct head pattern,* with *chestnut ear patch* and striped crown; *black tail with white corners;* white underparts with dark *central breast spot. Juvenile:* Head pattern duller, dusky streaks on breast. **VOICE:** Clear buzzing and churring passages, with pauses between. Call a sharp *tsip.* **SIMILAR SPECIES:** Vesper Sparrow. **HABITAT:** Open country with bushes, trees; pastures, farms, roadsides.

BELL'S SPARROW *Artemisiospiza belli* **Uncommon**

6–6¼ in. (15–16 cm). *Adult:* Generally darker and browner than Sage-brush Sparrow, with less streaking on back and heavier black whiskers. **VOICE:** Similar to Sagebrush Sparrow but higher pitched, less musical. **SIMILAR SPECIES:** Juvenile Black-throated Sparrow. Bell's from eastern part of range most similar to Sagebrush and can overlap on winter grounds. **HABITAT:** Dry brushy foothills, chaparral. Subspecies *clement-eae* of San Clemente Is., CA, threatened.

SAGEBRUSH SPARROW *Artemisiospiza nevadensis* **Uncommon**

6–6¼ in. (15–16 cm). Formerly conspecific with Bell's Sparrow (as "Sage Sparrow"). Note combination of *single breast spot* and *dark "whiskers" on sides of throat. Adult:* Gray head contrasts with browner back and wing. *White eye-ring,* touch of whitish over eye. *Juvenile:* Brown and streaked, has bold eye-ring. *Often runs on ground, with tail held high.* **VOICE:** Song four to seven musical notes, *tsit-tsoo-tseee-tsay* or *tsit, tsit, tsi you, tee a-tee;* recalls Western Meadowlark. Twittering call. **SIMILAR SPECIES:** Bell's Sparrow. Juvenile Black-throated Sparrow. **HABITAT:** Sage and saltbush flats; in winter, also creosote bush. Casual to Plains states.

BLACK-THROATED SPARROW *Amphispiza bilineata* **Fairly common**

5½ in. (14 cm). *Adult:* Note *white face stripes* and *jet-black throat and chest.* White corners to *distinct black tail.* Sexes alike. *Juvenile:* Seen into fall; *lacks* black throat but has similar head pattern; breast weakly streaked. **VOICE:** Song a sweet *cheet cheet cheeeeeeee.* Calls are light tinkling notes. **SIMILAR SPECIES:** Juvenile recalls juvenile Sage Sparrow but has a supercilium and black tail. **HABITAT:** Arid brush, creosote-bush and cactus deserts, juniper hillsides. Rare to casual vagrant to n. CA and northwest coast, largely first-fall birds.

FIVE-STRIPED SPARROW *Amphispiza quinquestriata* **Very rare, local**

6 in. (15 cm). *Dusky,* with *five white stripes* on head (white supercilium, subauricular streak, and throat), black whiskers, and single black spot on dark gray breast. Juvenile streaky; can have yellowish belly. **VOICE:** High-pitched, repeated, thrasherlike phrases. Call a sharp *tchak!* **SIMILAR SPECIES:** Black-throated and Sage Sparrows. **HABITAT:** Dense brushy canyon slopes, rocky hillsides.

BLACK-CHINNED SPARROW *Spizella atrogularis* **Uncommon**

5¾ in. (15 cm). Juncolike sparrow (but slimmer, with no white in tail); has streaked brown back, *head and underparts medium gray,* small pinkish bill. *Spring/summer male:* Bill encircled by bold *black chin and lores. Female and fall/winter male:* Most lack black face. Juvenile has indistinct streaks on head and breast. **VOICE:** Song a sweet series of clear notes, starting with several high notes, ending in rough trill: *sweet, sweet, sweet, weet-trrrrrrr.* **SIMILAR SPECIES:** Black-throated Sparrow, juncos. **HABITAT:** Brushy mountain slopes, chaparral, juniper; winters on brushy canyon slopes, usually in flocks. Casual vagrant north of range.

SPARROWS

first-year

adult

LARK SPARROW

BELL'S
SPARROW

SAGEBRUSH
SPARROW

juvenile

FIVE-STRIPED
SPARROW

BLACK-
THROATED
SPARROW

juvenile

BLACK-CHINNED
SPARROW

spring/
summer
male

fall/winter
female

AMERICAN TREE SPARROW *Spizelloides arborea* Uncommon

6¼ in. (16 cm). Note *dark "stickpin" on breast,* and *red-brown cap. Bill dark above, yellow below;* white wing bars; rufous wash on flanks. Ages and sexes rather similar (juvenile is streaked). **VOICE:** Song sweet, variable, opening on one or two high, clear notes. Call *tseet;* feeding call a musical *teelwit.* **SIMILAR SPECIES:** Field and Chipping Sparrows. **HABITAT:** Arctic and taiga scrub, willow thickets; in winter, brushy roadsides, weedy edges, cattail marshes. Casual vagrant well south of winter range.

CHIPPING SPARROW *Spizella passerina* Common

5½ in. (14 cm). *Spring/summer:* A small, slim, long-tailed, plain-breasted sparrow with bright *rufous cap, black eye line, white eyebrow. Fall/winter:* Duller; note *dark eyeline,* dirty grayish breast, *gray rump. Juvenile:* Has fine streaks on breast, rump not as gray; this plumage may be held through fall migration. **VOICE:** Song a dry chipping rattle on one pitch. Call a thin *tseet.* **SIMILAR SPECIES:** Clay-colored, Brewer's, Rufous-winged, and Swamp Sparrows. **HABITAT:** Open woods, especially pine, oak; orchards, farms, towns, lawns, feeders. Often forms flocks in fall and winter.

FIELD SPARROW *Spizella pusilla* Scarce, local

5¾ in. (15 cm). A small, slim, rusty-capped sparrow. Note small *pink bill,* white eye-ring, plain buffy breast; rusty upperparts, and weak face striping. *Juvenile:* Has finely streaked breast; plumage not held long. **VOICE:** Song an accelerating trill *psew-psew-psew-see-see-see-see* (ascending, descending, or on one pitch). Call *tseew.* **SIMILAR SPECIES:** American Tree, Chipping, and Brewer's Sparrows. **HABITAT:** Overgrown fields, pastures, brush, feeders. Casual vagrant to W. Coast.

CLAY-COLORED SPARROW *Spizella pallida* Uncommon

5½ in. (14 cm). Paler and buffier than fall/winter Chipping Sparrow, with paler lores, *more sharply outlined face pattern,* more-contrasting grayer nape, browner rump, whiter underparts; *eye-ring rather indistinct, broken.* Juvenile streaked below (held only briefly on breeding grounds). **VOICE:** Insectlike; three or four low, flat buzzes: *bzzz, bzzz, bzzz.* Call a thin *tseet,* like Chipping's but higher. **SIMILAR SPECIES:** Brewer's Sparrow. **HABITAT:** Scrub, brushy prairies, jack pines, weedy areas; in winter, open fields and brushlands, often with other Spizella sparrows. Scarce spring, fall, and winter visitor to W. Coast.

BREWER'S SPARROW *Spizella breweri* Fairly common

5½ in. (14 cm). A small, slim, pale, *nondescript* sparrow of sagebrush and desert scrub. Note pale lores, brownish rump, *distinct full whitish eye-ring,* and *lack of white central crown stripe.* "Timberline" subspecies (*taverneri*) has slightly bolder plumage; nests near tree line in n. Canadian Rockies and e. AK. Juvenile on breeding grounds streaked below. **VOICE:** Song long, musical buzzy trills on different pitches; canarylike. Call a thin *tsee.* **SIMILAR SPECIES:** Dull Chipping Sparrow redder on back, lacks eye-ring, has gray rump. Dull Clay-colored Sparrow buffier, head pattern and pale crown stripe usually more distinct. Caution: very dull Clay-coloreds can closely resemble Brewer's, but note especially *weaker eye-ring* on these. **HABITAT:** Nests in sagebrush, saltbush; winters in brushy plains and deserts, weedy fields. Casual vagrant to Plains states.

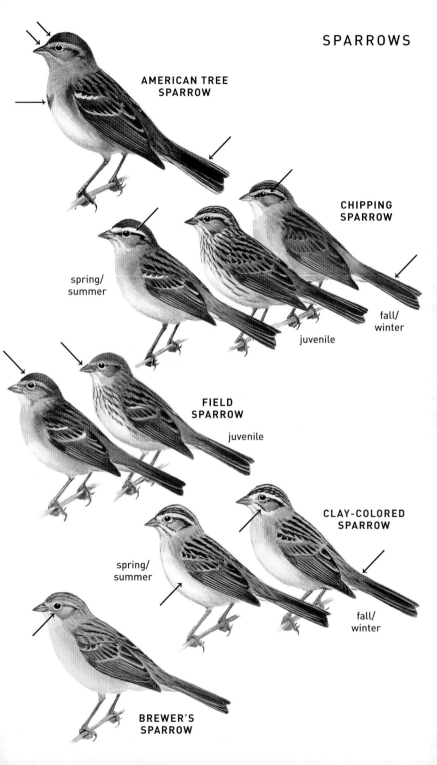

SPARROWS

AMERICAN TREE
SPARROW

CHIPPING
SPARROW

spring/
summer

juvenile

fall/
winter

FIELD
SPARROW

juvenile

CLAY-COLORED
SPARROW

spring/
summer

fall/
winter

BREWER'S
SPARROW

SAVANNAH SPARROW *Passerculus sandwichensis* **Common**

5½–5¾ in. (14–15 cm). An open-country sparrow with *yellowish on front of eyebrow, whitish stripe through crown,* and bright pink legs. Ages and sexes similar. Tail short, notched, the outer feathers palish but not bright white. "Large-billed" Savannah Sparrow (subspecies *rostratus*), a scarce post-breeding visitor to dry, sandy s. CA habitats, is paler with a larger bill. Darker "Belding's" Savannah Sparrow (*beldingi*) found in coastal salt marshes of cen.-s. CA. **VOICE:** Song a lisping, buzzy *tsit-tsit-tsit, tseeee-tsaaay.* Call a short *tseep* or light *tsu.* **SIMILAR SPECIES:** Song Sparrow darker, redder, with longer and rounded tail, duller pinkish legs. See Vesper Sparrow. Savannah's song similar to Grasshopper Sparrow's except for lower last note. **HABITAT:** Open fields, farms, meadows, salt marshes, prairies.

BAIRD'S SPARROW *Centronyx bairdii* **Scarce, local**

5½ in. (14 cm). An elusive, skulking prairie sparrow except when singing. *Adult:* Light breast crossed by *narrow band* of fine black streaks. Head flat, buff, streaked, with *ocher* median crown stripe and *double mustache stripes.* Juvenile (which can be found on migration) has a scaly pattern above. **VOICE:** Song two or three high musical *zips,* followed by trill on lower pitch. **SIMILAR SPECIES:** Savannah Sparrow has smaller bill, lacks dark marks at rear of auriculars and double mustache stripes. **HABITAT:** Native prairies; scattered bushes used as song perches. Accidental vagrant to the W. Coast.

GRASSHOPPER SPARROW *Ammodramus savannarum* **Uncommon**

5 in. (13 cm). Small, compact-bodied, with large and flat head and short and sharp tail; found in grasslands. Flight feeble. *Adult:* Crown with pale median stripe; *yellow lores; whitish eye-ring,* purplish-edged upperpart feathers; note relatively *unstriped buffy breast. Juvenile:* Less colorful, has dusky streaks on breast (found on migration). **VOICE:** Thin, dry, insectlike *pi-tup zeeeeeeeeeeee.* **SIMILAR SPECIES:** LeConte's Sparrow slimmer, longer tailed, smaller-billed; adult with orangier eyebrow; juvenile buffier, plainer faced. See Savannah Sparrow. **HABITAT:** Grasslands, hayfields, pastures, prairies.

LECONTE'S SPARROW *Ammospiza leconteii* **Uncommon**

5 in. (13 cm). A skulking sharp-tailed sparrow of prairie marshes. Note *bright orange* eyebrow and buffy breast (with streaks *confined to sides*), *purplish-chestnut streaks on nape,* stripes on back. Juvenile (can be found on migration) buffier overall, breast streaked. **VOICE:** Song consists of two extremely thin, grasshopper-like hisses. **SIMILAR SPECIES:** Nelson's Sparrow. Adult and juvenile Grasshopper Sparrow. **HABITAT:** Grassy marshes, tallgrass fields, weedy hayfields. Casual fall and winter vagrant to W. Coast.

NELSON'S SPARROW *Ammospiza nelsoni* **Scarce**

5 in. (13 cm). Note bright *orange on face,* completely surrounding gray ear patch. *Breast warm buff with faint blurry streaks,* stronger streaks on flanks, *unmarked gray nape,* back sharply striped with white. Ages and sexes similar. **VOICE:** Song a buzzy, two-part *shleeee-tup.* **SIMILAR SPECIES:** LeConte's Sparrow. **HABITAT:** In summer, prairie marshes. Very rare winter visitor to W. Coast salt marshes.

STREAK-BREASTED
GRASS SPARROWS

"Belding's"

SAVANNAH
SPARROW

typical

"Large-billed"

BAIRD'S
SPARROW

MARSH
SPARROWS

juvenile

GRASSHOPPER
SPARROW

LECONTE'S
SPARROW

NELSON'S
SPARROW

FOX SPARROW *Passerella iliaca* **Fairly common**

7 in. (18 cm). A large, plump sparrow, towheelike, kicking among dead leaves and other ground litter. *Breast heavily streaked* with triangular spots, often clustering on upper breast. Ages and sexes similar. Fox Sparrows vary widely: (1) "Red" northern and eastern subspecies (subspecies group *iliaca*): bright rusty with rusty back stripes (rare to W. Coast); (2) "Sooty" northwestern Pacific coastal subspecies (*unalaschcensis*): dusky or sooty head, back unstreaked, upper breast variably tinged reddish; (3) "Slate-colored" interior western subspecies (*schistacea*): gray-headed and gray-backed (unstreaked), yellowish-based bill; and (4) "Thick-billed" subspecies (*megarhyncha*) of s. Cascades and CA mts.: similar to Slate-colored but large-billed. Intermingle during winter. **VOICE:** Song a varied musical arrangement of short clear notes and sliding whistles. Calls a sharp *chink* (Thick-billed group) to flatter *chup* or *chick*. **SIMILAR SPECIES:** Song Sparrows in AK. **HABITAT:** Wooded undergrowth, brush, feeders.

SONG SPARROW *Melospiza melodia* **Common**

5¾–6½ in. (15–17 cm). This common sparrow has a *long rounded tail* and *heavy breast streaks* that merge into a *large central spot*. Broad grayish eyebrow. Juvenile more finely streaked. Vary in color and size, as shown, with many subspecies. **VOICE:** Song usually starts with three or four repetitious notes, *sweet sweet sweet,* etc., and ends in lower buzzy trill. Call a low, nasal *tchep.* **SIMILAR SPECIES:** Savannah, Lincoln's, and Swamp Sparrows. Some AK birds large, like Fox Sparrow, but not as red; bill smaller, with less-curved culmen. **HABITAT:** Thickets, brush, marshes, roadsides, gardens, feeders.

LINCOLN'S SPARROW *Melospiza lincolnii* **Fairly common**

5¾ in. (15 cm). Skulking, prefers to be near cover. Adult and juvenile similar to Song Sparrow, but smaller and trimmer, side of face grayer, sharp breast streaks *much finer* against *creamy buff* breast vs. whitish belly and throat; narrow whitish eye-ring; buffy mustache. **VOICE:** Song sweet and gurgling; starts with low passages, rises abruptly, drops. Calls a hard *tik* and buzzy *zzzeeet.* **SIMILAR SPECIES:** First-year Swamp Sparrow duller, darker, with blurrier streaks and rustier wing. Juvenile Swamp, Song, and Lincoln's Sparrows very similar: note differences in breast streaking, malar stripe, bill size and shape. **HABITAT:** Willow and alder thickets, mountain meadows; in winter, wet fields, brush, thickets, sometimes feeders.

SWAMP SPARROW *Melospiza georgiana* **Uncommon**

5¾ in. (15 cm). A plump, dark, *rusty-winged* sparrow with *broad black back striping. Adult male: White throat, rusty cap, blue-gray neck and breast. Female and first-year:* Variably average duller; *blackish* or dark rust crown, *olive-gray neck and breast;* dim flank streaking. Juvenile is heavily streaked. **VOICE:** Song a loose trill, sweeter than Chipping Sparrow's. Call a hard *cheep,* similar to Black Phoebe's. **SIMILAR SPECIES:** Song Sparrow larger, larger billed, longer tailed, has *heavier breast streaks,* lacks tawny flanks. Lincoln's Sparrow has buff breast with fine sharp streaks, finer bill. **HABITAT:** Nests in freshwater marshes; winters in fresh and salt marshes, pond edges, weedy ditches. Rare migrant in interior West and scarce winter visitor to CA.

"Red" (North and East)

"Slate-colored" (Rockies)

"Thick-billed" (CA)

STREAKED SPARROWS

ranges indicate breeding; these widely mix in winter

FOX SPARROW

"Sooty" (Northwest coast)

AK

Southwest

SONG SPARROW

typical

(typical)

SWAMP SPARROW

first-year female

adult

LINCOLN'S SPARROW

WHITE-THROATED SPARROW *Zonotrichia albicollis* Uncommon

6¾ in. (17 cm). *Spring/summer:* A gray-breasted sparrow with distinct white throat and yellow lores. Bill grayish. Polymorphic; head stripes vary in shades of black, brown, and tan; some adults have bold black-and-white head stripes, others duller brown and tan. Tan morph may be moderately streaked on breast; throat duller. Ages and sexes similar although first-fall birds and females average duller than adults and males within each morph. **VOICE:** Song several clear pensive whistles often rendered *old sam peabody peabody peabody*. Call a hard *chink*; also a thin, slurred *tseet*. **SIMILAR SPECIES:** White-crowned Sparrow. **HABITAT:** Thickets, brush, undergrowth of coniferous and mixed woodlands, feeders. Rare migrant in interior West; uncommon winter visitor to CA.

WHITE-CROWNED SPARROW *Zonotrichia leucophrys* Common

7 in. (18 cm). This species comprises multiple subspecies; birds of the East (subspecies *leucophrys*) and western mountains (*oriantha*) show black lores, those of the Pacific coast (*pugetensis* and *nuttalli*) show pale lores and yellow bills, and Great Basin and Canadian birds (*gambelli;* not shown) show pale lores and tawny bills. *Adult:* Clear breast, crown *striped with black and white. First-fall/winter:* Head stripes dark red-brown and light buff. **VOICE:** Song one or more clear, plaintive whistles, often *chew-chee-tzip-tzip-tzip tseew*, with many local dialects. Call a sharp *pink*. **SIMILAR SPECIES:** White-throated Sparrow has well-defined white throat, yellow spot before eye, grayish bill. First-fall/winter Golden-crowned Sparrow slightly larger, has *duskier bill and underparts,* more muted head pattern, usually with *dull yellowish forehead.* **HABITAT:** Brush, forest edges, thickets, chaparral; in winter, also farms, desert washes, gardens, parks, feeders.

GOLDEN-CROWNED SPARROW *Zonotrichia atricapilla* Fairly common

7¼ in. (18 cm). *Spring/summer*: Has *yellow central crown stripe,* bordered broadly with black. Dusky bill. *Fall/winter first-year:* May look like large female House Sparrow but usually with dull yellow suffusion on forehead; fall/winter adult similar but with blacker head stripes. **VOICE:** Song three to five high whistled notes of plaintive minor quality, *oh-dear-me.* Sometimes a faint trill. Call a sharp *tsew*. **SIMILAR SPECIES:** White-crowned Sparrow. **HABITAT:** Boreal and subalpine scrub, willow thickets, stunted spruces; in winter, similar to that of White-crowned (with which it is often found in mixed flocks), but favors denser shrubs.

HARRIS'S SPARROW *Zonotrichia querula* Uncommon

7½ in. (19 cm). Large; almost size of Fox Sparrow. *Adult: Black crown, face, and bib encircling pink bill. First-fall/winter:* Has *white on throat,* less black on crown, buffy brown on rest of head; blotched and streaked on breast. **VOICE:** Song has quavering quality of other *Zonotrichia* sparrows: one to three clear whistles, *peee* to *peee-pee-pee* on same pitch. Alarm call *wink*. **HABITAT:** Stunted boreal forests; in winter, brush, hedgerows, open woods. Very rare fall and winter visitor to W. Coast.

SPARROWS

tan-striped
morph

dull

white-striped
morph

**WHITE-THROATED
SPARROW**

first-fall/
winter

Pacific
coastal

adult

**WHITE-CROWNED
SPARROW**

Eastern and
Western
mountain

adult

first-fall/
winter

adult

**GOLDEN-
CROWNED
SPARROW**

spring/
summer

**HARRIS'S
SPARROW**

first-fall/
winter

DARK-EYED JUNCO *Junco hyemalis*   **Common**

6–6½ in. (15–16 cm). This familiar songbird is characterized by a variably darker-hooded appearance and *white outer tail feathers* that flash conspicuously in flight. Bill and belly white to whitish. Adult male has dark hood; first-year male and adult female slightly less so, and first-year female is drabbest. *Juvenile:* Finely streaked on head and breast but with characteristic junco white outer tail feathers. A complex species of distinct subspecies groups (often intergrading) as follows.

"Oregon" Junco (*oreganus* subspecies group) is the widespread subspecies in the West. Male has *rusty brown back* with *blackish hood* and *buffy, brownish, or rusty sides* (side color variable). Female duller, but note contrast between paler gray hood and brown back, convex shape to lower border of hood.

"Pink-sided" Junco (*mearnsi* group) breeds in the n. Prairie region and Great Basin, winters to south and west (rarely to W. Coast). Male has a gray hood, pink flanks, and black lores; female duller.

"Gray-headed" Junco (*caniceps* group) occurs in Great Basin and s. Rockies. Rufous patch on back of otherwise pale to medium gray plumage, with *gray sides* and *gray head, dark lores.* Breeders in Southwest have bicolored bill.

"Slate-colored" Junco (*hyemalis* group) is most northern and eastern subspecies, wintering mainly east of Rockies, sparingly westward. *Gray back and sides*, white belly. Female and first-year duller gray tinged brownish on back. Some particularly brownish young birds may be confused with Oregon Junco but usually have gray rather than brown or buff sides.

"White-winged" Junco (*aikeni* group) breeds in Black Hills region. A large, dark junco (resembling Slate-colored) with gray back; usually has *two whitish wing bars* and exhibits considerably more white in tail (four outer feathers on each side). Some female White-winged Juncos and some Slate-colored Juncos can have thin, weak, or broken wing bars, so caution is warranted.

VOICE: Song a loose trill, suggestive of Chipping Sparrow but more musical. Call a light *smack;* also clicking or twittering notes. **HABITAT:** Coniferous and mixed woods. In fall/winter season, open woods, undergrowth, roadsides, brush, parks, gardens, feeders; usually in flocks. In West, multiple subspecies can comingle.

YELLOW-EYED JUNCO *Junco phaeonotus*   **Uncommon, local**

6¼ in. (16 cm). Our only junco with *yellow eyes,* which give it a somewhat fierce look. Otherwise like "Gray-headed" Junco except slightly darker head contrasts with whiter throat; rufous on back *extends onto wing.* Ages and sexes vary but not as much as in Dark-eyed Juncos. Walks rather than hops. **VOICE:** Song musical, more complicated than Dark-eyed's, three-part: *chip chip chip, wheedle wheedle, che che che che che.* **HABITAT:** Coniferous forests, pine-oak woods; in winter, some come down to slightly lower elevations in canyons, including to feeders.

JUNCOS

DARK-EYED JUNCO

adult
female

"Oregon"
West

juvenile

adult
male

adult
male

N. Great
Basin
adult male

"Pink-sided"
N. Great Basin

adult
male

"Gray-headed"
S. Great Basin

"Slate-colored"

adult male
East

adult
female

"White-winged"
Black Hills region

ranges indicate
breeding; these
widely mix in
winter

adult
male

adult male

**YELLOW-EYED
JUNCO**

OLD WORLD SPARROWS Family Passeridae

Old World sparrows differ from our native sparrows (of the Passerellidae family) by having a more curved bill culmen (ridge). The widespread House Sparrow is well known. **FOOD:** Mainly insects, seeds. **RANGE:** Old World.

HOUSE SPARROW *Passer domesticus* Common, introduced
6¼ in. (16 cm). Introduced from Europe in 1840. Familiar to many people. *Male: Black throat, white cheeks, chestnut nape. Female and juvenile:* Lack black throat, have dingy breast, and dull eye stripe *behind eye only.* Note *single bold wing bar.* **VOICE:** Hoarse *chirp* and *shillip* notes, also a rising *sweep.* Song a series of such notes. **SIMILAR SPECIES:** Female Dickcissel, buntings, sparrows. **HABITAT:** Cities, towns, farms, feeders. Also introduced and common in HI (p. 412).

WEAVERS Family Ploceidae

Old World family. **FOOD:** Seeds, insects. **RANGE:** Africa.

NORTHERN RED BISHOP Uncommon, local, exotic
Euplectes franciscanus
4¼ in. (10 cm). Recently split from and sometimes still referred to as "Orange Weaver." This weaver is native to Africa but has been introduced in the Los Angeles area but it is not considered established. Short tail, large head, large bill. *Spring/summer male: Bright reddish body; black face, bill, belly. Female and fall/winter male:* Similar to Grasshopper Sparrow, but with larger, *paler bill, short tail.* Molting male may resemble House Finch.

ESTRILDID FINCHES Family Estrildidae

Old World family represented in N. America by escaped cage birds. A number of species introduced and established in HI (p. 410).

SCALY-BREASTED MUNIA Fairly common, local, exotic
Lonchura punctulata
4½ in. (11 cm). Known by several names, including "Nutmeg Mannikin." A small finch, native to se. Asia but introduced and now commonly established in s. CA as well as HI (p. 410). *Adult: Dark, cocoa brown body,* large dark bill, brown *belly checked with white.* Sexes similar. *Juvenile:* Very plain; pale brown overall, bill dark.

BULBULS Family Pycnonotidae

Native to Old World. One species introduced in CA. **FOOD:** Insects, fruit.

RED-WHISKERED BULBUL Uncommon, local, exotic
Pycnonotus jocosus
7 in. (18 cm). Note black crest, red cheek patch, black half-collar, and red undertail coverts; juvenile has duller head pattern. **VOICE:** Noisy chattering. **SIMILAR SPECIES:** Waxwings. **RANGE:** This native of se. Asia is established locally in the Los Angeles, CA, area where it has formed an established breeding population. **HABITAT:** Heavy vegetation in suburban neighborhoods.

MISCELLANEOUS SEED-EATING BIRDS

HOUSE SPARROW

male

female

spring/ summer male

female

NORTHERN RED BISHOP

juvenile

adult

SCALY- BREASTED MUNIA

adult

RED-WHISKERED BULBUL

FINCHES and ALLIES Family Fringillidae

Plump, small to medium-small birds with seed-cracking bills and relatively short, notched tails. Sexes usually differ. More arboreal than sparrows. **FOOD:** Seeds, insects, small fruit. **RANGE:** Worldwide, including HI (see p. 414).

BLACK ROSY-FINCH *Leucosticte atrata* Uncommon, local

6–6¼ in. (16 cm). Differs from other rosy-finches by male's blackish body color, feathering sometimes edged in gray. Female grayer; the only grayish rosy-finch; first-year female duller, less black in face. **VOICE:** High chirping notes. **SIMILAR SPECIES:** Other rosy-finches. **HABITAT:** Similar to other rosy-finches. Casual winter vagrant to s. CA, AZ.

BROWN-CAPPED ROSY-FINCH *Leucosticte australis* Uncommon, local

6–6¼ in. (16 cm). The plainest rosy-finch. Like Gray-crowned, but male with restricted gray on head, darker crown. Female much drabber than male. **VOICE:** As in Black Rosy-Finch. **SIMILAR SPECIES:** Other rosy-finches. **HABITAT:** Similar to other rosy-finches.

GRAY-CROWNED ROSY-FINCH *Leucosticte tephrocotis* Uncommon

6–8 in. (16–20 cm). Sparrow-sized birds of high snowfields and maritime tundra. *Male: Dark brown,* with *pinkish wash* on belly, wings, and rump. *Light gray patch* on back of head. Montane western and CA subspecies (*tephrocotis* group) are brown cheeked; those of coastal AK to WA ("Hepburn's," *littoralis* group) have gray cheeks and are widespread in winter. Females are duller; gray patch reduced or almost wanting. **VOICE:** As in Black Rosy-Finch. **SIMILAR SPECIES:** Other rosy-finches. **HABITAT:** Rocky summits, alpine cirques and snowfields; also rocky islands (off AK); winters in lower-elevation open country, regularly at feeders in mountain towns. Casual winter vagrant east of range; accidental to Plains states.

WHITE-WINGED CROSSBILL *Loxia leucoptera* Uncommon, irregular

6½ in. (17 cm). Distinguished from Red Crossbill by *bold white wing bars* (Red may have single weak bar) and white tertial tips in all plumages. *Adult male: Dull rose pink.* Female and first-year male olive-gray, with yellowish rump (see Red Crossbill). *Juvenile:* Heavily streaked. **VOICE:** Calls a liquid *peet* and a dry *chif-chif.* Song a succession of loud trills on different pitches. **SIMILAR SPECIES:** Red Crossbill. **HABITAT:** Spruce and fir forests, hemlocks. Irruptive winter visitor south of normal range.

RED CROSSBILL *Loxia curvirostra* Uncommon, irregular

5¾–7 in. (14–17 cm). Note *crossed mandibles* and *plain wings.* Usually found in *flocks. Adult male: Dull red,* brighter on rump. Second-year male often washed orange. *Female and first-year:* Dull olive-gray to mustard-yellow; yellowish on rump. *Juvenile:* Streaked, suggesting a large Pine Siskin. **VOICE:** Call a hard *jip-jip, kip-kip-kip, kwit-kwit,* or *kewp-kewp.* Song consists of a finchlike warbled *jip-jip-jip-jeeaa-jeeaa.* **SIMILAR SPECIES:** White-winged and Cassia Crossbills. **HABITAT:** Variety of conifers; rarely at feeders. Erratic and irruptive throughout range.

CASSIA CROSSBILL *Loxia sinesciuris* Fairly common, Local

6–7 in. (15–17 cm). Recently split from Red Crossbill. Resident to South Hills and Albion Mts., ID. Similar to Red Crossbill but bill much larger because of larger cones, resulting from the absence of squirrels within range. **VOICE:** Call more emphatic than Red Crossbills in area. **SIMILAR SPECIES:** Red Crossbill. **HABITAT:** Lodgepole pine forest.

ROSY-FINCHES AND CROSSBILLS

female

male

BLACK ROSY-FINCH

BROWN-CAPPED ROSY-FINCH

first-year female

"Hepburn's"

male

Gray-crowned Rosy-Finch

male

male

Pribilofs male

male

GRAY-CROWNED ROSY-FINCH

juvenile

adult male

WHITE-WINGED CROSSBILL

adult male

RED CROSSBILL

CASSIA CROSSBILL

adult female

adult male

juvenile

COMMON REDPOLL *Acanthis flammea* Uncommon, irregular

5¼ in. (13 cm). Small finch; note *bright red forehead* and *black chin*. *Adult male:* Has noticeable *pink breast*. *Adult female and first-year male:* Usually show a pink tinge; first-year female lacks pink. Often found in flocks. **VOICE:** Song a trill, followed by the rattling *chet-chet-chet*, the latter also given in flight. **SIMILAR SPECIES:** Hoary Redpoll, Pine Siskin. **HABITAT:** Birches, tundra scrub. In winter, weeds, brush, thistle feeders. Irruptive winter visitor south of normal range.

HOARY REDPOLL *Acanthis hornemanni* Scarce, irregular

5¼–5½ in. (13–14 cm). Look for a "frostier" bird with Commons, with whiter rump containing *little or no streaking; bill stubbier;* streaks on flanks and undertail coverts reduced. Females and first-year birds duller than males, can overlap in plumage with adult male Commons. **VOICE:** As in Common Redpoll. **SIMILAR SPECIES:** Common Redpoll. **HABITAT:** Same as Common Redpoll. Irruptive in winter, though not as much as Common.

HOUSE FINCH *Haemorhous mexicanus* Common

5¾–6 in. (14–15 cm). Slimmer than Purple and Cassin's Finches; tail longer, square-tipped. *Male:* Breast, forehead, stripe over eye, and rump vary from *red to orange to dull mustard yellow*. Sides and belly *streaks dark*. *Female:* Streaked brown; told from Purple Finch by paler brown coloration, smaller head and bill; *plainer face*; undertail coverts usually streaked. **VOICE:** Song bright finchlike notes; often ends in nasal *wheer.* Call a nasal, finchlike, *chirp*. **SIMILAR SPECIES:** Purple and Cassin's Finches. **HABITAT:** Cities, suburbs, farms, feeders; prefers drier habitats. Introduced and common in HI (p. 422).

PURPLE FINCH *Haemorhous purpureus* Fairly common

6 in. (15 cm). *Adult male:* Dull rose red, brightest on head, chest, and rump. Sides and flanks unstreaked. *Female and first-year male:* Heavily streaked, brown to olive-brown; undertail coverts usually lack streaks. **VOICE:** Song recalls Warbling Vireo but faster, bubblier; call a dull, flat, metallic *pik* or *tick*. **SIMILAR SPECIES:** Cassin's and House Finches. **HABITAT:** Woods, groves, riparian thickets, suburbs, feeders.

CASSIN'S FINCH *Haemorhous cassinii* Fairly common

6¼ in. (16 cm). Bill has *straighter ridge* than House and Purple Finches; wings longer. *Adult male:* Red of head and breast paler, more scarlet; *red crown contrasts* more with brown nape. *Female and first-year male:* Whiter underparts than Purple Finch, with sharper streaking above and below, streaked undertail coverts. **VOICE:** Song flutier and more varied than Purple's. Call a musical *chidiup*. **HABITAT:** Montane conifers; variably moves to lower elevations in winter. Casual to very rare winter vagrant to W. Coast and Plains states.

PINE GROSBEAK *Pinicola enucleator* Scarce

8¾–9 in. (23 cm). A large, plump, tame finch with dark, stubby bill, longish tail, dark wings with *two white wing bars*. *Adult male:* Dull *rose red*. *Female and first-fall/winter male:* Gray; head and rump tinged with dull mustard yellow; first spring/summer male can molt in scattered red feathers. **VOICE:** Song rich, rapid warbling: *richy-rich-chew-twee-chur-chur*. Call a musical *chee-vli*. **SIMILAR SPECIES:** Crossbills, Purple Finch. **HABITAT:** Lodgepole pines; only rarely irrupts in winter to lower-elevation habitats.

COMMON
REDPOLL

orange
variant

RED FINCHES,
ETC.

male

female

female

male

HOUSE
FINCH

male

adult
male

HOARY
REDPOLL

PURPLE
FINCH

female

adult
male

adult
male

female

CASSIN'S
FINCH

female

adult
male

PINE GROSBEAK

EVENING GROSBEAK
Uncommon, irregular

Coccothraustes vespertinus

8 in. (20 cm). Size of a starling. A *chunky, short-tailed* finch with *very large, pale, conical bill* (sometimes tinged greenish). *Male:* Deep yellow, with darker head, *yellow eyebrow. Female:* Silver gray, with yellow sides of neck, white patches in tail. Note sex-specific black-and-white wing patterns. **VOICE:** Song is repeated short trills. Calls distinctive: a ringing, finchlike *clee-ip* and a high, clear *thew.* **SIMILAR SPECIES:** Female crossbills. See Yellow Grosbeak. **HABITAT:** Coniferous and mixed forests; in winter, box elders, fruiting shrubs. Somewhat irruptive south of normal range.

AMERICAN GOLDFINCH   *Spinus tristis*
Common

5 in. (13 cm). Goldfinches are distinguished from warblers and other small birds by their short, conical bill and behavior. *Spring/summer male:* Bright yellow with black forehead and wings; tail also black; bill pale. *Spring/summer female:* Dull yellow-olive; darker above, with brownish-black wings and conspicuous wing bars. *Fall/winter:* Both sexes much like spring/summer female but bill dark; wings blacker in males. **VOICE:** Song clear, light, canary-like. Call, in undulating flight, each dip is punctuated by *ti-DEE-di-di* or *per-chik-o-ree* or *po-ta-to-chip.* **SIMILAR SPECIES:** Other goldfinches. **HABITAT:** Patches of thistles and weeds, roadsides, open woods, edges.

LESSER GOLDFINCH   *Spinus psaltria*
Fairly common

4½ in. (11 cm). *Male:* A very small finch with *black cap* and yellow underparts; white on wings. Males of subspecies *psaltria* (s. Rockies) have *black* back; males of western subspecies *hesperophilus* have *greenish* back. Some birds have mottled back. *Female:* Similar to fall/winter American Goldfinch, but usually yellower below, has *less contrasting wing bars, yellowish* (not white) *undertail coverts,* and *dark rump.* Calls differ. First-year female plain, dull greenish overall. **VOICE:** Sweet, plaintive, whiny notes, *tee-yee* (rising) and *tee-yer* (dropping). Song more phrased than American Goldfinch's. Will imitate other birds calls. **SIMILAR SPECIES:** Other goldfinches. **HABITAT:** Dry brushy and weedy country, open woods, wooded streams, towns, parks, gardens, feeders. Casual vagrant or visitor to Plains states.

LAWRENCE'S GOLDFINCH   *Spinus lawrencei*
Uncommon, irregular

4¾ in. (12 cm). Known in all plumages by *large amount of yellow in wings. Male:* Has bold *black face* (including chin). *Female: Plain and gray.* **VOICE:** Song similar to Lesser Goldfinch's, but with high tinkling notes and more mimicry. Call distinctive, thin *tink-oo.* **SIMILAR SPECIES:** Other goldfinches. **HABITAT:** Oak-pine and riparian woodland edges, chaparral, ranch yards, parks; often found near water such as stream pools, stock tanks, dripping faucets. Casual north and east of range, accidentally to TX.

PINE SISKIN   *Spinus pinus*
Fairly common

5 in. (13 cm). Size of a goldfinch. A small, dark, *heavily streaked* finch with deeply notched tail, sharply pointed bill. *Yellow bases to wings and tail* (more prominent in male than in female). Often first detected by voice, flying over. **VOICE:** Call a loud finchy *jjeee-ip;* also a light *tit-i-tit;* a buzzy *shreeeee.* Song suggests goldfinch, but coarser, wheezy. **SIMILAR SPECIES:** All other finches lack yellow in wings and tail. **HABITAT:** Conifers, mixed woods, alders, weedy areas, feeders.

YELLOW FINCHES,
ETC.

female

EVENING
GROSBEAK

male

AMERICAN
GOLDFINCH

fall/winter
male

spring/
summer
male

spring/
summer
female

female

adult
male

adult
male

LESSER
GOLDFINCH

black-backed

green-
backed

female

male

PINE
SISKIN

adult
male

female

LAWRENCE'S
GOLDFINCH

EUROPEAN GOLDFINCH *Carduelis carduelis* Scarce, exotic

5½ in. (14 cm). Occasional reports, mostly at feeders. Assumed to be escaped captive birds. Note red face, yellow wing patches.

BRAMBLING *Fringilla montifringilla* Rare vagrant

6¼ in. (16 cm). *Tawny* or *orangey buff* breast and shoulders, *whitish rump distinctive in flight. Spring/summer male:* Black head and back. *Female and fall/winter:* Gray cheek bordered by dark, flanks streaked or spotted. **VOICE:** Call a whiny *zweee;* in flight, a distinctive nasal, hollow *eck.* **RANGE:** Eurasian species; regular on w. AK islands, casual but widespread records elsewhere in N. America.

NORTH AMERICAN TANAGERS, CARDINALS, BUNTINGS, and ALLIES Family Cardinalidae

Medium-sized songbirds with heavy, fruit-eating or seed-crushing bills. Now incudes the N. American tanagers, as well as the crested cardinals, heavy-billed grosbeaks, smaller *Passerina* buntings, and the Dickcissel. **FOOD:** Seeds, fruit, insects. **RANGE:** New World.

ROSE-BREASTED GROSBEAK *Pheucticus ludovicianus* Fairly common

8 in. (20 cm). *Adult male:* Black and white, with large triangle of rose red on breast and thick pale bill. Underwing linings rose pink. Plumage fringed brown in fall/winter. *Female:* Streaked; recognized by large, pink, grosbeak bill, broad white wing bars, striped crown, and broad white eyebrow stripe. Underwing linings yellow. First-year male like female in first fall but has pink underwing lining; attains partial adult plumage by first spring/summer. **VOICE:** Similar to Black-headed Grosbeak. **SIMILAR SPECIES:** Purple Finch. Female and first-fall male differ from Black-headed Grosbeak in having *heavier streaks to paler* breast, paler bill; underwing pink in male. **HABITAT:** Deciduous woods, orchards, groves, thickets, sometimes at feeders. Scarce vagrant to W. Coast.

BLACK-HEADED GROSBEAK Fairly common
Pheucticus melanocephalus

8¼ in. (21 cm). A stocky bird, larger than a sparrow, with outsized bill. *Adult male:* Breast, collar, and rump *dull orange-brown.* Otherwise, black head and bold black-and-white wing and tail pattern are similar to those of Rose-breasted Grosbeak. In fall/winter, head striped with brown. *Female and first-fall male:* Largely brown, streaked above; head strongly patterned with light stripes and dark ear patch. Breast *washed with yellow-buff, ocher-buff, or butterscotch;* dark streaks on sides *fine,* nearly absent across middle of chest. Underwing linings yellow in all ages/sexes. *Maxilla dark.* First-spring/summer male adultlike but head variably mottled buff and wings brown rather than black. **VOICE:** Song consists of rising and falling passages; resembles American Robin's song, but more melodic. Call a flat *ick* or *eek.* **SIMILAR SPECIES:** Female and first-fall male Rose-breasted Grosbeak. Beware: some intermediates and hybrids also occur that can be difficult to identify. **HABITAT:** Deciduous and riparian woods; rarely at feeders in winter.

GROSBEAKS AND EURASIAN FINCHES

EUROPEAN GOLDFINCH

spring/summer male

female

fall/winter male

BRAMBLING

ROSE-BREASTED GROSBEAK

female

adult male

BLACK-HEADED GROSBEAK

female

adult male

YELLOW GROSBEAK *Pheucticus chrysopeplus* Casual vagrant

9¼ in. (24 cm). Size and shape of Black-headed Grosbeak. *Adult male:* Golden yellow and black; large, blackish grosbeak bill. *Female and first-year male:* Duller, with streaked back and crown. **VOICE:** Rich, whistly warble, similar to Black-headed Grosbeak: *cheer-reah, churr-weoh.* **SIMILAR SPECIES:** Evening Grosbeak lacks extensive yellow head; has different wing pattern. **RANGE:** Mexican species, casual visitor to sw. states. **HABITAT:** Deciduous woods, often near water. Escapees occasionally occur in CA and elsewhere.

NORTHERN CARDINAL Uncommon to fairly common
Cardinalis cardinalis

8¾ in. (22 cm). *Male:* An *all-red* bird with pointed *crest* and black patch at base of heavy, *triangular reddish bill. Female:* Brown tinged pinkish buff, with some red on wings and tail. *Crest, dark face,* and *heavy reddish orange bill* distinctive. *Juvenile:* Similar to female, but with blackish bill. **VOICE:** Song is clear, slurred whistles, repeated. Several variations: *what-cheer cheer cheer,* etc.; *whoit whoit whoit* or *birdy birdy birdy,* etc.; usually two-part. Call a short, sharp *tik.* **SIMILAR SPECIES:** Pyrrhuloxia. Male Summer and Hepatic Tanagers lack cardinal's crest and black face. **HABITAT:** Woodland edges, thickets, deserts, towns, gardens, feeders. Wanders casually well north and west of range. Introduced and fairly common in HI (p. 412).

PYRRHULOXIA *Cardinalis sinuatus* Uncommon to fairly common

8¾ in. (22 cm). *Male:* A *slender, gray and red bird,* with *long, spiky crest* and *pale yellowish,* stubby, almost parrotlike bill (strongly curved upper mandible). *Female:* Has gray back, buff breast, and touch of red in wings. Always note spiky crest and *stubby yellow bill.* **VOICE:** Song a clear *quink quink quink quink quink,* on one pitch; also a slurred, whistled *what-cheer, what-cheer,* etc., usually not two-part like Northern Cardinal's song. **SIMILAR SPECIES:** Best told from Northern Cardinal by bill color and shape, also by grayer color overall, spikier crest, lack of black mask in female, red face and throat in male. **HABITAT:** Mesquite, thorn scrub, deserts, feeders. Casual vagrant west and north of range.

BLUE GROSBEAK *Passerina caerulea* Uncommon

6¾ in. (17 cm). *Adult male:* Deep *dull blue,* with thick bill, *two broad rusty or chestnut wing bars.* Often *flips or twitches tail.* Head mottled brown in fresh fall/winter plumage. *Female and first-fall/winter male:* About size of Brown-headed Cowbird; warm or tawny brown, slightly lighter below, with two *rusty buff wing bars;* rump or tail may be tinged with blue. First-year male begins acquiring mottled blue plumage on winter grounds; by first spring/summer is a variable mixture of brown and blue. **VOICE:** Warbling song, phrases rising and falling; suggests Purple or House Finch, but slower, more guttural. Call a sharp *chink,* in flight a flat *bzzzt.* **SIMILAR SPECIES:** Female and first-year male Indigo Bunting show *weaker wing bars* and are *much smaller* and smaller billed. **HABITAT:** Thickets, hedgerows, riparian undergrowth, brushy hillsides, weedy ditches. Casual vagrant well north of range.

GROSBEAKS AND CARDINALS

YELLOW GROSBEAK

female

adult male

male

juvenile

NORTHERN CARDINAL

female

PYRRHULOXIA

female

male

BLUE GROSBEAK

female

adult male

INDIGO BUNTING *Passerina cyanea* Uncommon to scarce

5½ in. (14 cm). *Adult spring/summer male: Rich deep blue all over. First-spring/summer male:* Blue is duller and variably mottled brown. Fall/winter adult male brown, like female, but with more blue in wings and tail. *Female and first-fall/winter male:* Medium brown to olive-brown; breast with faint *blurry* streaks; paler wing bars indistinct. **VOICE:** Song similar to Lazuli Bunting's, but slower. Calls similar. **SIMILAR SPECIES:** Blue Grosbeak much larger; has rusty wing bars. Female and juvenile Lazuli Bunting slightly grayer brown above; more distinct, whitish wing bars; breast unstreaked and warmer-colored (except for juveniles, whose streaks are finer and sharper than Indigo's). Occasionally hybridizes with Lazuli Bunting where ranges overlap. **HABITAT:** Overgrown brushy fields, riparian thickets, bushy wood edges. Scarce vagrant and casual as breeder to W. Coast.

LAZULI BUNTING *Passerina amoena* Fairly common

5½ in. (14 cm). *Adult male:* A bright turquoise blue songbird with burnt orangey breast and white belly; *two white wing bars.* Fall/winter adult and first-spring/summer males mottled brownish. *Female and first-fall/winter male:* Unstreaked plain brown back and two pale wing bars (stronger than in female Indigo Bunting); breast washed deep buff, usually unstreaked except in juvenile, which may retain fine, sharp streaks into fall. **VOICE:** Song lively, high, and strident; measured phrases, usually paired: *sweet-sweet, chew-chew,* etc. Call a sharp, thin *spit* and a dry buzz (in flight). **SIMILAR SPECIES:** Female Indigo Bunting. **HABITAT:** Open brush, grassy hillsides with scattered oaks, riparian shrubs, chaparral, weedy fields and ditches.

PAINTED BUNTING *Passerina ciris* Rare

5½ in. (14 cm). The most gaudily colored N. American songbird. *Adult male:* A patchwork of *blue-violet* on head, *green* on back, *red* on rump and underparts, red orbital ring. *Female and first-year male:* Electric green above, paling to lemon-yellow below; *no other small finch is so green.* Juvenile is grayer above with only tinge of green, duller gray to buff below. **VOICE:** Song a wiry warble; suggests Warbling Vireo. Call a sharp *chip.* **HABITAT:** Riparian undergrowth, brushy or weedy fields; sometimes feeders. Widespread vagrant west and north of range, sometimes at feeders although beware cage bird escapees.

VARIED BUNTING *Passerina versicolor* Scarce, local

5½ in. (14 cm). *Adult male:* Plum purple body (looks black at a distance). Crown, face, and rump blue, with *bright red patch on nape. Female and first-year male:* Gray-brown with lighter underparts. *No strong wing bars, breast streaks, or distinctive marks of any kind.* Bill smaller and ridge more curved than other buntings. **VOICE:** Song thin, bright, more distinctly phrased, less warbled than Painted Bunting's; notes not as paired as Lazuli Bunting's. **SIMILAR SPECIES:** Female Indigo Bunting more olive-brown, with hint of blurry breast streaks. Female Lazuli paler and with noticeable wing bars. **HABITAT:** Riparian thickets, mesquite and other scrub in washes and lower canyons. Accidental vagrant to CA.

BUNTINGS

adult male

first-spring/
summer male

INDIGO
BUNTING

female

LAZULI
BUNTING

female

adult male

adult
male

PAINTED
BUNTING

female and
first-year
male

female and
first-year male

VARIED
BUNTING

adult male

HEPATIC TANAGER *Piranga flava* Uncommon

8 in. (20 cm). Male tanagers are brightly colored red; females and first-fall males greenish and yellow. Bills stout and notched. *Adult male:* Darker than Summer Tanager; orange-red, *brightest on crown and throat,* with *dark ear patch, dark bill, grayish flanks. Female and first-year male:* Dull yellowish and gray; dusky gray bill, cheeks, and flanks; yellow on throat may be tinged orange. First-year male becomes mixed red and yellow by spring. VOICE: Song very similar to Black-headed Grosbeak's. Call a single *chuck.* SIMILAR SPECIES: Summer Tanager. HABITAT: Open mountain woodlands with oaks, pines; occasionally to lowlands in winter. Casual vagrant well west and north of range.

SUMMER TANAGER *Piranga rubra* Uncommon

7¾ in. (20 cm). *Adult male:* Rose red all over, with *pale bill. Female and first-winter male:* Olive above, *mustard yellow* below; pale bill. First-spring/summer males become patched with red; adult females can have orangey wash to throat and undertail coverts. VOICE: Call a staccato *pi-tuk* or *pik-i-tuk-i-tuk.* Song robinlike phrases, richer and less nasal than Western Tanager's. SIMILAR SPECIES: Female Scarlet Tanager is yellow-green in color; wings darker; *underwing coverts whiter;* bill smaller, duskier. Hepatic Tanager has darker bill, cheeks, and flanks; brightest on crown and throat. HABITAT: Riparian woodlands, oaks. Rare to casual vagrant well north of range.

SCARLET TANAGER *Piranga olivacea* Rare vagrant

7 in. (18 cm). *Spring/summer male:* Flaming scarlet, with *jet black* wings and tail. *Female and fall/winter male:* Greenish olive above, variably *yellowish* below; dark *brownish to black wings.* VOICE: Call distinctive *chipburr.* SIMILAR SPECIES: Summer and Western Tanagers. HABITAT: In migrations, prefers leafy deciduous or mixed forests. Very rare vagrant to W. Coast.

WESTERN TANAGER *Piranga ludoviciana* Fairly common

7¼ in. (18 cm). Our only tanager with *strong wing bars. Adult male:* Yellow with black back, wings, and tail, two wing bars, and *reddish head.* Red is much reduced in fall and winter. *Female and first fall/winter male:* Yellow below with white belly but yellow undertail coverts; dull olive above, dull grayish "saddle" on back. VOICE: Song is short phrases; similar to American Robin's in form, but less sustained, hoarser. Calls a dry *pr-tee* or *pri-ti-tic* and breathy *whee?* SIMILAR SPECIES: Worn birds in late summer can have very faint wing bars and be confused with other tanagers. HABITAT: Nests in open coniferous or mixed forests; widespread in migration; a few winter in coastal CA.

FLAME-COLORED TANAGER *Piranga bidentata* Very rare vagrant

7¼ in. (18 cm). *Adult male:* Fire red with *streaked back, dark ear patch,* two white wing bars, and white tips on tertials and tail corners. *Female and first-fall/winter male:* Like female Western Tanager but note *back streaked, cheek patch dark,* pale tips on tertials and tail, and dark bill; hybrids known. VOICE: Like a slowed-down Western Tanager. RANGE: Casual spring and summer visitor from Mex. to mountains of se. AZ. HABITAT: Pine-oak forests.

TANAGERS

female

HEPATIC
TANAGER

adult
male

first-year
male

female

adult male

SUMMER
TANAGER

first-spring
male

female

molting

fall/winter
male

spring/
summer male

SCARLET
TANAGER

orange variant
spring male

female

adult male

FLAME-COLORED
TANAGER

female

spring/
summer male

WESTERN TANAGER

first-fall/winter male

DICKCISSEL *Spiza americana* Uncommon

6¼ in. (16 cm). *Adult male:* Note black bib, yellow chest, chestnut shoulder patch. In fall, bib obscure. *Female and first-year male:* Duller and plainer; dullest females recall female House Sparrow, but with bolder stripe over eye (often but not always tinged yellowish), touch of yellow on breast, and blue-gray bill. **VOICE:** Song a staccato *dick-ciss-ciss-ciss.* Flight call a short, hard buzz. **SIMILAR SPECIES:** Meadowlarks much larger. Female House Sparrow. **HABITAT:** Alfalfa and other fields, prairies, weedy patches; occasionally at feeders. Rare vagrant to W. Coast.

LARK BUNTING Fairly common
Calamospiza melanocorys (Family Passerellidae)

7 in. (18 cm). Note rather *heavy, blue-gray bill. Spring/summer male: Black,* with *large white wing patches. Female and fall/winter males:* Brown, streaked; *whitish* or *buffy white wing patches* and *tail corners.* In fall/winter adult males can be mottled black; otherwise, ages and sexes similar. **VOICE:** Display-flight song composed of musical slurs, unmusical *chugs,* piping whistles, trills; repeated. Call a flat, mellow *heew.* **SIMILAR SPECIES:** Spring/summer male Bobolink. Beware leucistic blackbirds. **HABITAT:** Plains, prairies; in winter, weedy desert lowlands, farm fields. Widespread vagrant north of range and to W. Coast.

BLACKBIRDS and ORIOLES Family Icteridae

Varied color patterns; sharp bills. Some black and iridescent; orioles are highly colored. Sexes usually unlike and, in most blackbirds and orioles, males are noticeably larger than females. **FOOD:** Insects, fruit, seeds, waste grain, small aquatic life. **RANGE:** New World; most species occur in Tropics.

WESTERN MEADOWLARK *Sturnella neglecta* Fairly common

9½ in. (24 cm). Chunky bird of grasslands, brown above, with darker crown, bright yellow breast crossed by black V; flanks buffier. Ages and sexes similar. When flushed, meadowlarks show conspicuous white sides on short tail. Flies with several shallow, snappy wingbeats alternating with short glides. Western nearly identical to Eastern Meadowlark, but paler above and on flanks; yellow of throat invades farther into malar area; crown stripes paler, more streaked with buff. Best identified by vocalizations. **VOICE:** Song variable; seven to ten flutelike notes, gurgling and double-note, unlike clear whistles of Eastern Meadowlark. Calls *chupp* or *chuck* and a dry rattle. Occasionally gives Eastern-like *dzzrt* call. **SIMILAR SPECIES:** In the Southwest, "Lilian's" Eastern Meadowlarks are as pale as Westerns but have much more white in the tail. **HABITAT:** Grasslands, cultivated fields and pastures, meadows, prairies, marshes. Introduced and fairly common on Kauai (p. 422).

EASTERN MEADOWLARK *Sturnella magna* Uncommon

9½ in. (24 cm). Nearly identical to Western Meadowlark, but darker and warmer (often reddish) above; malar area whiter, contrasting with yellow throat (beware: can be fringed yellowish in fall, when plumage fresh); vocalizations key. Southwestern U.S. "Lilian's" Meadowlark (subspecies *lilianae*) paler, like Western, but with more white in tail. **VOICE:** Song two clear, slurred whistles, *tee-yah, tee-yair* (last note slurred and descending). Call a rasping or buzzy *dzrrt;* also a guttural chatter. **SIMILAR SPECIES:** Western Meadowlark, Dickcissel. **HABITAT:** Similar to Western Meadowlark; Lilian's partial to grasslands. Accidental vagrant to CA.

OPEN FIELD BIRDS

DICKCISSEL

female

adult
male

fall/
winter

Bobolink
(p. 364) for
comparison

female and fall/
winter male

spring/
summer
male

LARK BUNTING

EASTERN
MEADOWLARK

WESTERN
MEADOWLARK

BOBOLINK *Dolichonyx oryzivorus* Uncommon, local

7 in. (18 cm). *Spring/summer male:* Our only songbird that is *solid black below and partially white above*; buff-yellow nape. Returning migrants in spring mottled brownish. *Female and fall/winter male:* Medium-small, rich buff-yellow, with dark striping on crown and back. Bill sparrowlike. Note pointed tail feathers. **VOICE:** Flight song a quivering descent, ecstatic and bubbling; starts low, rollicks upward. Flight call a clear *ink,* often heard in migration. **SIMILAR SPECIES:** Male Lark Bunting. Female Red-winged Blackbird longer-billed, less buff-yellow overall. Grasshopper Sparrow much smaller. **HABITAT:** Hayfields, weedy fields, tules. Scarce to rare vagrant or migrant to Southwest and W. Coast.

YELLOW-HEADED BLACKBIRD Fairly common
Xanthocephalus xanthocephalus

9–9¾ in. (23–25 cm). Gregarious. *Adult male:* A robin-sized blackbird, with *rich yellow head and breast;* in flight, shows *white wing patch. Female and first-year male:* Smaller (female) and browner; yellow confined to throat and chest; lower breast streaked white; white wing patch restricted. **VOICE:** Song of low, hoarse rasping notes produced with much effort; suggests rusty hinges. Call a low *kruck* or *kack.* **HABITAT:** Nests in freshwater marshes. Forages in farm fields, open country, feedlots. Often associates with other blackbirds in fall/winter flocks. Rare to casual vagrant to n. Pacific Coast.

RED-WINGED BLACKBIRD *Agelaius phoeniceus* Common

8½–8¾ in. (22 cm). *Adult male:* Black, with *bright red or orange-red, yellow-margined epaulets (wing-covert patches),* most conspicuous in breeding display. Red often concealed, only yellowish or off-whitish margin showing. "Bicolored" subspecies (*californicus*) in cen. CA lacks yellow margin. *First-year male:* Sooty brown, mottled (like larger version of female), but with dull red wing patch. *Female:* Brownish, with sharply pointed bill, "blackbird" appearance, and *well-defined dark streaking* below; adult females may have pinkish or dull red tinge to throat or shoulder. Travels and roosts in flocks during fall/winter season. **VOICE:** Calls a loud *check* and a high, slurred *tee-err.* Song a liquid, gurgling *konk-la-ree* or *o-ka-lay.* **SIMILAR SPECIES:** Other blackbird species, especially Tricolored Blackbird. **HABITAT:** Breeds primarily in marshes; forages in cultivated land, feedlots, towns, feeders, etc.

TRICOLORED BLACKBIRD *Agelaius tricolor* Uncommon, local

8½–8¾ in. (22 cm). Bill longer and proportionally thinner than in Red-winged; body averages slimmer, tail longer. *Adult male:* Similar to Red-winged Blackbird, but shoulder patch darker red, with conspicuous *white margin.* Overall plumage slightly glossier. *Female:* Darker than most subspecies of Red-winged, particularly on belly, and never has pinkish on throat, but can be difficult to identify. See voice. Highly gregarious; nests in dense colonies sometimes numbering in the thousands, whereas Red-winged is territorial. May segregate by sex in fall/winter. **VOICE:** More nasal than Red-winged: *on-ke-kaangh.* A nasal *kemp.* **SIMILAR SPECIES:** Red-winged Blackbird. **HABITAT:** Traditionally nested in cattail or tule marshes; more recently has also switched to blackberry patches, willows, and other scrubby habitats as marshes have been converted. In winter, forages in fields, farms, feedlots, park lawns.

ICTERIDS
(BLACKBIRDS, ETC.)

female

spring/
summer
male

BOBOLINK

fall/winter

adult
male

female

**YELLOW-HEADED
BLACKBIRD**

red epaulets
hidden

adult
male

female

**RED-WINGED
BLACKBIRD**

first-year
male

"Bicolored"
adult male
(CA)

adult
male

female

**TRICOLORED
BLACKBIRD**

RUSTY BLACKBIRD *Euphagus carolinus* — Scarce

9 in. (23 cm). Feathers fringed rusty only in fall and winter. *Spring/summer male:* A medium-sized black bird with pale yellow eye. Black head may show faint *greenish* gloss (not purplish). *Spring/summer female:* Slate colored, with *light eye. Fall/winter:* Feathers variably *fringed rusty,* creating overall rusty appearance; *buffy eyebrow, narrow dark patch through eye.* **VOICE:** Call *chack.* Also a split creak, like a rusty hinge: *kush-a-lee.* **SIMILAR SPECIES:** Brewer's Blackbird; Common Grackle much larger, bill much stronger. **HABITAT:** Wooded swamps, pond edges; in winter, also muddy fields, with other blackbirds. Very rare fall/winter vagrant to W. Coast.

BREWER'S BLACKBIRD *Euphagus cyanocephalus* — Common

9 in. (23 cm). A familiar blackbird in w. N. America. *Male:* All black, with whitish eye; in good light, *purplish* reflections on head and neck, greenish on body. *Fresh first-fall male:* Can be fringed olive-brown. *Female:* Brownish gray, usually with *dark* eye. **VOICE:** Song a harsh, wheezy, creaking *ksh-eee.* Call *chack.* **SIMILAR SPECIES:** Male Rusty Blackbird is flatter black with dull *greenish* head reflections; bill slightly longer. Female Rusty has *light* eye. Beware: first-fall male Brewer's can be fairly heavily fringed, like Rusty, but fringe color muddier brown, not rusty. **HABITAT:** Fields, mountain meadows, prairies, farms, feedlots, towns, parks, lawns, shopping malls, parking lots.

COMMON GRACKLE *Quiscalus quiscula* — Uncommon

12½ in. (32 cm). *Male:* A large, *iridescent,* yellow-eyed blackbird with long, *keel-shaped tail.* In good light, iridescent purple-blue on head. "Bronzed" Grackle (subspecies *versicolor*) found west of Appalachians deep bronze on back and belly. *Female:* Smaller and somewhat duller, with less wedge-shaped tail. Juveniles of both sexes are dull sooty brown with dark eyes. **VOICE:** Call *chuck* or *chack.* "Song" a split rasping note *zhreep zhrap,* etc. **SIMILAR SPECIES:** Great-tailed Grackle; Rusty and Brewer's Blackbirds. **HABITAT:** Cropland, towns, parks, feeders, groves; nests in conifers. Very rare vagrant to W. Coast.

GREAT-TAILED GRACKLE *Quiscalus mexicanus* — Common

Male 18 in. (46 cm); female 15 in. (38 cm). Like several other blackbirds, often found in large flocks, including while roosting, when they are quite noisy. *Male:* A very large, purple-glossed blackbird, distinctly larger than Common Grackle and with much longer, more ample tail. *Female:* Smaller than male; dark gray-brown above, warm brown below. Adults of both sexes have yellow eyes. Juveniles of both sexes have dark eyes and are indistinctly streaked below. **VOICE:** Harsh *check check check;* also a high *kee-kee-kee-kee.* Shrill, discordant notes, whistles, and clucks. A rapid, upward-slurring *ma-ree.* **SIMILAR SPECIES:** Common Grackle much smaller, tail not nearly as keel shaped; female blacker. **HABITAT:** Groves, farms, feedlots, towns, city parks, parking lots. Casual vagrant well north of range.

BLACKBIRDS AND GRACKLES

spring/summer
female

**RUSTY
BLACKBIRD**

spring/
summer
male

fall/
winter

first-fall/
winter male

female

male

**BREWER'S
BLACKBIRD**

**COMMON
GRACKLE**

"Purple"
male

female

"Bronzed"
male

male

female

**GREAT-TAILED
GRACKLE**

BROWN-HEADED COWBIRD   *Molothrus ater*   Common

7½ in. (19 cm). A small blackbird with sparrowlike bill. *Male:* Black with *brown head (appears all black in poor light).* *Female:* Gray-brown with lighter throat; note short *finchlike bill.* *Juvenile:* Paler than female. Buffy gray, with soft breast streaking and pale scaling above. *Molting first-fall male:* Splotched black. A nest parasite (never builds its own nest), juveniles are often seen being fed by smaller birds. Cowbirds feed on ground with tails lifted high. **VOICE:** Flight call *weee-titi.* Song a bubbly and creaky *glug-glug-gleeee.* Call *chuck.* **SIMILAR SPECIES:** Female told from female blackbirds by its *stubby bill* and smaller size. Juvenile cowbirds can resemble sparrows. **HABITAT:** In nesting season, forests and woodlands; also farms, fields, feedlots, roadsides, towns, parks, lawns, feeders.

BRONZED COWBIRD   *Molothrus aeneus*   Uncommon

8½–8¾ in. (21–22 cm). *Male:* Slightly larger and more *bull-headed* than Brown-headed Cowbird. Does *not* have brown head. Bill longer. *Red eye.* In breeding season, raises conspicuous *ruff* on nape. *Female:* Smaller nape ruff; dark brown to sooty overall, darker than female Brown-headed; eye reddish. Juvenile like large-billed juvenile Brown-headed. **VOICE:** High-pitched mechanical creakings. Male's display very animated. **SIMILAR SPECIES:** Brown-headed Cowbird. **HABITAT:** Cropland, brush, semiopen country, feedlots.

BULLOCK'S ORIOLE   *Icterus bullockii*   Fairly common

8¼–8½ in. (21–22 cm). The common oriole throughout the West. *Adult male:* Note *orange cheeks* and *dark eye line, large white wing patches, and black-tipped tail.* *Female and juvenile:* Dark eye line, yellowish supercilium, plain gray back, *whitish belly.* First-year male averages brighter orange than female, develops black in throat during first fall/winter. **VOICE:** Phrase of doubled musical whistles and rattles: *jet-jet whichy-whichy ju-ju tthat-tthat,* etc. Calls include a rough chatter and low *churp.* **SIMILAR SPECIES:** Baltimore Oriole; also Hooded and Orchard Orioles; Bullock's and Baltimore can hybridize where ranges meet. **HABITAT:** Deciduous and riparian woods, oaks, shade trees, ranch yards; small numbers winter in flowering trees of coastal CA.

BALTIMORE ORIOLE   *Icterus galbula*   Uncommon, local

8¼–8½ in. (21–22 cm). *Adult male:* Flame orange and black, with solid black head, tail boldly black and orange. *Adult female:* Olive-brown above, burnt orange-yellow below; two white wing bars; a variable amount of black on head, up to malelike partial hood; orange tail. *First-fall/winter:* Duller, with grayer back and some orange on underparts. Both sexes can develop partial to near-complete adultlike pattern by first spring. **VOICE:** Song rich, *hew-hee-hee-hew-hee-hew-hew,* etc. Call a low, whistled *hewli.* Chatter call not as rough as Bullock's. **SIMILAR SPECIES:** Dull first-fall Baltimore much like female Bullock's, but latter has more distinct dark eye line and yellowish supercilium, plainer gray back, whiter flanks contrasting more with yellowish undertail coverts. **HABITAT:** Shade trees. Rare vagrant to W. Coast.

BROWN-HEADED COWBIRD

molting first-fall male

juvenile

male

female

female

BRONZED COWBIRD

male

BULLOCK'S ORIOLE

adult male

juvenile and female

adult female

adult male

BALTIMORE ORIOLE

juvenile and first-fall/winter

SCOTT'S ORIOLE *Icterus parisorum* Uncommon

8¾–9 in. (22–23 cm). *Adult male:* Note solid black head and back; *lemon-yellow* underparts. *Female:* More greenish yellow below and more olive-gray and streaked above than other female orioles. *Juvenile and first-year:* Both sexes lack black at first but variably develop blackish in throats (female) and/or heads (male) by spring. **VOICE:** Song composed of rich fluty whistles; suggests Western Meadowlark. Call a harsh *chuck.* **SIMILAR SPECIES:** Female Hooded and Bullock's Orioles. **HABITAT:** Dry desert montane scrub, yucca forests, Joshua trees, pinyon-juniper, sugar-water feeders. Also eucalyptus and date palms in winter. Casual vagrant well north of range.

ORCHARD ORIOLE *Icterus spurius* Uncommon, local

7–7¼ in. (18 cm). A small, short- and straight-billed oriole. Often flicks tail sideways. *Adult male:* All dark; rump and underparts *deep chestnut.* *Female and juvenile:* Olive or greenish gray above, yellowish below; two white wing bars. *First-year male:* develops black bib in fall/winter, usually in Tropics. **VOICE:** Song a fast-moving outburst interspersed with piping whistles and guttural notes, ending with strident slurred *wheeer!* Call a soft *chuck.* **SIMILAR SPECIES:** Baltimore Oriole slightly larger and more orange. Female and first-year male Orchard and Hooded Orioles difficult to separate but note Hooded's thinner-based and more curved bill, longer tail, weaker wing bars, and *quite different calls.* Developing juvenile Hooded Orioles only rarely overlap in range with Orchard Orioles in summer. **HABITAT:** Wood edges, orchards, shade trees; more likely than other orioles to be seen in brushy areas. Rare vagrant and winter visitor to W. Coast.

HOODED ORIOLE *Icterus cucullatus* Fairly common

7½–8 in. (19–20 cm). *Adult male:* Orange and black, with black throat and *orange crown.* In winter, back scaled yellow or orange. *Female:* Similar to female Bullock's Oriole, but bill longer, slightly curved; back olive-gray; head, tail, and underparts more extensively greenish yellow. Call very different. *First-year male:* Like female; develops black throat during first winter. **VOICE:** Song rambling, of grating notes and piping whistles: *chut chut chut whew whew;* opening notes throaty. Call a distinctive, up-slurred, whistled *eek* or *wheenk.* **SIMILAR SPECIES:** Orchard and Scott's Orioles. **HABITAT:** Palm trees, shade trees, towns, gardens. Casual vagrant well north of range.

STREAK-BACKED ORIOLE *Icterus pustulatus* Very rare vagrant

8¼ in. (21 cm). This Mexican oriole resembles Hooded or first-year male Bullock's, but has a *streaked back,* much white in wing. *Adult male:* Basically yellow-orange, head much deeper orange. Female, first-year birds, and juvenile are duller but streaking still obvious; juvenile lacks black on throat. **VOICE:** Rich warble, similar to Baltimore or Bullock's Oriole. **SIMILAR SPECIES:** Adult male Hooded Oriole in winter has scaled or scalloped black back pattern, not streaked, and bill not as thick at base. **RANGE:** Very rare visitor from Mex., mostly in fall and winter, to AZ; casual west to CA and east to TX. **HABITAT:** Arid scrub, woodland edges.

ORIOLES

SCOTT'S ORIOLE

female

adult male

first-fall

first-year male

adult male

ORCHARD ORIOLE

juvenile and female

first-year male

juvenile and female

adult male

HOODED ORIOLE

adult male

STREAK-BACKED ORIOLE

BIRDS OF
HAWAII

RESIDENT HAWAIIAN WATERFOWL

HAWAIIAN GOOSE *Branta sandvicensis*　　Uncommon, endangered

23–27 in. (58–69 cm). A distinctive small goose found primarily in upland areas away from water. Face, cap, and throat black; *neck buff with distinct dark furrows*; black ring around base of neck; body brownish, irregularly barred dark. Bill and legs black; feet with reduced toe webbing. Ages and sexes similar. **VOICE:** High-pitched whiney *ee-ehh* and small squeaks, often double-noted, giving rise to popular Hawaiian name, "Néné." **SIMILAR SPECIES:** Hawaiian Goose lacks dark body plumage of Brant and black neck and white cheek patch of Cackling Goose. **HABITAT:** Open upland pastures and lava flows (Hawaii I. and Maui) and lowland fields (Kauai, Molokai). Individuals disperse after breeding season; occasionally found in coastal areas; rarely flies between islands.

HAWAIIAN DUCK *Anas wyvilliana*　　Locally uncommon, endangered

18–19 in. (45–48 cm). Like a small version of Mallard; plumage of both sexes resembles female Mallard, but darker with more distinct dark chevrons; *tail and bill darker*, speculum greenish blue, legs duller orange. *Male:* Bill tinged yellowish, crown often with dark green tinge in adults. *Female:* Bill dark with orange tip, speculum duller. Hybridizes fairly extensively with feral Mallards, resulting in a mixture of characteristics; conservation efforts ongoing to restore genetic purity of Hawaiian Ducks. Known as "Koloa" in Hawaiian. **VOICE:** Calls softer than those of Mallard, and given less frequently. **SIMILAR SPECIES:** Mallard. Laysan Duck, but ranges do not overlap. **HABITAT:** Marshes, ponds, wooded streams (especially on Kauai).

LAYSAN DUCK *Anas laysanensis*　　Very local, endangered

17–18 in. (43–45 cm). A small duck resembling a dark female Mallard but with variable conspicuous *white patch around eye*. Speculum dark green with broad white tips, bill dark, legs bright orange. Sexes similar except adult male can have dark green tinge to crown and head and averages larger eye patch and brighter speculum; bill tinged dark yellowish in male, dark orange in female. **VOICE:** Calls softer than Mallard's, given less frequently. **SIMILAR SPECIES:** Mallard much larger and lacks eye patch. See Hawaiian Duck. **HABITAT:** Central brackish lagoon (Laysan I.). Recently introduced to man-made wetlands on Midway and Kure Atolls.

MALLARD *Anas platyrhynchos*　　Uncommon exotic and rare vagrant

See also p. 26. Introduced to the Hawaiian Is. during the 1800s; feral populations now thrive on most se. Hawaiian Is. Found in various levels of domestication in parks, wetlands, and refuges. Hybridizes extensively with Hawaiian Duck; control efforts have reduced populations of pure Mallards and hybrids. Also a rare vagrant to the nw. Hawaiian Is., presumably from continental populations; wild birds likely occur undetected in se. Hawaiian Is. as well.

MUSCOVY DUCK *Cairina moschata*　　Local, exotic

Domesticated flocks of white morphs occur in parks, neighborhoods.

RESIDENT HAWAIIAN WATERFOWL

HAWAIIAN GOOSE (NÉNÉ)

HAWAIIAN DUCK

female

male

LAYSAN DUCK
male

hybrid male Hawaiian Duck with Mallard

female

MALLARD

male

domestic variation

MUSCOVY DUCK

REGULAR MIGRATORY WATERFOWL
in HAWAII

Most migratory swans, geese, ducks, and mergansers have occurred in HI as regularly wintering, casual-to-scarce vagrant, or accidental species.

CACKLING GOOSE *Branta hutchinsii* Scarce

See p. 18. Annual in small numbers, some remaining for years. Smallest subspecies *minima* ("Ridgway's") and subspecies *leucopareia* ("Aleutian") most commonly observed. A flock of feral Canada Geese (p. 18) occurs in Hilo, Hawaii I.; otherwise Canada Goose accidental in HI.

BRANT *Branta bernicla* Scarce

See p. 18. One to five "Black Brants" (subspecies *nigricans*) annually in se. Hawaiian Is., in wetlands, coastal areas, occasionally on ocean.

NORTHERN PINTAIL *Anas acuta* Fairly common

See p. 24. The most common migratory waterfowl throughout Hawaiian Is. Formerly much more common; more recently groups of up to 30 (occasionally more than 100) found in lakes and wetlands.

NORTHERN SHOVELER *Spatula clypeata* Fairly common

See p. 28. Found throughout Hawaiian Is. Formerly much more common; more recently groups of up to two dozen found in lakes and wetlands.

AMERICAN WIGEON *Mareca americana* Uncommon

See p. 24. Usually found with pintails and shovelers in small numbers (fewer than ten). Gadwall (p. 26) very rare in HI.

EURASIAN WIGEON *Mareca penelope* Scarce

See p. 24. Often with American Wigeon. Rare in se. Hawaiian Is. but more regular in nw. Hawaiian Is., where American is rare.

BLUE-WINGED TEAL *Spatula discors* Scarce

See p. 28. Found occasionally in wetlands. Has bred on Hawaii I.

GREEN-WINGED TEAL *Anas crecca* Uncommon

See p. 28. Groups of up to a dozen found in Hawaiian Is. with other migratory ducks. "American" subspecies regular in se. Hawaiian Is. "Eurasian" subspecies (p. 28) regular in nw. Hawaiian Is.

LESSER SCAUP *Aythya affinis* Fairly common

See p. 30. Flocks of up to 40 on lakes, reservoirs, and ponds. Greater Scaup (p. 30), Tufted Duck (p. 50), and other *Aythya* ducks very rare among Lesser Scaup and Ring-necked Ducks in Hawaiian Is.

RING-NECKED DUCK *Aythya collaris* Uncommon

See p. 30. Up to a dozen can be found, usually among Lesser Scaup.

BUFFLEHEAD *Bucephala albeola* Scarce

See p. 38. Found occasionally on lakes, usually female-plumaged.

PIED-BILLED GREBE *Podilymbus podiceps* Scarce

See p. 56. Found occasionally in lakes and rivers. Has bred on Hawaii I. Most other N. American grebe species (p. 56) accidental in HI.

REGULAR MIGRATORY
WATERFOWL

"Aleutian"

CACKLING
GOOSE

"Ridgway's"

adult

"BLACK"
BRANT

first-
year

NORTHERN
PINTAIL

female

male

AMERICAN
WIGEON

male

NORTHERN
SHOVELER

female

male

BLUE-WINGED
TEAL

female

male

female

male

EURASIAN
WIGEON

female

GREEN-WINGED
TEAL

female

American male

RING-NECKED
DUCK

female

male

LESSER SCAUP

male

female

male

BUFFLEHEAD

female

fall/winter
adult

spring/
summer adult

PIED-BILLED
GREBE

ALBATROSSES and LARGE PETRELS in HAWAII

LAYSAN ALBATROSS *Phoebastria immutabilis* **Fairly Common**
See p. 70. Breeds abundantly in nw. Hawaiian Is. and on Kauai and Oahu (present late Oct. through July; absent Aug. through mid-Oct.). Uncommon at sea in HI waters except near breeding sites. Hybrids with Black-footed Albatross occur where both species breed.

SHORT-TAILED ALBATROSS *Phoebastria albatrus* **Rare, endangered**
See p. 70. Prospective breeding and courting birds occur regularly in very small numbers in nw. Hawaiian Is. (present late Oct. through June). Single pair has recently bred on Midway Atoll and others attempted breeding on Kure.

BLACK-FOOTED ALBATROSS *Phoebastria nigripes* **Uncommon**
See p. 70. Breeds commonly in nw. Hawaiian Is. (present late Oct. through July; absent Aug. through mid-Oct.). Uncommon at sea off se. Hawaiian Is.

HAWAIIAN PETREL **Uncommon, endangered**
Pterodroma sandwichensis
17–18 in. (43–46 cm). Blackish to brownish upperparts with slightly darker M-pattern; *black hoodlike cap* with broad *white patch around bill*; broad dark diagonal *underwing carpal bars*. Breeding endemic to se. Hawaiian Is.; ranges at sea throughout ne. Pacific to N. American coast (see p. 66). Arrives and departs colonies at night. Uncommon in waters off colonies; most frequently observed from shore near sunset off e. Kauai in Apr.–Sept. **VOICE:** Primary vocalization above colonies at night *ooo-aah-ooo*, begetting Hawaiian name "U'au"; also shorter, low-pitched and high-pitched calls at nests. **SIMILAR SPECIES:** Juan Fernández Petrel, White-necked Petrel. **HABITAT:** Open ocean; breeds colonially in dry high-elevation habitats.

JUAN FERNÁNDEZ PETREL *Pterodroma externa* **Uncommon**
17–18 in. (43–46 cm). Similar in size and shape to Hawaiian Petrel but bill larger, less dark to head, white to partially white uppertail coverts, *almost completely white underwing*, without or with very narrow and indistinct carpal bars. White-necked Petrel similar but nape usually whiter; back paler and grayer than upperwings; underwing carpal mark thicker and longer; uppertail coverts with little or no white. **RANGE:** Breeds in Juan Fernández Is. off Chile, ranges widely into tropical and subtropical Pacific. Scarce in se. Hawaiian waters, primarily in summer/fall; can be observed from shore from north tip of Hawaii I. in Aug.–Nov. Accidental vagrant to AZ.

WHITE-NECKED PETREL *Pterodroma cervicalis* **Uncommon**
17–18 in. (43–46 cm). Similar in size and shape to Hawaiian and Juan Fernández Petrels. Distinguished by broad white nape collar (beware: Juan Fernández can have narrow collar); *gray back contrasts with blackish upperwing*; underwing carpal bar narrower than in Hawaiian, broader and longer than in Juan Fernández. **RANGE:** Breeds in Kermadec Is. off New Zealand, ranges widely into tropical and subtropical Pacific. Uncommon in HI waters, year-round but most often in late fall and winter. Accidental vagrant to w. Mex.

ALBATROSSES AND LARGE PETRELS

second-year

adult

SHORT-TAILED ALBATROSS

LAYSAN ALBATROSS

BLACK-FOOTED ALBATROSS

HAWAIIAN PETREL

JUAN FERNANDEZ PETREL

WHITE-NECKED PETREL

SHEARWATERS and SMALL PETRELS in HAWAII

BLACK-WINGED PETREL *Pterodroma nigripennis* **Fairly common**
10–11 in. (25–29 cm). Medium-small petrel, *pale gray crown and upper-parts* with moderately distinct M pattern and *bold black underwing carpal bar*. Bill fairly stout. When worn, upperwing becomes dark, obscuring M pattern. **SIMILAR SPECIES:** Bonin, Cook's, and Mottled Petrels. **RANGE:** Breeds near New Zealand; found regularly year-round in HI waters.

MOTTLED PETREL *Pterodroma inexpectata* **Scarce to uncommon**
See p. 66. Passage migrant through HI waters during short windows in Mar.–Apr. and Oct.–Nov. Similar to Black-winged Petrel but dark belly patch (occasionally extending to head) usually obvious.

COOK'S PETREL *Pterodroma cookii* **Scarce**
See p. 66. Passage migrant through HI waters in spring and fall. Stejneger's Petrel (*P. longirostris*; not shown), very rare migrant through HI waters (and casual off CA), has similar underwing pattern but has dusky to black crown.

BONIN PETREL *Pterodroma hypoleuca* **Common, local**
11–12 in. (29–31 cm). Medium-small petrel; dark grayish brown head pattern and upperparts, underwing with dark carpal bar and *extensive black patch* to under-primaries. Legs pinkish with black toes. Abundant breeder in nw. Hawaiian Is. (Oct.–Apr.); absent in se. Hawaiian waters. **VOICE:** Raspy descending *keeekekh* calls at colonies. **SIMILAR SPECIES:** Crown and underwing pattern unique among *Pterodroma* petrels. **HABITAT:** Breeds in sandy burrows on atolls; uncommonly seen at sea.

WEDGE-TAILED SHEARWATER *Ardenna pacifica* **Common**
16–18 in. (41–46 cm). Breeds throughout Hawaiian Is.; most common tubenose offshore. A lanky shearwater with long, *thin grayish bill*, tipped dark; *pale fringes to upperpart feathers*; long wedge-shaped tail. Legs and feet pinkish. Light morph a common breeder and offshore in HI; dark-morph rare in s. HI waters. **VOICE:** Haunting, drawn-out *oooooo-ahhh* given by courting adults. Squeaky calls given by chicks. **SIMILAR SPECIES:** Light morph similar to Pink-footed Shearwater (p. 68; accidental in HI) but bill thinner and grayer, tail longer, and flight floppier. Dark morph larger, underwing dark, flight more buoyant than in Sooty Shearwater; bill grayer and thinner than in Flesh-footed Shearwater (p. 68). Newell's Shearwater smaller, shorter-tailed, more contrasting; flight stiffer. **HABITAT:** Breeds in sandy coastal areas, offshore islets. Casual vagrant to CA.

NEWELL'S SHEARWATER *Puffinus newelli* **Uncommon, endangered**
13–14 in. (33–36 cm). Contrasting *black-and-white* pattern and rapid shallow wingbeats. Similar to Manx Shearwater (p. 68) but tail longer, *distal half of undertail coverts dark*, sides of rump with white patches. **VOICE:** A raspy bray, *heecha-heecha-heecha,* given over colonies at night. **SIMILAR SPECIES:** Wedge-tailed Shearwater. **HABITAT:** Breeds in mid- to high-elevation fern tangles. Uncommon in HI waters; best observed near sunset off e. Kauai in Apr.–Sept. Accidental in CA.

BULLER'S SHEARWATER *Ardenna bulleri* **Scarce**
See p. 68. Scarce passage migrant through HI waters in spring and late fall.

SHEARWATERS AND SMALL PETRELS

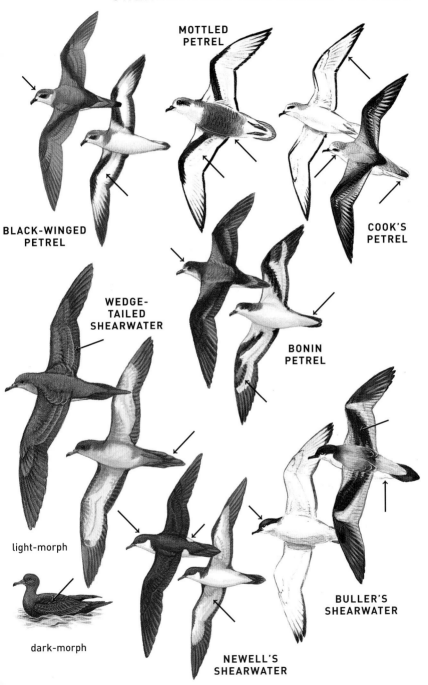

MOTTLED PETREL

COOK'S PETREL

BLACK-WINGED PETREL

WEDGE-TAILED SHEARWATER

BONIN PETREL

light-morph

dark-morph

BULLER'S SHEARWATER

NEWELL'S SHEARWATER

DARK-BODIED TUBENOSES in HAWAII

CHRISTMAS SHEARWATER *Puffinus nativitatis* Scarce, local

14–16 in. (35–39 cm). A small shearwater with fast shallow wingbeats as typical of *Puffinus*. Plumage *entirely dark brown*, including underwing; bill short and black; feet pink with black toe tips. **VOICE:** Moaning calls similar to those of Wedge-tailed Shearwater. Also short nasal *kowp* calls at colonies. **SIMILAR SPECIES:** Dark Wedge-tailed and Sooty Shearwaters larger, the latter with pale underwing; Bulwer's Petrel smaller, longer tailed, has pale brown upperwing bar. **HABITAT:** Open ocean. Breeds in sandy burrows in nw. and a few se. Hawaiian islets.

SOOTY SHEARWATER *Ardenna grisea* Uncommon

See pp. 68. Uncommon to fairly common passage migrant in HI waters in spring and fall; occasionally seen in large flocks and/or from shore. Short-tailed Shearwater (p. 68) uncommon in se. Hawaiian Is. waters, primarily late fall.

BULWER'S PETREL *Bulweria bulwerii* Uncommon

11–12 in. (28–31 cm). Small-bodied petrel with proportionally *long tapered tail*; uniformly brown with usually *distinct pale brown upperwing carpal bar*. Legs grayish to pinkish with darker toes. Unique size, smaller than other petrels but larger than storm-petrels. **VOICE:** Repeated barking, doglike *coorp* notes at breeding burrows. **SIMILAR SPECIES:** Christmas Shearwater. Tristram's Storm-Petrel smaller, grayer; tail shorter and forked. **HABITAT:** Breeds in rocky coastal and offshore-islet crevices. Uncommon offshore throughout most of Hawaiian Is. (primarily May–Sept.); absent in Nov.–Mar.

TRISTRAM'S STORM-PETREL Uncommon, local
Oceanodroma tristrami

10 in. (25–26 cm). A large storm-petrel, grayish (fresh) to brownish (worn), head often glossier and grayer, *uppertail coverts paler forming indistinct band*, tail forked. Flies low to the water with more flapping than other storm-petrels. **VOICE:** Muted *cooo* notes at breeding burrows. **SIMILAR SPECIES:** Bulwer's Petrel. No other "dark-rumped" storm petrel occurs in HI. **HABITAT:** Breeds in sandy burrows; fairly common offshore of low-lying nw. Hawaiian Is. atolls in Sept.–Mar.; virtually unrecorded in se. Hawaiian Is. Accidental in CA.

LEACH'S STORM-PETREL *Oceanodroma leucorhoa* Uncommon

See p. 72. Fairly common migrant and uncommon winter visitor to HI waters in Sept.–Apr. (vs. Apr.–Sept. for Band-rumped); only white-rumped Leach's recorded (see p. 72).

BAND-RUMPED STORM-PETREL *Oceanodroma castro* Scarce

8½–9 in. (21–23 cm). Very similar to Band-rumpeds found elsewhere. **VOICE:** Quick, ascending *rechy-rechy-rich* given at and above colony areas, likened to the sound of a finger rubbing wet glass. **SIMILAR SPECIES:** Leach's Storm-Petrel similar but note white uppertail coverts broadly tipped dark, resulting in white "band" as opposed to double-oval patches in Leach's, which also is found primarily in winter rather than summer. **HABITAT:** Breeds along high-elevation ridges of se. Hawaiian Is., most notably on Kauai; nesting sites largely unknown. At sea, most often observed off Kauai and Hawaii Is. in May–Sept.; occasionally rafts.

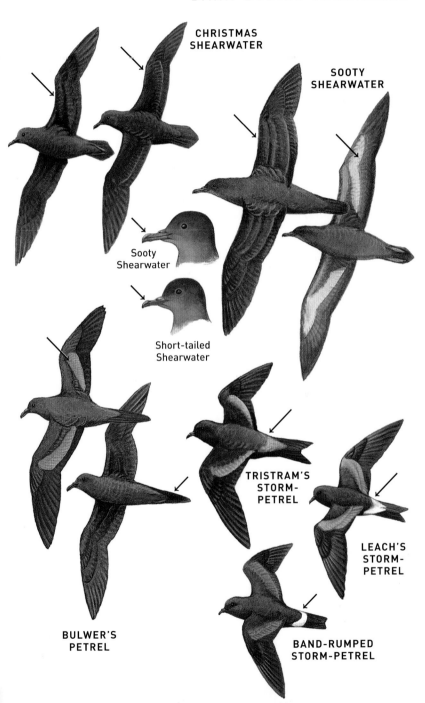

DARK-BODIED TUBENOSES

CHRISTMAS SHEARWATER

SOOTY SHEARWATER

Sooty Shearwater

Short-tailed Shearwater

TRISTRAM'S STORM-PETREL

LEACH'S STORM-PETREL

BULWER'S PETREL

BAND-RUMPED STORM-PETREL

BOOBIES, TROPICBIRDS, and FRIGATEBIRDS in HAWAII

BROWN BOOBY *Sula leucogaster*   **Fairly common**

See also p. 76. Breeds fairly commonly throughout Hawaiian Is.; "Brewster's Booby" (subspecies *brewsteri*), p. 76, found rarely in HI waters and in breeding colonies. **VOICE:** Female gives descending game-bird-like honks and grunts; male gives raspy whistling sounds. **HABITAT:** Often seen sitting on buoys off coast. Nests on ground (nw. Hawaiian Is.) or along remote rocky cliffs (se. Hawaiian Is.).

RED-FOOTED BOOBY *Sula sula*   **Common**

See also p. 76. White morph breeds commonly throughout Hawaiian Is.; white-tailed brown-morph adults occasionally recorded. **VOICE:** Descending clacking and rasping notes, males with squealing quality, quicker tempo than Brown Booby. **HABITAT:** Nests in bushes, at times in large colonies, where protected habitat occurs; locally common offshore.

MASKED BOOBY *Sula dactylatra*   **Uncommon, local**

See also p. 76. Breeds uncommonly throughout Hawaiian Is. Nazca Booby (*S. granti;* not shown) adults, with orange-tinged bills, accidental in HI waters and at Masked Booby colonies. **VOICE:** Female a ducklike *caup*; male a descending whistle. **HABITAT:** Nests on ground in nw. Hawaiian Is. and at only one locality (off Oahu) in se. Hawaiian Is. Uncommonly encountered in offshore waters.

WHITE-TAILED TROPICBIRD *Phaethon lepturus*   **Fairly common**

Breeds fairly commonly throughout se. Hawaiian Is. Red-billed Tropicbird (p. 74) rare in HI. **VOICE:** Sharp ternlike notes given when courting near nest sites. **HABITAT:** Breeds along steep vegetated ridges in se. Hawaiian Is., in craters on Hawaii I.; small numbers in large introduced trees on Midway Atoll. Fairly common in offshore waters.

RED-TAILED TROPICBIRD *Phaethon rubricauda*   **Fairly common**

See also p. 74. Breeds commonly throughout nw. Hawaiian Is., locally in se. Hawaiian Is. **VOICE:** Raspy, loud ternlike *krrek* notes given when courting; startling, explosive squawks near nests. **HABITAT:** Breeds on ground under bushes and trees in nw. Hawaiian Is., in rocky ocean-facing crevices in se. Hawaiian Is. Fairly common in offshore waters.

GREAT FRIGATEBIRD *Fregata minor*   **Fairly common**

34–41 in. (86–105 cm); wingspan 6½–7½ ft. (205–230 cm). Similar to Magnificent Frigatebird (p. 78) but slightly smaller and stockier in flight; white streaks usually present in axillars; adults with glossier green backs and red orbital skin; adult male has more-prominent brown upperwing carpal bar; adult female has grayish throat; juvenile has cinnamon-to-rufous head. Can take up to ten years to develop adult plumages. **VOICE:** A cooing whinny, bill clapping during display. **SIMILAR SPECIES:** Magnificent Frigatebird not recorded in HI. Lesser Frigatebird (*F. ariel;* not shown), rare in nw. Hawaiian Is. (has bred once), smaller; adult (especially male) has more solid white spurs on axillars; female has black throat, more extensive white to nape and axillars; juvenile similar in plumage. **HABITAT:** Fairly common breeder in nw. Hawaiian Is. Roosts on offshore islets but does not breed in se. Hawaiian Is., where less common from NW to SE in chain; seen more frequently over islands during storms.

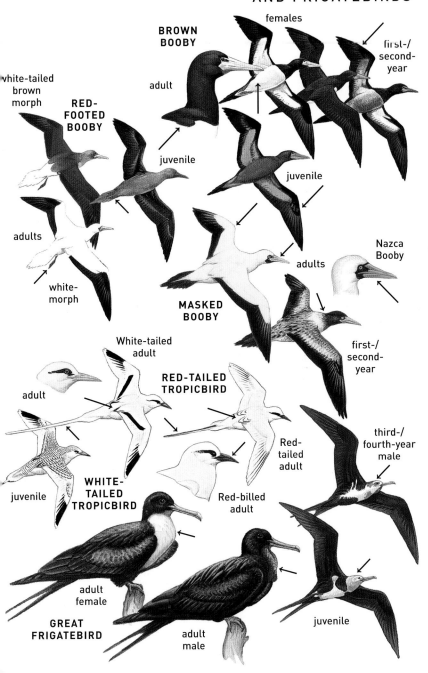

BOOBIES, TROPICBIRDS, AND FRIGATEBIRDS

BROWN BOOBY

females

first-/second-year

white-tailed brown morph

RED-FOOTED BOOBY

adult

juvenile

juvenile

adults

white-morph

adults

Nazca Booby

MASKED BOOBY

first-/second-year

White-tailed adult

RED-TAILED TROPICBIRD

adult

Red-tailed adult

adult

third-/fourth-year male

WHITE-TAILED TROPICBIRD

juvenile

Red-billed adult

adult female

GREAT FRIGATEBIRD

adult male

juvenile

GULLS and JAEGERS in HAWAII

Gulls rare in warm tropical and subtropical waters, including in Hawaii, where they are scarce in winter, despite 14 species having been recorded. In Hawaii, gulls are found in ports, along beaches, in coastal wetlands, and occasionally on the open ocean. First-years and second-years are most common.

LAUGHING GULL *Leucophaeus atricilla*   Scarce

See pp. 84 and 92. The most regular gull species in HI, with up to ten found together, often with other gull species. Adults in spring/summer plumage (p. 84) very rare in HI. Found in calm bays and coastal wetlands of se. Hawaiian Is., rare in nw. Hawaiian Is.

FRANKLIN'S GULL *Leucophaeus pipixcan*   Scarce

See pp. 84 and 92. Irregular spring migrant throughout the Hawaiian Is., with the majority of records in mid-Apr. through mid-May. Up to 15 observed in some years, none in others. Unlike Laughing Gull, most are adults in spring/summer plumage; very few records at other times of year. Favors coastal sandy habitats.

BONAPARTE'S GULL *Chroicocephalus philadelphia*   Rare

See pp. 84 and 92. First-winter birds found rarely in winter in se. Hawaiian Is., most frequently on coastal mudflats, wetlands, and ponds. Black-headed Gull and Black-legged Kittiwake (pp. 84, 86, and 92) are casual vagrants, largely to the nw. Hawaiian Is.

RING-BILLED GULL *Larus delawarensis*   Scarce

See pp. 86 and 92. Annual in se. Hawaiian Is. in small numbers. Usually found in coastal wetlands, occasionally in bays. Mew Gull (pp. 86 and 92) and California Gull (pp. 86 and 94) are extremely rare in HI; most initially identified as these species turn out to be Ring-billeds.

HERRING GULL *Larus argentatus*   Rare

See pp. 88 and 94. In se. Hawaiian Is., only first-winter birds recorded, primarily of N. American subspecies. Siberian subspecies (*vegae*) a bit darker backed and with white-based tail in first-year; all ages recorded more frequently in nw. Hawaiian Is. Found in harbors, mudflats; sandy beaches on northwestern atolls.

GLAUCOUS-WINGED GULL *Larus glaucescens*   Scarce

See pp. 88 and 96. Scarce but annual winter visitor throughout the Hawaiian Is., almost all in first-year or second-year plumages. Often found on beaches, as well as in harbors. Glaucous Gull (pp. 88 and 96) is a much rarer winter visitor.

SLATY-BACKED GULL *Larus schistisagus*   Scarce

See p. 90. Regular in nw. Hawaiian Is.; much rarer in se. Hawaiian Is. Most birds in first-winter and second-winter plumages, similar to those shown for Kelp Gull (p. 98) but with dark pink legs. Western and Lesser Black-backed Gulls (pp. 90 and 94) are accidental vagrants to HI.

POMARINE JAEGER *Stercorarius pomarinus*   Uncommon

See p. 78. Pomarine is the most regular of the jaegers and skuas to be found in Hawaiian waters in fall, winter, and spring. Parasitic and Long-tailed Jaegers (p. 80), and South Polar Skua (p. 78), all encountered more rarely and in smaller numbers.

GULLS AND JAEGERS

LAUGHING GULL

juvenile

first-year

juvenile

fall/winter

FRANKLIN'S GULL

BONAPARTE'S GULL

first-year

spring/summer adults

first-year

adult

variation in first- years

male

RING-BILLED GULL

first-year

first-year

HERRING GULL

female

SLATY-BACKED GULL

adult

first-year

second-year

light-morph adult

GLAUCOUS-WINGED GULL

first-year

second-year

POMARINE JAEGER

juvenile

first-year

second-year

second-year

MIGRATORY TERNS in HAWAII

Terns in Hawaii include both migrants and vagrants from N. America or Asia, and tropical breeding species, the latter including both year-round residents and those found in summer only. Migratory species can occur at all times of year, and most species are usually found in coastal ponds and wetlands, occasionally along beaches. Individuals of some species can stay for long periods, up to several years, once they have reached Hawaii.

CASPIAN TERN *Hydroprogne caspia* — Scarce

See p. 102. Individuals arriving to se. Hawaiian Is. can stay for multiple years, molting from summer to winter plumages. Found in freshwater coastal wetlands, often with gulls. Elegant Tern (p. 102) and Sandwich Tern (*Thalasseus sandvicensis*; not shown) are accidental vagrants to HI.

COMMON TERN *Sterna hirundo* — Rare

See p. 100. A rare visitor in most years, often in winter. First-year birds sometimes stay through summer. Usually found in coastal wetlands, sometimes along beaches. Siberian subspecies (*longipennis*) a casual vagrant to nw. Hawaiian Is.; Gull-billed Tern (p. 102) an accidental vagrant to se. Hawaiian Is.

ARCTIC TERN *Sterna paradisaea* — Scarce

See p. 100. Encountered primarily as an offshore migrant through Hawaiian waters, strictly in spring and fall, occasionally in numbers. Mostly adults in spring, adults and juveniles in fall; very rare ashore or at other times of year.

BLACK TERN *Chlidonias niger* — Very rare

See p. 104. Found occasionally over coastal wetlands and ponds. Usually first-year birds that can remain through their first spring and summer, gaining partial mottled black plumage; occasional fall/winter adults occur as well. White-winged Tern (p. 104) and Whiskered Tern (*C. hybrida*; not shown) are accidental vagrants to HI.

LEAST TERN *Sternula antillarum* — Scarce to uncommon

See p. 104. Annual in spring, summer, and fall; occasionally breeds in coastal wetlands throughout nw. and se. Hawaiian Is. Can be found in groups of up to ten in late summer, often including both adults and juveniles. Rare individuals remain through early winter. Little Tern (*S. albifrons*; not shown), a rare vagrant and breeder to nw. Hawaiian Is., best separated from Least by its uniformly white rump and tail, and single-note call.

MIGRATORY TERNS

CASPIAN TERN

spring/summer adult

first-year

spring/summer adult

COMMON TERN

adults

first-year

spring/summer adults

ARCTIC TERN

first-year

first-year

spring/summer adult

fall/winter

spring/summer adult

LEAST TERN

juvenile

spring/summer adult

fall/winter birds

BLACK TERN

BREEDING PACIFIC TERNS in HAWAII

SOOTY TERN *Onychoprion fuscatus*   Common, local

See also p. 104. Summer breeder in large colonies in nw. Hawaiian Is. and on islets off e. Oahu; arrives early spring. **VOICE:** Nasal *wide-a-wake* at colonies and occasionally over se. Hawaiian Is. **SIMILAR SPECIES:** See Gray-backed Tern. **HABITAT:** Breeds on flats of atolls and islets; fairly common offshore over tuna schools.

GRAY-BACKED TERN *Onychoprion lunatus*   Uncommon, local

14–15 in. (35–38 cm). Usually breeds near Sooty Terns, about one percent as commonly. Sparse in Hawaiian waters in Mar.–Oct. *Adult:* Back pale gray; cap black; white eyeline extends well behind eye. *Juvenile:* Crown, back, and wing coverts barred dusky, brown, and white. **VOICE:** Nasal *aay-eear* and other ternlike notes. **SIMILAR SPECIES:** Sooty Tern. **HABITAT:** Breed on edges of Sooty colonies.

BROWN NODDY *Anous stolidus*   Fairly common, local

Breeds throughout nw. Hawaiian Is. and on islets off e. Oahu. Found sparingly at sea. **VOICE:** Ripping *karrrrk* or *arrrrowk;* a harsh *eye-ak*. **SIMILAR SPECIES:** Black Noddy smaller, smaller billed, darker (also has grayer rump and orange legs in se. Hawaiian Is.). Brown Noddy flies low to the water. **HABITAT:** Breeds colonially on ground or singly on wide branches in trees.

BLACK NODDY *Anous minutus*   Fairly common, local

Subspecies *marcusi* in nw. Hawaiian Is. has more restricted white cap, uniform dark back and tail, and dark gray legs; *melanogenys* in se. Hawaiian Is. has gray cap extending to nape, paler and grayer tail, orange legs. **VOICE:** A rapid chattering *ah-ah-ah*, slower and more varying in se. Hawaiian Is. **SIMILAR SPECIES:** Brown Noddy. **HABITAT:** Nests in trees in nw. Hawaiian Is., along rocky cliffs in se. Hawaiian Is. Forages at sea and sometimes over coastal ponds.

BLUE-GRAY NODDY *Anous ceruleus*   Scarce, local

10–11 in. (25–28 cm). Summer breeder only on rocky nw. Hawaiian Is., most commonly Necker and Nihoa. A very delicate tern, with frosty pale gray head and underparts, darker gray back, and dusky wings. Ages similar. **VOICE:** A shrill, wavering, screamlike *eee-ah*. **SIMILAR SPECIES:** White Tern. **HABITAT:** Breeds on rocky islands. Rarely observed at sea; accidental in se. Hawaiian waters.

WHITE TERN *Gygis alba*   Fairly common, local

10½–11½ in. (27–29 cm). Common in nw. Hawaiian Is. and w. Oahu in se. Hawaiian Is.; year-round but more abundant in spring and summer. *Adult:* Entirely white with blue-black eye and bill. *Juvenile:* Upperpart feathers fringed pale brown. **VOICE:** Raspy chuckling *er-er-ear-ear-ear.* **SIMILAR SPECIES:** Blue-gray Noddy. White Tern more slender and buoyant than white Rock Pigeon. **HABITAT:** Lays eggs in tree crotches and on structures. Courts high in air; fairly common at sea with other pelagic terns.

BREEDING PACIFIC TERNS

SOOTY TERN
adult
juvenile

GRAY-BACKED TERN
adult
adult

BROWN NODDY

BLACK NODDY
se. Hawaiian Is.
nw. Hawaiian Is.

WHITE TERN

BLUE-GRAY NODDY

MORE-COMMON MIGRATORY
SHOREBIRDS to HAWAII

PACIFIC GOLDEN-PLOVER *Pluvialis fulva* **Common**

See p. 108. Winters commonly throughout nw. and se. Hawaiian Is. in wetlands and fields, including ball parks, cemeteries, and lawns. Adults molt into spring/summer plumage before departure in Apr. Oversummering first-year birds regular, often in winter or partial-summer plumages. Known as "Kolea" in Hawaiian. American Golden-Plover (p. 108) not yet recorded in HI.

BLACK-BELLIED PLOVER *Pluvialis squatarola* **Scarce**

See p. 108. Scarce to uncommon in HI, on beaches or in wetlands, often with Pacific Golden-Plovers.

SEMIPALMATED PLOVER *Charadrius semipalmatus* **Scarce**

See p. 110. Scarce to uncommon in HI, in wetlands, often with other shorebirds. Common-ringed Plover (p. 110), Lesser Sand-Plover (p. 140), and Killdeer (p. 110) rare vagrants to HI.

WANDERING TATTLER *Tringa incana* **Fairly common**

See p. 116. Fairly common in winter in HI, on beaches, rocky shores, and wetlands. A few remain through summer in winterlike plumages. Call note begets Hawaiian name "Ulili." Gray-tailed Tattler (p. 144) and Spotted (p. 124), Common (p. 144), and Terek (p. 144) Sandpipers are accidental to rare vagrants to HI.

RUDDY TURNSTONE *Arenaria interpres* **Common**

See p. 116. Common in winter in HI, on mudflats, beaches, wetlands, and fields. Based on calls, known as "Akekeke" in Hawaiian. Surfbird (p. 116) is an accidental vagrant to HI but Black Turnstone (p. 116) unrecorded.

SANDERLING *Calidris alba* **Fairly common**

See p. 118. Fairly common in winter in HI, on beaches, wetlands. Known as "Hunakai" in Hawaiian, which means blowing sea foam. Red-necked Stint (p. 144) and Red Knot (p. 118) are very rare vagrants to HI.

BRISTLE-THIGHED CURLEW *Numenius tahitiensis* **Uncommon**

See p. 142. Fairly common in nw. Hawaiian Is., uncommon in se. Hawaiian Is., on beaches, coastal dunes, fields. Primarily in winter but oversummers regularly in smaller numbers; most easily seen in n. Oahu and on Molokai. Known as "Kioea" in Hawaiian, which means "standing tall" but also could indicate the species' call.

WHIMBREL *Numenius phaeopus* **Scarce**

See p. 114. Scarce in winter in HI, but individuals often return for multiple years. Often found with Bristle-thighed Curlews. Both N. American (*hudsonicus*) and Eurasian (*variegatus*) subspecies occur with near-equal frequency. Far Eastern Curlew (*N. madagascariensis*, not shown) accidental in nw. Hawaiian Is.

MORE-COMMON MIGRATORY SHOREBIRDS

juveniles

BLACK-BELLIED PLOVER

fall/winter

PACIFIC GOLDEN-PLOVER

fall/winter

spring/summer

juvenile

fall/winter

spring/summer

WANDERING TATTLER

fall/winter

SEMIPALMATED PLOVER

spring/summer

fall/winter

juvenile

spring/summer

fall/winter

spring/summer

RUDDY TURNSTONE

SANDERLING

North American

Eurasian

WHIMBREL

BRISTLE-THIGHED CURLEW

RARER MIGRATORY SHOREBIRDS to HAWAII

LESSER YELLOWLEGS *Tringa flavipes*   Scarce

See p. 128. Scarce fall migrant to HI, rarer in winter and spring. Greater Yellowlegs (p. 128), Wilson's Phalarope (p. 130), and most other *Tringa*-like shorebirds (pp. 128 and 130) are accidental to rare vagrants to HI.

BAR-TAILED GODWIT *Limosa lapponica*   Scarce

See p. 142. Asian subspecies a scarce migrant, more common in the nw. Hawaiian Is. Occasionally winters, regularly on Laysan I. All three other godwit species (pp. 114 and 142) are accidental vagrants in HI.

LONG-BILLED DOWITCHER *Limnodromus scolopaceus*   Uncommon

See p. 126. Regular winter visitor in small numbers (flocks of up to 20), in se. Hawaiian Is. Scarcer in nw. Hawaiian Is. Short-billed Dowitcher (p. 126) is a very rare vagrant in HI; most reports turn out to be Long-billeds.

WILSON'S SNIPE *Gallinago delicata* (see also p. 136)   Uncommon

See p. 126. Small numbers winter annually throughout Hawaiian Is., though often difficult to find. Common Snipe (p. 146 also a casual vagrant. Pin-tailed Snipe (*G. stenura*, not shown) accidental.

DUNLIN *Calidris alpina* (see also p. 138)   Scarce

See p. 118. Small numbers winter throughout Hawaiian Is., occasionally in groups of up to ten. N. American subspecies (*pacifica*) most regular.

WESTERN SANDPIPER *Calidris mauri*   Rare

See p. 120. One or two found during most winters, primarily se. Hawaiian Is. Semipalmated Sandpiper (p. 120), White-rumped Sandpiper (p. 122), and Red-necked and Little Stints (p. 144) casual vagrants to HI.

LEAST SANDPIPER *Calidris minutilla*   Scarce

See p. 120. One to a few found in se. Hawaiian Is. during most winters. Long-toed Stint (p. 144) is an accidental vagrant.

PECTORAL SANDPIPER *Calidris melanotos*   Scarce to uncommon

See p. 122. Annual irregular migrant, occasionally in flocks of dozens, exceptionally over 100. Found throughout HI although more regular in se. Hawaiian Is. Scarce in winter. Baird's Sandpiper (p. 122) and Buff-breasted Sandpiper (p. 124) are very rare vagrants to HI.

SHARP-TAILED SANDPIPER *Calidris acuminate* Scarce to uncommon

See p. 146. Status similar to Pectoral Sandpiper (more than 100 occasionally encountered), but more common in nw. Hawaiian Is. than Pectoral. Long-toed Stint (p. 144) is an accidental vagrant to the nw. Hawaiian Is.

RUFF *Calidris pugnax*   Scarce

See p. 146. Somewhat irregular vagrant throughout Hawaiian Is. About half of recorded fall birds remain to overwinter.

RED PHALAROPE *Phalaropus fulicarius*   Uncommon

See p. 130. Probably regular in migration and winter in surrounding pelagic waters; sometimes encountered in multiples. Rarely seen ashore. Wilson's and Red-necked Phalaropes (p. 130) are rare vagrants.

RARER MIGRATORY SHOREBIRDS

LESSER YELLOWLEGS

BAR-TAILED GODWIT

fall/winter

juvenile

LONG-BILLED DOWITCHER

juvenile

fall/winter

WILSON'S SNIPE

DUNLIN

fall/winter

fall/winter

juvenile

WESTERN SANDPIPER

LEAST SANDPIPER

fall/winter

juvenile

juvenile

PECTORAL SANDPIPER

juvenile

juvenile

fall/winter

RUFF

juvenile male

spring/summer female

SHARP-TAILED SANDPIPER

RED PHALAROPE

RESIDENT WETLAND BIRDS in HAWAII

BLACK-NECKED STILT · *Himantopus mexicanus* · Fairly common

See also p. 112. "Hawaiian Stilt" (subspecies *knudseni*) breeds commonly throughout se. Hawaiian Is. Darker on head and neck than N. American stilts. Known as "A'eo" in Hawaiian. **VOICE:** Sharp yipping: *kyip, kyip, kyip,* a distinctive loud sound in HI coastal wetlands. Black-winged Stilt (*H. himantopus*, not shown) of Asia a vagrant to nw. Hawaiian Is. Hawaiian populations endangered.

CATTLE EGRET · *Bubulcus ibis* · Common, introduced and vagrant

See also p. 150. Common throughout lowland agricultural areas, parks, and roadsides of se. Hawaiian Is. and scarce migrant to nw. Hawaiian Is.; has bred on Midway. Cattle Egrets in HI often stained with red dirt. Snowy and Great Egrets (p. 150), accidental vagrants to HI, are larger, longer necked, have different bill and/or leg colors.

BLACK-CROWNED NIGHT-HERON · Fairly common
Nycticorax nycticorax

See also p. 152. Indigenous to HI. Fairly common in lowland marshes, estuaries, marinas, and aquafarms throughout se. Hawaiian Is.; most common on Kauai and Oahu. Occasionally found in higher-elevation forested streams. Predates tern chicks on offshore islets. Known as "Auku'u" in Hawaiian. Great Blue Heron (p. 148) and Green Heron (p. 152) are rare vagrants to HI.

WHITE-FACED IBIS · *Plegadis chihi* · Scarce

See p. 154. Scarce in HI but flocks of up to 11 birds have been recorded and, once having arrived, they often stay for years. Found in wetlands throughout se. Hawaiian Is.

HAWAIIAN COOT · *Fulica alai* · Fairly common, endangered

14–15½ in. (36–39 cm). *Adult:* Very similar to American Coot (p. 158), which has no confirmed records in HI, but adult has either a white shield that is more extensive than in American or a brighter red-topped shield than in American. Juveniles and first-year birds more similar to American Coot, with developing small dark red shields. Known as "Alae kea" in Hawaiian. **VOICE:** Similar to American Coot's. **SIMILAR SPECIES:** Common (Hawaiian) Gallinule. **HABITAT:** Coastal wetlands throughout se. Hawaiian Is., occasionally in upland ponds. Migrates between islands and has been recorded as a casual vagrant throughout nw. Hawaiian Is.

COMMON GALLINULE · *Gallinula galeata* · Fairly common, local

See also p. 158. "Hawaiian Gallinule" (subspecies *sandvicensis*), which is endangered, is very similar to N. American Common Gallinule. Found locally in freshwater wetlands of Kauai and Oahu. Known as "Alae ula" in Hawaiian.

RESIDENT WETLAND BIRDS

CATTLE EGRET

BLACK-NECKED (HAWAIIAN) STILT

males

nonbreeding

breeding

WHITE-FACED IBIS

juvenile

adult

adult

BLACK-CROWNED NIGHT-HERON

first-year and small red-shielded adult

HAWAIIAN COOT

white-shielded adult

chick

large red-shielded adult

adult

juvenile

adult

COMMON GALLINULE

chick

INTRODUCED GAME BIRDS in HAWAII

CHUKAR *Alectoris chukar*   Locally fairly common, introduced

See p. 170. Found fairly commonly at higher elevations of the six largest se. Hawaiian Is.; most common on Maui and Hawaii I.

GRAY FRANCOLIN   Locally common, introduced

Francolinus pondicerianus

11–13 in. (28–33 cm). Francolins are medium-sized, ground-dwelling game birds found primarily in cen. Asia; Gray Francolin was introduced to HI from India in 1958–1962. Drab, grayish brown, with *buff to tawny forehead and throat*; reddish back; pink to orangish legs. Sexes similar. **VOICE:** Loud, ringing *dee-luku-dee-luku* repeated up to many times. Can be similar to calls of Common Myna but more regular. **SIMILAR SPECIES:** Chukar more boldly marked with red bill. Female Black Francolin has rufous patch on nape, otherwise lacks tawny in face and reddish in upperparts. **HABITAT:** Confined to drier coastal and lowland areas; brushy regions, resorts, golf courses.

BLACK FRANCOLIN   Locally fairly common, introduced

Francolinus francolinus

12–14 in. (30–36 cm). Introduced to HI from India or Nepal in 1959–1962. *Male:* Striking game bird with *black head and underparts*, chestnut neck, white *cheek patch* and spots to sides, and bright orange legs. *Female:* Brown with dark eyeline though *pale face, rufous patch on hind neck*, dull orange legs. **VOICE:** Distinctive, insectlike *dzee-dee-dee—dee-de-dit*. **SIMILAR SPECIES:** For female, see Gray Francolin, Erckel's Francolin. **HABITAT:** Lowland and mid-elevation drier grasslands, brushy fields. Skulking; can be difficult to see except when male perches to sing.

JAPANESE QUAIL   Locally scarce to uncommon, introduced

Coturnix japonica

7–8 in. (18–20 cm). Introduced to HI from Japan in 1921 and 1929–1930. By far the smallest game bird in HI; *resembles a small buffy Northern Bobwhite* but patterns often difficult to observe on this elusive species. Male slightly brighter than female and with more striking head pattern. **VOICE:** A subtle but distinctive (once learned), raspy ascending two-note or three-note *pratch-wheeth* or *pratch-a-wirth*. Call may be best way to detect this species. **SIMILAR SPECIES:** Smaller than California Quail; poses lower to ground and more skulking. **HABITAT:** Grasslands and edges to fields, both lower and higher elevations. Has declined in HI during late twentieth century; now uncommon on Kauai (and possibly Niihau), rare or extirpated on other islands.

CALIFORNIA QUAIL   Locally common, introduced

Callipepla californica

See p. 172. Common at low and high elevations of Molokai, Maui, and Hawaii Is. Rare on Kauai; absent from Oahu and Lanai.

GAMBEL'S QUAIL *Callipepla gambelii*   Locally uncommon, introduced

See p. 172. Uncommon to fairly common on Lanai and Kahoolawe Is.

SMALL INTRODUCED
GAME BIRDS

GRAY
FRANCOLIN

CHUKAR

BLACK
FRANCOLIN

female

female

JAPANESE
QUAIL

male

male

female

female

GAMBEL'S
QUAIL

CALIFORNIA
QUAIL

male

male

ERCKEL'S FRANCOLIN
Locally fairly common, introduced

Pternistis erckelii

14–16 in. (36–41 cm). Introduced to HI from Africa in 1957. A large, dumpy game bird; primarily *gray with rufous crown and streaks*. Bill strong and hooked, legs yellow. Sexes alike. **VOICE:** Ducklike quacking sounds; explosive descending cackles. **SIMILAR SPECIES:** Larger than other francolins in HI. Female Ring-necked Pheasant has longer tail, not as boldly streaked. **HABITAT:** Mid- to higher- (occasionally lower-) elevation grasslands and scrubby drier forests; common on Hawaii I., less common elsewhere.

KALIJ PHEASANT *Lophura leucomelanos*
Uncommon, introduced

Male 24–29 in. (65–73 cm); female 21–23 in. (53-58 cm). Introduced to Hawaii I. in 1962, probably from Nepal. A relatively small pheasant. *Male:* Glossy *black and silver* plumage. Long spiky crest and *arched tail*, bare red face. *Female:* Brown with white scaling; short *crest; arched tail*. **VOICE:** Subtle clucks and squeals, given primarily in courtship or with chicks. **SIMILAR SPECIES:** Female darker, smaller, and/or more-elongated than female Ring-necked Pheasant and Red Junglefowl, has crest. **HABITAT:** Mid- to higher-elevation forests. Becoming established in nw. Oahu and recently observed in upland Maui.

RING-NECKED PHEASANT
Fairly common, introduced

Phasianus colchicus See p. 170. Found fairly commonly in open areas of six larger se. Hawaiian Is.

INDIAN PEAFOWL *Pavo cristatus*
Locally uncommon, introduced

Male 75–90 in. (190–229 cm); female 35–40 in. (90–102 cm). Introduced to HI as early as 1860. Large, pheasantlike bird, often domesticated but wild populations established in remote areas of the four larger se. Hawaiian Is. and Niihau. *Male:* Familiar "peacock" with bright *iridescent blue body* and *long green and blue train* (uppertail coverts). *Female:* Smaller and browner than male, *greenish head and neck, white belly*. **VOICE:** Loud repeated *carauww*, heard over great distances. **SIMILAR SPECIES:** Much larger than Ring-necked Pheasant and walks upright. See female Wild Turkey. **HABITAT:** Dry lowland and mid-elevation forested areas; semi-domesticated birds also encountered in park and suburban settings.

WILD TURKEY *Meleagris gallopavo*
Fairly common, introduced

See also p. 162. Found fairly commonly in open woodlands of most se. Hawaiian Is.

RED JUNGLEFOWL *Gallus gallus*
Locally fairly common, introduced

Male 24–29 in. (60–73 cm); female 16–18 in. (41–46 cm). Introduced by Polynesian settlers as early as 1500 years ago. Original junglefowl populations have been extirpated or diluted by more-recent strains throughout most of se. Hawaiian Is., but wild strains persist in upland areas of Kauai. *Male:* Colorful *orange and glossy purplish* with long glossy dark green uppertail coverts and red head combs. *Female:* Smaller, variably brown, *short blackish tail*. **VOICE:** Familiar *cock-a-doodle-doo*, various repeated *clucks* by females and *cheeps* by chicks. **SIMILAR SPECIES:** Ring-necked Pheasant, female Kalij Pheasant. **HABITAT:** Upland open forests and edges, especially in Kokee State Park. Domesticated strains frequently encountered elsewhere in HI.

LARGE INTRODUCED GAME BIRDS

ERCKEL'S FRANCOLIN
female
male

KALIJ PHEASANT
female
male

INDIAN PEAFOWL
female
male

RING-NECKED PHEASANT
male
female

RED JUNGLEFOWL
female
male

WILD TURKEY
female
male display

HAWKS, OWLS, SANDGROUSE, and DOVES in HAWAII

HAWAIIAN HAWK *Buteo solitarius*   Uncommon, endangered

16–18 in. (41–46 cm). Endemic to Hawaii I. Similar to Broad-winged Hawk (p. 188) in size. Adult plumage dimorphic. *Juvenile and first-year:* Dark hood; sides of breast streaked. **VOICE:** Repeated *kee-oo* begetting Hawaiian name "'Io." **SIMILAR SPECIES:** See Short-eared Owl. **HABITAT:** Forests, open fields, lava flow areas; virtually all elevations and habitats on Hawaii I.

SHORT-EARED OWL *Asio flammeus*   Uncommon

See also p. 204. Endemic subspecies (*sandwichensis*) uncommon throughout se. Hawaiian Is. over agricultural fields, wetlands. Known locally as "Pueo." Averages smaller and darker than continental subspecies, a casual winter vagrant to nw. Hawaiian Is. Wing shape and flight differ from Hawaiian Hawk's; note dark commas to underwings.

CHESTNUT-BELLIED SANDGROUSE   Locally uncommon, introduced
Pterocles exustus

11–13 in. (28–33 cm). Introduced to Hawaii I. from India in 1961–1962. A distinctively shaped, streamlined bird with small head and long pointed tail. *Male: Sandy colored with pale tawny face* and neck, dark chestnut abdomen. *Female:* Similar to male but *heavily barred* above and below. **VOICE:** Low-pitched gobbling notes. **SIMILAR SPECIES:** Spotted Dove has broader tail and wings, does not fly in flocks. **HABITAT:** Dry ranchlands, especially near dawn and dusk along highway south of Waimea.

ROCK PIGEON (ROCK DOVE, DOMESTIC PIGEON)
Columba livia   Common, introduced

See also p. 214. Common throughout se. Hawaiian Is., in agricultural areas, towns, cities; abundant in Honolulu. Plumages variable with many "typical" birds as well as white, blackish, and reddish variants. See White Tern, which can be mistaken for white Rock Pigeon in Honolulu.

SPOTTED DOVE *Streptopelia chinensis*   Common, introduced

See also p. 214. Introduced to HI from China prior to 1855. Found commonly on all se. Hawaiian Is., primarily in lowlands. Larger size, *broad collar of black and white spots on hindneck. Juvenile:* Lacks collar. **VOICE:** *Coo-whooo-coo*, the second note guttural. **SIMILAR SPECIES:** Mourning Dove. Courting Spotted Doves can resemble raptors. **HABITAT:** Agricultural fields, residential areas, parks, open forests.

MOURNING DOVE *Zenaida macroura*   Uncommon, introduced

See p. 216. Uncommon in lowlands and mid-elevation open areas of se. Hawaiian Is., most regularly found on Hawaii I. and Maui.

ZEBRA DOVE *Geopelia striata*   Common, introduced

8–9½ in. (20–24 cm). Introduced to HI from se. Asia in the 1920s. Now one of the most abundant species in se. Hawaiian Is. lowlands. Resembles Inca Dove (p. 216) in size and shape but head with pale bluish gray, *underparts distinctly barred black.* **VOICE:** Sharp, flutelike *pi-too-pi-poo-poo-poo-poo*, a very familiar sound in HI. **SIMILAR SPECIES:** Spotted Dove much larger. **HABITAT:** Residential and cultivated areas, parks, city streets; underfoot at outdoor eateries.

HAWK, OWL, SANDGROUSE, AND DOVES

HAWAIIAN HAWK

dark-morph adult

juvenile

dark morph

light-morph adult

SHORT-EARED OWL

fly on awkward stiff wings, often at dusk

CHESTNUT-BELLIED SANDGROUSE

female

female

male

SPOTTED DOVE

male

MOURNING DOVE

male

plumages variable

ROCK PIGEON

female

typical form

ZEBRA DOVE

SWIFTS, FALCONS, PARROTS, and CROW in HAWAII

MARIANA SWIFTLET
Aerodramus bartschi

Very local, introduced, endangered

4–5 in. (10–12 cm). Introduced to Oahu from Guam in 1962 to control mosquitoes. A small established population of 100 to 200 birds has remained stable in size. Similar to Chimney Swift (p. 230) in appearance and habits. **VOICE:** Twittery clicking notes. **SIMILAR SPECIES:** The only *small aerial bird* species in Hawaii. **RANGE AND HABITAT:** Sparsely distributed over forested southwestern slopes of cen. Oahu.

PEREGRINE FALCON *Falco peregrinus*

Uncommon

See p. 198. Annual in migration in HI in small numbers. Tundra subspecies (*tundrius*) most common during migration; small numbers of this and other subspecies overwinter. Seen most commonly over coasts and wetlands; also at sea. Smaller Merlin (p. 200) casual in winter in HI.

RED-CROWNED PARROT
Amazona viridigenalis

Locally established, introduced

See also p. 220. Population established by escapees on Oahu in late 1960s. Found primarily in vicinity of Pearl City; overall population of 150–200 birds estimated. The only short-tailed parrot established in HI.

ROSY-FACED LOVEBIRD *Agapornis roseicollis*

Exotic

See also p. 220. Escaped populations near Kihei, Maui, beginning in mid-2000s, increasing toward establishment.

RED-MASKED PARAKEET
Psittacara erythrogenys

Locally established, introduced

12–14 in. (30–35 cm). Increasing populations since the late 1980s found east of Honolulu and along Kona Coast, Hawaii I. Native of S. America. Green with red bend of underwing and *extensive red patch on crown and around face.* Juvenile entirely green and can be confused with other escaped parakeets. **VOICE:** Medium-pitched cackles. **SIMILAR SPECIES:** Mitered Parakeet (p. 220) has a small, controlled population on the n. Maui coast has less red in head as adult and lacks red to forepart of underwing. **HABITAT:** Large fruiting trees, residential areas, coastal habitats; forested slopes of Hawaii I.

ROSE-RINGED PARAKEET *Psittacula krameri*

Common, introduced

See also p. 220. A large, long-tailed, and conspicuous parakeet. Populations established on Kauai in the 1960s and Oahu in the 1970s, where now common to abundant. Seen in large flocks going to roost at sunset. Has become an agricultural pest on Kauai.

HAWAIIAN CROW
Corvus hawaiiensis

Extirpated from wild, endangered

12–14 in. (47–51 cm). Formerly an uncommon endemic resident on Hawaii I., primarily at mid-elevations on western slopes. Captive population of over 100 birds exist for future propagation. A large-billed, raven-like corvid, slightly browner than N. American ravens and crows. **VOICE:** Variety of sounds: *wree-o-wreep, kwak,* upslurred *kaaak,* etc. **SIMILAR SPECIES:** The only *large blackish bird* in HI. One record of Common Raven (p. 278) in nw. Hawaiian Is. **HABITAT:** Forested slopes with fruiting trees.

SWIFT, FALCON, PARROTS, AND CROW

MARIANA
SWIFTLET

PEREGRINE
FALCON

juvenile

adults

RED-MASKED
PARAKEET

RED-CROWNED
PARROT

ROSY-FACED
LOVEBIRD

ROSE-RINGED
PARAKEET

HAWAIIAN
CROW

ENDEMIC HAWAIIAN MONARCHS, SOLITAIRES, and *ACROCEPHALUS* WARBLER

KAUAI ELEPAIO *Chasiempis sclateri* **Fairly common, local**

5½–6½ in. (14–16 cm). Elepaios are small, variably plumaged, and active birds, *frequently flicking wings and cocking tails*. Kauai Elepaio is plainest of three species. *Adult:* Gray above, *white rump* and throat, cinnamon breast, *wings dark with bold white wing bars and spots* (sexes similar). In all three elepaio species, juveniles dull brown with buff spotting and first-years similar but without buff spots (sexes similar); second-years have plumage variably intermediate between first-year and adult of each sex. **VOICE:** Elepaios give distinctive three- to five-note *el-e-PAI-o*; also short squeaks and chatters. Kauai Elepaio song shorter and without emphasis. **SIMILAR SPECIES:** Juvenile Puaiohi larger, less active. **HABITAT:** Wet, dense, native forest; less common in drier lower-elevation forests.

OAHU ELEPAIO *Chasiempis ibidis* **Scarce, local, endangered**

5½–6½ in. (14–16 cm). Populations fragmented and declining. *Adult male:* Browner above than Kauai Elepaio and with variably extensive *black in face and throat*; adult female similar but with less black. **VOICE:** See Kauai Elepaio; Oahu's song longer (often five notes), emphasis on second and fourth notes. **SIMILAR SPECIES:** Chinese Hwamei much larger. **HABITAT:** Native and non-native forests of mid-elevation valleys.

HAWAII ELEPAIO *Chasiempis sandwichensis* **Fairly common**

5½–7 in. (14–18 cm). *Adults:* Similar to Oahu Elepaio but *ruddier; increasing amounts of white in head*, from wetter eastern slopes to drier western slopes to mesic high-elevation areas; male has more black in throat than female. **VOICE:** Classic four-note *el-e-PAI-o*. **SIMILAR SPECIES:** Juvenile Omao larger, duller, less active, lacks white. **HABITAT:** Mid- to high-elevation native forests, common on wetter slopes; local in higher-elevation mesic forest.

OMAO *Myadestes obscurus* **Fairly common**

6½–7½ in. (17–19 cm). Endemic to Hawaii I.; very similar to three now-extinct species that occurred on Oahu, on Molokai and Lanai, and on Kauai. *Adult:* A plump, short-tailed, dark brown-and-gray thrush with buff wing stripe in flight. Juvenile similar but with pale spotting (see Puaiohi). **VOICE:** Jumbled thrushlike song: *wheech-eech-chup-chup-weechy-chup*. Also dry rattle, "police whistle," mew, etc. **SIMILAR SPECIES:** Hawaii Elepaio. Chinese Hwamei redder with distinct eye markings. **HABITAT:** High-elevation wet forests; locally in mesic scrub.

PUAIOHI *Myadestes palmeri* **Uncommon, local, endangered**

6–7 in. (16–18 cm). The remaining thrush on Kauai. *Adult:* Similar to Omao but smaller, with *distinct whitish eye-ring*. *Juvenile:* Similar to adult but with buff spotting above, mottling below, pale tips to wing coverts. **VOICE:** Tremulous, flutelike *jeer-jure-weet*; call a dry buzzy *jjjent*. **HABITAT:** Wet native-forest gulches.

MILLERBIRD *Acrocephalus familiaris* **Local, endangered**

4½–5 in. (11–12 cm). Endemic to nw. Hawaiian Is. Recently reintroduced from Nihoa to Laysan after extirpated from latter in 1923. Small, *plain brown* bird (ages and sexes alike). **VOICE:** Song recalls Marsh Wren's (p. 288). Also a dry *jat*. **HABITAT:** Low-lying scrub.

MONARCHS, SOLITAIRES, AND *ACROCEPHALUS* WARBLER

first-year

KAUAI ELEPAIO

adult

adult male

juvenile

OAHU ELEPAIO

second-year male

adult female wet side

second-year female wet side

adult female high elevation

adult male wet side

adult male dry side

HAWAII ELEPAIO

OMAO

PUAIOHI

juvenile

MILLERBIRD

INTRODUCED SCRUB and FOREST PASSERINES in HAWAII

NORTHERN MOCKINGBIRD *Mimus polyglottos* Uncommon, introduced

See p. 268. Introduced to HI from N. America in 1928. Found in dry lowlands. **SIMILAR SPECIES:** Common Myna darker, plumper.

WHITE-RUMPED SHAMA Fairly common, introduced
Copsychus malabaricus

8½–10½ in. (22–27 cm). Introduced to Kauai from India in 1931 and to Oahu from Indonesia in 1938; has spread to Molokai, Lanai, and w. Maui. *Adult male: Slender, long-tailed*, dark glossy blue above; *belly orange*; white rump. Female duller; juvenile with buff spots. **VOICE:** Flutelike whistles and notes; call a short *tick*. **HABITAT:** Lowland wet forests.

JAPANESE BUSH WARBLER Fairly common, introduced
Horornis diphone

5½–6 in. (14–16 cm). Introduced to Oahu from Japan in 1929; spread to other se. Hawaiian Is. More often heard than seen. A small, *plain brownish bird* with *pale supercilium and dark eyeline* (ages and sexes similar). **VOICE:** Distinctive haunting *hooo-hweeeo*. **HABITAT:** Mid- to high-elevation ridgeline scrub; in winter to lower elevations.

JAPANESE WHITE-EYE *Zosterops japonicus* Common, introduced

4½ in. (11–12 cm). Introduced from Japan in 1929–1937. Small, active, *bright green above*, yellow and white below; *bold white eye-ring* (ages and sexes similar). Often in small groups. **VOICE:** Series of high-pitched *jeet* notes. **SIMILAR SPECIES:** Greenish Hawaiian finches duller, lack white eye-ring. **HABITAT:** All low- to high-elevation habitats in HI.

GREATER NECKLACED LAUGHINGTHRUSH Uncommon, introduced
Ianthocincla pectoralis

11–13 in. (28–34 cm). Introduced to Kauai from Asia in 1919. A jaylike babbler, *brownish olive above*, white below, with patterned cheeks and neck (ages and sexes similar). Travels in loose flocks. **VOICE:** Loud pure whistles; *wheet* contact calls. **HABITAT:** Lowlands of ne. Kauai.

HWAMEI *Garrulax canorus* Uncommon, introduced

8–10 in. (21–25 cm). Introduced from China in 1890s–1920s. Reddish brown with distinct *pale blue eye patch* (ages and sexes similar). **VOICE:** Song a series of chucks, jeers, and whistles; heard more than seen. **HABITAT:** Moist forests, primarily in upland regions.

RED-BILLED LEIOTHRIX Uncommon to common, introduced
Leiothrix lutea

5½–6 in. (14–15 cm). Introduced in 1918–1929; now extirpated from Kauai. Medium-small, colorful, with *bright red bill* (ages and sexes similar). Travels in groups. **VOICE:** Pleasing series of whistles, similar to Chinese Hwamei but less jeering. **HABITAT:** Mid- to upper-elevation forests.

EURASIAN SKYLARK *Alauda arvensis* Uncommon to common, introduced and vagrant

See p. 326. Introduced to HI in 1870. Accidental in nw. Hawaiian Is. Found most commonly mid- to high-elevation pastures of Maui and Hawaii I.

INTRODUCED PASSERINES

NORTHERN MOCKINGBIRD

wing-flashing

juvenile

Kauai adult

Oahu adult

WHITE-RUMPED SHAMA

JAPANESE BUSH-WARBLER

JAPANESE WHITE-EYE

GREATER NECKLACED LAUGHING-THRUSH

HWAMEI

RED-BILLED LEIOTHRIX

EURASIAN SKYLARK

INTRODUCED ESTRILDIDAE FINCHES
in HAWAII

Estrildid finches are popular, small-bodied, active cage birds originally from Africa and Asia. Ages and/or sexes similar unless noted.

LAVENDER WAXBILL Scarce to uncommon, introduced
Estrilda caerulescens
4–4½ in. (10–11 cm). Introduced in 1965. *Pale lavender-gray* with thin black mask and *dark red tail*. Found singly or in small groups. **VOICE:** Two- to three-note *tsee-tsee-tseer*. **HABITAT:** Dry residential areas, scrub.

ORANGE-CHEEKED WAXBILL *Estrilda melpoda* Uncommon, exotic
4 in. (10 cm). Introduced to Maui in 1989, where population is declining. *Adult:* Gray and brown with *round orange cheek patch*, red bill, *red rump*. Juvenile browner with pale cheek patch. **VOICE:** Rapid series of *cheeps*. **SIMILAR SPECIES:** Common Waxbill barred, has red mask, lacks red vent. **HABITAT:** Dry residential areas and scrub.

COMMON WAXBILL *Estrilda astrild* Common, introduced
4–5 in. (10–12 cm). Introduced in 1973; rapidly expanding. *Adult:* Gray crown, white throat, red bill, *elongated red mask*; body brownish, *finely barred black*. Juvenile brown, often with dull red eye patch. **VOICE:** Raspy *jee-jeh-jeya*; constant *jeps*, drier than Orange-cheeked Waxbill. **HABITAT:** Grassy fields; movements respond to tall-grass seed production.

RED AVADAVAT *Amandava amandava* Fairly common, introduced
3½–4 in. (9–10 cm). Introduced in early 1900s. *Adult male:* Primarily *dark red with white spots*; black wings and tail, white wing bars and spots. *Adult female:* Gray with black and white wings; red bill and rump. Juvenile brown with dark bill, buff wing bars. **VOICE:** High-pitched *cheets*. **HABITAT:** Grassy fields, responding to grass-seed production.

AFRICAN SILVERBILL *Euodice cantans* Fairly common, introduced
4–5 in. (10–12 cm). Introduced in 1960s. Pale brown head, *white underparts*, dark brown wings and tail, *silver bill*. **VOICE:** Distinctive metallic *pit* notes in flight. **HABITAT:** Scrublands, more common in dry areas.

JAVA SPARROW *Lonchura oryzivora* Fairly common, introduced
5½–6½ in. (14–17 cm). Introduced in 1960s. *Adult: Black head with white face patch*; back and breast gray; belly pinkish; *large red bill*. *Juvenile:* Browner, cheek patch paler, bill dull red. **VOICE:** Melodic jumbled *pseeps* and whistled *pseews*; call a dry *chep*. **SIMILAR SPECIES:** Juvenile Chestnut Munia. **HABITAT:** Grassy fields, residential areas, bird feeders.

SCALY-BREASTED MUNIA *Lonchura punctulata* Common, introduced
See p. 346. Introduced in 1866. Found in grassy fields, cemeteries, lawns, and forest edges up to medium-high elevations.

CHESTNUT MUNIA *Lonchura atricapilla* Fairly common, introduced
4½–5 in. (11–12 cm). Introduced in 1959; recent emigrant to Hawaii I. *Adult:* Chestnut body, black head, large silver bill. *Juvenile:* Brown with gray bill. **VOICE:** Nondescript *tips* and *cheps*. **SIMILAR SPECIES:** Juvenile Java Sparrow. **HABITAT:** Weedy fields, residential areas.

INTRODUCED ESTRILDIDAE FINCHES

LAVENDER WAXBILL

ORANGE-CHEEKED WAXBILL

COMMON WAXBILL

RED AVADAVAT

adult male

adult female

juvenile

AFRICAN SILVERBILL

adult

JAVA SPARROW

juvenile

SCALY-BREASTED MUNIA

adult male

CHESTNUT MUNIA

juvenile

adult

INTRODUCED OLD WORLD SPARROW, CARDINALS, and TANAGERS in HAWAII

HOUSE SPARROW *Passer domesticus*   Common, introduced
See p. 346. Introduced in 1866–1871. Found in urban, pastoral, and some rural habitats throughout se. Hawaiian Is.

NORTHERN CARDINAL   Fairly common, introduced
Cardinalis cardinalis
See p. 356. Introduced in 1929. Found in suburban and scrubby habitats of se. Hawaiian Is.; accidental vagrant to Nihoa, nw. Hawaiian Is.

RED-CRESTED CARDINAL *Paroaria coronata*   Common, introduced
7–8 in. (18–20 cm). This and the following three species are in the New World tanager family, Thraupidae, from S. America. Red-crested Cardinal introduced in 1928; currently a vagrant to Hawaii I. *Adult:* Gray and white with *noticeably crested red head* extending to center breast. *Juvenile:* Similar but head brown. A tame and confiding species in HI. **VOICE:** Pure melodius two-note whistles, vireo-like phrases. Call a short ascending *waenk*. **SIMILAR SPECIES:** Yellow-billed Cardinal. **HABITAT:** Open parks, coastal strands, residential areas to restricted lowlands.

YELLOW-BILLED CARDINAL *Paroaria capitata*   Common, introduced
6–7 in. (16–18 cm). Introduced in 1960s. Replaces Red-crested Cardinal on Hawaii I. *Adult:* Dark gray and white with *dark red head* and black throat extending to center breast; *bill orange-yellow. Juvenile:* Similar but head brown, bill duller with black tip. **VOICE:** Clear, high-pitched series of whistles, including double-noted *whee-cheer* frequently repeated; call a harsh *craark*. **SIMILAR SPECIES:** Red-crested Cardinal has noticeable crest (lacking in Yellow-billed Cardinal), red (not black) point extends to breast. **HABITAT:** Scrubby forest along coastal strands, beach parks.

SAFFRON FINCH *Sicalis flaveola*   Uncommon to common, introduced
5½–6½ in. (14–16 cm). Introduced in 1965 (on Oahu and Hawaii I., where now common) and 2004 (on Kauai, where uncommon). *Adult male:* Bright lemon yellow head and underparts, with *orange wash to forecrown and throat*; upperparts greenish yellow, flight feathers blackish with yellow edging. *Juvenile:* Largely brownish with dark streaking to back and patches of yellow; *faint or no malar streak and supercilium.* Adult female similar to juvenile but brighter, back greenish, lower mandible yellow. **VOICE:** Song a series of clear, high-pitched *seep-seeup-tsee-tseep*, etc. Calls a single- or double-note *tseep* or *tsee-tseeup*. **SIMILAR SPECIES:** Yellow-fronted Canary (p. 422) has much more distinct dark malar streak and pale supercilium than juvenile Saffron Finch. **HABITAT:** Lowland residential areas, coastal strands, city and beach parks.

YELLOW-FACED GRASSQUIT *Tiaris olivaceus*   Scarce, exotic
3½–4½ in. (9–11 cm). Introduced in 1974. *Adult male:* Largely olive and gray with distinct *yellow supercilium and throat and black forecrown, face, and breast. Juvenile and female:* Pale grayish olive with *pale yellow lores*, whitish supercilium and throat, and *pale crescent above and below eye.* **VOICE:** Very rapid and high-pitched trill, *ti-ti-ti-ti-ti-ti.* **SIMILAR SPECIES:** Juvenile Saffron Finch and Yellow-fronted Canary larger, usually with faint to distinct dark streaks. **HABITAT:** Weedy or grassy fields. Only sporadically observed, singly or in pairs.

INTRODUCED OLD WORLD SPARROW, CARDINALS, AND TRUE TANAGERS

HOUSE SPARROW

female

male

NORTHERN CARDINAL

female

male

RED-CRESTED CARDINAL

adult

juvenile

YELLOW-BILLED CARDINAL

adult

juvenile

SAFFRON FINCH

juvenile

adult

YELLOW-FACED GRASSQUIT

female

adult male

ENDEMIC HAWAIIAN FINCHES

Hawaiian finches form a large diverse group of the family Fringillidae (p. 348) that became established in the Hawaiian Is. 3 to 7 million years ago and has since shown spectacular adaptive radiation in bill forms.

LAYSAN AND NIHOA FINCHES
Local, endangered

Telespiza cantans and *T. ultima*

6–7½ in. (15–19 cm). Endemics to nw. Hawaiian Is. *Adult male:* Bright *yellow head and underparts*, black flight feathers fringed yellow. *Adult female:* Duller, variable. *Juvenile: Streaked* brown. Nihoa Finch (not shown) slightly smaller, bill stubbier. **VOICE:** Tinkling songs and calls. **HABITAT:** Laysan: scrub, beaches; Nihoa: rocks.

PALILA *Loxioides bailleui*
Uncommon, endangered

6–7½ in. (16–19 cm). Endemic to Hawaii I. *Adult:* Bright *yellow head and breast;* gray back; *black parrotlike bill.* Female slightly duller, juvenile more so. **VOICE:** Distinctive *pa-li-la* or *pa-li-la-la.* **HABITAT:** Dry forest.

MAUI PARROTBILL
Scarce, local, endangered

Pseudonestor xanthophrys

5–6 in. (13–15 cm). *Adult male:* Olive above; yellow *supercilium* and underparts; *parrotlike bill. First-year female:* Duller, lacks yellow. Adult female, first-year male intermediate. **VOICE:** Song recalls Canyon Wren's (p. 288). Calls *chet* and *see-uw.* **HABITAT:** Wet upland forest.

AKOHEKOHE *Palmeria dolei*
Uncommon, local, endangered

6½–7 in. (16–18 cm). *Adult: Blackish* starlinglike bird, white crest and streaks; *orange eye patch and nape* (sexes similar). *Juvenile:* Duller overall, reduced crest. **VOICE:** Variable shrieks, whistles, a guttural *ako-he-ko-he,* etc. **HABITAT:** Wet upland forest.

APAPANE *Himatione sanguinea*
Fairly common to common

4½–5½ in. (12–14 cm). The most common Hawaiian finch. *Adult: Dark red;* brighter face; black wings and tail; *white vent;* curved black bill (sexes alike). *Juvenile:* Pale brown; molting birds mottled *brown and red.* **VOICE:** Jumbled *kee-chew-rich-choo-choo-jit-choo-chi-chi-chi. Cheet* flight calls. **SIMILAR SPECIES:** Iiwi has a red bill, white-edged tertials, lacks white vent. **HABITAT:** Upland native forest; flowering Ohia trees.

IIWI *Drepanis coccinea*
Uncommon to fairly common

5½–6 in. (14–16 cm). Iconic Hawaiian finch, absent or rare on Molokai, Lanai, and Oahu; uncommon to fairly common on Kauai, Maui, and Hawaii Is. *Adult:* Scarlet with black wings and tail; *bill strongly decurved, bright orange-red* (sexes alike). *Juvenile:* Greenish yellow with black wings; molting birds mottled *green and red.* **VOICE:** Distinctive *cheree, che-choo, jaaa, cho-chee,* with "rusty gate" quality; also a whistled *pee-er.* **SIMILAR SPECIES:** Apapane. **HABITAT:** Upland forest; flowers, berries.

HAWAII AKEPA *Loxops coccineus*
Uncommon, local, endangered

4–5 in. (11–13 cm). Small. *Adult male:* Bright *orange* with dusky wings and tail; bill small, *siskinlike, pale,* slightly crossed. *Adult female:* Grayish and olive with yellow-orange breast. *First-year:* Dull olive. *Second-year male:* Yellowish or duller orange than adult male. **VOICE:** High, tinkling *tseedle-lee-tseedle-lee,* not as monotone as Hawaii Creeper's song. Calls of same quality. **HABITAT:** Upland forest; forages in leaf crowns.

ENDEMIC HAWAIIAN FINCHES

LAYSAN FINCH

Nihoa Finch is similar (see text)

PALILA

juvenile

adult male

adult female

first-year female

MAUI PARROTBILL

AKOHEKOHE

adult male

adult

juvenile

adult

IIWI

juvenile

molting first-year

first-year

adult

juvenile

molting first-year

APAPANE

adult male

female

second-year male

HAWAII AKEPA

GREEN-and-YELLOW HAWAIIAN FINCHES on KAUAI and OAHU

AKIKIKI *Oreomystis bairdi*   Scarce, local, endangered

5–5½ in. (12–14 cm). Formerly "Kauai Creeper." Endemic to Kauai. *Adult:* Plain, *grayish olive above*, whitish below; *short decurved pink bill. Juvenile:* Has *white spectacles.* Creeps nuthatchlike on larger branches. **VOICE:** Wood-warblerlike *we-see-se-see-we-see,* sometimes rising. Call *tseet* or *tse-wee.* **HABITAT:** Wet, native forest.

ANIANIAU *Magumma parva*   Uncommon, local

4–4½ in. (10–11 cm). Endemic to Kauai; declining. Small. *Adult male:* Uniformly *bright yellow; short curved beak. Female and first-year male:* Slightly duller. **VOICE:** Similar to Akikiki but more melodic. **SIMILAR SPECIES:** Akekee and Kauai Amakihi have black lores. **HABITAT:** Wet, native forest; flowering trees and shrubs.

AKEKEE *Loxops caeruleirostris*   Scarce, local, endangered

4–5 in. (10–12 cm). Formerly "Kauai Akepa"; Oahu Akepa (*L. wolstenholmei*) and Maui Akepa (*L. ochraceous*) last recorded in 1893 and ca. 1980, respectively. Endemic to Kauai. *Adult male:* Olive above with *yellow rump*, underparts yellow; *black face mask.* Bill sharp, pale bluish. Female and first-year male slightly duller. **VOICE:** Song slightly more monotone than Akikiki's, often dropping: *tsee-tsee-tsee-tsu-tsu-tsee.* **SIMILAR SPECIES:** Anianiau and Kauai Amakihi have curved bills, lack yellow in rumps. **HABITAT:** Wet, native forest; feeds in canopy.

KAUAI AMAKIHI *Chlorodrepanis stejnegeri*   Fairly common, local

4–5 in. (11–12 cm). Endemic to Kauai. *Adult male:* Somewhat bright olive and yellow; *small black face mask.* Bill large and decurved. Female and first-year duller. **VOICE:** A rapid trill on plane or slightly descending *tse-tse-tse-tse-tsip-tsip* or *tseewe-tsewe-tsewe.* Calls nasal finchlike *churee* or *chewip,* or gnatcatcher-like *cheaaah.* **SIMILAR SPECIES:** Anianiau, Akekee. **HABITAT:** Upland native forest; flowers.

OAHU AMAKIHI *Chlorodrepanis flava*   Fairly common

4–4½ in. (11–12 cm). Endemic to Oahu. *Adult male:* Similar to Kauai Amakihi but bill smaller; indistinct malar streak sometimes present. *Adult female:* Olive-gray above, pale greenish below; indistinct pale yellow to whitish wing bars. *Juvenile:* Grayer than female, more-distinct wing bars. **VOICE:** As in Kauai Amakihi. **SIMILAR SPECIES:** Japanese White-eye. **HABITAT:** Native and non-native forests, arboretums; flowering trees and shrubs. Moves to lower elevations in winter.

GREEN-AND-YELLOW FINCHES
Kauai and Oahu

adult

juvenile

AKIKIKI

first-year
female

adult
male

ANIANIAU

AKEKEE

adult male

adult
male

**KAUAI
AMAKIHI**

juvenile

molting
first-year

OAHU AMAKIHI

GREEN-and-YELLOW HAWAIIAN FINCHES
on MOLOKAI, MAUI, and HAWAII IS.

AKIAPOLAAU *Hemignathus wilsoni*   Uncommon, local, endangered

5–6 in. (13–15 cm). Endemic to Hawaii I. *Adult male:* Yellow; black lores; *upper mandible long and curved, lower mandible short and chisel-like. First-year female:* Duller; underparts olive. Adult female and first-year male intermediate, some with green bodies and bright yellow throats. **VOICE:** Distinctive, melodic series of 10–12 notes, *which-chu-chwee-chu,* often ending with two- to three-note *chwee-chwee.* Common call a pure *chuwee.* **SIMILAR SPECIES:** Beware Hawaii Amakihis with deformed upper mandibles are not infrequent. **HABITAT:** Wet upland forest (formerly dry high-elevation forest). The similar but extinct Oahu Nukupuu (*H. lucidus,* not shown) and Kauai Nukupuu (*H. hanapepe,* not shown) were last collected in 1838–1841 and 1899, respectively.

HAWAII AMAKIHI *Chlorodrepanis virens*   Uncommon to common

4–4½ in. (11–12 cm). Common on Maui and Hawaii I.; uncommon on Molokai; extirpated from Lanai. *Adult male:* Similar to Kauai Amakihi but bill smaller. *Adult female:* Duller, less yellow. *Juvenile:* Dull greenish with indistinct wing bars. Females on Maui and Molokai (subspecies *wilsoni*) grayer. **VOICE:** As in Kauai Amakihi. **SIMILAR SPECIES:** Japanese White-eye. Maui Alauahio lacks mask, has straighter bill. Hawaii Creeper more olive; mask broader; bill slightly straighter, forages on branches. **HABITAT:** Wet to dry native forests; flowering trees and shrubs, where primarily a nectar feeder. Can be found in non-native, low-elevation forests in winter. Larger, extinct, Greater Amakihi (*Viridonia sagittirostris*) last collected on Hawaii I. in 1902.

MAUI ALAUAHIO *Paroreomyza montana*   Fairly common

4–4½ in. (11–12 cm). Formerly "Maui Creeper" although only occasionally creeps. Found on Maui; extirpated from Lanai. Plump. *Adult male:* Rather bright olive above and yellow below; bill fairly straight, pale. *First-year female:* Much duller, olive above, grayish below. Adult female and first-year male intermediate. Often in family groups. **VOICE:** Melodic, repeated *cheep-pur wee-da,* more musical than amakihi. Call a distinctive short *chep.* **SIMILAR SPECIES:** Hawaii Amakihi. **HABITAT:** High-elevation wet native and non-native forests. Forages primarily in leaves, on branches.

HAWAII CREEPER *Loxops mana*   Uncommon, endangered

4½–5 in. (11–13 cm). Endemic to Hawaii I. Olive above with gray-washed crown; dull, pale greenish to brownish below; small *squarish black mask;* bill *thin, sharp, slightly decurved* (sexes similar). *Juvenile and first-year:* Grayer, reduced or no blackish mask, pale supercilium. Often creeps horizontally along branches. **VOICE:** Quiet trill: *che-che-che-she-she,* often slightly descending. Call slightly nasal *cheit* or *cheerit.* **SIMILAR SPECIES:** Hawaii Amakihi. **HABITAT:** High-elevation native forests.

GREEN-AND-YELLOW FINCHES
Molokai, Maui, and Hawaii Island

AKIAPOLAAU

first-year female

adult male

HAWAII AMAKIHI

juvenile

MAUI ALAUAHIO

first-year female

adult female

adult male

adult male

juvenile/ first-year

adult

HAWAII CREEPER

EXTINCT HAWAIIAN BIRDS

Thirty-six endemic Hawaiian species and subspecies are now extinct. Many other species are known only from fossils. This represents the greatest loss of avian diversity in the world. Here we show a cross-section of extinct taxa.

LAYSAN RAIL *Zapornia palmeri*
A flightless species formerly on Laysan I. (last seen 1923) and introduced to Midway Atoll (last seen in 1944). Hawaiian Rail (*Z. sandwichensis*) was a forest species last collected in 1884.

BISHOP'S OO *Moho bishopi*
Formerly on Molokai (last seen 1903–1904). The similar Oahu Oo (*M. apicalis*), Hawaii Oo (*M. nobilis*), and Kauai Oo (*M. braccatus*) were last recorded in 1837, 1902, and 1987, respectively.

KIOEA *Chaetoptila angustipluma*
Little-known species from Hawaii I.; last collected about 1859.

POO-ULI *Melamprosops phaeosoma*
Unique Hawaiian finch discovered on Maui in 1973. Went extinct in 2004.

KAKAWAHIE *Paroreomyza flammea*
Dark reddish alauahio of Molokai last seen in 1963. Oahu Alauahio (*P. maculata*) was last collected on that island in 1968.

KONA GROSBEAK *Chloridops kona*
Formerly found in dry high-elevation forests of Hawaii I. This species, the Greater Koa-Finch (*Rhodacanthis palmeri*), and the Lesser Koa-Finch (*R. flaviceps*) were last collected in these forests in 1891–1896.

ULU-AI-HAWANE *Ciridops anna*
Only five specimens of this elegant Hawaiian finch were collected from Hawaii I., the last in 1892. It fed in native palm tree species.

BLACK MAMO *Drepanis funerea*
This black relative of the Iiwi was found only in dense, ridgeline scrub forests of Molokai, where it was last collected in 1907. The Hawaii Mamo (*D. pacifica*), of Hawaii I. (last collected in 1898), had a bright yellow rump, vent, and bend of wing.

OU *Psittirostra psittacea*
Formerly very common in lowland forests but last recorded on Oahu (in 1893), Maui (1901), Molokai (1907), Lanai (1931), Hawaii I. (1986), and Kauai (1989).

LANAI HOOKBILL *Dysmorodrepanis munroi*
Known from only one specimen, collected on Lanai in 1913. Illustration based on specimen, an adult of unknown sex; thus, plumage variation by age and sex unknown.

KAUAI AKIALOA *Akialoa stejnegeri*
Spectacularly long-billed Hawaiian finch, last recorded on the Alakai Plateau in 1969. The similar Oahu Akialoa (*A. ellisiana*) of Oahu, Maui-nui Akialoa (*A. lanaiensis*) of Lanai, and Lesser Akialoa (*A. obscura*) of Hawaii I. were last seen in 1892, 1894, and 1903, respectively.

EXTINCT HAWAIIAN BIRDS

LAYSAN RAIL

BISHOP'S OO

adult

KIOEA

KAKAWAHIE

adult male

POO-ULI

KONA GROSBEAK

BLACK MAMO

LANAI HOOKBILL

adult male

adult male

OU

ULU-AI-HAWANE

KAUAI AKIALOA

adult male

INTRODUCED FINCHES, MEADOWLARK, MYNA, and BULBULS in HAWAII

HOUSE FINCH *Haemorhous mexicanus*   Common, introduced

See p. 350. Introduced to HI in 1859. Found in dry, open, rural and suburban habitats throughout se. Hawaiian Is.; casual vagrant to nw. Hawaiian Is. Yellow-headed variants more frequent in HI than in N. America.

YELLOW-FRONTED CANARY   Common, introduced
Crithagra mozambica

4½–5 in. (11–13 cm). This African Fringillid finch was introduced to Oahu in 1964 and Hawaii I. in 1966. Head gray and yellow with dark lores and malar stripe creating *distinctly patterned face*; back olive; wings and tail dark; *rump and underparts bright yellow* (ages and sexes similar). **VOICE:** Song a series of *tsees* and warbles. Call *tsee-lee*. **SIMILAR SPECIES:** Juvenile Saffron Finch. **HABITAT:** Lowland parks, residential areas.

ISLAND CANARY *Serinus canaria*   Local, introduced

5–5½ in. (12–14 cm). Native to the Canary and Azores Is., this popular cage bird was introduced to Midway Atoll in 1909, where it increased after rats were eradicated in 1997. The cage-bird variant predominates: *entirely pale yellow* or with bleached whitish wings and tail; juveniles and some adults have variable brown-streaked patches of original native stock. **VOICE:** Melodic tinkling *tsee-tsee-tseew-tseew-tsip-tsip-tsip*. **HABITAT:** Ironwood trees; residential areas; open sandy fields.

WESTERN MEADOWLARK   Fairly common, introduced
Sturnella neglecta

See p. 362. Introduced from N. America to Kauai in 1928. Found in pastures and open fields throughout lowlands; may be declining.

COMMON MYNA *Acridotheres tristis*   Common, introduced

Introduced from Asia to Oahu in 1866 and had spread to all other se. Hawaiian Is. by the 1880s and to Midway in the 1970s. Found abundantly and conspicuously in urban and rural lowland habitats of Hawaii, less commonly to high-elevation pastures and forests. Gregarious; sometimes found in large flocks. White patches in wings characteristic (although see Northern Mockingbird).

RED-VENTED BULBUL *Pycnonotus cafer*   Common, introduced

8–9 in. (20–23 cm). A cage-bird species from India that escaped on Oahu in 1966 and is now abundant there; occasionally reported from other islands. *Black head with prominent crest*; gray body; *white rump*; red vent (ages and sexes similar). **VOICE:** A husky, guttural *chwee-juu-wur*, repeated sporadically as song. **SIMILAR SPECIES:** Red-whiskered Bulbul is slightly smaller; has a patterned white, black, and red face; and lacks a white rump. **HABITAT:** Lowland residential areas, parks, scrub.

RED-WHISKERED BULBUL   Fairly common, introduced
Pycnonotus jocosus

See also p. 346. Asian cage-bird species escaped on Oahu in 1965 and is now fairly common although, unlike Red-vented Bulbul, found more commonly on mid-elevation slopes, in residential areas and parks that include large trees. **SIMILAR SPECIES:** Red-vented Bulbul.

INTRODUCED FINCHES, MEADOWLARK, MYNA, AND BULBULS

orange variant
male

**HOUSE
FINCH**

female

male

**YELLOW-FRONTED
CANARY**

**ISLAND
CANARY**

**WESTERN
MEADOWLARK**

**COMMON
MYNA**

**RED-
WHISKERED
BULBUL**

**RED-VENTED
BULBUL**

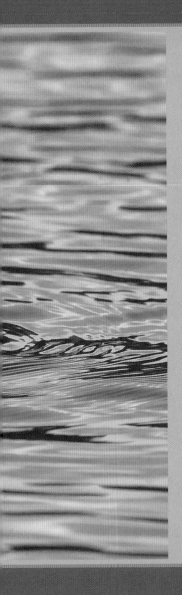

LIFE LIST
INDEX

LIFE LIST

The following pages contain the American Birding Association's Checklist as of December 2018 (also available online at http://listing.aba.org/aba-checklist/). The ABA Checklist "includes ABA-area breeding species, regular visitors, and casual and accidental species from other regions that are believed to have strayed here without direct human aid, and well-established introduced species that are now part of our avifauna."

Scientific names are not given below but can be found in the species accounts throughout the book. Note that the sequence here does not follow that of the plates in this book, which have been arranged as much for ease of identification as in accordance with our understanding of current (and frequently changing) phylogenetic sequence.

DUCKS, GEESE, AND SWANS (ANATIDAE)

_____ Black-bellied Whistling-Duck

_____ Fulvous Whistling-Duck

_____ Emperor Goose

_____ Snow Goose

_____ Ross's Goose

_____ Graylag Goose

_____ Greater White-fronted Goose

_____ Lesser White-fronted Goose

_____ Taiga Bean-Goose

_____ Tundra Bean-Goose

_____ Pink-footed Goose

_____ Brant

_____ Barnacle Goose

_____ Cackling Goose

_____ Canada Goose

_____ Hawaiian Goose

_____ Mute Swan

_____ Trumpeter Swan

_____ Tundra Swan

_____ Whooper Swan

_____ Egyptian Goose

_____ Common Shelduck

_____ Muscovy Duck

_____ Wood Duck

_____ Baikal Teal

_____ Garganey

_____ Blue-winged Teal

_____ Cinnamon Teal

_____ Northern Shoveler

_____ Gadwall

_____ Falcated Duck

_____ Eurasian Wigeon

_____ American Wigeon

_____ Laysan Duck

_____ Hawaiian Duck

_____ Eastern Spot-billed Duck

_____ Mallard

_____ American Black Duck

_____ Mottled Duck

_____ White-cheeked Pintail

_____ Northern Pintail

_____ Green-winged Teal

_____ Canvasback

_____ Redhead

_____ Common Pochard

_____ Ring-necked Duck

_____ Tufted Duck

_____ Greater Scaup

_____ Lesser Scaup

_____ Steller's Eider

_____ Spectacled Eider

_____ King Eider

_____ Common Eider

_____ Harlequin Duck

_____ Labrador Duck

_____ Surf Scoter

_____ White-winged Scoter

_____ Common Scoter

_____ Black Scoter

_____ Long-tailed Duck

_____ Bufflehead

_____ Common Goldeneye

_____ Barrow's Goldeneye

_____ Smew

_____ Hooded Merganser

_____ Common Merganser

_____ Red-breasted Merganser

_____ Masked Duck

_____ Ruddy Duck

CURASSOWS AND GUANS (CRACIDAE)

_____ Plain Chachalaca

NEW WORLD QUAIL (ODONTOPHORIDAE)

_____ Mountain Quail

_____ Northern Bobwhite

_____ Scaled Quail

_____ California Quail

_____ Gambel's Quail

_____ Montezuma Quail

PARTRIDGES, GROUSE, TURKEYS, AND OLD WORLD QUAIL (PHASIANIDAE)

_____ Chukar

_____ Gray Francolin

_____ Black Francolin

_____ Erckel's Francolin

_____ Himalayan Snowcock

_____ Gray Partridge

_____ Red Junglefowl

_____ Kalij Pheasant

_____ Ring-necked Pheasant

_____ Indian Peafowl

_____ Ruffed Grouse

_____ Greater Sage-Grouse

_____ Gunnison Sage-Grouse

_____ Spruce Grouse

_____ Willow Ptarmigan

_____ Rock Ptarmigan

_____ White-tailed Ptarmigan

_____ Dusky Grouse

_____ Sooty Grouse

_____ Sharp-tailed Grouse

_____ Greater Prairie-Chicken

_____ Lesser Prairie-Chicken

_____ Wild Turkey

FLAMINGOS (PHOENICOPTERIDAE)

_____ American Flamingo

GREBES (PODICIPEDIDAE)

_____ Least Grebe

_____ Pied-billed Grebe

_____ Horned Grebe

_____ Red-necked Grebe

_____ Eared Grebe

_____ Western Grebe

_____ Clark's Grebe

SANDGROUSES (PTEROCLIDAE)

_____ Chestnut-bellied Sandgrouse

PIGEONS AND DOVES (COLUMBIDAE)

_____ Rock Pigeon

_____ Scaly-naped Pigeon

_____ White-crowned Pigeon

_____ Red-billed Pigeon

_____ Band-tailed Pigeon

_____ Oriental Turtle-Dove

_____ European Turtle-Dove

_____ Eurasian Collared-Dove

_____ Spotted Dove

_____ Zebra Dove

_____ Passenger Pigeon

_____ Inca Dove

_____ Common Ground-Dove

_____ Ruddy Ground-Dove

_____ Ruddy Quail-Dove

_____ Key West Quail-Dove

_____ White-tipped Dove

_____ White-winged Dove

_____ Zenaida Dove

_____ Mourning Dove

CUCKOOS, ROADRUNNERS, AND ANIS (CUCULIDAE)

_____ Common Cuckoo

_____ Oriental Cuckoo

_____ Yellow-billed Cuckoo

_____ Mangrove Cuckoo

_____ Black-billed Cuckoo

_____ Greater Roadrunner

_____ Smooth-billed Ani

_____ Groove-billed Ani

GOATSUCKERS (CAPRIMULGIDAE)

_____ Lesser Nighthawk

_____ Common Nighthawk

_____ Antillean Nighthawk

_____ Common Pauraque

_____ Common Poorwill

_____ Chuck-will's-widow

_____ Buff-collared Nightjar

_____ Eastern Whip-poor-will

_____ Mexican Whip-poor-will

_____ Gray Nightjar

SWIFTS (APODIDAE)

_____ Black Swift

_____ White-collared Swift

_____ Chimney Swift

_____ Vaux's Swift

_____ White-throated Needletail

_____ Mariana Swiftlet

_____ Common Swift

_____ Fork-tailed Swift

_____ White-throated Swift

_____ Antillean Palm-Swift

HUMMINGBIRDS (TROCHILIDAE)

_____ Mexican Violetear

_____ Green-breasted Mango

_____ Rivoli's Hummingbird

_____ Plain-capped Starthroat

_____ Amethyst-throated Hummingbird

_____ Blue-throated Mountain-Gem

_____ Bahama Woodstar

_____ Lucifer Hummingbird

_____ Ruby-throated Hummingbird

_____ Black-chinned Hummingbird

_____ Anna's Hummingbird

_____ Costa's Hummingbird

_____ Bumblebee Hummingbird

_____ Broad-tailed Hummingbird

_____ Rufous Hummingbird

_____ Allen's Hummingbird

_____ Calliope Hummingbird

_____ Broad-billed Hummingbird

_____ Berylline Hummingbird

_____ Buff-bellied Hummingbird

_____ Cinnamon Hummingbird

_____ Violet-crowned Hummingbird

_____ White-eared Hummingbird

_____ Xantus's Hummingbird

RAILS, GALLINULES, AND COOTS (RALLIDAE)

_____ Yellow Rail

_____ Black Rail

_____ Corn Crake

_____ Ridgway's Rail

_____ Clapper Rail

_____ King Rail

_____ Virginia Rail

_____ Rufous-necked Wood-Rail

_____ Sora

_____ Laysan Rail

_____ Hawaiian Rail

_____ Paint-billed Crake

_____ Spotted Rail

_____ Purple Gallinule

_____ Western Swamphen

_____ Common Gallinule

_____ Common Moorhen

_____ Eurasian Coot

_____ Hawaiian Coot

_____ American Coot

SUNGREBES (HELIORNITHIDAE)

_____ Sungrebe

LIMPKINS (ARAMIDAE)

_____ Limpkin

CRANES (GRUIDAE)

_____ Sandhill Crane

_____ Common Crane

_____ Whooping Crane

THICK-KNEES (BURHINIDAE)

_____ Double-striped Thick-knee

STILTS AND AVOCETS (RECURVIROSTRIDAE)

_____ Black-winged Stilt

_____ Black-necked Stilt

_____ American Avocet

OYSTERCATCHERS (HAEMATOPODIDAE)

_____ Eurasian Oystercatcher

_____ American Oystercatcher

_____ Black Oystercatcher

LAPWINGS AND PLOVERS (CHARADRIIDAE)

_____ Northern Lapwing

_____ Black-bellied Plover

_____ European Golden-Plover

_____ American Golden-Plover

_____ Pacific Golden-Plover

_____ Lesser Sand-Plover

_____ Greater Sand-Plover

_____ Collared Plover

_____ Snowy Plover

_____ Wilson's Plover

_____ Common Ringed Plover

_____ Semipalmated Plover

_____ Piping Plover

_____ Little Ringed Plover

_____ Killdeer

_____ Mountain Plover

_____ Eurasian Dotterel

JACANAS (JACANIDAE)

_____ Northern Jacana

SANDPIPERS, PHALAROPES, AND ALLIES (SCOLOPACIDAE)

_____ Upland Sandpiper

_____ Bristle-thighed Curlew

_____ Whimbrel

_____ Little Curlew

_____ Eskimo Curlew

_____ Long-billed Curlew

_____ Far Eastern Curlew

_____ Slender-billed Curlew

_____ Eurasian Curlew

_____ Bar-tailed Godwit

_____ Black-tailed Godwit

_____ Hudsonian Godwit

_____ Marbled Godwit

_____ Ruddy Turnstone

_____ Black Turnstone

_____ Great Knot

_____ Red Knot

_____ Surfbird

_____ Ruff

_____ Broad-billed Sandpiper

_____ Sharp-tailed Sandpiper

_____ Stilt Sandpiper

_____ Curlew Sandpiper

_____ Temminck's Stint

_____ Long-toed Stint

_____ Spoon-billed Sandpiper

_____ Red-necked Stint

_____ Sanderling

_____ Dunlin

_____ Rock Sandpiper

_____ Purple Sandpiper

_____ Baird's Sandpiper

_____ Little Stint

_____ Least Sandpiper

_____ White-rumped Sandpiper

_____ Buff-breasted Sandpiper

_____ Pectoral Sandpiper

_____ Semipalmated Sandpiper

_____ Western Sandpiper

_____ Short-billed Dowitcher

_____ Long-billed Dowitcher

_____ Jack Snipe

_____ Eurasian Woodcock

_____ American Woodcock

_____ Solitary Snipe

_____ Pin-tailed Snipe

_____ Common Snipe

_____ Wilson's Snipe

_____ Terek Sandpiper

_____ Common Sandpiper

_____ Spotted Sandpiper

_____ Green Sandpiper

_____ Solitary Sandpiper

_____ Gray-tailed Tattler

_____ Wandering Tattler

_____ Lesser Yellowlegs

_____ Willet

_____ Spotted Redshank

_____ Common Greenshank

_____ Greater Yellowlegs

_____ Common Redshank

_____ Wood Sandpiper

_____ Marsh Sandpiper

_____ Wilson's Phalarope

_____ Red-necked Phalarope

_____ Red Phalarope

PRATINCOLES (GLAREOLIDAE)

_____ Oriental Pratincole

SKUAS AND JAEGERS (STERCORARIIDAE)

_____ Great Skua

_____ South Polar Skua

_____ Pomarine Jaeger

_____ Parasitic Jaeger

_____ Long-tailed Jaeger

AUKS, MURRES, AND PUFFINS (ALCIDAE)

_____ Dovekie

_____ Common Murre

_____ Thick-billed Murre

_____ Razorbill

_____ Great Auk

_____ Black Guillemot

_____ Pigeon Guillemot

_____ Long-billed Murrelet

_____ Marbled Murrelet

_____ Kittlitz's Murrelet

_____ Scripps's Murrelet

_____ Guadalupe Murrelet

_____ Craveri's Murrelet

_____ Ancient Murrelet

_____ Cassin's Auklet

_____ Parakeet Auklet

_____ Least Auklet

_____ Whiskered Auklet

_____ Crested Auklet

_____ Rhinoceros Auklet

_____ Atlantic Puffin

_____ Horned Puffin

_____ Tufted Puffin

GULLS, TERNS, AND SKIMMERS (LARIDAE)

_____ Swallow-tailed Gull

_____ Black-legged Kittiwake

_____ Red-legged Kittiwake

_____ Ivory Gull

_____ Sabine's Gull

_____ Bonaparte's Gull

_____ Gray-hooded Gull

_____ Black-headed Gull

_____ Little Gull

_____ Ross's Gull

_____ Laughing Gull

_____ Franklin's Gull

_____ Belcher's Gull

_____ Black-tailed Gull

_____ Heermann's Gull

_____ Mew Gull

_____ Ring-billed Gull

_____ Western Gull

_____ Yellow-footed Gull

_____ California Gull

_____ Herring Gull

_____ Yellow-legged Gull

_____ Iceland Gull

_____ Lesser Black-backed Gull

_____ Slaty-backed Gull

_____ Glaucous-winged Gull

_____ Glaucous Gull

_____ Great Black-backed Gull

_____ Kelp Gull

_____ Brown Noddy

_____ Black Noddy

_____ Blue-gray Noddy

_____ White Tern
_____ Sooty Tern
_____ Gray-backed Tern
_____ Bridled Tern
_____ Aleutian Tern
_____ Little Tern
_____ Least Tern
_____ Large-billed Tern
_____ Gull-billed Tern
_____ Caspian Tern
_____ Black Tern
_____ White-winged Tern
_____ Whiskered Tern
_____ Roseate Tern
_____ Common Tern
_____ Arctic Tern
_____ Forster's Tern
_____ Royal Tern
_____ Great Crested Tern
_____ Sandwich Tern
_____ Elegant Tern
_____ Black Skimmer

TROPICBIRDS (PHAETHONTIDAE)

_____ White-tailed Tropicbird
_____ Red-billed Tropicbird
_____ Red-tailed Tropicbird

LOONS (GAVIIDAE)

_____ Red-throated Loon
_____ Arctic Loon
_____ Pacific Loon
_____ Common Loon
_____ Yellow-billed Loon

ALBATROSSES (DIOMEDEIDAE)

_____ Yellow-nosed Albatross
_____ White-capped Albatross
_____ Chatham Albatross

_____ Salvin's Albatross
_____ Black-browed Albatross
_____ Light-mantled Albatross
_____ Wandering Albatross
_____ Laysan Albatross
_____ Black-footed Albatross
_____ Short-tailed Albatross

SHEARWATERS AND PETRELS (PROCELLARIIDAE)

_____ Northern Fulmar
_____ Great-winged Petrel
_____ Providence Petrel
_____ Kermadec Petrel
_____ Trindade Petrel
_____ Herald Petrel
_____ Murphy's Petrel
_____ Mottled Petrel
_____ Bermuda Petrel
_____ Black-capped Petrel
_____ Juan Fernández Petrel
_____ Hawaiian Petrel
_____ White-necked Petrel
_____ Bonin Petrel
_____ Black-winged Petrel
_____ Fea's Petrel
_____ Zino's Petrel
_____ Cook's Petrel
_____ Stejneger's Petrel
_____ Tahiti Petrel
_____ Bulwer's Petrel
_____ Jouanin's Petrel
_____ White-chinned Petrel
_____ Parkinson's Petrel
_____ Streaked Shearwater
_____ Cory's Shearwater
_____ Cape Verde Shearwater
_____ Wedge-tailed Shearwater

_____ Buller's Shearwater

_____ Short-tailed Shearwater

_____ Sooty Shearwater

_____ Great Shearwater

_____ Pink-footed Shearwater

_____ Flesh-footed Shearwater

_____ Christmas Shearwater

_____ Manx Shearwater

_____ Newell's Shearwater

_____ Bryan's Shearwater

_____ Black-vented Shearwater

_____ Audubon's Shearwater

_____ Barolo Shearwater

SOUTHERN STORM-PETRELS (OCEANITIDAE)

_____ Wilson's Storm-Petrel

_____ White-faced Storm-Petrel

_____ Black-bellied Storm-Petrel

NORTHERN STORM-PETRELS (HYDROBATIDAE)

_____ European Storm-Petrel

_____ Fork-tailed Storm-Petrel

_____ Ringed Storm-Petrel

_____ Swinhoe's Storm-Petrel

_____ Leach's Storm-Petrel

_____ Townsend's Storm-Petrel

_____ Ashy Storm-Petrel

_____ Band-rumped Storm-Petrel

_____ Wedge-rumped Storm-Petrel

_____ Black Storm-Petrel

_____ Tristram's Storm-Petrel

_____ Least Storm-Petrel

STORKS (CICONIIDAE)

_____ Jabiru

_____ Wood Stork

FRIGATEBIRDS (FREGATIDAE)

_____ Magnificent Frigatebird

_____ Great Frigatebird

_____ Lesser Frigatebird

BOOBIES AND GANNETS (SULIDAE)

_____ Masked Booby

_____ Nazca Booby

_____ Blue-footed Booby

_____ Brown Booby

_____ Red-footed Booby

_____ Northern Gannet

CORMORANTS (PHALACROCORACIDAE)

_____ Brandt's Cormorant

_____ Neotropic Cormorant

_____ Double-crested Cormorant

_____ Great Cormorant

_____ Red-faced Cormorant

_____ Pelagic Cormorant

DARTERS (ANHINGIDAE)

_____ Anhinga

PELICANS (PELECANIDAE)

_____ American White Pelican

_____ Brown Pelican

BITTERNS, HERONS, AND ALLIES (ARDEIDAE)

_____ American Bittern

_____ Yellow Bittern

_____ Least Bittern

_____ Bare-throated Tiger-Heron

_____ Great Blue Heron

_____ Gray Heron

_____ Great Egret

_____ Intermediate Egret

_____ Chinese Egret

_____ Little Egret

_____ Western Reef-Heron

_____ Snowy Egret

_____ Little Blue Heron

_____ Tricolored Heron

_____ Reddish Egret

_____ Cattle Egret

_____ Chinese Pond-Heron

_____ Green Heron

_____ Black-crowned Night-Heron

_____ Yellow-crowned Night-Heron

IBISES AND SPOONBILLS (THRESKIORNITHIDAE)

_____ White Ibis

_____ Scarlet Ibis

_____ Glossy Ibis

_____ White-faced Ibis

_____ Roseate Spoonbill

NEW WORLD VULTURES (CATHARTIDAE)

_____ Black Vulture

_____ Turkey Vulture

_____ California Condor

OSPREYS (PANDIONIDAE)

_____ Osprey

HAWKS, KITES, EAGLES, AND ALLIES (ACCIPITRIDAE)

_____ White-tailed Kite

_____ Hook-billed Kite

_____ Swallow-tailed Kite

_____ Golden Eagle

_____ Double-toothed Kite

_____ Northern Harrier

_____ Chinese Sparrowhawk

_____ Sharp-shinned Hawk

_____ Cooper's Hawk

_____ Northern Goshawk

_____ Black Kite

_____ Bald Eagle

_____ White-tailed Eagle

_____ Steller's Sea-Eagle

_____ Mississippi Kite

_____ Crane Hawk

_____ Snail Kite

_____ Common Black Hawk

_____ Great Black Hawk

_____ Roadside Hawk

_____ Harris's Hawk

_____ White-tailed Hawk

_____ Gray Hawk

_____ Red-shouldered Hawk

_____ Broad-winged Hawk

_____ Hawaiian Hawk

_____ Short-tailed Hawk

_____ Swainson's Hawk

_____ Zone-tailed Hawk

_____ Red-tailed Hawk

_____ Rough-legged Hawk

_____ Ferruginous Hawk

BARN OWLS (TYTONIDAE)

_____ Barn Owl

TYPICAL OWLS (STRIGIDAE)

_____ Oriental Scops-Owl

_____ Flammulated Owl

_____ Western Screech-Owl

_____ Eastern Screech-Owl

_____ Whiskered Screech-Owl

_____ Great Horned Owl

_____ Snowy Owl

_____ Northern Hawk Owl

_____ Northern Pygmy-Owl

_____ Ferruginous Pygmy-Owl

_____ Elf Owl

_____ Burrowing Owl

_____ Mottled Owl

_____ Spotted Owl

_____ Barred Owl

_____ Great Gray Owl

_____ Long-eared Owl

_____ Stygian Owl

_____ Short-eared Owl

_____ Boreal Owl

_____ Northern Saw-whet Owl

_____ Northern Boobook

TROGONS (TROGONIDAE)

_____ Elegant Trogon

_____ Eared Quetzal

HOOPOES (UPUPIDAE)

_____ Eurasian Hoopoe

KINGFISHERS (ALCEDINIDAE)

_____ Ringed Kingfisher

_____ Belted Kingfisher

_____ Amazon Kingfisher

_____ Green Kingfisher

WOODPECKERS AND ALLIES (PICIDAE)

_____ Lewis's Woodpecker

_____ Red-headed Woodpecker

_____ Acorn Woodpecker

_____ Gila Woodpecker

_____ Golden-fronted Woodpecker

_____ Red-bellied Woodpecker

_____ Williamson's Sapsucker

_____ Yellow-bellied Sapsucker

_____ Red-naped Sapsucker

_____ Red-breasted Sapsucker

_____ American Three-toed Woodpecker

_____ Black-backed Woodpecker

_____ Great Spotted Woodpecker

_____ Downy Woodpecker

_____ Nuttall's Woodpecker

_____ Ladder-backed Woodpecker

_____ Red-cockaded Woodpecker

_____ Hairy Woodpecker

_____ White-headed Woodpecker

_____ Arizona Woodpecker

_____ Northern Flicker

_____ Gilded Flicker

_____ Pileated Woodpecker

_____ Ivory-billed Woodpecker

CARACARAS AND FALCONS (FALCONIDAE)

_____ Collared Forest-Falcon

_____ Crested Caracara

_____ Eurasian Kestrel

_____ American Kestrel

_____ Red-footed Falcon

_____ Merlin

_____ Eurasian Hobby

_____ Aplomado Falcon

_____ Gyrfalcon

_____ Peregrine Falcon

_____ Prairie Falcon

PARAKEETS, MACAWS, AND PARROTS (PSITTACIDAE)

_____ Monk Parakeet

_____ Carolina Parakeet

_____ Nanday Parakeet

_____ Green Parakeet

_____ Thick-billed Parrot

_____ White-winged Parakeet

_____ Red-crowned Parrot

LORIES, LOVEBIRDS, AND AUSTRALASIAN PARROTS (PSITTACULIDAE)

_____ Rose-ringed Parakeet

_____ Rosy-faced Lovebird

BECARDS, TITYRAS, AND ALLIES (TITYRIDAE)

_____ Masked Tityra

_____ Gray-collared Becard

_____ Rose-throated Becard

TYRANT FLYCATCHERS (TYRANNIDAE)

_____ Northern Beardless-Tyrannulet

_____ Greenish Elaenia

_____ White-crested Elaenia

_____ Dusky-capped Flycatcher

_____ Ash-throated Flycatcher

_____ Nutting's Flycatcher

_____ Great Crested Flycatcher

_____ Brown-crested Flycatcher

_____ La Sagra's Flycatcher

_____ Great Kiskadee

_____ Social Flycatcher

_____ Sulphur-bellied Flycatcher

_____ Piratic Flycatcher

_____ Variegated Flycatcher

_____ Crowned Slaty Flycatcher

_____ Tropical Kingbird

_____ Couch's Kingbird

_____ Cassin's Kingbird

_____ Thick-billed Kingbird

_____ Western Kingbird

_____ Eastern Kingbird

_____ Gray Kingbird

_____ Loggerhead Kingbird

_____ Scissor-tailed Flycatcher

_____ Fork-tailed Flycatcher

_____ Tufted Flycatcher

_____ Olive-sided Flycatcher

_____ Greater Pewee

_____ Western Wood-Pewee

_____ Eastern Wood-Pewee

_____ Cuban Pewee

_____ Yellow-bellied Flycatcher

_____ Acadian Flycatcher

_____ Alder Flycatcher

_____ Willow Flycatcher

_____ Least Flycatcher

_____ Hammond's Flycatcher

_____ Gray Flycatcher

_____ Dusky Flycatcher

_____ Pine Flycatcher

_____ Pacific-slope Flycatcher

_____ Cordilleran Flycatcher

_____ Buff-breasted Flycatcher

_____ Black Phoebe

_____ Eastern Phoebe

_____ Say's Phoebe

_____ Vermilion Flycatcher

SHRIKES (LANIIDAE)

_____ Red-backed Shrike

_____ Brown Shrike

_____ Loggerhead Shrike

_____ Northern Shrike

VIREOS (VIREONIDAE)

_____ Black-capped Vireo

_____ White-eyed Vireo

_____ Thick-billed Vireo

_____ Cuban Vireo

_____ Bell's Vireo

_____ Gray Vireo

_____ Hutton's Vireo

_____ Yellow-throated Vireo

_____ Cassin's Vireo

_____ Blue-headed Vireo

_____ Plumbeous Vireo

_____ Philadelphia Vireo

_____ Warbling Vireo

_____ Red-eyed Vireo

_____ Yellow-green Vireo

_____ Black-whiskered Vireo

_____ Yucatan Vireo

JAYS AND CROWS (CORVIDAE)

_____ Canada Jay

_____ Brown Jay

_____ Green Jay

_____ Pinyon Jay

_____ Steller's Jay

_____ Blue Jay

_____ Florida Scrub-Jay

_____ Island Scrub-Jay

_____ California Scrub-Jay

_____ Woodhouse's Scrub-Jay

_____ Mexican Jay

_____ Clark's Nutcracker

_____ Black-billed Magpie

_____ Yellow-billed Magpie

_____ Eurasian Jackdaw

_____ American Crow

_____ Northwestern Crow

_____ Tamaulipas Crow

_____ Fish Crow

_____ Hawaiian Crow

_____ Chihuahuan Raven

_____ Common Raven

MONARCH FLYCATCHERS (MONARCHIDAE)

_____ Kauai Elepaio

_____ Oahu Elepaio

_____ Hawaii Elepaio

LARKS (ALAUDIDAE)

_____ Eurasian Skylark

_____ Horned Lark

SWALLOWS (HIRUNDINIDAE)

_____ Purple Martin

_____ Cuban Martin

_____ Gray-breasted Martin

_____ Southern Martin

_____ Brown-chested Martin

_____ Tree Swallow

_____ Mangrove Swallow

_____ Violet-green Swallow

_____ Bahama Swallow

_____ Northern Rough-winged Swallow

_____ Bank Swallow

_____ Cliff Swallow

_____ Cave Swallow

_____ Barn Swallow

_____ Common House-Martin

CHICKADEES AND TITMICE (PARIDAE)

_____ Carolina Chickadee

_____ Black-capped Chickadee

_____ Mountain Chickadee

_____ Mexican Chickadee

_____ Chestnut-backed Chickadee

_____ Boreal Chickadee

_____ Gray-headed Chickadee

_____ Bridled Titmouse

_____ Oak Titmouse

_____ Juniper Titmouse

_____ Tufted Titmouse

_____ Black-crested Titmouse

VERDIN (REMIZIDAE)

_____ Verdin

BUSHTITS (AEGITHALIDAE)

_____ Bushtit

NUTHATCHES (SITTIDAE)

_____ Red-breasted Nuthatch

_____ White-breasted Nuthatch

_____ Pygmy Nuthatch

_____ Brown-headed Nuthatch

CREEPERS (CERTHIIDAE)

_____ Brown Creeper

WRENS (TROGLODYTIDAE)

_____ Rock Wren

_____ Canyon Wren

_____ House Wren

_____ Pacific Wren

_____ Winter Wren

_____ Sedge Wren

_____ Marsh Wren

_____ Carolina Wren

_____ Bewick's Wren

_____ Cactus Wren

_____ Sinaloa Wren

GNATCATCHERS AND GNATWRENS (POLIOPTILIDAE)

_____ Blue-gray Gnatcatcher

_____ California Gnatcatcher

_____ Black-tailed Gnatcatcher

_____ Black-capped Gnatcatcher

DIPPERS (CINCLIDAE)

_____ American Dipper

BULBULS (PYCNONOTIDAE)

_____ Red-vented Bulbul

_____ Red-whiskered Bulbul

KINGLETS (REGULIDAE)

_____ Golden-crowned Kinglet

_____ Ruby-crowned Kinglet

BUSH WARBLERS (SCOTOCERCIDAE)

_____ Japanese Bush Warbler

LEAF WARBLERS (PHYLLOSCOPIDAE)

_____ Willow Warbler

_____ Common Chiffchaff

_____ Wood Warbler

_____ Dusky Warbler

_____ Pallas's Leaf Warbler

_____ Yellow-browed Warbler

_____ Arctic Warbler

_____ Kamchatka Leaf Warbler

SYLVIID WARBLERS (SYLVIIDAE)

_____ Lesser Whitethroat

_____ Wrentit

WHITE-EYES (ZOSTEROPIDAE)

_____ Japanese White-eye

LAUGHINGTHRUSHES (TIMALIIDAE)

_____ Greater Necklaced Laughingthrush

_____ Chinese Hwamei

_____ Red-billed Leiothrix

REED WARBLERS (ACROCEPHALIDAE)

_____ Thick-billed Warbler

_____ Millerbird

_____ Sedge Warbler

_____ Blyth's Reed Warbler

GRASSBIRDS (LOCUSTELLIDAE)

_____ Middendorff's Grasshopper-Warbler

_____ River Warbler

_____ Lanceolated Warbler

OLD WORLD FLYCATCHERS (MUSCICAPIDAE)

_____ Gray-streaked Flycatcher
_____ Asian Brown Flycatcher
_____ Spotted Flycatcher
_____ Dark-sided Flycatcher
_____ White-rumped Shama
_____ European Robin
_____ Siberian Rubythroat
_____ Bluethroat
_____ Siberian Blue Robin
_____ Rufous-tailed Robin
_____ Red-flanked Bluetail
_____ Narcissus Flycatcher
_____ Mugimaki Flycatcher
_____ Taiga Flycatcher
_____ Common Redstart
_____ Stonechat
_____ Northern Wheatear
_____ Pied Wheatear

THRUSHES (TURDIDAE)

_____ Eastern Bluebird
_____ Western Bluebird
_____ Mountain Bluebird
_____ Townsend's Solitaire
_____ Brown-backed Solitaire
_____ Kamao
_____ Amaui
_____ Olomao
_____ Omao
_____ Puaiohi
_____ Orange-billed Nightingale-Thrush
_____ Black-headed Nightingale-Thrush
_____ Veery
_____ Gray-cheeked Thrush
_____ Bicknell's Thrush
_____ Swainson's Thrush
_____ Hermit Thrush
_____ Wood Thrush
_____ Eurasian Blackbird
_____ Eyebrowed Thrush
_____ Dusky Thrush
_____ Fieldfare
_____ Redwing
_____ Mistle Thrush
_____ Song Thrush
_____ Clay-colored Thrush
_____ White-throated Thrush
_____ Rufous-backed Robin
_____ American Robin
_____ Red-legged Thrush
_____ Varied Thrush
_____ Aztec Thrush

MOCKINGBIRDS AND THRASHERS (MIMIDAE)

_____ Blue Mockingbird
_____ Gray Catbird
_____ Curve-billed Thrasher
_____ Brown Thrasher
_____ Long-billed Thrasher
_____ Bendire's Thrasher
_____ California Thrasher
_____ LeConte's Thrasher
_____ Crissal Thrasher
_____ Sage Thrasher
_____ Bahama Mockingbird
_____ Northern Mockingbird

STARLINGS (STURNIDAE)

_____ European Starling
_____ Common Myna

WAXWINGS (BOMBYCILLIDAE)

_____ Bohemian Waxwing

_____ Cedar Waxwing

HAWAIIAN MOHOS (MOHOIDAE)

_____ Kauai Oo

_____ Oahu Oo

_____ Bishop's Oo

_____ Hawaii Oo

_____ Kioea

SILKY-FLYCATCHERS (PTILIOGONATIDAE)

_____ Gray Silky-flycatcher

_____ Phainopepla

OLIVE WARBLERS (PEUCEDRAMIDAE)

_____ Olive Warbler

ACCENTORS (PRUNELLIDAE)

_____ Siberian Accentor

WAXBILLS (ESTRILDIDAE)

_____ Common Waxbill

_____ Red Avadavat

_____ African Silverbill

_____ Java Sparrow

_____ Scaly-breasted Munia

_____ Chestnut Munia

OLD WORLD SPARROWS (PASSERIDAE)

_____ House Sparrow

_____ Eurasian Tree Sparrow

WAGTAILS AND PIPITS (MOTACILLIDAE)

_____ Eastern Yellow Wagtail

_____ Citrine Wagtail

_____ Gray Wagtail

_____ White Wagtail

_____ Tree Pipit

_____ Olive-backed Pipit

_____ Pechora Pipit

_____ Red-throated Pipit

_____ American Pipit

_____ Sprague's Pipit

FRINGILLINE AND CARDUELINE FINCHES AND ALLIES (FRINGILLIDAE)

_____ Common Chaffinch

_____ Brambling

_____ Evening Grosbeak

_____ Hawfinch

_____ Common Rosefinch

_____ Pallas's Rosefinch

_____ Poo-uli

_____ Akikiki

_____ Oahu Alauahio

_____ Kakawahie

_____ Maui Alauahio

_____ Palila

_____ Laysan Finch

_____ Nihoa Finch

_____ Kona Grosbeak

_____ Lesser Koa-Finch

_____ Greater Koa-Finch

_____ Ula-ai-hawane

_____ Akohekohe

_____ Laysan Honeycreeper

_____ Apapane

_____ Iiwi

_____ Hawaii Mamo

_____ Black Mamo

_____ Ou

_____ Lanai Hookbill

_____ Maui Parrotbill

_____ Kauai Nukupuu

_____ Oahu Nukupuu

_____ Maui Nukupuu

_____ Akiapolaau

_____ Lesser Akialoa

_____ Kauai Akialoa

_____ Oahu Akialoa

_____ Maui-nui Akialoa

_____ Anianiau

_____ Hawaii Amakihi

_____ Oahu Amakihi

_____ Kauai Amakihi

_____ Greater Amakihi

_____ Hawaii Creeper

_____ Akekee

_____ Oahu Akepa

_____ Maui Akepa

_____ Hawaii Akepa

_____ Pine Grosbeak

_____ Eurasian Bullfinch

_____ Asian Rosy-Finch

_____ Gray-crowned Rosy-Finch

_____ Black Rosy-Finch

_____ Brown-capped Rosy-Finch

_____ House Finch

_____ Purple Finch

_____ Cassin's Finch

_____ Oriental Greenfinch

_____ Yellow-fronted Canary

_____ Common Redpoll

_____ Hoary Redpoll

_____ Red Crossbill

_____ Cassia Crossbill

_____ White-winged Crossbill

_____ Eurasian Siskin

_____ Pine Siskin

_____ Lesser Goldfinch

_____ Lawrence's Goldfinch

_____ American Goldfinch

_____ Island Canary

LONGSPURS AND SNOW BUNTINGS (CALCARIIDAE)

_____ Lapland Longspur

_____ Chestnut-collared Longspur

_____ Smith's Longspur

_____ McCown's Longspur

_____ Snow Bunting

_____ McKay's Bunting

EMBERIZIDS (EMBERIZIDAE)

_____ Pine Bunting

_____ Yellow-browed Bunting

_____ Little Bunting

_____ Rustic Bunting

_____ Yellow-throated Bunting

_____ Yellow-breasted Bunting

_____ Gray Bunting

_____ Pallas's Bunting

_____ Reed Bunting

TOWHEES AND SPARROWS (PASSERELLIDAE)

_____ Olive Sparrow

_____ Green-tailed Towhee

_____ Spotted Towhee

_____ Eastern Towhee

_____ Rufous-crowned Sparrow

_____ Canyon Towhee

_____ California Towhee

_____ Abert's Towhee

_____ Rufous-winged Sparrow

_____ Botteri's Sparrow

_____ Cassin's Sparrow

_____ Bachman's Sparrow

_____ American Tree Sparrow

_____ Chipping Sparrow

_____ Clay-colored Sparrow

_____ Brewer's Sparrow

_____ Field Sparrow

_____ Worthen's Sparrow

_____ Black-chinned Sparrow

_____ Vesper Sparrow	_____ Orchard Oriole
_____ Lark Sparrow	_____ Hooded Oriole
_____ Five-striped Sparrow	_____ Streak-backed Oriole
_____ Black-throated Sparrow	_____ Bullock's Oriole
_____ Sagebrush Sparrow	_____ Spot-breasted Oriole
_____ Bell's Sparrow	_____ Altamira Oriole
_____ Lark Bunting	_____ Audubon's Oriole
_____ Savannah Sparrow	_____ Baltimore Oriole
_____ Grasshopper Sparrow	_____ Black-backed Oriole
_____ Baird's Sparrow	_____ Scott's Oriole
_____ Henslow's Sparrow	_____ Red-winged Blackbird
_____ LeConte's Sparrow	_____ Tricolored Blackbird
_____ Seaside Sparrow	_____ Tawny-shouldered Blackbird
_____ Nelson's Sparrow	_____ Shiny Cowbird
_____ Saltmarsh Sparrow	_____ Bronzed Cowbird
_____ Fox Sparrow	_____ Brown-headed Cowbird
_____ Song Sparrow	_____ Rusty Blackbird
_____ Lincoln's Sparrow	_____ Brewer's Blackbird
_____ Swamp Sparrow	_____ Common Grackle
_____ White-throated Sparrow	_____ Boat-tailed Grackle
_____ Harris's Sparrow	_____ Great-tailed Grackle
_____ White-crowned Sparrow	

_____ Golden-crowned Sparrow

_____ Dark-eyed Junco

_____ Yellow-eyed Junco

SPINDALISES (SPINDALIDAE)

_____ Western Spindalis

YELLOW-BREASTED CHATS (ICTERIIDAE)

_____ Yellow-breasted Chat

BLACKBIRDS (ICTERIDAE)

_____ Yellow-headed Blackbird

_____ Bobolink

_____ Eastern Meadowlark

_____ Western Meadowlark

_____ Black-vented Oriole

WOOD-WARBLERS (PARULIDAE)

_____ Ovenbird

_____ Worm-eating Warbler

_____ Louisiana Waterthrush

_____ Northern Waterthrush

_____ Bachman's Warbler

_____ Golden-winged Warbler

_____ Blue-winged Warbler

_____ Black-and-white Warbler

_____ Prothonotary Warbler

_____ Swainson's Warbler

_____ Crescent-chested Warbler

_____ Tennessee Warbler

_____ Orange-crowned Warbler

_____ Colima Warbler

_____ Lucy's Warbler

_____ Nashville Warbler

_____ Virginia's Warbler

_____ Connecticut Warbler

_____ Gray-crowned Yellowthroat

_____ MacGillivray's Warbler

_____ Mourning Warbler

_____ Kentucky Warbler

_____ Common Yellowthroat

_____ Hooded Warbler

_____ American Redstart

_____ Kirtland's Warbler

_____ Cape May Warbler

_____ Cerulean Warbler

_____ Northern Parula

_____ Tropical Parula

_____ Magnolia Warbler

_____ Bay-breasted Warbler

_____ Blackburnian Warbler

_____ Yellow Warbler

_____ Chestnut-sided Warbler

_____ Blackpoll Warbler

_____ Black-throated Blue Warbler

_____ Palm Warbler

_____ Pine Warbler

_____ Yellow-rumped Warbler

_____ Yellow-throated Warbler

_____ Prairie Warbler

_____ Grace's Warbler

_____ Black-throated Gray Warbler

_____ Townsend's Warbler

_____ Hermit Warbler

_____ Golden-cheeked Warbler

_____ Black-throated Green Warbler

_____ Fan-tailed Warbler

_____ Rufous-capped Warbler

_____ Golden-crowned Warbler

_____ Canada Warbler

_____ Wilson's Warbler

_____ Red-faced Warbler

_____ Painted Redstart

_____ Slate-throated Redstart

CARDINALS, *PIRANGA* TANAGERS, AND ALLIES (CARDINALIDAE)

_____ Hepatic Tanager

_____ Summer Tanager

_____ Scarlet Tanager

_____ Western Tanager

_____ Flame-colored Tanager

_____ Crimson-collared Grosbeak

_____ Northern Cardinal

_____ Pyrrhuloxia

_____ Yellow Grosbeak

_____ Rose-breasted Grosbeak

_____ Black-headed Grosbeak

_____ Blue Bunting

_____ Blue Grosbeak

_____ Lazuli Bunting

_____ Indigo Bunting

_____ Varied Bunting

_____ Painted Bunting

_____ Dickcissel

TANAGERS AND ALLIES (THRAUPIDAE)

_____ Red-crested Cardinal

_____ Yellow-billed Cardinal

_____ Saffron Finch

_____ Red-legged Honeycreeper

_____ Bananaquit

_____ Yellow-faced Grassquit

_____ Black-faced Grassquit

_____ Morelet's Seedeater

INDEX

SHORE SILHOUETTES

1 Forster's Tern
2 Black Tern
3 Herring Gull
4 Cormorant
5 Loon
6 Great Blue Heron
7 Mallard
8 Pied-billed Grebe
9 Marbled Godwit
10 Greater Yellowlegs
11 Dowitcher
12 Clapper Rail
13 Whimbrel
14 Black-bellied Plover
15 Turnstone
16 Night-Heron
17 Phalarope
18 Least Sandpiper
19 Semipalmated Plover
20 Sanderling
21 Spotted Sandpiper
22 Killdeer
23 Coot
24 Green-backed Heron

FLIGHT SILHOUETTES

1 Barn Swallow
2 Cliff Swallow
3 Purple Martin
4 Chimney Swift
5 Starling
6 Common Grackle
7 Blackbird
8 Bluebird
9 Robin
10 Goldfinch
11 House Sparrow
12 Belted Kingfisher
13 Blue Jay
14 Flicker
15 Mourning Dove
16 Meadowlark
17 Bobwhite
18 Ruffed Grouse
19 Pheasant
20 Nighthawk
21 Crow
22 Sharp-shinned Hawk
23 Kestrel
24 Killdeer
25 Wilson's Snipe
26 Woodcock

Pages listed are first occurrences.